Stop, Thief!

Editor: Sasha Lilley

Spectre is a series of penetrating and indispensable works of, and about, radical political economy. Spectre lays bare the dark underbelly of politics and economics, publishing outstanding and contrarian perspectives on the maelstrom of capital—and emancipatory alternatives—in crisis. The companion Spectre Classics imprint unearths essential works of radical history, political economy, theory and practice, to illuminate the present with brilliant, yet unjustly neglected, ideas from the past.

Spectre

Greg Albo, Sam Gindin, and Leo Panitch, *In and Out of Crisis: The Global Financial Meltdown and Left Alternatives*

David McNally, *Global Slump: The Economics and Politics of Crisis and Resistance*

Sasha Lilley, *Capital and Its Discontents: Conversations with Radical Thinkers in a Time of Tumult*

Sasha Lilley, David McNally, Eddie Yuen, and James Davis, *Catastrophism: The Apocalyptic Politics of Collapse and Rebirth*

Peter Linebaugh, *Stop, Thief! The Commons, Enclosures, and Resistance*

Spectre Classics

E.P. Thompson, *William Morris: Romantic to Revolutionary*

Victor Serge, *Men in Prison*

Victor Serge, *Birth of Our Power*

Stop, Thief!

The Commons, Enclosures, and Resistance

Peter Linebaugh

ISBN: 978-1-60486-747-3
Library of Congress Control Number: 2013911523

Cover by John Yates / Stealworks
Interior design by briandesign

10 9 8 7 6 5 4 3 2

PM Press
PO Box 23912
Oakland, CA 94623
www.pmpress.org

Printed in the USA by the Employee Owners of Thomson-Shore in Dexter, Michigan.
www.thomsonshore.com

To Kate and Riley, sisters

Contents

The "USA"

"First Nations"

Acknowledgments

I thank and acknowledge Celia Chazelle, an editor of *Why the Middle Ages Matter: Medieval Light on Modern Injustice* (London: Routledge, 2012) for whom I wrote the essay on Wat Tyler.

I thank and acknowledge Amy Chazkel, editor of special issue on the enclosures of the *Radical History Review* 108 (Fall 2010), for which I wrote "Enclosures from the Bottom Up."

I thank Jeffrey St. Clair and the late Alexander Cockburn of *CounterPunch*, who first published "The Commons, the Castle, the Witch, and the Lynx" (2009).

I thank the Ireland Institute's *The Republic*, where I published "The Red-Crested Bird and Black Duck" (Spring–Summer 2001).

I thank especially Sasha Lilley for commissioning my introduction to the PM Press edition of E.P. Thompson's biography of William Morris and for her help with it.

I thank Verso Books for the republication of my introduction to its Thomas Paine anthology (2009).

I thank Ana Mendez de Andes of Traficantes de Sueños for "The City and the Commons," first presented at the Museo Nacional Centro de Arte Reina Sofia in Madrid (2013).

I thank the genial Barry Maxwell of the Institute of Comparative Modernities at Cornell University, who organized two important conferences, one on "primitive accumulation" (2004) and the other on "globalizing anarchism" (2012), which produced a scholarly commons.

I thank Silke Helfrich and David Bollier for their active inter-commoning.

I thank Gustavo Esteva, Kevin Whelan, Staughton Lynd, Manuel Yang, John Roosa, Marcus Rediker, Silvia Federici, Dan Coughlin, and Dave Riker for friendly inspiration.

Some of the essays contain specific acknowledgments. Thus for "Karl Marx, the Theft of Wood, and Working-Class Composition" (1976) I thanked Bobby Scollard, Gene Mason, and Monty Neill, all of the New England Prisoner's Association.

I thank Alan Haber—comrade, neighbor, and pal—for commissioning two pieces.

I thank a group of artists, scholars, and archivists at the Blue Mountain Center in the Adirondacks, including Malav Kanuga and George Caffentzis for help with "The Invisibility of the Commons."

I thank Iain Boal of Birkbeck College, University of London, for publishing "Ned Ludd & Queen Mab" and for road trips to the serpent mound in Chillicothe, Ohio, and to the Brecklands, Norfolk, UK.

For all-round encouragement I thank the anti-enclosing, thief-stopping comrades of Ypsilanti Occupy, Jeff Clark and Quemadura, and for anti-war leadership I thank Libby Hunter, Gordon Bigelow, and the Liberty Street Agitators.

I thank Ramsey Kanaan and Sasha Lilley, my PM Press editors, who have been unfailingly prompt, helpful, and encouraging.

I thank Riley Linebaugh for clarifying discussions, helpful suggestions, and *joie de vivre*. Finally, I offer deep and tender thanks to my compañera, Michaela Brennan, with whom I've shared these journeys arm in arm.

Introduction

WOBBLY SOAP-BOXERS WERE ABLE TO GET A CROWD'S ATTENTION WITH THE SIMPLE street cry, "Stop, thief!" With the crowd's attention thereby obtained, the soap-boxer continued, "I've been robbed. I've been robbed by the capitalist system . . ." and then into his spiel.[1]

I wrote *Stop, Thief!* to join the alarm against neoliberalism which steals our land, our lives, and the labors of those preceding us.

The fifteen essays were written against enclosure, the process of privatization, closing off, and fencing in. Enclosure is the historical antonym and nemesis of the commons. *Stop, Thief!* is intended to help put an end to legal fibs and ideological fables that cover up truths such as, for example, that the enclosers are thieves who make laws which say that we are the thieves! A well-known but anonymous English poem expresses this truth which my essays merely elaborate.

> The law locks up the man or woman
> Who steals the goose from off the common,
> But lets the greater villain loose
> Who steals the common from the goose.

Most every student of "the commons" comes across this quatrain sooner or later. The charm of the lines arises from the crime against the goose, as if it were a sound bite from the Animal Liberation Front. But with a moment's thought we understand that the key term is not "goose" but "the common."

There are two thoughts. The first one is true enough, and a generation of English social historians have done much to reestablish it, that imprisonment grew with enclosures replacing the old chastisements, like the stocks. A massive prison construction program accompanied the enclosure of agricultural production. In addition this scholarly literature established that the man or woman locked up had been a commoner, not a villain at all.[2]

The second thought is the thought of expropriation or privatization. It says that a greater but nameless villain has stolen the common. Fences, ditches, walls, hedges, razor wire, and the like demark the boundaries of private property. They were built "lawfully" by Act of Parliament when Parliament was composed exclusively of landlords. They called it "improvement," and today they call it "development" or "progress." Just as the emperor has no clothes, these words are naked of meaning.

The "greater villains" aim to take land. In the Ohio valley, in Bengal, in the English midlands, in west Africa, in Chiapas, in Borneo, Indonesia. Why? They want what's underneath: gold, coal, oil, iron, what have you. They also create the proletariat, i.e., you! This taking, this expropriating the common, is a process of war, foreign and domestic.

I said it was an English quatrain. But I have found that it was known in Ireland in the seventeenth century, the century of English settlement or plantation, prefiguring that of North America. So we need to see it as anti-imperialist. In this case, the "greater villains" were English settlers and planters, and the Irish "man and woman" were losers.

Let's go back to the two thoughts. In the technical terms of rhetoric the second thought is an *enthymeme* because it contains a hidden premise, namely the reasoning that says stealing commons is worse than taking a goose. The success of the *enthymeme* depends on assent from the hearer, even though the suppressed premise does not need to be stated. That is the case here. We then wonder why the suppression is necessary. The premise subverts dominant, conventional thinking.

As Woody Guthrie put in the mouth of Pretty Boy Floyd, the Oklahoma bandit, "Some rob you with a six-gun, some with a fountain pen."

We know that the stealing was done by legislators, in fact the same legislators, who locked up "the man or woman." Those legislators were the thieves. Thus hidden within the quatrain is not only a story about the commons; it is also about law and class struggle. To restrict ourselves to the terms of the poem, there are two conceptions of law, one is statute law or law of the state, and the other is the rules of the commons. In actuality, the process contrasts law and custom, or statute and commoning. Is there a higher law? Is there a revolutionary law, a restorative requisitioning? Who makes law? Who upholds that law?

The commons is destroyed in two ways, by imprisonment and privatization. Each process produces its requisite emotional environment, wrath and fear. Those in prison are angry, those with property are fearful. Restorative justice therefore must include both the restoration of the commons and the restoration of liberty to the prisoner. This cannot be done as long as commoners are locked up. Since the commons and liberation are inseparable, the abolition of privatized, capitalist property and the abolition of prison must go together.

To shout "Stop, thief!" is to assume that someone is listening. It is to assume that the crowd agrees. As the miscreant flees, the crowd will trip him up, or remember his license plate, or otherwise initiate action needed to restore the commons. We can throw the rascals out of office; we can expropriate the rich; we can pull down fences. To make this cry, this shout, requires that we're standing on firm ground, some kind of commons. The essays in this book provide not the particulars for a bill of indictment against "the greater villains" but a reminder that history gives us, "the man or woman," ground to stand on.

Speaking loosely, these essays fall into five categories: the commons, Marx, the UK, the USA, and the first nations or indigenous people. Certainly they don't have to be read in order. The categories are unstable to begin with and are bound to change if not collapse. The UK and the USA were creations of the 1790s, and they will not last forever. Eternal existence is a fantasy of ruling classes, which is why they are afraid of history. Listen to Shelley.

> I met a traveller from an antique land,
> Who said—"Two vast and trunkless legs of stone
> Stand in the desert . . . near them, on the sand,
> Half sunk a shattered visage lies, whose frown,
> And wrinkled lips, and sneer of cold command,
> Tell that its sculptor well those passions read
> Which yet survive, stamped on these lifeless things,
> The hand that mocked them, and the heart that fed;
> And on the pedestal these words appear:
> 'My name is Ozymandias, King of Kings,
> Look on my Works ye Mighty, and despair!'
> Nothing beside remains. Round the decay
> Of that colossal Wreck, boundless and bare
> The lone and level sands stretch far away."

While Ozymandias might wish his stone image to last forever, the drip-drip of the waters of time, not to mention the sandblast of the raging winds of history, turn it to dust. The categories have their histories and these histories originated in conflict.

In assembling these essays I was struck by how important the region of the Great Lakes has been to me, the "burned-over district" of western New York, and the rust belt of Toledo and Detroit. My home has been in these parts of "that colossal wreck." The former region is called the "burned-over district" for two reasons. The first is that the barren spiritual movements—the table-tapping séances of the Fox sisters, the Second Coming of the Millerites, the golden plates of Mormons—originated there in the early nineteenth century.

The second arises from the deep trauma effected on the land by the massacres, holocausts, and ethnic murders of the eighteenth century, a trauma which not even American pride in deliberate historical ignorance could erase. I shall come back to this.

The region has had biographical, professional, and historical importance to me. My parents are buried in Seneca ground, Cattaraugus, New York. My mother was raised in Cattaraugus, studied in the region at Wells College, and admired Edmund Wilson's *Apologies to the Iroquois* (1959). For many years I worked in the area too at the University of Rochester on the Genesee River. With family and friends I used to spend long harvest weekends in Letchworth Gorge, the sixteen-mile-long chasm of the Genesee River in western New York. Later I learned that the Haudenosaunee, or Iroquois confederation, had been deeply influential to the German communists, Frederick Engels and Karl Marx, in understanding the origin of private property, patriarchy, and the state.

There was a great wave of enclosure at the sixteenth-century birth of the aggressive European nation-state. There was another wave led by Parliament in the eighteenth century. A third wave wrought planetary damage beginning in the late twentieth century.[3] The following essays came out of this third historical wave of enclosure with the notable exception of one, "Karl Marx, the Theft of Wood, and Working-Class Composition," which appeared a quarter of a century earlier, in 1976. Nevertheless, it anticipated the themes of the later essays.

Karl Marx was not just a German professor but an exiled immigrant and a Londoner whose name on census records was spelled "Charles Marks." I lived not far from Highgate cemetery and studied *Das Kapital* every Sunday afternoon with an extraordinary group of people as we "discovered" a Marx unknown to the economistic readers or the vanguard politicos, a Marx unknown to, or at least autonomous from, the New Left or the CP. The great communist had roots in the river and forest commons and said so. While his individual identity might have various translations, the principles that he fought for had a longer temporality.

"Karl Marx, the Theft of Wood, and Working-Class Composition" was written at the University of Rochester in a math professor's office in a building erected upon a Indian burial ground which had once been recognized by a historical marker, just as in those years over a bridge crossing the Genesee River was a graffiti quotation from Langston Hughes, "I've Known Rivers." To me these were significant markings. Both signs have vanished though their meanings abide.

My article attempted to link the ideas of Marx with what I had learned from E.P. Thompson and the scholars associated with him at the University of Warwick in England. Our work published in 1975 in *Whigs and Hunters* and *Albion's Fatal Tree* were expressed in what Thompson called "the empirical idiom," which required that we eschew Marxist "theory." I was working in a history department at Rochester led by Eugene Genovese, who brazenly proclaimed his "Marxism" turning it to advantage. Either you had to bypass Marxism (Thompson) or turn it into a brand (Genovese). This was my quandary and to it I found resolution that began with ghosts.

Susan B. Anthony (feminist), Frederick Douglass (abolitionist), and Lewis Henry Morgan (anthropologist) were buried in the graceful, intricate landscapes of Mount Hope Cemetery, which happened to be located right behind the Rochester history department. Their graves became a frequent destination of pedagogical pilgrimages. The gravel paths, the unmowed tall grass, the prolific wild flowers, and abundant insect life did not produce a place conducive to book-reading and note-taking, so I began to explain things quickly and simply—Wobbly style—on the palm of a hand or with lines drawn by a stick in the dirt. I needed to learn about women and feminists, about African Americans and abolitionists, about the Iroquois and the origins of privatization and to express what I learned clearly and succinctly for I had begun to teach at Attica penitentiary, not so far from Letchworth Gorge.

All that transpired in the mid-1970s. While comprehending the interrelationship between prison and enclosure, the emphasis in "Karl Marx, the Theft of Wood, and Working-Class Composition" was, in keeping with the times when it was written, on criminalization and the proletariat. However, with the advent of the third historical wave of enclosures the emphasis had to change to the commons.

The collapse of the Soviet Union (1990) on the one hand and the advent of the Zapatistas (1994) and their people's army on the other changed the atmosphere of scholarly investigation in America. On the one hand it became possible to think of communism without the totalitarian state, and on the other hand the issue of the commons had become an actual source of armed struggle in many parts of the world. The discourse of the commons somewhat hesitatingly could be heard in the 1990s, as the *ejido* was taken at U.S. command from the Mexican Constitution, as the jackals of Silicon Valley gathered around the software of the computer beast, as ocean, atmosphere, forest—those elements of Nature which had been taken as axioms or the *donnés* of existence (you know, *our world*)—were taken or poisoned. Cattle ranching, timber interests began to tear apart the forests of Amazonas, Java, Congo, and Sumatra. The "greater villains" were loose upon the world.

We didn't have communism to fall back on; the war against Yugoslavia and the demise of the USSR returned the Red again to utopia, that "good place" or "no place" so called. The common ground, what Dene political scientist Glenn Coulthard calls grounded normativity, fast disappeared in the ugly pompous lexicon of neoliberalism—privatization, commodification, proletarianization, feminization, financialization, globalization—turning important nouns into verbs and then back again into hideous mouthfuls, as if to assert that the action and the struggle signified by the verb was over. Nationalization has two meanings—state ownership and making a nation—and we're back to Ozymandias, king of kings.

Prompted by E.P. Thompson's *Customs in Common*, I began to think about these two issues, communism and the commons, in 1993 in an article called "Commonists of the World Unite!"[4] The slogan of the communists had been "From each according to their ability, to each according to their need." The means of attaining it was supposed to be the state, or the "nationalization of the means of production, distribution, and exchange." The Zapatistas required us to think about forms of government.

"Frau Gertrude Kugelmann and the Five Gates of Marxism" was written much later for a conference at Cornell University in Ithaca, New York, also on former Iroquois land. I searched for a short mnemonic to introduce the main ideas of Marx as I had learned them from comrades in Detroit, Padua, London, and Brooklyn but with a historical eye. Furthermore I was slowly becoming aware of the inimitable relation that women had to the commons. So I wanted to investigate the role that the various women played in the life of Marx. I soon discovered that these two searches in fact were one.

(Those German revolutionaries of Frau Kugelmann's generation were jailed in the Spandau prison in Berlin where they were forced to make furniture. More than a century later I lectured on the commons at Cornell University and learned that upstairs from the lecture hall was a chair made in the nineteenth century in that very Berlin prison and cunningly attached to it was a message. The message was protected by foil and hidden in a medallion, which was accidentally exposed at a Board of Trustees meeting in the 1920s, revealing its contents: "Go out into the world and testify to what is born even in prison walls, from strength, from patience, and from loving toil. [signed] The United Workingmen."[5])

The first two essays were written at the request of Alan Haber, the first president of SDS (Students for a Democratic Society), the radical organization which sought to link the civil rights struggle in the American south to the anti-war and anti-poverty struggles of the American north in the early 1960s. Fifty years later Alan was still at it. One essay ("Some Principles") was for the Gray Panthers of Ann Arbor, Michigan, and the other from which this book takes its title was written as part of Alan's campaign against turning over to "developers" much of our town of Ann Arbor so that it can be further asphalted as parking lots. Because Ann Arbor is a book-loving town, the article recommends readings on the commons.

As for the United Kingdom, or the UK, like the USA, it is the name more of an administrative entity than a country. It used to be four kingdoms (England, Wales, Scotland, Ireland) but by 1801 they'd disappeared, the Irish being the last to be swallowed up in the maw of empire. The abbreviation "UK" was a counter-revolutionary figure from the start, as the Irish rebellion was suppressed in a few weeks of unprecedented terror in the summer of 1798. "The Red-Crested Bird and Black Duck" arose from my encounter with Ireland and its eloquent scholarship. It describes the depth of hope, the varieties of commons, and the trans-Atlantic transmission of subversive knowledge (west to east) in the teeth of terror and the night of carnage.

There was a startling ascent of prosperity to Ireland, a veritable pot of gold, then just as suddenly it collapsed and the pot emptied, which threw intellectual life into some confusion. On the day of the Good Friday Agreement of 1998, the major development in the Irish peace process, I found myself speaking in Dublin Castle with a notable group of other scholars, one still wearing the white flannels required in the cricket match in which he had just been batting.

With geographer, historian of technics and science, art critic, and Ulster man Iain Boal, I drove to Toronto to meet David Noble, the late historian of machines and their bad effects on workers and human life generally. To get there we traveled near the River Thames where Tecumseh was killed in battle defending the Indian commons and the goal of confederation of the Indian nations. At his request I wrote "Ned Ludd & Queen Mab," trying to link the English romantic poets with the working-class underground.

Even J.S. Mill referred with horror to "a world with nothing left to the spontaneous activity of nature with every foot of land brought into cultivation . . . and scarcely a place left where a wild shrub or flower could grow."[6] The passionate idealism and the belief that we make our own destiny were the props upholding William Morris's great tent of communizing (he made communism a verb!) as well as to the history writing of E.P. Thompson whose feet in walking upon the ancient times showed us the commons even in the wild flowers. Only three qualities were needed to achieve equalization, Thompson and Morris agreed, "intelligence enough to conceive, courage enough to will, and power enough to compel."

"Enclosures from the Bottom Up" reminds us that there's a hole in every wall, and thus a commons behind every enclosure. This is even the case with terror, which frequently accompanies enclosure. The destruction of the Iroquois commons was at the specific order of George Washington, known in the language of the Haudenosaunee, not as the "father of his country," but as "Town Destroyer." In 1779 George Washington ordered Major General John Sullivan to terrorize the Iroquois. Accordingly Sullivan deliberately destroyed the crops, uprooted the orchards, burnt the houses, and massacred every man, woman, and child of the six nations of the Iroquois confederacy until September 15, when he was exhausted by the effort not far from Letchworth Gorge.

"Wat Tyler Day: The Anglo Juneteenth" was written for scholars committed to the relevance of the struggles of medieval times to our own. Both essays were attempts to begin the vast and exciting project of rewriting history from the standpoint of the commons. The commons may have its own temporality. For example, although "The Anglo Juneteenth" brings together three historical events, each separated by centuries (Magna Carta in 1215, the Peasants' Revolt of 1381, and the American Civil War of 1865) they are united by legal, idealist, and working-class struggle. The essay results in a proposal for an international holiday.

The state plays a decisive role in enclosure: its servants and warriors write the letters of blood and fire. It surely is "the greater villain." In the European Renaissance, when the aggressive European nation-states were formed, the rulers of each were guided by how-to-govern books, most notably Machiavelli's *The Prince*. In England Thomas Elyot wrote *The Governor* (1536) for this purpose. This was the era of peasant revolts to restore the commons and the greatest was in Germany under the rainbow sign. *The Governor* begins with a condemnation of the commons and execration of communism, as I was able to explain in my preface to the Korean translation of *The Magna Carta Manifesto*.

The "USA," or United States of America, although a neologism of Thomas Paine, was grandiose and false from the start. "United" it was not, as the Civil War would demonstrate, and "America" it was not, at least not exclusively, considering Canada or Mexico or Brazil. Honored by Verso Publishers to write an introduction to its anthology of Thomas Paine, I was guided into the Brecklands and the Norfolk broads by Iain Boal and began to understand that the reality of several forms of commoning experienced by the great Atlantic revolutionary depended on locality.

The essay called "Meandering at the Crossroads of Communism and the Commons" returned me to New York State, not to the burned-over district but to the Adirondack Mountains and the hospitality of the Blue Mountain Center. John Brown could not be far from one's historical thinking among these mountains as they provided the protection for the runaway slaves in his army of abolition. It was first published by Massimo D'Angelis and his website The Commoner.

"The Commons, the Castle, the Witch, and the Lynx" reported on an international conference held in Westphalia. It provided a caution against idealizing the Seneca commons which during the crisis of the 1790s was infested by fire-water and suffered from the violence of patriarchy.

The scholar who searches for the commons and rests interpretation upon it is not alone. V. Gordon Childe did work in the Orkney Islands in the North Sea above Scotland. George Thomson did work in the Blasket Islands southwest of mainland Ireland in the Atlantic.[7] One was an archaeologist, the other a classicist, both were deeply influenced by Karl Marx. Their subsequent scholarly careers flourished on different subjects, Thomson on Greek tragedy and Childe as a historiographer of the early history of mankind. They wrote in the 1930s and 1940s. Though they did not write directly about the commons, and certainly not as an embracing conceptual tool, it may be that their work in the Orkney and Blasket islands was partly inspired by an anti-capitalist quest for "primitive communism" in their own backyards so to say. My Madrid lecture, "The City and the Commons," was directly inspired by the movements of the circles and the squares as well as the quest of these earlier scholars.

As the son of an American diplomat and his wife—or, as I should say, as the son of two diplomats, one of whom was unpaid—I was raised by representatives of the USA. Consequently I learned "to think like a state." It is taking me a lifetime to think otherwise, that is, to think in common, of the commons, and for the commons. Mary Jemison has helped.

Earlier I noted the importance of the burned-over district and the rust belt to the composition of these essays. Also while putting them together I learned about Mary Jemison, an unsung inhabitant of the region. I conclude this introduction by briefly telling her story because it seems so well to summarize the personal, professional, and theoretical themes of *Stop, Thief!*

She was born at sea as her parents fled the Irish famine of 1741. Her father cleared land in western Pennsylvania to become a flax farmer supplying the Irish linen industry and thus part of the Atlantic system. During the French and Indian War of mid-century the Shawnee killed him and his family, excepting Mary who, according to their custom, was adopted by Seneca women as a replacement of a brother who had been killed. She learned a new language and adopted a new name, Deh-he-wä-mis. Mary learned common field horticulture cultivating the "three sisters": corn, squash, and beans. Whether gathering wood for the woodpile or hoeing weeds in the field or husking corn, her work was in common with the other women.

Mary Jemison fled to Letchworth Gorge from the terrorizing onslaught in 1779 of General Sullivan who killed and burnt everything—corn, orchards, cabins, men, women, and children—of the Iroquois. With two children on her back and three trailing behind she found refuge in the relatively inaccessible gorge where two runaway African American former slaves made her welcome. They lived in common for several years.

Given the opportunity in 1797 to return to so-called "white" society, she refused. That was at the peak of the second historical wave of enclosures. Despite the settlers' terror, the commons was preserved by the unexpected endeavors of a commons of Irish, Iroquois, and African people. Her white, Anglo editor of 1824 agreed that "she was the protectress of the homeless fugitive, and made welcome the weary traveller."[8]

It was the women of the Haudenosaunee who preserved the commons in the midst of the expropriations attendant on the creation of the USA. It is the women of the world who continue to do so in the midst of our dark times.

The Commons

CHAPTER ONE

Some Principles of the Commons

HUMAN SOLIDARITY AS EXPRESSED IN THE SLOGAN "ALL FOR ONE AND ONE FOR ALL" is the foundation of commoning. In capitalist society this principle is permitted in childhood games or in military combat. Otherwise, when it is not honored in hypocrisy, it appears in the struggle contra capitalism or, as Rebecca Solnit shows, in the disasters of fire, flood, or earthquake.

The activity of commoning is conducted *through* labor *with* other resources; it does not make a division between "labor" and "natural resources." On the contrary, it is labor which creates something as a resource, and it is by resources that the collectivity of labor comes to pass. As an action it is thus best understood as a verb rather than as a "common pool resource." Both James Lovelock's "Gaia Hypothesis" and the environmentalism of Rachel Carson were attempts to restore this perspective.

Commoning is primary to human life. Scholars used to write of "primitive communism." "The primary commons" renders the experience more clearly. Scarcely a society has existed on the face of the earth which has not had at its heart the commons; the commodity with its individualism and privatization was strictly confined to the margins of the community where severe regulations punished violators.

Commoning begins in the family. The kitchen is where production and reproduction meet, and the energies of the day between genders and between generations are negotiated. The momentous decisions in the sharing of tasks, in the distribution of product, in the creation of desire, and in sustaining health are first made here.

Commoning is historic. The "village commons" of English heritage or the "French commune" of the revolutionary past are remnants from this history, reminding us that despite stages of destruction parts have survived, though often in distorted fashion as in welfare systems, or even as their opposite as in the realtor's gated community or the retailer's mall.

Commoning has always had a spiritual significance expressed as sharing a meal or a drink, in archaic uses derived from monastic practices, in recognition of the sacred *habitus*. Theophany, or the appearance of the divine principle, is apprehended in the physical world and its creatures. In North America ("Turtle Island") this principle is maintained by indigenous people.

Commons is antithetical to capital. Commoners are quarrelsome (no doubt), yet the commons is without class struggle. To be sure, capital can arise from the commons, as part is sequestrated off and used against the rest. This begins with inegalitarian relations, among the Have Lesses and the Have Mores. The means of production become the way of destruction, and expropriation leads to exploitation, the Haves and Have Nots. Capital derides commoning by ideological uses of philosophy, logic, and economics which say the commons is impossible or tragic. The figures of speech in these arguments depend on fantasies of destruction—the desert, the life-boat, the prison. They always assume as axiomatic that concept expressive of capital's bid for eternity, the ahistorical "Human Nature."

Communal values must be taught, and renewed, continuously. The ancient court leet resolved quarrels of overuse; the *panchayat* in India did the same, like the way a factory grievance committee is supposed to be; the jury of peers is a vestigial remnant which determines what a crime is as well as who's a criminal. The "neighbor" must be put back into the "hood," as they say in Detroit, like the people's assemblies in Oaxaca.

Commoning has always been local. It depends on custom, memory, and oral transmission for the maintenance of its norms rather than law, police, and media. Closely associated with this is the independence of the commons from government or state authority. The centralized state was built upon it. It is, as it were, "the preexisting condition." Therefore, commoning is not the same as the communism of the USSR.

The commons is invisible until it is lost. Water, air, earth, fire—these were the historic substances of subsistence. They were the archaic physics upon which metaphysics was built. Even after land began to be commodified during English Middle Ages it was written,

> But to buy water or wind or wit or fire the fourth,
> These four the Father of Heaven formed for this earth in common;
> These are Truth's treasures to help true folk

We distinguish "the common" from "the public." We understand the public in contrast to the private, and we understand common solidarity in contrast to individual egotism. The commons has always been an element in human production even when capitalism acquired the hoard or laid down the law. The boss might "mean business" but nothing gets done without respect. Otherwise, sabotage and the shoddy result.

Commoning is exclusive inasmuch as it requires participation. It must be entered into. Whether on the high pastures for the flock or the light of the computer screen for the data, the wealth of knowledge, or the real good of hand and brain, requires the posture and attitude of working alongside, shoulder to shoulder. This is why we speak neither of rights nor obligations separately.

Human thought cannot flourish without the intercourse of the commons. Hence, the first amendment linking the rights of speech, assembly, and petition. A moment's thought reveals the interaction among these three activities which proceed from lonely muttering to poetic eloquence to world changing, or

> Bing! Bing! the light bulb of an idea
> Buzz! Buzz! talking it over with neighbors or co-workers
> Pow! Pow! telling truth to power.

Ann Arbor
January 2010

CHAPTER TWO

Stop, Thief! A Primer on the Commons & Commoning

WE'RE LOSING THE GROUND OF OUR SUBSISTENCE TO THE PRIVILEGED AND THE mighty. With the theft of our pensions, houses, universities, and land, people all over the world cry, "Stop, thief!" and start to think about the commons and act in its name. But what is the commons? Its twenty-first-century meaning is emerging from the darkness of centuries past.

Primers were once prayer books for the laity. Usually "primer" refers to the elementary book used to teach children to read. In another meaning of the word the primer is that which ignites the blasting powder in the old, revolutionary flintlock rifles.

So here is a primer on the commons and commoning. It does not contain prayers, though the matter here is solemn enough. It also has a list of books from the simple to the complex. Finally, if this primer leads to action, detonating greater energy or exploding for the common good, so much the better.

This short primer notes eighteen of the common places in this discussion (food, health, etc.) and sixteen books.

Food: The potluck, the principle of BYO, the CSA (community supported agriculture), the kitchen, are the profoundest human expressions of commoning. The extra seat at the table, the principle of hospitality, are inseparable from human community. The meal is at the heart of every religion. Our daily bread. Food was "rations" on the unhappy ship, on the happy one food was the sailor's commons.

Health: Public health, exercise, sports, prevention of accidents and disease, access to hospitals are dire needs. There was a time when hospitals were places of reception for guests, for strangers, for travelers. The practice of the hospital was the embodiment of the principle of hospitality. *Salus publica populi romani* referred to the goddess of health and well-being, "the public health of the Roman people." Surely, her worship in our day has fallen on evil times, as medical, pharmaceutical, and insurance companies in league with government strangle her in their coils. Once the woodlands were a common pharmacopeia not the private property of Big Pharma.

Security: Militarism and money do not safeguard us. On 9/11 the most expensive military in the world failed to protect the American people or even its own HQ. Instead, citizen passengers after twenty-three minutes of deliberation and voting were able collectively to disarm United Airlines flight 93. A sacrificial collective was formed for the common good. As for the Pentagon, the conclusion is obvious. Our protection is our mutuality.

Housing: Squatting, the group house, intentional communities, the hobo's jungle, the boarding house, the homeless camps are rarely anyone's idea of utopia yet they meet real needs, they arise from direct actions, they are actual mutualism, they enliven dead spaces, they are cooperative.

Gender: Birth, nurturance, neighborhood, and love are the beginnings of social life. The commons of the past has not been an exclusively male place. In fact, it is one very often where the needs of women and children come first. And not "needs" only but decision-making and responsibility have belonged to women from the neighborhoods of industrial "slums" to the matriarchy of the Iroquois confederation to the African village.

Ecology: Look! Look at Tahrir Square. Look at the young and old people in Athens. Look at the popular mobilizations in Spain. People are creating spaces in the urban environment where it becomes possible to engage in the conversation and debate that is essential to commoning. The barber shop, the corner grocery, the church basement, the ice-cream parlor, the local co-op may not be available. The town hall has gone and the town square has become a parking lot. So the first step in commoning is to find a locale, a place, and if one is not easily to hand, then to create one. The emerging geography of the future requires us actively to common spaces in our factories and offices.

Knowledge: The commons grows without copyright; lighting your candle from mine does not diminish me or put my candle out. As Thomas Jefferson said, "He who receives an idea from me, receives instruction himself without lessening mine; as he who lites his taper at mine, receives light without darkening me." Conversation and just talk, or rapping, was once the people's internet. Common sense arises from the web of family and neighborhood relationships. But we need a place to meet! How about the school? Rage, rage against the dying of the light.

Semantics: The gigantic *Oxford English Dictionary* has four to five pages on the word "common," beginning with, "belonging equally to more than one." We get some of our most powerful words from the commons, such as community, communal, commonage, commonality, commune, communion with their social, political, and spiritual overtones and histories. Etymologically, these words are the offspring, so to speak, of two Latin parents, *com* meaning together, and *munis* meaning some kind of obligation. Of course we don't need to stay with English and Latin. In the Andes mountain range, for instance, the *allyus* is the key word; in Mexico the *ejido* was the key word. The word "commons" can be tricky, subject to double-talk or the forked tongue, as when it is used for its opposite as in the privatized housing tract (gated community) or the privatized market (the mall) which will call themselves "the common" but which are actually based on exclusivity unless you possess the do re mi!

Working class: The Supreme Court has ruled against class action by women workers. Let us, the entire working class, employed and unemployed, men and women, rise from our slumbers and show that we do not wait on the Supreme Court for permission to act as a class!

Some say the precariat has replaced the proletariat. This simply means that life for us, the common people, has become more insecure, more uncertain, and more precarious. Whether we are old or whether we are young, whether we are poor or getting by, the institutions that used to help us have disappeared and their names have become bad words, like "welfare" or "social security." As we have learned from our experiences of Katrina or the mortgage crisis, neither government nor corporations are able to abate the situation. As the disasters accumulate we are left more and more to our own devices and find we must dig deeper. The remembered commons of old as well as the spontaneous commons of now need to be available when need arises. Who runs the workplaces anyway?

Being: The commons refers neither to resources alone nor to people alone but to an intermixture of them both. The commons is not only "common pool resources" nor is the commons purely "the people." In other words it is not a thing but a relationship. In medieval Europe the forests, the hills, the coasts, the estuaries were locations of commoners who were respectively foresters, shepherds, fishers, and reed people. The commoner was the person who *commoned* in such lands, and one parish to another parish *intercommoned*, and the bullying giants of legend, the lords and ladies, *discommoned*. In this struggle our landscapes were formed, even our human "nature," as well as Nature herself.

Knowing: Often you don't know of the commons until it is taken away. The neighborhood without sidewalks, the water fountain that has gone dry, the land that once your family could use, the fresh air that used to renew your spirit—gone! They are taking liberties with what we took for granted. No more! Stop, thief!

Politics: The commons is outside the government. Commons provides its own security. Custom, or habit and socialization, rather than police force, regulate relations, as anyone knows who has organized a neighborhood softball game or football in the street. In English history, politics began as a negotiation between lords and commoners. This is why there is a House of Lords and a House of Commons.

Law: Generally custom, rather than law, safeguards and defines commons. Custom is local, it is held in memory, and the elders are the keepers of community memory. From Africa and Latin America we learn that this may be another guise of patriarchy and privilege. Thus while we respect custom, we do not romanticize it.

Economy: The commons is often outside of the realm of buying and selling or the realm of the commodity; it is where life is conducted face to face. The commons is neither a gift economy nor potlatch. No, not everything is free, but yes, everything may be shared. It is a place of reciprocities. This economy is not grounded in those triplets of evil named by Dr. Martin Luther King Jr., namely, militarism, racism, and consumerism. The Industrial Revolution was neither. Quite the contrary. In England mechanization was actually *counter*-revolutionary and what it produced, besides soot and grime, was the opposite of industry: misery for workers and idleness for the rulers. Talk about oxymorons!

History: The commons is old and it is all over, from Iraq to Indiana, from Afghanistan to Arizona, it is associated with indigenous people and it has many recent modifications. History is not a story of simple progress along a straight line of stages or up the rungs of a ladder. There have been many stages, overlapping, returning, leap-frogging, if never actually disappearing. Beneath the radar there have been many communities, commoning along. Besides, progress for whom?

Religion: The good Samaritan, the principle of all things in common. The Franciscans say *juri divino omni sunt communia*, or by divine law all things are common. The Christian New Testament reports that the early Christians held all things in common. Marie Chauvet, the Haitian novelist and observer of voudou, writes, "Someone touched the calabash tree, my Lord God! . . . Someone touched the calabash tree . . . someone touched the calabash tree. . . . You cut down all the trees, and the earth is no longer protected. Look, she's going away and shows you her teeth in revenge."

Poets and Writers: our poets and theorists, our revolutionaries and reformers, have dreamt of it. Henry David Thoreau, Walt Whitman, Maya Angelou, Thomas Paine, Karl Marx, Peter Kropotkin, Claude McKay, Tom McGrath, Marge Piercy . . . oh, the list goes on and on, from the mystics to the romantics to the transcendentalists, from the democrats to the anarchists, from the socialists to the communitarians, from the Wobblies to the reds, from the folkies to the rockers.

England: Some associate the commons with England's so-called "green and pleasant land" and are apt to quote the following as an ancient bit of wisdom.

> The law locks up the man or woman
> Who steals the goose from off the common
> But lets the greater villain loose
> Who steals the common from the goose.

True enough, certainly prisons and the loss of the commons went together in English history, though it was an Irishman who composed this bit of wit. Who are the geese in today's world? In England at the time of the enclosures of commons and prison construction in the 1790s, the Romantic Revolt poured out a huge expression of opposition. Samuel Coleridge writing at the time gave us a few spiritual lines which we can quote as a take away.

> Return, pure Faith! Return, meek piety!
> The kingdoms of the world are yours: each heart
> Self-governed, the vast Family of Love
> Rais'd from the common earth by common toil,
> Enjoy the equal produce . . .

Further Reading

The books on this list may not be easily acquired just because bookstores are closing, libraries face budget cutbacks, and schools supplant the page with the screen, or the book with the computer. But if you've read this far you already know that knowledge, like a place to meet, can be obtained with patience, resourcefulness, and working with others. I have listed the books in rough order of difficulty.

Robert Fulghum, *All I Really Need to Know I Learned in Kindergarten* (New York: Ballantine Books, 1983)
Share everything, play fair, don't hit people, clean up your own mess, put things back where you found them, say sorry when you hurt someone, don't take things that aren't yours, and when going into the world hold hands, stick together, and look both ways!

Jay Walljasper, ed., *All That We Share: A Field Guide to the Commons* (New York: The New Press, 2010)
An anthology in ten chapters, with helpful lists, dictionary, solutions, by noted scholars and thinkers. This is a good place to start because it is practical, simple, and short.

Raj Patel, *The Value of Nothing: How to Reshape Market Society and Redefine Democracy* **(New York: Picador, 2009)**
The author became, despite himself, subject of a messianic cult, but don't worry, this is a sensible introduction saying that the age of *homo economicus* is past and that we are all commoners now.

"p.m.," *bolo bolo* **(New York: Autonomedia, 2011)**
A new edition of this beautifully creative and visionary set of practical suggestions, full of sweet delight for readers from twelve to seventy and up with lovely new words for new roles and lifestyles in the comedy of life.

Rebecca Solnit, *A Paradise Built in Hell: The Extraordinary Communities That Arise in Disaster* **(New York: Viking, 2009)**
Mrs. Anna Amelia Holshouser dressed properly, combed her hair, and applied her make-up before descending the shaking stairs into the maelstrom of the San Francisco earthquake of 1906. Immediately, she began helping her neighbors, and soon the Mizpah Café was feeding thousands. Her extraordinary story is of commoning amidst disasters—Mexico, Halifax, New York, San Francisco, New Orleans—and of the clumsy, counterproductive efforts of authorities who generally make the mess worse.

David Bollier, *Silent Theft: The Private Plunder of Our Common Wealth* **(New York: Routledge, 2002)**
One of the earliest responses to the onslaught of privatization, especially strong on the internet, influenced by Ralph Nader, well written with the intensity of thorough and quiet conviction. Bollier is a worldwide activist on behalf of commoning.

Iain Boal, Janferie Stone, Michael Watts, and Cal Winslow, eds., *West of Eden: Communes and Utopia in Northern California* **(Oakland: PM Press, 2011)**
Documents the commoning projects in northern California in the 1960s and '70s, including the free theatre in San Francisco parks; Native American occupation of Alcatraz; Black Panther breakfast program; rusticating hippies and back-to-the-landers; the Pacifica Radio network.

Silvia Federici, *Caliban and the Witch: Women, the Body, and Primitive Accumulation* **(New York: Autonomedia, 2004)**
Beautifully illustrated, already a classic text, passionately conceived, it helps to reconceptualize the relations among racism, sexism, and capitalism by locating the historical trauma against women and the commons.

Maria Mies and Veronika Bennholdt-Thomsen, *The Subsistence Perspective: Beyond the Globalised Economy*, trans. Patrick Camiller, Maria Mies, and Gard Wieh (New York: Zed Books, 1999)
Written by European feminists with strong ties to Bangladesh the authors act locally and think globally and vice versa! They provide alternatives to the axioms of capitalism and patriarchy: humans are selfish, resources are scarce, needs are infinite, the economy must grow. They teach standing on our own feet, speaking in our own voices.

Peter Linebaugh, *The Magna Carta Manifesto: Liberties and Commons for All* (Berkeley: University of California Press, 2008)
Declared by the *Nation* magazine as "the year's most lyrical and necessary book on liberty." Three chapters on American history, one on India, and several on English history, with song, drama, paintings, and murals. Found to be useful to the briefs of the Center for Constitutional Rights in the Gitmo cases.

Lewis Hyde, *Common as Air: Revolution, Art, and Ownership* (New York: Farrar, Straus and Giroux, 2010)
This is a superior book in defense of the cultural commons. It takes on the absurdities of branding, copyright, and privatization of ideas, thoughts, and beauty. It has splendid chapters on Benjamin Franklin and Thomas Jefferson. Its twenty-first-century concept of civic virtue calls on us to resist enclosure.

Michael Hardt and Antonio Negri, *Commonwealth* (Cambridge: Harvard University Press, 2009)
The concluding volume of a trilogy of high academic theory and challenging philosophy which names the republic, modernity, and capital as three obstructions to the commons. It has a terminology of its own. Love is the process of creating the commons and overcoming the solitude of individualism.

Elinor Ostrom, *Governing the Commons: The Evolution of Institutions for Collective Action* (New York: Cambridge University Press, 1990)
She won the Nobel Prize and this book possesses the strengths of American social science. She takes "the tragedy of the commons" and "the prisoner's dilemma," and demonstrates their shallowness by logic and empirical inquiry into communal tenure in Switzerland and Japan, fishery commons in Turkey, Nova Scotia, and Sri Lanka.

Herbert Reid & Betsy Taylor, *Recovering the Commons: Democracy, Place, and Global Justice* **(Urbana: University of Illinois Press, 2010)**
A political scientist and a cultural anthropologist do their thing for advanced students of political theory and philosophy with surprising and welcome derivations from their experiences in the Appalachian mountains and with the Appalachian people.

Ann Arbor
July 2011

CHAPTER THREE

The City and the Commons:
A Story for Our Times

THE MUNICIPAL OCCUPATIONS AND THE URBAN ENCAMPMENTS OF 2011 PROVIDE THE starting point for these reflections on the city and the commons, and for a story.[1]

Taksim Square, Tahrir Square, Syntagma Square, Puerto del Sol, Zuccotti Park, Oscar Grant Plaza, St. Paul's Cathedral: historically, the city grew around these places expanding concentrically. They came alive again as gathering places whose primary purpose was to spark discussion locally and globally.[2] They were a commons inasmuch as internal relations were not those of commodity exchange, an anti-hierarchical ethos, or "horizontalism," prevailed, and basic human needs such as security, food, waste disposal, health, knowledge, and entertainment were self-organized.

These campings took place amid an international conversation about the commons initiated by the Zapatistas of Mexico after the repeal of Article 27 of the Mexican Constitution, providing for common lands in the village, the *ejido*. The South American discussion combined constitutional discourse with the commoning practices of indigenous peoples. The Nobel Prize in Economics was awarded in 2009 to Elinor Ostrom for "her analysis of economic governance, especially the commons." It is significant that the award went to a woman precisely because the commons historically was the domain where women enjoyed some parity with men, as Jeannette Neeson showed in her study *Commoners*.[3]

The paradox of Occupy was the conscious human attempt to common the privatized heart of the city when the evidence of history apparently would deem this to be an impossibility, indeed a contradiction. In an important article published in 1950 the influential archaeologist and pre-historian V. Gordon Childe, described a new economic stage in social evolution beginning about five thousand years ago, the city, or "the urban revolution" as he called it, or the creation of the city.[4] It contrasted with the Paleolithic and Neolithic stages (corresponding somewhat with the eighteenth- and nineteenth-century stages of "savagery" and "barbarism"). Whether characterized by roving bands of hunters and gatherers or by small villages subsisting by the domestication of plants and animals, neither privatization nor enclosure of property prevailed in either of these earlier stages. Instead society depended on cooperative labor, common resources, and communal distribution. Or what we may call "the commons."

Court, Fort, and Port

Thus, the city and the commons appear to be opposite. The city is a place where food is consumed, the country commons is a place of its production. The city-state precedes the nation-state but not the commons.

Originally surrounded by walls, the city expressed antagonism with the countryside. John Horne Tooke, the imprisoned radical and etymologist of the 1790s, believed that the word "town" derived from Anglo-Saxon meaning inclosed, encompassed, or shut in.[5] In contrast we have tended to see the commons without enclosures and in open relation with land, forest, mountain, rivers, and seas. The city is the location of markets, the destination of caravans, the terminus of ships, the home of specialized craftspeople, so commerce and the city are intertwined. The city fulfilled several functions: of fortification against servile rebellion and foreign invasion, of law and sovereignty, and of trade and commerce. As a fort, as a court, and as a port, the city has embodied in all of these functions the principle of enclosure.

We can't think of the city except in terms of class. Traditionally, its population was divided in three, the patricians, the plebeians, and the proletariat. When the peasants demanded the return of their commons, they went to the city as they did to London during the great Peasants' Revolt (1381). They freed prisoners and destroyed written evidence of the expropriation of commons.

Freedom to the capitalist meant freedom from the restrictions on commerce, markets, and production that characterized the medieval city. Freedom also meant freedom of movement. This entailed a contradiction, however. The principle of movement was opposed by the principle of enclosure. Capitalists "sought to demolish the old structures" including the circumambient walls. The vector between town and country was the wheeled vehicle and the road, or the in the case of colony and metropolis, the sea-lanes and the ship. In the countryside the road became the scene of robberies, memorialized in the name of the "highwayman." Highway robbery became synonymous with profiteering. Hermes was god of both thievery and trade. The street becomes the thoroughfare. The meaning of "traffic" changed from commodity exchange to vehicular motion on the roadways linking forever speed, avarice, and congestion. By the 1790s directional orientation on the streets was determined: on the right for France and its colonies, on the left in Britain and its colonies.[6]

Just as some walls come down, others go up. The great age of confinement begins—the hospital, the factory, the barracoon, the prison, the ship, insane asylum, old age home, the crèche, the school, barracks—become sealed capsules where the commanding principle (as Bentham termed it) prevailed.[7]

The urban theatre of power joined the urban spectacle of commodities with the result that the city became a matrix of pain—the stocks, whipping posts, the gallows, the gibbet, the lock-ups, houses of correction, workhouses, and dungeons provided focal points of public gathering. At the junction point between the city and the county stood the gallows, called Tyburn, where thousands perished.

In England, Scotland, Wales, and Ireland a vast process of enclosure was taking place. We are familiar with this as it concerned land: Acts of Parliament in England and Wales, clearances in the Scottish Highlands, Penal Laws in Ireland. We are less familiar with the enclosure in the factory, the prison, and urban infrastructures. The walls which once defended the city from enemies coming from the countryside now were interiorized to enclose urban wealth from the creation of commons in the city by workers who had lost their commons in the country.

Childe contrasted the "urban revolution" with the Neolithic revolution preceding it and what he called (following the wisdom of the time) the "industrial revolution." If the wheel, the plough, and the sail boat were the technological signature of the urban revolution, then the steam engine, or the heat engine, of the late eighteenth century transformed all three and made possible a "great transformation" in the human relation to the earth and to each other.[8] This took place first in England.

Two hundred years ago London was the largest city in the world, and commanded it. As the center of world banking it transferred wealth from country to city, from colony to metropolis. Its shipping was greatest, hundreds of vessels arrived from around the world every year; its population was numerous, divided between the squares of the West End and the slums of the East End. It was the headquarters of government, church, army, and navy.

Three great walls summarize London at the time. First, Thomas Dancer redesigned Newgate prison after it was destroyed in the Gordon riots of 1780. Second, he cooperated with John Soane, the architect of the Bank of England. By 1796 they had demolished neighboring residences and built a high defensive screen wall, sealing off the hoards of gold, silver, cash, and paper records of the national debt. An 1803 London guidebook, compared it to "the enclosure of a gaol, an immense pile of wall, almost bullet-proof."[9] Third, the wall of the West India docks and the London Docks, were "inclosed and surrounded by a strong brick or stone Wall not less than 30 feet high . . . and immediately without the Wall, there shall be a Ditch of the width of 12 feet . . . to be always kept filled with water 6 feet deep, and no House or Building shall be erected within 100 yards of the outside of the Wall." Law, money, commodity: the walled prison, bank, and port.

The military planners of the defense of London in 1801 no longer relied on the wall. Fortification of London as a whole was too expensive. Instead, in the words of George Hanger, "every enclosed field is a natural fortification: the ditch is the fossé, the bank the parapet, and the hedge on top of it a natural abbatis." "I mean to contend every inch of ground with them for miles, through these inclosed natural fortresses." He believed the enemy will attack from the common or common-field.[10]

The street was part of the urban commons. It was not only the place of traffic, or the movement of commodities. It joined producer and consumer, and it joined the producers of various components in separated workshops. It was the site of sport, of theater, of carnival, of song. The cries of London street sellers provided a permanent part of the sounds of the city. By venerable urban custom the puppeteer could set up his Punch-and-Judy show in the middle of the street. The street was erotic, the streetwalker a synonym for the sex worker. Along with the street was the evolution of the sidewalk or "pavement." Wheeled and foot traffic were demarcated corresponding to a division between "economy" and "society" or between economic production and social reproduction.

The ancient antagonism between town and country is parallel to the more recent antagonism between colony and imperial metropolis. The city has attracted the young and energetic of the countryside, just as the metropolis has been the destination of the poor from the colonized parts of the world, the wretched of the earth in Fanon's phrase. The city of the global North brings together people from the global South—Asia, America, and Africa—where forms of commoning have persisted into the twenty-first century. Marx and Engels wrote in *The Communist Manifesto*, "Just as it [capitalism] has made the country dependent on the towns, so it has made barbarian and semi-barbarian countries dependent on the civilized ones, nations of peasants on nations of bourgeois, the East on the West."

Ireland & Haiti, Edward & Catherine

Ireland was the oldest colony of England. Haiti was the richest colony of France. France and England were engaged in a long, and world war, part of an old conflict and, more important to us, a war of ideas, a war between *liberté*, *égalité*, and *fraternité* on the one hand and Church, King, and Property on the other. Each colony revolted. Haiti against France in August 1791, Ireland forming a revolutionary organization in October of the same year, and finally goaded into revolt against England in 1798. The periphery thus threatened the center. The commons had a geopolitical dynamic.

Edward Marcus Despard, and his wife, Catherine, an African American woman, embodied these challenges. He was born in Ireland in 1750. He sailed for Jamaica in 1765 and he remained in the Caribbean or Central America until 1790. He returned to British Isles and was to spend the next dozen years, perhaps the most revolutionary of human history, in London prisons (apart from Shrewsbury)—King's Bench, Coldbath Fields, the Tower, Tothill Fields, Newgate, and Horsemonger Lane.

He was an active revolutionary for an independent republican Ireland, and she was a woman with roots in the struggle against slavery. They had valuable experience in forms of the commons which they brought to England at a crucial time when the rate of dispossession from common lands and common rights was extremely high. Despard was imprisoned as a revolutionary in March 1798 and he suffered a traitor's death five years later. He was charged with conspiring to lead an urban insurrection by attacking Windsor Castle (the court), the Bank of England (the port), and the Tower of London (the fort). The insurrectionary project thus aimed at the threefold essence of the city by besieging three of its most monumental buildings. It aimed to take these over rather than to abolish their principles of war, money, and law, and therefore it did not threaten that "urban revolution." Yet the commons did pose such a threat.

Even with the noose around his neck, as it was on February 21, 1803, Despard sought to change the course of history. He spoke as "a friend to truth, to liberty, and to justice." As a friend to "the poor and oppressed" he anticipated the triumph of the "principles of freedom, of humanity, and of justice" against the principles of falsehood, tyranny, and delusion. He suffered death for endeavoring to procure health, happiness, and freedom for the human race.

The gallows speech became one of the great sites of human eloquence. The United Irishmen could turn defeat into condemnation of the oppressor. He did not turn the tables alone. Catherine helped him with his rhetorical triads. We find similar triads in Thomas Spence (his followers met in 1801 as the "Real Friends to Truth, Justice, and Human Happiness") and in Frederick Engels criticizing the utopian socialists ("socialism is the expression of absolute truth, reason, and justice").

His judge hanged him for espousing "the wild and Leveling principle of Universal Equality." Edward Law or Lord Ellenborough on behalf of landlords, stock-jobbers, and capitalists summed up the danger of the revolutionary commons. This is the key point about the Despard conspiracy. It is ambivalent, on the one side it is an insurrectionary attempt to take the city, on the other hand, it is "wild," that is, linked with "savagery" and "barbarism," it is "leveling," that is, it is connected to the Levellers and Diggers of the seventeenth-century English revolution, it is part of the universal upsurge beginning in France and continuing in Haiti.

The year 1803 was a historic moment, or "spot in time," with an Hegelian, a Marxist, and a Thompsonian meaning. Moved by the struggle against slavery in Haiti, Hegel came to understand universal history of freedom in the dialectics of the master-slave.[11] Engels was fond of the "utopian" socialists of the time (Saint Simon and Robert Owen) faulting them only for living before the industrial proletariat matured to develop the "science" of socialism.[12] Thompson showed that, driven by the prohibition of trade unions and the persecution of political reformers, the working-class movement in England formed a political underground which enabled it to survive but destroyed an opportunity to connect with the ideas of the romantic poets. Hegel gave us dialectics, Engels gave us historical materialism, and Thompson the working class. Hegel leads us to the slaves, the utopian socialists lead us to the indigenous peoples, and Thompson leads us to the underground.

"A Red Round Globe Hot Burning"

Knowledge of the commons grows with expansion of imperialism. A single term, "the commons," expresses, first, that which the working-class lost when subsistence resources were taken away and, second, the idealized visions of *liberté*, *égalité*, and *fraternité*. Winstanley, for instance, who in 1650 said that the earth is a common treasury for all, or Rousseau whose *Discourse on Inequality* (1755) made the commons the starting point of the human story. While the romantic poets inflated the notion of the commons they disengaged it from material practice.

The English romantic poets arose precisely at the moment of maximum antagonism between commons and privatization. What was nature to them? "[The common] is one of the bridges from Jacobinism and utopian communism to nature," wrote E.P. Thompson in 1969 although Thompson did not linger on this bridge in his subsequent work.[13] Yet this is the bridge we must cross.

The most influential writer of the time, Thomas Paine, was familiar with both river and pasturage commons in his town, Thetford, and with the commons of the Iroquois during the War of Independence. He wrote, "the earth in its natural uncultivated state was, and ever would have continued to be, the *common property of the human race* . . . that the system of landed property, by its inseparable connection with cultivation, and with what is called civilized life, has absorbed the property of all those whom it dispossessed, without providing, as ought to have been done, an indemnification for that loss."

Here is Coleridge in 1795 combining ideas of politics, natural resources, human labor, and justice:

> . . . each heart
> Self-governed, the vast Family of Love
> Rais'd from the common earth by common toil,
> Enjoy the equal produce . . .

And here is Wordsworth cautious,

> . . . something there was holden up to view
> Of a republic, where all stood thus far
> Upon common ground, that they were brothers all.
> (*The Prelude*, lines 226–31, 1805)

His poetry attacked manufactories and workhouses, prisons and soup kitchens. His story of the abandoned woman as Wordsworth's main plot for his poetry of the 1790s hits the nail on the head, for in the commons woman's place could be on a par with men. His 1802 preface to *Lyrical Ballads* was a manifesto, to use "the real language of men" and to choose subjects from "low and rustic life."

William Blake put it simply, "the Whole Business of Man Is The Arts & All Things Common," and then prayed on it, "Give us the Bread that is our due & Right, by taking away Money, or a Price, or Tax upon what is Common to all in thy Kingdom."[14] Thus "the commons" was in the air, and so was its opposite, enclosure. For Blake enclosure leads to death and to ecocide:

> They told me that I had five senses to inclose me up,
> And they inclos'd my infinite brain into a narrow circle,
> And sunk my heart into the Abyss, a red round globe hot burning
> Till all from life I was obliterated and erased.[15]

The Manifold of the Commons

From the standpoint of stadial history (such as V. Gordon Childe exemplified), the commons is a vestige of savagery or a relic of barbarism. From the standpoint of capitalist development the commons is the waste from manufactures or the by-products of handicrafts. In short, the commons are either leftovers or holdouts deserving at best a heritage niche. The manifold of the commons means to bring together the resistances to enclosures no matter their geographic provenance or their economic function.[16] It opposes Blake's "red round globe hot burning."

William Blake was inspired by the "thirty towns." They were based upon Guaraní practices of common land in South America and by Christian ideas of all things in common. The common land was called God's property or *tupam-baé*. Montesquieu praised them; Voltaire mocked them; William Robertson wrote, "The produce of their fields, together with the fruits of their industry of every species, was deposited in common storehouses, from which each individual received everything necessary for the supply of his wants."[17]

America was the seed-bed of European models of utopia since 1516 when Thomas More published *Utopia*. Here there is neither private property nor rich and poor.[18] America in this sense replaced the Golden Age that had persisted from antiquity. The Golden Age was an aristocratic vision, Utopia was a bourgeois vision. Shakespeare drew upon both in his treatment of American colonization in *The Tempest* (1609), "All things in common Nature should produce without sweat or endeavor."

"The dish with one spoon" is a rhetorical figure of the Haudenosaunee expressing the unity of the five nations of the Iroquois confederacy with the commons of the Great Lakes. The same region produced the warrior leader, Tecumseh, who also struggled for confederation in the name of the "commons." In 1789 the indigenous people of Connecticut lamented, "the times are turned upside down. . . . They had no contention about their lands, for they lay in common; and they had but one large dish, and could all eat together in peace and love."[19] It is a lament heard over and over again in this decade from the romantic *Lyrical Ballads* to the prisons of London.

All the Atlantic mountains, to paraphrase Blake, had begun to shake with the Tupac Amarú revolt in the Andes of 1780. At the *cerro ricco* in Potosí, the source of the world's silver and the universal equivalent of all commodities, the murderous *mita* deformation of cooperative labor prevailed.[20] Direct appropriation was criminalized. The 1780 revolt has been likened to "a great Civil War" whose drama, mobilization, and consequences rank with those of the Haitian revolution of 1791–1803. In Haiti Moreau described a "kind of republic" in the estuary of the Artibonite River where property was not inherited by their offspring but returned to the community. The slaves defended customary rights to common provision grounds of potatoes and manioc. Polverel, one of the French commissioners, issued a proclamation in August 1793 saying that the plantation belonged "in common" to the "universality" of the "warriors" and eligible "cultivators."[21]

Despite the land transfers following the conquests by Cromwell and William III, commoning retained its existence in Ireland. Despard grew up with it. Typical to the eighteenth century was the rundale-and-clachan pattern of settlement in the west and in the uplands of Ireland. Tenants holding partnership leases and inhabiting housing clusters regulated communal grazing (*buaile* or "booley") in the uplands, turbary rights in the bogland, and foreshore rights (*cearta trá*, or seaweed rights) by the strand. The strips of communal infield were rotated annually (rundale) to ensure ecological egalitarianism of all types of soil—deep, shallow, sandy, dry. This form of commoning, therefore, was a response to commercial expansion in the lowlands, and should be seen as part of "modernism" rather than as a vestige from a mythic past.[22] Despard's counterparts in Ireland opposed rampant privatization, including Thomas Reynolds and Robert Emmet, who were to suffer hanging later in 1803. Russell considered the "thirty towns" as "beyond compare the best, the happiest, that ever has been instituted." Anything short of "Celtic communism," according to James Connolly, "is only national recreancy" or cowardly faithlessness. In Scotland 1792 was called "the year of the sheep" when the Cheviot sheep was brought to the highlands and the first wave of clearances began. The Highland clearances destroyed the tenants who drew lots for strips in runrig agriculture and the cotters who lost their common of grazing, kail-yard, and potato patch. Eviction, burning, riot, and exile was the result.[23]

In 1793 the Governor-General of Bengal, Charles Cornwallis, proclaimed the Permanent Settlement which installed a regime of private property.[24] The same man at the same time started the fight on his estate against Mary Houghton, the gleaner's queen. Notwithstanding several thousand years of human history to the contrary, the English court declared that gleaning was not a common right. The attack on English agrarian customs was deep, vicious, and widespread. The Charters of Liberty had protected some of them since the Middle Ages; Magna Carta acknowledged the widow's "estovers in the common" (fuel) while its companion, the Charter of the Forest, protected pannage (pig's food). The lexicon of the agrarian commons (turbary, piscary, herbage, etc.) is obscure, forgotten, local, or arcane. Much commoning is durable to the extent it is invisible.

By enclosure we include the complete separation of the worker from the means of production—this was most obvious in the case of land (the commons)—it also obtained in the many trades and crafts of London, indeed it was prerequisite to mechanization. The shoemaker kept some of the leather he worked with ("clicking"). The tailor kept cloth remnants he called "cabbage." The weavers kept their "fents" and "thrums" after the cloth was cut from the loom. Servants expected "vails" and would strike if they were not forthcoming. Sailors treasured their "adventures." Wet coopers felt entitled to "waxers." The ship-builders and sawyers took their "chips." The dockers (or longshoremen) were called "lumpers," and worked with sailors, watermen, lightermen, coopers, warehousemen, porters, and when the containers of the cargo broke or the cargo spilled they took as custom their "spillings," "sweepings," or "scrapings." The cook licked his own fingers.[25]

Alexander von Humboldt, the aristocratic savant, journeyed to America, 1799–1804. "The gentle character of the Guanches was the fashionable topic, as we in our times, land the Arcadian innocence of the inhabitants of Otaheite." The mutiny on the *Bounty* arose from the crew's opposition to the division between Captain Bligh's "oeconomy," his money economy and their customs of the sea.[26] In Tahiti this division opened into a cruel gulf between the two civilizations. "To the Europeans theft was a violation of legal ownership. . . . To the Tahitians it was a skillful affirmation of communal resources."[27]

To sum up. The loss of commons included a manifold of practices from the country, from the "barbarian" and "semi-barbarian" nations (Marx), from customary trade practices, and urban "criminality." Where or how could these practices be compared? How might the various commons become subject to synthesis? Paradoxically one such place was prison.

The Prison *Encuentro*

France and England were the empires locked in war. George Lefebvre tells us that the existence of the French peasantry depended on collective rights: access to common land for pasture, access to woodlands for fuel and building materials, and the right of gleaning after the harvest.[28] The encroachment upon these common customs led to the uprisings of the summer of 1789. Jules Michelet counted thirty prisons in Paris in the eighteenth century. The Bastille had walls thirty feet thick and more than a hundred feet high. Under Louis XVI its interior garden was enclosed against the prisoners and the windows walled up.[29] The enclosure of the commons and the storming of the Bastille started the revolution. William Hazlitt, the English radical, likened the liberation of the Bastille to the jubilee; Thomas Paine called it "the high altar and castle of despotism" producing only doubt and despair; John Thelwall spoke of its "bars, iron doors, and caves forlorn" in his first sonnet from prison.[30]

In *The State of Prisons* (1776) John Howard exposed the hunger, cold, damp, vermin, noise, irreligion, profanity, and corruption of prisons. He advised no fees, early rising, uniforms, soap and cold water, prayers, Bible reading, solitary nighttime cellular confinement, frequent inspection, constant day-time work, and classification in order to prevent communication. The goal was repentance, or penance, hence "the penitentiary." His solution helped to destroy the inmate order or the prisoner's forms of self-governance where a vibrant political culture could flourish. In Newgate, feminists, millenarians, vegetarians, antinomians, prophets, poets, philosophers, historians, healers, and doctors gathered, "guests of His Majesty."

Lord George Gordon was at the center of the "London's notorious prison republic." He "divided his substance with those who had no money. . . . He clothed the naked, and fed the hungry," his secretary wrote, and described the prisoners, "They were composed of all ranks . . . the jew and the Gentile, the legislator and the laboring mechanic, the officer and the soldier, all shared alike; liberty and equality were enjoyed in their full extent, as far as Newgate would allow."[31] James Ridgway was imprisoned 1793–1797 in Newgate, "From his cell poured forth a stream of works on the French Revolution, tyranny, war with France, peace, the rights of women, America, religious freedom, slavery, army-navy reform, Ireland, as well as some novels and several plays."[32] Dr. James Parkinson, the republican, democrat, and leveler, wrote his *Remarks on Scurvy* (1797) while in the Tower.[33] Coldbath Fields was opened in 1794, one of the "reformed" penitentiaries, soon nicknamed the Bastille or simply the "Steel." Coleridge wrote,

> As he went through Coldbath Fields he saw
> A solitary cell;
> And the Devil was pleased, for it gave him a hint
> For improving his prisons in Hell.

Up the Chimney and the Hollow Quill

Thomas Spence and Gracchus Babeuf were the leading communists of the 1790s in England and France respectively. Babeuf was an insurrectionist and journalist, Spence a propagandist by song, graffiti, coin, and drink. They participated in revolutionary movement, they espoused the universalism of communism, and they had actual experience of the commons.

Francis Place, still active in the L.C.S. and with the committee supporting the prisoners, describes how writings were smuggled into Coldbath Fields prison. They were rolled up and stuck into a quill, and the quill was inserted into a joint of roast meat close to the bone to avoid overheating.[34] One imagines Catherine Despard crossing the several miles from the patrician squares of upper Berkeley Street to the narrow winding streets and alleys of plebeian Clerkenwell in order to deliver dinner, and Spence's plan.

Spence brings together the practicalities of customary rights of the commons with the idealities of universal equality. He drew on several traditions, the Garden of Eden, Jubilee, the Golden Age, utopian, Christian, Jewish, American Indian, millenarian, Dissenting. All of these ideas were experienced in a context of the commons of the sea (his mother was from the Orkney Islands) and of the land (the Newcastle Town Moor not yet enclosed).

He first enunciated his plan that the land should revert to parish ownership to the Newcastle Philosophical Society in 1775. He moved to London, joined the London Corresponding Society, and over the course of the next

decade developed his schemes, how to put his plan into operation, revolutionary insurrection, general strike, equality for women, and "rich confiscations."
His most enduring song was "The Jubilee Hymn," sung to the tune of "God
Save the Queen," the actual jubilee arising as a compromise some five thousand years earlier between the Neolithic and the Urban "stages."

Arriving in London he countermarked the coin of the realm. It was a
period of severe shortage in small copper coinage, so tradesmen issued their
own tokens. Spence soon began to do so too.[35] The pennies and halfpennies displayed radical mottoes ringed around the coin's edge: "If rents I once
consent to pay My Liberty is past away," or "Man over Man He Made Not
Lord." On one side of a penny entitled "Before the Revolution" is the image
of a chained skeletal prisoner in a stone dungeon gnawing on a bone while
on its obverse side, titled "After the Revolution," is a man happily feasting at
table while three figures gaily dance beneath a leafy tree.

He sold a drink called "salop," a concoction made from powder ground
from the root-tubers of the early-purple orchid and then infused in warm milk,
honey, and spices. This orchid is "one of the few orchids that fairly be called
common." Also called dogstones, goosey ganders, kettle cases, etc. (orchis
means testicles), it became popular as an aphrodisiac.[36] Did Spence venture
out into the earth's commons to gather his own orchidaceous samples, or did
he acquire his supplies from one of the knowing herb women of the London
streets and markets?

Thomas Spence was also committed to the "Steel" but not before Despard
was removed to another new penitentiary, Shrewsbury, where Spence was
removed too only after Despard had left. The revolutionary soldier and the
English communist crossed paths in institutions designed to suppress revolution, the commons, and talk! If ideas of communism reached Despard in
a hollow quill, ideas of anti-imperialism did so from the chimney, for that is
where Arthur O'Connor's book was hidden in Coldbath Fields. It is a classic
of the literature of national liberation.

Arthur O'Connor (1763–1852) was a member of the Directory of the
United Irishmen. He was a wealthy landowner. He negotiated with France in
1795 and 1796. He believed "there were 200,000 men in London so wretched
that in rising in the morning they were not sure to find dinner in the day."[37] He
was arrested and imprisoned in Dublin Castle where in six months he wrote
The State of Ireland, which was distributed in February 1798. He was arrested
in England en route to France along with other United Irishmen and charged
with treason. Interrogated by the Privy Council, including the Prime Minister,
the Home Secretary, and the Lord Chancellor he was sent to Coldbath Fields
prison. "Of all the furies I ever met," he wrote later, "the wife of the gaoler

was the greatest." Yet his book became part of the clandestine prison library hidden up a chimney, as the Attorney General revealed in Parliamentary debate.

Addressing England, O'Connor wrote, "O Ignorance! Thou guardian of bastilles! Thou parent of famine! Thou creator of slaves, and supporter of despots, thou author of every mischief and every ill! How long must we bear thy accursed dominion?" The Irish people were "worse housed, worse clad, worse fed" of any people in Europe. "Your corn, your cattle, your butter, your leather, your yarn," all the produce of the land is exported. He praised Irish hospitality, the absolute axiom of the commons. He opposed mechanization, monopoly, high grain prices, and primogeniture. He castigated British imperialism not only for its crimes in Ireland but "in every quarter of the globe, pillaging, starving, and slaughtering the unoffending inhabitants of the East Indies; lashing the wretches they have doomed to slavery in the West Indies." As his modern editor writes, "The only logical antidote to the pathologies of the state of Ireland was a democratic, socially egalitarian republic."[38] Arthur O'Connor himself wrote "Redress means restoration of plunder and restoration of rights."

Sir Francis Burdett, M.P., accompanied Catherine on her visits to Despard. Once he left three guineas for the "mutineers." A good third of the British fleet mutinied the previous year over arrears of pay, forced labor, bloody discipline, and systemic cheating. A hundred ships raised the red flags of defiance. Among their demands was to have sixteen ounces to the pound. Thirty-six mutineers were hanged, including Richard Parker, president of the fleet. The United Irishmen were prominent among the agitators below decks including the Belfast man, Valentine Joyce.[39] Thirty-three of the mutineers were still imprisoned in Coldbath Fields by the time Despard arrived. The prison and the ship were conduits in the manifold of the commons where experiences in Ireland, the Caribbean, and Britain could be compared.

Entrepreneurs of Enclosure: A Gang of Four

The open fields were enclosed. Factories began to enclose handicrafs. Markets were replaced by shops. The penitentiary replaced outdoor punishments. Even the gallows on Tyburn Road was closed and reopened inside Newgate prison. Sexuality was repressed. The mind-forged manacles locked shut but not without help from the mind manaclers who forge ruling ideas still.

Bentham, Young, Colquhoun, and Malthus triumphed in the battle of ideas. Bentham was a founder of utilitarianism, Arthur Young was an agronomist, a development specialist, Colquhoun was a founder of police, and Malthus a founder of population studies. The ideas of the utilitarian, the agronomist, the demographer, and the police man reflected dominant historical trends, and erected social and intellectual structures which have persisted into the twenty-first century. They were not only men of the study, they were men of affairs, and appealed to practical, commanding men who paid them.

Arthur Young was the advocate of land privatization; the earth became a capitalist asset. Thomas Malthus sought to show that famine, war, and pestilence balanced a fecund population. Patrick Colquhoun was the magistrate and government intelligence agent who organized the criminalization of London custom. Jeremy Bentham contrived the architectural enclosure of the urban populations with his "panopticon."

They were international. Malthus became the professor at the College of the East India Company. Jeremy Bentham's notion of the panopticon originated from a trip to Russia. Colquhoun's formative years were passed in Virginia and later he advised the West India interest and had a stake in Jamaican plantations. Arthur Young's first survey of agriculture was the result of a tour in Ireland. They are global thinkers of counter-revolution against *liberté*, *égalité*, and *fraternité*.

They present their policies as "law." The law of property with Bentham, the law of police with Colquhoun, the laws of political economy with Young, the laws of nature in Malthus. Bentham will have institutions for orphans and "wayward" women. Malthus will recommend the postponement of marriage. Colquhoun inveighed against brothel and ale-house. Arthur Young takes the ground from under the feet of the women whose pig-keeping, chicken minding, and vegetable patch depended on common right. They are concerned with the reproduction of the working class.

Arthur Young toured Norfolk in 1803 and published the results in 1804. He visited approximately seventy-nine parishes which suffered enclosure and precisely describes the common rights lost.[40] The number of enclosure acts more than doubled from 1789 when thirty-three were passed to the middle of the 1790s (seventy-seven) and then almost doubled again by the year 1801 with a hundred and twenty-two enclosure acts. In 1801 Parliament passed the General Enclosure Act (41 George III, c. 109). Perhaps three million acres were enclosed between 1800 and 1815.[41] In 1800 he published *The Question of Scarcity* in which he advocated a potato and rice diet as the solution to the bread crisis. He taught the poor religious obedience because otherwise they would become "the rancorous children of the rights of man."[42]

Thomas Malthus published *An Essay on the Principle of Population* in 1798, and a second edition appeared in 1803. Malthus argued that "self-love [is] the main-spring of the great machine" (i.e., human beings) and that "all cannot share alike the bounties of nature." Patrick Colquhoun in *The Police of the Metropolis* (1800) advocated a "General Police Machine" and enforced the view that not all could share in the bounties of commerce.[43] "Light horsemen" robbed at night, "heavy horsemen" in the day, conveying away the goods in secret pockets, narrow pouches, and bell-bottom pants. This coffee or sugar could then be bartered for rent, drink, food, clothing at the innumerable old iron shops, grocers, publicans, brothel keepers, chandlers, and other receivers. "For this species of traffic, there are multitudes of open doors in every Street," wrote Colquhoun. Dockland communities were a hydra, and the hydra was the commons.[44]

Jeremy Bentham (1748–1832), published in 1802 *Panopticon versus New South Wales; or, The Panopticon Penitentiary System and the Penal Colonization System Compared*. He proposed it as an institution of discipline for schools, factories, poorhouses, hospitals, asylums, barracks, orphanages, and prisons. He called it "a mill for grinding rogues honest, and idle men industrious." In fact the treadmill was recently installed in Coldbath Fields prison. Bentham likened the panopticon to the ghosts of a haunted house. This gothic epitome of enclosure referred not only to loss of land but to fundamental change in relation to planet earth unparalleled since the Urban Revolution of five thousand years previous. The incessant accumulation of "industrial" subjects required their enclosure from the cradle to the grave. To be ruled the population of civil society had to be confined and to be confined it had to be brought under complete surveillance.

Cricket and Catherine Curtail the Closures

The panopticon was defeated by a combination of forces. Mrs. Despard was part of it as she lobbied Parliament, penned letters to the newspapers, petitioned the Home Secretary, worked with the wives of the other prisoners, visited Edward, and challenged the governor of the "Steel." The cricketers and commoners of Westminster also opposed it. As a boy, Jeremy Bentham boarded at the Westminster School between 1755 and 1760. He wrote his former headmaster for help in building a panopticon on Tothill Fields. As a boy Sir Francis Burdett, Catherine's colleague, also boarded at this school until he was expelled in 1786 for refusing to submit to the headmaster and inform against the fellow boys who had smashed windows in their boarding house.[45]

The land was "in the state of Waste which might be subject to the rights of common." The parishioners of St. Margaret's and St. James's, enjoyed common of pasture. *The Gentleman's Magazine* said "it was in no neighborhood." It was a cricket ground from "time immemorial" for the boys of Westminster School. Bentham appealed to the Westminster scholars offering to find them a new pitch so that he could build his prison. "Whatever benefit they reap from the use of that dreary and ill-looking expanse, in the way of sport and exercise, is subject to the perpetual intrusion of *mean dangerous* and *unwelcome* company, of all sorts."[46] One of Spence's political halfpennies from the mid-1890s depicted a "Westminster scholar" wearing academic robes and a scholarly bonnet on one side and on the obverse a "Bridewell boy" wearing trousers or *sans-culottes*.

A Parliamentary Select Committee on Public Walks and Places of Exercise heard testimony in 1833. "I have witnessed dissatisfaction at being expelled from field to field, and being deprived of all play places." Hundreds used to play cricket every summer night in the fields in the back of the British Museum. Popular recreation was undergoing profound repression by evangelicals, landlords, and industrialists. Pugilism, pedestrianism, football, and dancing also suffered.[47] C.L.R. James writes of cricket, "It was created by the yeoman farmer, the gamekeeper, the potter, the tinker, the Nottinghamshire coal-miner, the Yorkshire factory hand. These artisans made it, men of hand and eye."[48] James describes the game in the terms of Wordsworth's Preface to *Lyrical Ballads*. The cricketer maintains human beauty and dignity against the "savage torpor" of urban, uniform occupation.

Burdett and Bentham fought over Tothill Fields. Burdett and Catherine prevailed against the panopticon. As a viable historical event, rather than a philosophical concept, the panopticon was defeated by June 1803 when prime minister Addington informed Bentham that he was unwilling to finance it.[49] In 1810 the Dean of Westminster and former head of the school "paid a man with a horse and plough to drive a furrow around ten acres and the following year gates and rails were erected."[50] At some indeterminate date following, the "Westminster scholars" began to refer to the former commoners as "Sci's," short for Volscis, the people whose conquest in 304 B.C.E., they learned in Latin classes, initiated the expansion of Rome.

When dispossession met the opposition of commoners we get evidence of the composition of a class of servants, craftsmen, slaves, parents, laborers, and sailors. Their experience had included revolution whose violence had scarred many of them and whose dreams had inspired a significant few. It was the confluence of practical commoning "from below" with Enlightenment hopes "from on high" that led to the origins of the romantic movement and the communist movement.

The Despard Moment

We do not need to see the "moment" as that of the Peace of Amiens when Britain and France ceased fire for a year. We do not see it either as the removal of government to Washington, DC, and the expansion of the slave regime through the Louisiana Purchase. We do not see it even as the moment of victory against slavery and the triumph of the "Army of the Incas" (as

Dessalines called his army) in Haitian independence. It included these plus the romantic's discovery of nature.

What did "nature" mean in 1802? Taking from farmer and sailor knowledge of the clouds, taking from the miner and the navvy knowledge of the underground, taking from the peasant knowledge of the land, taking from the indigenous knowledge of plants, the moment of 1802–3 saw a vast change in the social relations of human knowledge.[51] From the clouds in the sky to the strata underground to the life-forms between earth and the heavens, the "world" was undergoing transformation in human understanding.[52] Ballooning aeronauts saw the earth as a giant organism. They gave us the bird's-eye view, or the supra-terranean perspective, just as the coal miners gave us the subterranean view. "Geology" as a word to describe the subterranean science came into existence in 1795. In 1801 "Strata" Smith published the first map of the underworld of England and Wales. He was inspired as a child by the fossils he found after the ditching and hedging of his village fields upon their enclosure in 1787.[53]

Ivan Illich finds that "life, as a substantive notion, makes its appearance around 1801."[54] Reacting against mechanistic classification, Lamarck coined the term "biology" that year. "Life" is talked about as property. *Homo economicus* was born as a life form, and labor-power as a machine. The month before Despard suffered, Giovanni Aldini, a professor of anatomy from Bologna, attempted to revive the body of a murderer, Thomas Forster, by the application of electrical charges after he had been hanged at Newgate. A fortnight after Despard was sentenced to be hanged, beheaded, disemboweled, and quartered, the man devising this punitive butchery, Edward Law ("Lord Ellenborough"), introduced the bill in Parliament that made abortion for the first time in statute law a capital offense. The attempt was made to enclose not just the land of England, its handicrafts, its transport, its mind, but the womb as well.

As Despard took his last breath in February 1803 and Toussaint Louverture perished a month later, other tribunes of the revolutionary moment fell silent. Volney went to work for Napoleon; Thomas Paine set sail in September 1802 to an unwelcome in America; in 1801 Thelwall left the hustings of the open field and opened a school of elocution.

Since the city, in the sense of law, force, and commodity, has abolished the countryside commons and the "bourgeois" nations destroyed the "barbarian" ones, the commoners of the world can no longer retire to the forest or run to the hills. Unprecedented as the task may historically be, the city itself must be commonized.

Dublin
May–June 2013

"Charles Marks"

CHAPTER FOUR

Karl Marx, the Theft of Wood, and Working-Class Composition: A Contribution to the Current Debate

I

The international working-class offensive of the 1960s threw the social sciences into crisis from which they have not yet recovered.[1] The offensive was launched in precisely those parts of the working class that capital had formerly attempted to contain within silent, often wageless reserves of the relative surplus population, that is, in North American ghettoes, in Caribbean islands, or in "backward" regions of the Mediterranean. When that struggle took the form of the mass, direct appropriation of wealth, it became increasingly difficult for militants to understand it as a "secondary movement" to the "real struggle" that, it was said, resided only in the unions and the plants. Nor could it be seen as the incidental reactions of "victims" to an "oppressive society," as it was so often by those organizations left flat-footed by the power of an autonomous Black movement and an autonomous women's movement.

This is not the place to elaborate on the forms that the struggles have taken in the direct appropriation of wealth, nor how these were able to circulate within more familiar terms of struggle.[2] We must note, however, that they thrust the problem of crime, capital's most ancient tool in the creation and control of the working class, once again to a prominent place in the capitalist relation. As the political recomposition of the international working class threw into crisis the capitalist organization of labor markets, so that part of traditional social science, criminology, devoted to studying one of the corners in the labor market, "criminal subcultures" and street gangs, had to face a crisis of its own.

George Jackson recommended burning the libraries of criminology. Young criminologists began to question the autonomous status of criminology as a field of study.[3] Accompanying both the internal and external critique of criminology has been a recovery of interest in the treatment of crime within the Marxist tradition. Yet that tradition is by no means accessible or complete and in fact contains contradictory strains within it, so that one cannot be completely unqualified in welcoming it.

In stating our own position let us try to be as clear as possible even at the risk of overstatement. We wish to oppose the view that fossilizes particular compositions of the working class into eternal, even formulaic, patterns. We must, in particular, combat the view that analyzes crime (or much else indeed) in the nineteenth-century terms of a "lumpenproletariat" versus an "industrial proletariat." It is to be regretted that despite the crisis of criminology and the experience of struggle that gave rise to it, some militants can still speak of the "lumpenproletariat" *tout court* as though this were a fixed category of capitalist relations of power. When neither the principle of historical specification nor the concept of class struggle is admitted there can be no useful analysis of class strategy, howsoever exalted the methodology may be in other respects.[4]

In the rejection of various idealist interpretations of crime including their "marxist" variants, there is, perforce, a revival of interest in the situation of the problem within specified historical periods, that is, within well-constituted phases of capitalist accumulation. In this respect the recent work appearing in these pages that discusses the problem in terms of original accumulation must be welcomed.[5] At the same time we must express the hope that this analysis may be extended to the discussion of the appropriation of wealth and of crime at other periods of the class relation. The contribution of those whose starting point in the analysis of crime is the concept of "marginalization."[6] This leads us to an analysis of the capitalist organization and planning of labor markets, certainly an advance in comparison to those for whom capital remains de-historicized and fixed in the forms of its command. Still, one cannot help but note the unilateral nature of the concept, the fact that it entails an approach to the question that must accept capital's point of view without adequately reconstituting the concept with working-class determinants. One remembers that the life and works of Malcolm X and George Jackson, far from being contained within incidental, "marginal sectors," became leading international reference points for a whole cycle of struggle.

The recent publication of the English translation of Marx's early writings on the criminal law and the theft of wood provides us with a propitious moment for another look at the development of Marx's thinking on the question of crime.[7] We hope that some suggestions for placing those articles within the context of the real dynamics of capitalist accumulation may not only allow us to specify the historical determinants of class struggle in the 1840s, but— what is of far greater importance—may make a contribution to the present debate, a debate which in its abandonment of "criminology" as traditionally constituted in favor of an analysis of the political composition of the working class has more than a few similarities with Marx's own development after 1842.

II

It would not be much of an exaggeration to say that it was a problem of theft that first forced Marx to realize his ignorance of political economy, or to say that class struggle first presented itself to Marx's serious attention as a form of crime. Engels had always understood Marx to say that it was the study of the law on the theft of wood and the situation of the Moselle peasantry that led him to pass from a purely political viewpoint to the study of economics and from that to socialism.[8] Marx's own testimony is no less clear. In the 1859 preface to his *Contribution to the Critique of Political Economy* he wrote,

> In 1842–43, as editor of the *Rheinische Zeitung*, I found myself embarrassed at first when I had to take part in discussions concerning so-called material interests. The proceedings of the Rhine Diet in connection with forest thefts and the extreme subdivision of landed property; the official controversy about the condition of the Mosel peasants into which Herr von Schaper, at that time president of the Rhine Province, entered with the *Rheinische Zeitung*; finally, the debates on free trade and protection, gave me the first impulse to take up the study of economic questions.[9]

Faced with his own and Engels's evidence, we must therefore beware of those accounts of the development of Marx's ideas that see it in the exclusive terms of either the self-liberation from the problematics of Left Hegelianism or the outcome of a political collision that his ideas had with the French utopian and revolutionary tradition that he met during his exile in Paris. The famous trinity (French politics, German philosophy, and English political economy) of the intellectual lineages of Marx's critical analysis of the capitalist mode of production appears to include everything but the actual, material form in which class struggle first forced itself to the attention of the young radical in 1842.

Our interest, however, is not to add the footnote to the intellectual biography of Marx that his ideas, too, must be considered in relation to their material setting. Our purpose is different. We wish to find out why, as it was his inadequate understanding of crime that led him to the study of political economy, Marx never again returned to the systematic analysis of crime as such. As we do this we shall also find that the mass illegal appropriation of forest products represented an important moment in the development of German capitalism, and that it was to the partial analysis of that moment that a good part of the work of some founders of German criminology was devoted. The same moment of struggle in German agrarian relations produced contradictory results among those attempting to understand it: on the one hand, the formation of criminology, and on the other, the development of the revolutionary critique of capitalism.

III

Between October 25 and November 3, 1842, Marx published five articles in the *Rheinische Zeitung* on the debates about a law on the theft of wood that had taken place a year and a half earlier in the Provincial Assembly of the Rhine.[10] The political background to those debates has been described several times.[11] Here we need only point out that the "liberal" emperor, Frederick William IV, following his accession, attempted to make good on a forgotten promise to call a constitutional convention, by instead reconvening the provincial assemblies of the empire. Though they had little power, their opening, together with the temporarily relaxed censorship regulations, was the occasion for the spokesmen of the Rhenish commercial and industrial bourgeoisie to stretch their wings in the more liberal political atmosphere. The *Rheinische Zeitung*, staffed by a group of young and gifted men, was their vehicle for the first, hesitant flights against the Prussian government and the landed nobility. Characterized at first by "a vague liberal aspiration and a veneration for the Hegelian philosophy,"[12] the journal took a sharper turn under Marx's editing, and it was his articles on the theft of wood that caused von Schaper to write the Prussian censorship minister that the journal was now characterized by the "impudent and disrespectful criticism of the existing government institutions."[13]

Though containing passages of "exhilarating eloquence,"[14] the articles as a whole suffer from an uncertainty as to their central subject. Is it the appropriation of wood, legal or illegal? Is it the equity of the laws of property governing that appropriation? Or, is it the debates with their inconsistencies and thoughtlessness that took place in the assembly before the law was passed? Marx is least confident about the first subject; indeed, we learn little about the amounts and types of direct appropriation. He really warms to the second as it allows him to expound on the nature of the state and the law. On the third his characteristic wit and sarcasm come into full play. Despite these ambiguities, the articles as a whole are united by the theme of the contradiction between private self-interest and the public good. He objects, in particular, to nine provisions in the new law:

1. It fails to distinguish between the theft of fallen wood and that of standing timber or hewn lumber.
2. It allows the forest warden to both apprehend wrongdoers and evaluate the stolen wood.
3. It puts the tenure of the appointment of the forest warden entirely at the will of the forest owner.
4. Violators of the law are obliged to perform forced labor on the roads of the forest owner.

5. The fines imposed on the thief are remitted to the forest owner (in addition to compensation for damaged property).
6. Costs of defense incurred at trial are payable in advance.
7. In prison, the thief is restricted to a diet of bread and water.
8. The receiver of stolen wood is punished to the same extent as the thief.
9. Anyone possessing wood that is suspected must prove honest title to it.

Young Marx was outraged by the crude, undisguised, self-interested provisions of punishment established by this law. He was no less indignant with its substantive expansion of the criminal sanction. His criticism of the law rested upon an *a priori*, idealist conception of both the law and the state. "The law," he wrote, "is the universal and authentic exponent of the rightful order of things." Its form represents "universality and necessity." When applied to the exclusive advantage of particular interests—the forest owners—then "the immortality of the law" is sacrificed and the state goes "against the nature of things." The "conflict between the interest of forest protection and the principles of law" can result only in the degradation of "the idea of the state." We stress that this criticism applied to both the substantive and the procedural sections of the law. In the latter case, "public punishment" is transformed "into private compensation." "Reform of the criminal" is attained by the "improvement of the percentage of profit" devolving on the forest owner. The attack on the substantive part of the law rests on similar arguments. "By applying the category of theft where it ought not to be applied you exonerate it." "All the organs of the state become ears, eyes, arms, legs, and means by which the interest of the forest owner hears, sees, appraises, protects, grasps and runs." "The right of human beings gives way to the right of trees." As he stated this, Marx also had to ask, which human beings? For the first time he comes to the defense of the "poor, politically and socially propertyless" when he demands for the poor "a customary right."

On what basis is the demand made? Some confusion results as Marx, only a few years away from his Berlin studies of the pandects and jurisprudence, attempts to solve the problem. First, he justifies it on the basis that the law must represent the interests of all "citizens," that is, he refers to the classical arguments of natural justice. Second, and not altogether playfully, he says that "human poverty . . . deduces its right to fallen wood" from the natural fact that the forests themselves present in the contrast between strong, upright timber to the snapped twigs and wind-felled branches underneath an "antithesis between poverty and wealth." Third, in noting that the inclusion of the appropriation of fallen wood with that of live and hewn timber under the rubric of the criminal sanction is inconsistent with both the sixteenth-century penal code and the ancient "Germanic rights" (*leges barbarorum*), he suggests the greater force of these feudal codes.

It is true that Marx understands that these changes of law correspond, over the centuries, to changes in property relations: "all customary rights of the poor were based on the fact that certain forms of property were indeterminate in character, for they were not definitely private property, but neither were they definitely common property, being a mixture of private and public right, such as we find in all the institutions of the Middle Ages." Accumulation has in these articles no separate existence apart from the law which indeed determines it as Marx implies when he says that it was the introduction of the Roman law that abolished "indeterminate property." Powerless to resist, as it were, the tide of a millennium of legal development, Marx seeks to defend the "customary right" by fleeing the seas of history altogether and placing his defense upon the *terra firma* of nature itself. There are objects "which by their elemental nature and their accidental mode of existence" must defy the unitary force of law which makes private property from "indeterminate property," and the forests are one of these objects.

Appeal as he might to the "universal necessity of the rightful order of things" or to the bio-ecology of the forest, neither of these lofty tribunals could so much as delay, much less halt, the swift and sharp swath that the nobility and burgomasters in Dusseldorf were cutting through the forests of the Rhineland. Fruitless as such appeals had to be, Marx could not even understand, by the idealist terms of his argument, why it was that the rich Rhenish agriculturalists found it necessary to pass such a law at that time thus expanding the criminal sanction. Nor—and this was far dearer to his interests—could he analyze the historical forces that propelled the Rhenish cotters to the direct appropriation of the wood of the forests. To be sure, we know from passing remarks made in other articles of the 1842–1843 period that Marx understood that the parceling of landed property, the incidence of taxation upon the vineyards, the shortages of firewood, and the collapsing market for Moselle wines were all elements of a single situation that he could, however, only see from the partial, incomplete standpoint of natural justice.

IV

When looking at these articles from the standpoint of Marx's later works, we can see that he analyzes only the contradictory appearance of the struggle. Having no concept of class struggle or capitalist accumulation he treats the Rhenish peasantry with a democratic, egalitarian passion, but still as an object external to the actual forces of its development. Unable to apprehend the struggle as one against capitalist development, he assumes that a reasoned appeal to the agrarian lords of the forest, or to their sympathetic brethren in Cologne, will find sympathetic ears. Thus real development occurs, he thought, at the level of the state which only needed to be reminded of its own inherent benevolence to reverse the course of the law and of history.

Precisely this viewpoint, though in an inverted form, dominated the work of the early German criminologists.[15] Like the young Marx, they separated the problem of the state and crime from the class relations of accumulation. They saw crime from a unilateral, idealist viewpoint. However, for them it was less a question of state benevolence than it was of the malevolence of the working class. They sought to determine the "moral condition of the people" by the classification, tabulation, and correlation of "social phenomena." The work produced in this statistical school sought to find "laws" that determined the relative importance of different "factors" (prices, wages, extension of the franchise, etc.) that accounted for changes in the amounts and types of crime. Like the young Marx, they were unable to ask either why some forms of appropriation became crimes at specified periods and others not, or why crimes could at some times become a serious political force imposing precise obstacles to capitalist reproduction.

The problem of the historical specification of class relations and in particular those as they were reflected in Marx's articles, can be solved only from the standpoint of his later work, especially the first volume of *Capital*. There we learn that in discussing the historical phases of the class relation it is necessary to emphasize the forms of divisions within the working class that are created by combining different modes of production within the social division of labor. This is one of the lessons of chapter XV. The effect of the capitalist attack managed by means of the progressive subordination of living labor to machines is to extend and intensify "backward" modes of production in all of their forms. This is one of the weapons capital enjoys in establishing a working class articulated in a form favorable to it. Another is described in chapter XXV of *Capital*, a chapter that is often read as a statement of a dual labor market theory, that is, that capital in maintaining both an active and a reserve front in its social organization of labor-power creates the mechanism for reducing the value of necessary labor. In fact, the "relative surplus population" is maintained in several different forms, forms determined precisely by the combination of different modes of production. With the reproduction of capital and the struggles against it, that combination constantly changes. The chapter begins with a difficult, apparently technical, section on the value composition of capital that reminds us that the configuration of the working class cannot be analyzed exclusively in terms of its attachments to different "sectors" or "branches" of the social division of labor. Even while accounting for divisions in the class that rest upon its relation to capitals with variant compositions, the political composition of the working class must always be studied from the additional viewpoint of its ability to use these divisions in its attack upon capital. These are divisions whose determinations are not merely the relation to the labor process (employed or unemployed), but divisions based upon the quantitative and qualitative form of the value of labor-power.

Lenin, in his analysis of the development of capitalism in Russia and, generally, in his polemics with the "legal Marxists" of the 1890s, was forced to cover much of this ground. "As for the forms of wage-labor, they are extremely diverse in a capitalist society, still everywhere enmeshed in survivals and institutions of the pre-capitalist regime."[16] In contrast to the Narodnik econo-mists who considered the size of the proletariat exclusively as current factory employment, Lenin was forced to remind militants that the working class must be considered only in its relation to capital and in its ability to struggle against capital, regardless of the forms in which capital organizes it within particular productive settings. From a quantitative point of view the timber and lumber workers of post-Reform Russia were next in importance only to agricultural workers. The fact that these belonged to the relative redundant population, or that they were primarily local (not migratory) workers, or that a propor-tion of their income did not take the form of the wage made them no less important from either the standpoint of capitalist accumulation or from that of the working-class struggle against it. Although "the lumber industry leaves all the old, patriarchal way of life practically intact, enmeshing in the worst forms of bondage the workers left to toil in the remote forest depths," Lenin was forced to include his discussion of the timber industry in his section on "large-scale machine industry." He did so not on the grounds of the quantita-tive scale of lumber workers within the proletariat as a whole, but because the qualitative extension of such work remained a condition of large-scale indus-try in fuel, building, and machine supplies. Under these circumstances it was not possible to consider the two million timber workers as the tattered edges of a dying "feudalism." Forms of truck payment and extra-economic forms of bondage prevailed not as mere remnants from a pre-capitalist social forma-tion, but as terms of exploitation guaranteeing stability to capitalist accumu-lation. This was made clear in the massive agrarian unrest of the years 1905–1907 when the illicit cutting of wood was one of the most important mass actions against the landowners.[17]

Let us return, at this point, to the development of capitalism in the Rhineland and, in sketching some elements of the class relation, see if we can throw some light upon the historical movement of which Marx's articles were a partial reflection.

V

Capitalist development in Germany, at least before 1848, is usually studied at the level of circulation as the formation of a national market. In 1818, 1824, and 1833, at the initiative of Prussia, a series of commercial treaties were signed creating a customs union, the Zollverein, that sought to restore the larger market that Napoleon's "continental system" had imposed. The treaties removed restrictions on communications and transport. They abolished internal customs, established a unified external tariff, and introduced a common system of weights and measures. "In fact," as a British specialist stated in 1840, "the Zollverein has brought the sentiment of German nationality out of the regions of hope and fancy into those of positive material interests."[18] In 1837 and 1839 treaties with the Netherlands abolishing the octroi and other Dutch harbor and navigation duties established the Rhine as the main commercial artery of western Prussia.[19] Indeed, the Zollverein was only the most visible aspect of the offensive launched by German capital, providing as it did the basis for a national banking and credit market, a precondition of the revolutions in transportation of the 1830s and 1840s, and the basis of the expansion in trade that found some of its political consequences in the establishment of Chambers of Commerce, the consolidation of the German bourgeoisie, and the liberal initiatives of the young Frederick William IV.

VI

The reforms in internal and foreign commercial arrangements, together with the reforms of the Napoleonic period that created a free market in land and "emancipated" the serfs, provided the foundations not only of a national market but laid the basis within a single generation for rapid capitalist development. Older historians, if not more recent ones, clearly understood that those changes "far from bringing into being the anticipated just social order, led to new and deplorable class struggles."[20] The expropriation of the serfs and their redeployment as wage laborers are of course logically and historically distinct moments in the history of capital. During the intermediating period the articulation of the working class within and without capitalist enterprises must present confusions to those attempting to analyze it from the framework established during other periods of working-class organization. A consideration of the working class that regards it only when it is waged or only when that wage takes an exclusively monetary form is doomed to misunderstand both capitalist accumulation and the working-class struggle against it. To consider our period alone, those who find class struggle "awakened" only after the 1839 strike of gold workers at Pfortsheim and the Berlin cotton weavers' and Brandenburg railway workers' strikes will not be able to understand why, for all their faults, Marx's articles on the theft of wood expressed an important moment in the dynamics of accumulation and class relations. In the following pages we can only suggest some elements of those dynamics.

The recomposition of class relations in the Rhineland during the 1830s and '40s was not led, as in England at the time, by the introduction of large-scale machinery. German manufacture was nevertheless deeply affected. From the point of view of class relations, manufacturing capital was organized in two apparently opposite ways. On the one hand the changes in transportation required massive, mobile injections of labor willing to accept short-term employments. Under state direction the great railway boom of the 1830s more than quadrupled the size of the railway system. River transport also changed—steam-powered tugs replaced the long lines of horses pulling laden barges on the Rhine. These changes provided, as it were, the material infrastructure to the possibilities made available by the Zollverein. On the other hand, the capitalist offensive against traditional handicraft and small workshop production met setbacks that were partially the results of workers' power in the detail of the labor process or of the obstacles remaining in the traditional, often agrarian, relations that engulfed such productive sites.

What Banfield, the English free-trader, wrote of the foremen of the Prussian-owned coal mines of the Ruhr applied equally well to most forms of Rhenish manufacture in the 1840s: "Their business they generally understand, but the discipline, which is the element by which time is played off against money, and which allows high wages to coexist with large profits, does not show itself."[21] Only a visitor from England with two or three generations of experience in the organization of relative surplus value, could have so clearly enunciated this fundamental principle of capitalist strategy. In Prussia the height of political economy stopped with the observation that the state organization of the home market could guarantee accumulation. In the silk and cotton weaving districts of Elberfeld where outwork and task payments prevailed, workers' power appeared to capital as short-weighting of finished cloth, "defective workmanship," and the purloining of materials. The handworkers of the Sieg and Ruhr—wire-drawers, nail-makers, coppersmiths, etc.—prevented the transition to large-scale machinery in the forge industries. Linen workers and flax farmers prevented the introduction of heckling and scutching machines. Alcoholism and coffee addiction were regarded as serious impediments to the imposition of higher levels of intensity in work. Of course, another aspect of this power to reject intensification in the labor process was a stagnation that brought with it low wages and weaknesses in resisting the prolongation of the working day which, in cotton textiles, had become sixteen hours by the 1840s. Such were the obstacles to accumulation throughout Rhenish manufacture—the Lahn valley zinc works, the sugar refineries of Cologne, the rolling mills and earthenware factories of Trier and the Saarbrucken, the fine steel trades of Solingen, as well as in coal, weaving, and forge work.

These apparently opposite poles of the labor market in Rhenish manufacturing—the "light infantry," mobile, massive, and sudden, of railway construction and the stagnant, immobile conditions of small-scale manufacturing—were in fact regulated by the rhythms of agrarian relations. The point needs to be stressed insofar as many tend to make an equivalence between agriculture and feudalism on one hand and manufactures and capitalism on the other, thus confusing a primary characteristic of the social (and political) division of labor under capitalism with the transition to capitalist dominance in the mode of production as a whole. Both the form of the wage and the labor markets of manufacture were closely articulated to agrarian relations. Remuneration for work in manufacturing was in part made either by the allotment of small garden plots or by a working year that permitted "time off" for tending such plots. Other non-monetary forms of compensation, whether traditional perquisites in manufacture or common rights in forests, provided at once an obstacle to capitalist freedom in the wage and, at the pivot of the capitalist relation, a nodal point capable of uniting the struggles of workers in both agrarian and manufacturing settings. This mutual accommodation between manufacturing and agriculture could sometimes present bottlenecks to accumulation, as in the Sieg valley, where village control over the woodlands guaranteed that timber exploitation would remain more an aspect of working-class consumption than in industrial fuel in the metal trades. Macadamization of the roads to the foundries allowed owners to buy and transport fuels, at once releasing them from the "parsimony" of village controlled wood supplies and providing the basis for the reorganization of the detail of the labor process.[22] Thus we can begin to see that technical changes in transportation are as much a weapon against the working class as they are adjuncts to the development of circulation in the market.

The progressive parceling of arable and forest lands in the Rhine, the low rates of agricultural growth, as well as the mixed and sometimes sub-subsistence forms of compensation provided a dispersed and extensive pool for the intensive and concentrated labor requirements of the railway and metallurgical industries, and concurrently established (what was well known at the time) a form of agrarian relations wherein political stability could be managed.[23] The "latent" and "stagnant" reserves of proletarians were regulated, in part, by the institutions designed to control mendicity and emigration.

The emigration of German peasants and handicraft workers doubled between 1820 and 1840. Between 1830 and 1840 it actually tripled as on average forty thousand German speaking emigrants a year jammed the main ports of embarkation (Bremen and Le Havre) awaiting passage.[24] The areas with the most intense emigration were the forest regions of the upper Rhine.[25] A lucrative business existed in Mainz for the factors who organized the shipping of the peasants of the Odenwald and the Moselle across the Atlantic to Texas and Tennessee. Pauperization records are no less indicative of active state control of the relative surplus population than they are of the magnitude of the problem. Arrests for mendicity increased between 1841 and 1842 in Franconia, the Palatinate, and Lower Bavaria by 30 to 50 percent.[26] In the 1830s one in four people in Cologne were on some form of charitable or public relief.[27]

Emigration policies and the repression of paupers alike were organized by the state. The police of western Prussia were directed to prevent the accumulation of strangers. The infamous Frankfurt Assembly of 1848 devoted much of its work to the encouragement and regulation of emigration. What early German criminologists were to find in the inverse relation between the incidence of emigration and that of crime had already become an assumption of policy in the early 1840s. The agrarian proletariat of the Rhine was thus given four possible settings of struggle during this period: emigration, pauperization, the immiseration of the "dwarf economy," or the factory. Its history during that period is the forms of its refusal of the last, the least favorable terrain of struggle. Of course to many contemporaries these problems appeared to be the result of "overpopulation" whose solution might have been sought in Malthusian remedies were it not for the fact that the struggles of the Rhenish proletariat for the reappropriation of wealth had already forced the authorities to consider them as a major problem of "crime and order."

The organization of agriculture in the Rhineland during the 1830s and 1840s was characterized by the open-field system regulated by the *Gemeinde* or village association on the one hand, and by the progressive parceling (or even pulverization) of individual ownership on the other. Friedrich List called it the "dwarf economy."[28] Since the time of the French occupation of the Rhine when cash payments replaced labor dues, the first historic steps were taken in the "emancipation of the peasantry." The "two forms of agrarian relations were complementary: the *Gemeinde* tended to encourage parceling, and thus one would be mistaken to consider the property relation of the *Gemeinde* opposed to the development of private property. Parceling and the concurrent development of a free land-market in Rhenish Prussia wrought "devastation among the poorer peasantry."[29]

The village system of farming, still widespread in the 1840s, was the "most expensive system of agriculture" according to one of its nineteenth-century students. It was argued that the distance separating the individual's field from his dwelling caused a waste of time, and that the tissue of forest and grazing rights and customs caused a duplication of effort, constituting an impediment to "scientific" farming. Similarly, common rights in the mill were an inefficient deployment of resources and an obstacle to innovations. Side by side with the *Gemeinde* existed the enormous number of small allotment holders who, living at the margin of subsistence, were intensely sensitive to the slightest changes in prices for their products and to changes in interest rates at seeding or planting time. On ten million arable acres in the Rhineland, there were eleven million different parcels of land.[30] As a result of the opening of the Rhineland to competition from east Prussian grain and the extension of the timber market, small allotment holders could neither live on the lower prices received for their products nor afford the higher prices required for fuel. Under this progressive erosion of their material power, a life and death struggle took place for the reappropriation of wealth, a struggle that was endemic, highly price sensitive, and by no means restricted to timber and fuel rights.

"In summer many a cow is kept sleek on purloined goods."[31] In the spring women and children ranged through the fields along the Rhine and its tributaries; the Moselle, the Ahr, and the Lahn, cutting young thistles and nettles, digging up the roots of couch-grass, and collecting weeds and leaves of all kinds to turn them to account as winter fodder. Richer farmers planted a variety of lucernes (turnips, Swedes, wurzel), but they had to be ever watchful against the industrious skills of their neighbors, skills that often "degenerated into actual robbery." It must be remembered that a good meal in the 1840s consisted of potato porridge and sour milk, a meal that depended upon the keeping of a cow and on access to fodder or grazing rights that had become increasingly hard to come by.

The terms of cultivation among the orchards were similar to conditions of grazing and foraging—operose work and a suspicious eye. The size of orchards was determined not by the topography of the land but by the walking powers of the *gardes champêtres* who provided "inefficient protection against the youth or loose population of the surrounding country." At harvest time cherries, apples, pears, walnuts, and chestnuts were guarded by their owners who rested on beds of straw during evening vigils. The expansion of the field police in the 1830s did nothing to reduce the complaints of depredations. A "man of weight" in the Moselle valley provides us with this description:

> The disorderly habits that have such an influence in after life, it may safely
> be asserted have their root in the practice of sending children to watch
> the cattle on the (uninclosed) stubbles. Big and little meet here together.
> The cattle are allowed to graze for the most part on other people's lands;

little bands are formed, where the older children teach the younger their
bad habits. Thefts are discussed and planned, fighting follows, then come
other vices. First, fruit and potatoes are stolen, and every evening at
parting the wish is entertained that they may be able to meet again the
next. Neither fields, gardens, nor houses are eventually spared, and with
the excuse of this employment it is scarcely possible to bring the children
together to frequent a summer day-school, or to attend on Sundays to
the weekly explanation of the Christian doctrines.[32]

We note that in these observations no fine distinction can be drawn
between the struggle to retain traditional common rights against their recent
expropriation and the endemic depredations that were executed without cover
of that appeal to legitimacy, nor should we expect it. In viticulture, garden,
and orchard farming the transformation of the market, the fall of prices, the
stringencies of credit, especially during the period of 1839–1842, intensified
the immiserations of the Rhenish agrarian population which still accounted
for about 73 percent of employments.

Traditionally, one of the most important cushions to natural and cycli-
cal disaster was the widespread existence of common rights in private and
corporate forests. Despite the relatively high levels of population density and
manufacturing development in western Prussia, the proportion of forest to
arable lands was three to four, in contrast to Prussia as a whole where it was
about one to two. The riches of the forests could provide not only fuel, but
also forage, materials for houses, farm equipment, and food. The crisis hitting
the Rhenish farming population made these riches all the more necessary
to survival. At the same time, access to them was becoming progressively
restricted with the inexorable expropriation of forest rights.

The forest, one knows, had supported a complex society both within
its purviews and in the neighboring terrain: woodcutters, charcoal-burners,
coopers, sabot-makers, basket-makers, joiners, tanners, potters, tile-makers,
blacksmiths, glass-makers, lime-burners—the list is limited only by the limits
of the uses of wood. Particular use-rights in the traditional forest economy
had a social life of their own prescribed in a "tissue of customary rights" that
defy the norms and clarities of private property. All rights were governed by
two principles. First, that "no Man can have any Profit or Pleasure in a Forest
which tends to the Destruction thereof," in the words of a sixteenth-century
treatise.[33] Second, the forms of human appropriation were designed to guarantee and preserve the stability and hierarchy of class relations which guaranteed to the lord his liberty in the hunt and mastery of the chase and to the
poor particular inalienable usages. Assart of the forest, rights of agistment,

rights of pannage, estovers of fire, house, cart or hedge, rush, fern, gorze and sedge rights, rights to searwood, to windfalls, to dotards, rights of lops and tops—in all, the overlapping vocabulary of natural and social relations recall a forgotten world, easily romanticized by those first criticizing the simplicities of *meum et tuum*. Indeed such romanticism is provoked by the harshness of the opposite view that said the existence of such rights "hindered intensive silviculture, disturbed the progress of orderly cutting, prevented natural regeneration of the forest and depleted the fertility of the forest soil."[34]

Forest relations in the Rhineland had already changed considerably by the time that Karl Marx took up his angry pen in 1841. The parceling off of large forest estates, the buying and selling of woodlands, the expropriation of forest usufructs had all well progressed by the 1840s. The movement to abolish forest rights really began with the French Revolution. The Prussian agrarian edict of 1811 removed all restrictions that encumbered the free, private exploitation of forest properties.

The first forty years of the century were characterized by a secular appreciation in the value of timber relative to the value of other agrarian products. This may be attributed to the markets encouraged by the Zollverein, to the demands of railway construction, to the increasing demand for machinery (oak was still widely used), and to the burgeoning market for both individual and productive fuel consumption, itself the result in part of the expropriation of forest usufructs. Dutch shipbuilding, traditionally dependent on the wide rafts of oak brought down the Rhine, remained active. British shipbuilding relied in part on Rhenish hardwoods—oak, elm, cherry, and ash—for its supply of spars, masts, yards, staves, and knees.[35] Industrial and commercial building in Cologne and the Ruhr was dependent on Rhenish timber. The discovery of the deep seams in 1838 that launched the great expansion of the Ruhr coalfields brought with it an equally sudden rise in the demand for mining timbers.[36] Timber prices rose no less in the fuel market where beech was extensively used as an industrial firing fuel, and where timber remained the main source of working-class fuel consumption despite the growing importance of coal. The price of beech tripled between the beginning of the century and 1841. Between 1830 and 1841 it doubled, rising in part due to the demand for railway ties.[37] Constructional timber prices rose by 20 percent during the same period.

This secular trend in forest prices and the struggle of the "peasant proletariat" against it brought about a real crisis in legitimate appropriation that required the active intervention of the state.[38] That which exports to Belgium and Holland started, the wind and the sun completed, and hundreds of years of soil and mulch in the Rhenish broadleaf forests were destroyed in the first part of the century.[39] The free alienation of forest lands, their subdivision and parceling, and the violent, unplanned clearing of the woods threatened both part of the livelihood of an entire class in the Rhineland and sound principles of sustained yield management. Without succumbing to the romanticism of the forest which seems everywhere to accompany its destruction (e.g., Chateaubriand, "forests preceded people, deserts followed them"), we must note that on the vanguard of the movement to "preserve" the German woods was the Prussian state anxious to socialize the capital locked up in private forest acres.

For a start, the state reduced the clearing of its own forests and expanded the proportion of forests it owned relative to private, corporate and village forests. By the summer of 1841 more than half of the Rhenish forests were Prussian owned or controlled. Under state encouragement an apparatus, independent of particular capitalists, was developed for the scientific study and management of timber. G.L. Hartig (1764–1837), organizer of the Prussian Forest Service, and Heinrich Cotta (1763–1844), founder of the Forest Academy at Tharandt (the oldest such school in the world), pioneered the development of scientific silviculture. Partially under their influence, the free assart and clearing of the forest was subjected to state supervision in order to prevent the further depredation of the woods. The schools established in this movement produced a forest police expert in soil rent theory, actuarial calculations, afforestation scheduling, and cutting according to age-class composition. Not until the end of the century had the Germans lost their pre-eminence in sustained yield management.[40]

Enforcing the plans developed by these specialists in sustained yield and capital turnover against a working population increasingly ready to thwart them, stood the cadres of the police and the instruments of law. "No state organization was more hated," a Prussian silviculturist wrote, "than the forest police."[41] At the end of the nineteenth century the mere listing of the manuals and books of the Prussian forest police filled sixty-one pages in a standard bibliography.[42] The law that these cadres enforced, in state *and* corporate and village forests, was the result of some centuries of development. Nothing could be more misleading than to regard the legislation criticized by Marx as law that with a single stroke cut through the thicket of feudal rights in order to establish the property law of the bourgeoisie. That process had been going on for a long time, at least since the forest ordinances of 1515 which, more than anything else, had abolished the unwritten, communal norms of the Carolingian period. The revisions of the law which Marx criticized were modifications of the main legal instrument concerning Prussian forests, the Forestal Theft Act of 1837.[43] Several other German states had recently reorganized their forest police and revised their written codes. That of Baden, for example, enacted in 1833, contained 220 sections establishing rules and punishments for nearly every detail of forest appropriation. In Thuringia and Saxe-Meiningen similar codes were established. Written permits were required for berry and mushroom gathering. Dead leaves and forest litter could be gathered for fodder only "in extreme cases of need." The topping of trees for May poles, Christmas trees, rake handles, wagon tongues, etc., was punishable by fine and prison. By the 1840s most forests of Prussia had become subject to the police and deputies of the *Forstmeister* of the Ministry of Interior in Berlin.[44] The moment of class relations reflected in Marx's articles was not that of the transition from feudalism to capitalism or even one whose reflection in the law marked a transition from Teutonic to Roman conceptions of property. Each of these had occurred earlier. Nevertheless, it was an important moment in class relations which is to be measured not only by its intensity for which there is ample evidence, but also by its victories, an aspect of which must be studied in the obstacles placed upon the creation of a factory proletariat in the 1840s.

The countryman had a tenacious memory. "The long vanished days when in the teeming forests anyone who wished might load his cart with wood, remained unforgotten throughout Germany."[45] Of course, *anyone* could never have loaded his cart with wood. That some could think so is testimony to the power of the movement in the 1830s and 1840s that was able to confuse the issue of lost rights with the direct appropriation regardless of its ancient legitimacy. Lenin in a similar context warned against accepting those "honeyed grandmothers' tales" of traditional "paternal" relations, a point that must be stressed even while we note that such tales have a way of becoming a force in themselves.

One need not be a specialist in nineteenth-century German folklore to recognize that much of the imagination of the forester expressed hostility to the forces transforming the forests and their societies. In these imaginary worlds the trees themselves took sides with the cotters against their oppressors. Michael the Woodman roamed the forests of the Odenwald selecting trees destined for export on which to place his mark. Such trees were fated to bring misfortune upon their ultimate users: the house built of them would burn, the ship would sink.[46] Knorr in the Black Forest played pranks on travelers. The wild Huntress in the same place gave strangers wrong directions. Particular trees were endowed with marvelous powers. A cherry whose loose boughs provided the cradle of a lost infant, a walnut that withstood the sieges of tumultuous gales, these could confer unexpected generosities upon neighboring peasants. Others exercised capricious malevolence against wayfarers, travelers or others strange to the woods. The legends and stories of the forests testified to the fact that poor woods-people and the peasants of the purlieus could find friends in the densest regions of the forest against the oppressions not only of princes and seigneurs but also of their more recent enemies-the tax collector, the forest police, and the apostles of scientific forest management.

By the end of the 1830s the forests of the Rhineland were haunted by more effectual dangers than the evil spirits of popular imagination, Thus in 1842 a Prussian guidebook warned travelers:

> Keep as much as possible to the highways. Every side path, every woodway, is dangerous. Seek herbage in towns when possible, rather than in villages, and never, or only under the most urgent necessity, in lonely ale-houses, mills, wood-houses, and the like. . . . Shouldst thou be attacked, defend thyself manfully, where the contest is not too unequal; where that is the case, surrender thy property to save thy life.[47]

The real dangers in the forests before the revolution of 1848 were not those that Michael the Woodman might effect upon wayfarers but those that a mass movement for the appropriation of forest wealth placed upon capitalist accumulation. In 1836, of a total of 207,478 prosecutions brought forward in Prussia, a full 150,000 were against wood pilfering and other forest offenses.[48] In Baden in 1836 there was one conviction of woodstealing for every 6.1 inhabitants. In 1841 there was a conviction for every 4.6 inhabitants, and in 1842 one for every four.[49]

So widespread was this movement that it would not be much of an exaggeration to say that German criminology cut its teeth in the tabulation of this movement. From the standpoint of later bourgeois criminology their works appear crude methodologically and in their substance, so many trivialities. Dr. Georg Mayr, for instance, one of the first academic statisticians of criminology and the Zollverein, discovered that the more difficult it is to gain a livelihood in a lawful manner, the more crimes against property will be committed. Hence property crimes will vary directly with the price of provisions and inversely with the level of wages. He discovered that wood pilfering was likely to be greater in regions where privately owned forests prevailed over corporate and communal forests.[50] Wilhelm Starke studied the theft of wood in Prussia between 1854 and 1878. He concluded that the theft of wood was greater during the winter than the summer, and greater in cold years than in warm ones.[51] Ludwig Fuld made painstaking calculations to show that in Prussia between 1862 and 1874 there was a significant positive correlation between the price of rye and the number of convictions for the theft of wood. Valentini, the director of prisons in Prussia, discovered that within the eight districts of Prussia that he studied, the amount of crimes recorded varied according to the forms of land tenure prevalent in each. He found that in the "dwarf economy" of the Rhineland, where the parceling of land had been carried to its extremes, pauperism was highest and the pilfering of wood the greatest, though these high rates did not hold for other types of crimes "against property."[52] However, objectionable as such work may appear to the more sophisticated calculators of crime, one must stress that it reflects in part a real social analysis of the wage, or a decisive form of income, for a large part of the western Prussian proletariat. It is just as much an indication of that struggle as the "honeyed grandmothers' tales." In fact, we could say that the development of scientific silviculture and of positivist criminology were two sides of the same coin: one studying sustained yield and the other the endemic ("moral," as they would say) obstacles to that yield.

If we take a glance forward to the revolution of 1848 a number of our problems become clarified. First, the great rural jacqueries of March that swept southwestern Germany were in part united by their common attempts to reappropriate the wealth of the forests, sometimes under the slogan calling for the recovery of lost rights and other times not. The attempts were geographically widespread and common to several juridically distinct sectors of the agrarian population—feudal tenants, day laborers, crofters, and cotters alike.[53] Second, this movement defies a rigid separation between a class of "rural peasants" and "urban workers," as the coordination and leadership of them was the responsibility of itinerant handworkers, loggers, rivermen, bargemen, teamsters, and wagoners, precisely those categories of workers with a foot both in the "country" and the "city." Furthermore, the working class that was locked within "backward" settings of manufacture and domestic industry burst out in flashes of destruction against factories and machines, a movement that paralleled the struggle against the forest police, enclosures, functionaries, tax collectors, and forest owners, a movement that in the Rhineland certainly was often united by the same personnel.[54] This is not the place to consider the strengths and weaknesses of the revolutionary working class of 1848 as a whole, nor do we mean to replace as its revolutionary subject the eastern textile workers or the Berlin craftsmen with the south German agrarian masses. We only wish to indicate that the relation between the "latent" and "stagnant" labor reserves to capitalist development in the Rhineland, some of whose unities we've tried to suggest, had their political analogues in 1848. The Frankfurt Assembly of 1848 found that the work of its Agriculture and Forestry Commission overlapped with that on Workers' Conditions and that the problems of repression of autonomous rural and urban movements were similar.[55]

The defeat of these movements, more than anything else, paved the way for the advanced assault of German industrialization. Only after 1848 do those familiar indices of capitalist power against the working class (spindles per factory, number of steam engines employed, output of pig iron, etc.) begin to "take off." In light of that it is especially poignant to find that it was not until late into the Nazi period that the full expropriation of forest rights was completed, a time, in other words, when they had long ceased to be a principal terrain of struggle.[56] It is a fact worth considering nevertheless by those who consider the final expropriation of such rights as the decisive moment in the birth of capitalism.

VII

In sketching the dynamics of the class struggle in western Prussia during the 1840s, we've tried to show that the problem of the theft of wood should be seen neither as a problem of primary accumulation in the expropriation of a feudal peasantry nor as a problem of an anarchic, individualized "lumpen-proletariat." Instead, we've attempted to present the elements of an analysis that cast the problem in a different light. In particular, we've seen in it a struggle to maintain and increase one of the forms of value of the working class, a form that enabled it for a time to reject those terms of work and exploitation that German capital was seeking to make available in the factory. We recall that the detonators of the working-class explosion in the spring of 1848 were precisely various categories of workers, agrarian and urban, within different forms of the relative redundant population. Marginal, to be sure, from the point of view of Siemens or Krupps, but a historic mass vanguard nevertheless. Other recent examples come easily to mind. We may end by noting that the author of *Capital*, the work that is the starting point of the working-class critique of the capitalist mode of production and that provides us with the concepts for at once analyzing the forms of the divisions within the working class and the conditions for using these within the revolutionary struggle against capital, dedicated his work to a Silesian peasant, Wilhelm Wolff, "the brave, noble fighter in the vanguard of the proletariat."

Rochester
1976

REFERENCES

Adelman, Gerhard. "Structural Change in the Rhenish Linen and Cotton Trades at the Outset of Industrialization." In *Essays in European Economic History, 1789–1914*, edited by François Crouzet, W.H. Chaloner, and Walter M. Stern. London: Arnold, 1969.

Ainlay, John. Review of Ian Taylor, Paul Walton, and Jock Young, *The New Criminology* (1973) in *Telos* 26 (1975): 213–25.

Banfield, T.C. 1846. *Industry of the Rhine. Series 1: Agriculture; Series 2: Manufactures*. London: C. Knight & Co., 1846–1848.

Bonger, William Adrian. *Criminalité et conditions économique*. Amsterdam: G.P. Tierie, 1905.

Bowring, John. "Report on the Prussian Commercial Union," Parliamentary Papers, XXI. 1840.

Cornu, Auguste. *Karl Marx et Friedrich Engels: Leur vie et leur oeuvre*. 3 vols. Paris: Presses Universitaires de France, 1958.

Crime and Social Justice Collective. "The Politics of Street Crime." *Crime and Social Justice* 5 (Spring–Summer 1976): 1–4.

Currie, Elliott. "Review: The New Criminology." *Crime and Social Justice* 2 (Fall–Winter 1974): 109–13.

Deveze, Michel. *La Vie de la Forêt Française au XVIe siècle*. 2 vols. Paris: SEVPEN, 1961.

Droz, Jacques. *Les Revolutions Allemandes de 1848*. Paris: Presses Universitaires de France, 1957.

Endres, Max. *Handbuch der Forstpolitik*. Berlin: J. Springer, 1905.

Fernow, Bernhard E. *Economics of Forestry: A Reference Book for Students of Political Economy*. New York: T.W. Crowell & Co, 1902.

Fuld, Ludwig. *Der Einfluss der Lebensmittelpreise auf die Bewegung der Strafbaren Handlungen*. Mainz: J. Diemer, 1881.

Hamerow, Theodore S. *Restoration, Revolution, Reaction: Economics and Politics in Germany, 1815–1971*. Princeton: Princeton University Press, 1958.

Henderson, W.O. *The Zollverein*. Cambridge: Cambridge University Press, 1939.

———. *The Rise of German Industrial Power, 1834–1914*. Berkeley: University of California Press, 1975.

Heske, Franz. *German Forestry*. New Haven: Yale University Press, 1938.

Hirst, Paul Q. "Marx and Engels on Law, Crime and Morality." *Economy and Society* 1 (February 1972): 28–56.

———. "The Marxism of the 'New Criminology.'" *The British Journal of Criminology* 8, no. 4 (October 1973): 396–98.

Howitt, William. *Rural and Domestic Life in Germany*. London: Longman, Brown, Green, and Longmans, 1842.

Hughes, C.E. *A Book of the Black Forest*. London: Methuen & Co., 1910.

König, Hermann. *Die Rheinische Zeitung von 1842–43 in ihrer Einstellung zur Kulturpolitik des Preussischen Staates*. Munster: F. Coppenrath, 1927.

Lenin, Vladimir I. *The Development of Capitalism in Russia*. Moscow: Foreign Languages Publishing House, 1899.

Lengerke, Alexander Von. *Die Ländliche Arbeiterfrage*. Berlin: Büreau des Königl. Ministeriums für landwirtschaftliche Angelegenheiter, 1849.

Manwood, John. *Manwood's Treatise of the Forest Laws*. 4th ed. Edited by William Nelson. London: B. Lintott, 1717.

Marx, Karl. 1842. "Proceedings of the Sixth Rhine Province Assembly." 3rd article. *Debates on the Law of the Theft of Wood*. Karl Marx and Frederick Engels: Collected Works, Volume 1. New York: International Publishers, 1975.

———. *A Contribution to the Critique of Political Economy*, translated by N.I. Stone. Chicago: Charles H. Kerr, 1904.

———. *Capital: A Critical Analysis of Capitalist Production*, Volume 1. Translated by Samuel Moore and Edward Aveling. London: George Allen & Unwin, 1938.

Mayr, Georg. *Statistik der Gerichtlichen Polizei im Königreiche Bayern*. Munich: J. Gotteswinter & Möessl, 1867.

Mehring, Franz. *Karl Marx: The Story of His Life*. Translated by Edward Fitzgerald. Ann Arbor: University of Michigan Press, 1962.

Melossi, Dario. "The Penal Question in *Capital*." *Crime and Social Justice* 5 (Spring–Summer 1976): 26–33.

Milward, Alan S., and S.B. Saul. *The Economic Development of Continental Europe, 1780–1870*. Totowa, NJ: Rowman and Littlefield, 1973.

Noyes, P.H. *Organization and Revolution: Working-Class Associations in the German Revolutions of 1848–1849*. Princeton: Princeton University Press, 1966.

Palgrave, R.H. Inglis. *Dictionary of Political Economy*. 3 volumes. London: Macmillan and Co., 1912.

Perrie, Maureen. "The Russian Peasant Movement of 1905–1907: Its Social Composition and Revolutionary Significance." *Past & Present*, 57 (November 1972): 123–55.

Phillipson, Michael. "Critical Theorising and the 'New Criminology.'" *The British Journal of Criminology* 8, no. 4 (October 1973): 398–400.

Schwappach, Adam. *Forstpolitik, Jagd- und Fischereipolitik*. Leipzig: C.L. Hirschfeld, 1894.

Schwendinger, Herman, and Julia R. Schwendinger. "Delinquency and the Collective Varieties of Youth." *Crime and Social Justice* 5 (Spring–Summer 1976): 7–25.

Starke, Wilhelm. *Verbrechen und Verbrecher in Preussen 1854–1878*. Berlin: T.C.F. Enslin, 1884.

Stein, H. "Karl Marx et le pauperisme rhénan avant 1848." Jahrbuch des Kölnischen Geschichtsvereins, XIV (1972).

Taylor, Ian, Paul Watson, and Joch Young. "Rejoinder to the Reviewers," *The British Journal of Criminology* 13, no. 4 (October 1973): 400–403.

Treitschke, Heinrich von. *A History of Germany in the Nineteenth Century*. Translated by Eden and Cedar Paul. 7 volumes. New York: McBride, Nast & Co., 1919.

U.S. Department of State. *Forestry in Europe: Reports from the Consuls of the United States*. Washington, DC: Government Printing Office, 1887.

Valentini, Hermann von. *Das Verbrecherthum im preussischen Staat*. Leipzig: J.A. Barth, 1869.

Vigouroux, Camille. "Karl Marx et la législation forestière rhénane de 1842." *Revue d'histoire économique sociale* 43, no. 2 (1965): 222–33.

Wilson, Edmund. *To the Finland Station*. New York: Harcourt, Brace and Co., 1940.

CHAPTER FIVE

Frau Gertrude Kugelmann and
the Five Gates of Marxism

A HUNDRED AND FORTY YEARS AGO, IN APRIL 1867, HAVING VISITED THE PAWN SHOP to redeem his clothes and watch, Karl Marx left London suitably accoutered for Hamburg with the manuscript of *Das Kapital* in hand.[1]

It was a year when David Livingston sought out the source of the Nile, and presumably the secrets of humanity's origin but actually it was a step toward the Scramble to come. It was the year of the invention of barbed wire, a means of enclosing cheaper, speedier, and nastier than any other. It was the year of the founding in Louisiana of the Knights of the White Camelia, a terrorist organization of white supremacy. In 1867 Alfred Nobel's "safety-powder" was patented as dynamite. *Das Kapital* thus came forth in a year of imperialism, enclosure, racism, and bombing.

The "fearful weather and gales" of the voyage across the North Sea sent most passengers below. A few were not incapacitated by sea-sickness: Marx, a cattleman, a clockmaker, a Texan, a strong-stomached woman, and a man returning from fifteen years roaming in unmapped areas of Peru who regaled the others with accounts of "the sexual depravities of savages." Marx summed up this American and an indigenous story for Engels. "He was received in a hut where a woman was giving birth. The afterbirth is roasted and—supreme expression of hospitality—he is obliged to partake of the SWEET-BREAD." Perhaps Engels remembered something Marx had written him a year earlier. Referring to a gigantic manuscript unfit for publishing Marx wrote that he "began the business of copying out and *polishing the style* on the dot of January first, and it all went ahead swimmingly, as I naturally enjoy licking the infant clean, after long birth-pangs. But then the carbuncle intervened again . . ." and he had to stop.[2]

Marx delivered his manuscript to Otto Meissner, his Hamburg publisher, who promptly put it in his safe, and then prepared to wait to correct the proof-sheets sent up from the printer in Leipzig (in Hamburg "the proofreaders were insufficiently learned"). Meanwhile, Marx waited in Hanover as the guest of Dr. Ludwig Kugelmann, an eminent gynecologist, and his wife, Gertrude.

"Splendid people," "exceptionally kind" is how Marx described them to Engels. Kugelmann was a former member of the Communist League and a follower of Marx and Engels from 1847. He had been one of Marx's correspondents who elicited from "the Moor" the most illuminating of letters.[3] Kugelmann was successful in many respects, esteemed by his colleagues and responsible for technical innovations, though I don't know whether he actually delivered babies. He certainly was a help in delivering *Das Kapital*. During the previous year Marx had asked him twice for help in obtaining a personal loan in Germany. Dr. Kugelmann was active in trying to obtain reviews of it in Germany, and was second only to Engels in launching the "damned book." The inflamed suppurating carbuncles, the begging letters, rheumatism, toothache, the dunning creditors, the adolescent daughters denied pretty treats, the winter cold with neither money nor coal in the house.

Kugelmann's character is revealed by a gift he sent. On Christmas day 1867 as Marx lay groaning on his back from the incessant pains and as the females below stairs were preparing pudding for desert there arrived a tremendous bust of *Jupiter Tonans*, a grandiose gift from Dr. Kugelmann. (It was one of two gifts, the other being a tapestry which had hung in the study of Leibniz.) Zeus the sky god hurtles his thunder upon the weaker beings and when Kugelmann did this on his wife it ended the friendship with Marx. But I get ahead of myself.

Marx arrived on April 16 and he stayed a month, conscious of the "economic advantages." He wrote Engels that it was here on his birthday, May 5, that he corrected the first sheet of *Das Kapital* as sent by the printer.[4] Gertrude Kugelmann took an interest in the book a well. How could she not? Its author corrected the page proofs in her house while she anticipated his every need for more than a month. It was "one of the happiest and most agreeable oases in the desert of life," as he later wrote. Although bored by the enthusiasm of Kugelmann, he was charmed by the warmth and friendship of Frau Gertrude Kugelmann, and interested in another houseguest, Therese Tenge (née Bolongaro-Crevenna), wife of a Westphalian landowner, who was a great musician, an atheist, and inclined to socialism. "She is a superior woman," he wrote to Laura, his middle daughter, denying that he flirted with her.

It was here too, that the activist and theorist of the proletarian revolution expressed his hope "that I shall be able to fundamentally rectify my financial affairs and at last stand on my own feet again."[5] Surely, the hope of proletarians all over the world could not be expressed better. To fundamentally rectify our financial affairs and at last stand on our own feet again.

Ah, where did we go wrong?

Das Kapital was published in September, and in this "the Bible of the working class," as Engels would call it, is an answer.

It has thirty-three chapters and they are arranged into eight parts. Some of these chapters are very short, some are difficult. The subtitle calls it "A Critical Analysis of Capitalist Production," but the subtitle of the second German edition changed this to "A Critique of Political Economy." Political economy must be critiqued before the analysis of capitalist production can become sufficiently critical to propose communism. Otherwise, we think that concepts of political economy are eternal. There has been a lot of confusion about what kind of book it is, theory or history, critique or criticism, anti-capitalist or anti-economics. I emphasize history, as Marx did too to the gynecologist's wife.

In November 1867 Marx wrote to Kugelmann, "Please be so kind as to tell your good wife that the chapters on the "Working Day," "Cooperation," "The Division of Labor," "Machinery," and finally on "Primitive Accumulation" are the most immediately readable. You will have to explain any incomprehensible terminology to her. If there are any other doubtful points, I shall be glad to help."[6]

The longest ones, oddly, are the Gertrude Kugelmann chapters, those which are "immediately readable." For something to be "immediately readable" a number of conditions need to be met: First, the diction must be familiar and this would exclude both obtuse philosophical terminology and the jargon of political economy. Second, the subject matter must be contemporary. Finally, if there is a shared experience between the reader and the author, then again the material will be immediately readable, especially if the author is putting that experience into words for the first time as far as the reader is concerned. With the addition of one chapter and the conjoining of another, these Kugelmann chapters provide us with the five gates of Marxism.

Our conference refers to one of these gates: Part VIII, "The So-Called Primitive Accumulation." He is not talking about a piggy bank or a pile of coconuts. No, he is talking about our world. We have a problem of translation. In German, Part VIII is *Die Sogenannte Ursprüngliche Akkumulation*, and *ursprüngliche* may be translated as "source," "original," or "primary". I want us to approach the idea historically but not rigidly; the primary accumulation continues beyond the "primitive stage," so to speak. Our understanding need not be confined to the sixteenth century; even advanced capitalism includes the primary accumulation of capital. Our own world is incomprehensible unless we understand its source; this is its base. It unifies terror and accumulation.

Four points need to be emphasized. First, primary accumulation is worldwide. "The discovery of gold and silver in America, the extirpation, enslavement, and entombment in mines of the aboriginal population, the beginning of the conquest and looting of the East Indies, the turning of Africa into a warren for the commercial hunting of black-skins, signalized the rosy dawn of the era of capitalist production. These idyllic proceedings are the chief momenta of primary accumulation. On their heels treads the commercial war of the European nations, with the globe for a theatre."

The second characteristic of primary accumulation is its violence, its "merciless Vandalism." The violence of primary accumulation is a history of expropriation "and the history of this, their expropriation, is written in the annals of humanity in letters of blood and fire." "Great masses of men are suddenly and forcibly torn from their means of subsistence . . . the expropriation of the agricultural producer, of the peasant, from the soil, is the basis off the whole process." The violence occurs as imperialism in its two ways, as commercial competition among the European nation-states and as conquest of the societies of Africa, Asia, and America. The organization of this "brute force" requires an army and navy, a centralized taxation system, public debt, a state bank, and international financial understandings.

It is within this classic form that the importance of the Enclosures occurs. The enclosure of England is protracted from the sixteenth to the nineteenth century. The first phase was done by church and king, the second by Parliament. Phase one was accompanied by an ideological offensive, the Protestant Reformation. Phase two no less was accompanied by an ideological offensive, three stooges called Improvement, Progress, and Development. The agricultural population was removed from the land by the spoliation of church property, the colossal theft of state lands, the systematic robbery of communal land, the clearing of the highlands of Scotland, or the usurpation of clan property, and the *défrichement* of the forests. These are assisted by the criminal code, new courts, the development of cadre of attorneys, the establishment of universities, new philosophy and the destruction of other ways of thinking. Even in its classic, English, form we need to augment his account with new chapters. These have been written. The violence against woman's body. The violence of the African slave trade. Racism and misogyny, racist accumulation and misogynist accumulation.[7]

Marx is sarcastic. His rhetoric throughout is powerful. Primary accumulation has a theological and philosophical aspect. He compares it to original sin. "Adam bit the apple, and thereupon sin fell on the human race." Its origin is supposed to be explained when it is told as an anecdote of the past, but primary accumulation is not a thing of the past alone. Moreover, not all suffer the same consequences from original sin. In Protestant theology an "elect" of the intelligent and frugal become rulers, while the rest by reason of laziness must be forced to eat bread in the sweat of their brows. Here his sarcasm begins to mount, as he tears into theology with his bare teeth. This is the final feature of his discussion that stands out.

Archaeologists inform us that the Garden of Eden is a fable arising during the transition from hunting-and-gathering to settled agriculture, that it belongs to the Neolithic revolution of eight to ten thousand years ago. We know it to have been in Mesopotamia. There have been many sins since the first taste of the apple of knowledge. Who is going to pay? At the high church ceremony in Westminster Abbey the other day celebrating the abolition of the slave trade two hundred years ago Mr. Agbetu interrupted the solemn and sacred proceedings, striding to the front to tell her majesty, "You, the Queen, should be ashamed," and to tell the prime minister, "You should say sorry." Mr. Agbetu tells a truth in the highest English Christian sacred place. When Engels refers to *Das Kapital* as the Bible of the working class he need not mean merely that it was authoritative. First of all is the implication that the Bible itself was the ideological Capital of the ruling class: a Jahwist story of an exclusive hill-tribe followed by the story of the carpenter's son with his unique strategy against empire. There is not atonement without making amends which necessarily includes the restoration of surplus value.

When Hugo Gellert sought to illustrate *Das Kapital* in 1933 ("like the X-ray it discloses the depths below the surface") he drew sixty lithographs, more than half of them from what we can call the Kugelmann chapters pointing the way to the five gates. He began the illustrated interpretation with the final gate, part VIII, which he also calls primary accumulation.[8]

Karl Korsch, the German council communist, wrote an introduction to a 1932 Berlin edition of *Das Kapital*.[9] Volume one "impresses us both in form and content, as a finished and rounded whole." In this context of trying to understand *Das Kapital* as a "scientific work of art" that Korsch introduces Marx's recommendations to Mrs. Kugelmann. The description is so vivid, the narrative so gripping. This is true, but there is more. "I want to recommend to the beginner an approach that diverges somewhat from Marx's advice on a suitable start for the ladies (wherein we may sense a certain deference to the prejudices of his own time!)." We are supposed to smile in the condescending recognition that Marx was a male chauvinist. Be that as it may. We do not smile.

We must see Gertrude Kugelmann as a "lady." We need to also understand that Marx treated her as a comrade. We can resist the temptation to think of her as a midwife.

He sent her a photogram of his daughter Laura in June, and in January of the next year of his other daughters, Jenny and Eleanor. In July he wrote promising to send Mrs. Kugelmann a membership card for the International Working Men's Association, formed earlier. Ever since the IWMA was formed in 1864 Marx had busied himself with these cards. An individual membership in the IWMA cost 1s.1d. a year. "The cards served as a passport abroad." He also sent a card to Therese Tenge.

"I hope that I have not fallen into disfavour with your dear wife," he wrote in October 1868 not having heard from Kugelmann. "À propos: the International Women's Association . . . has sent an epistle to the Brussels Congress, enquiring whether ladies may join. The answer, of course, was a courageous affirmative. Should you therefore persist in your silence, I shall send your wife a mandate as correspondent of the General Council." This was not entirely a joke. In December he wrote that Madame Law was elected to be a member of the General Council. He reported as well that "great progress was evident in the last Congress of the American "Labour Union" in that, among other things, it treated working women with complete equality." He wrote, "Anybody who knows anything of history knows that great social changes are impossible without the feminine ferment."[10]

When Marx chose those particular chapters for Mrs. Kugelmann to read, he referred to capitalist production not to political economy. Similarly, when he asked his daughters to help his research he did not put them onto "theoretical discourses" but right into the crimes of the capitalist mode of production as revealed in the Blue Books. Laura assisted him at the Reading Room of the British Museum lying about her age in order to qualify for a reader's ticket. Jenny acted as a part-time secretary and did research for him in the great library of Bloomsbury. The latest Blue Books arrive. What do they say? They must be read. Their own suffering is placed in perspective. The material goes into the chapter on machinery and the chapter on the general law of accumulation. "Deviling" was the slang in Victorian literary production of doing professional work for a barrister or literary man without fee. Marx himself delayed the completion of *Das Kapital* in order to incorporate the findings of the latest (5th) *Report of the Children's Employment Commission* and the (8th) *Board of Health Report*, an inquiry into housing.

Marx finds evidence how a technical advance in one area leads to degradation in another. Britain was the worldwide emporium of the rag trade importing from Japan, South America, Egypt, Russia, for the paper industry. The girls employed as rag-sorters were infected by small pox and other infectious diseases. The same report gives him evidence of "overcrowded habitations absolutely unfit for human beings." Twenty such colonies of 10,000 persons each in London were "nothing short of infernal."

The *5th Report* is cited in chapter 15, and the Bethnal Green public market where children hire themselves out to work for the silk manufacturers for 1s.8d. a week, on mechanization of brick-making, the replacement of stitching by riveting in the Leicestershire shoemaking trade, on the worker's name for the print shops of books and newspapers, i.e. "slaughter-houses," on the drunkenness of the "brickie," how ocean navigation has "swept away the technical basis on which seasonal work was supported," on the desirability of combining "some work as well as play to give variety to schooling," the torturous, monstrous tension of the ten-year-old boys in the Coventry ribbon looms where "the boy is a mere substitute for steam-power," how the parents exploit their children without limit possessing "the absolute power of making children mere machine"—"a pestiferous source of corruption and slavery."

The 6th Report of the Children's Employment Commission was published in March, and Marx cites it in ch. 25. How the girls of an agricultural village "live like pigs" and that depression and death often follow incest. How the gang system of agricultural work prevails in eastern England forty to fifty women and children (six to thirteen years of age) led by a gang-master, over-work, enormous marches, demoralization. He is the "democratic emperor" of these Sodoms and Gomorrahs.

These two chapters, these two subjects rather, were so important to Marx that he was willing to delay submitting his manuscript to get the latest information. Doing so was a family labor, and he relied on the intelligence, eye-sight, and study habits of his daughters. In July 1867 when he was back in London he wrote the preface to Das Kapital presupposing "a reader who is willing to learn something new and therefore to think for himself." Surely, Mrs. Kugelmann was among those at the back of his mind?

Years later in 1874 Kugelmann persuaded Marx to attend the spa at Carlsbad. They quarreled, the grounds being the incessant, bullying, pedantry Kugelmann displayed towards his wife. Jupiter Tonans returned. The "foreign workers" of Moscow gave this account of the quarrel, "Although a sincere believer in the ultimate triumph of socialism, he rejected the proletarian class struggle and expected the realization of his ideal in a purely reformist way." Eleanor, who accompanied Marx to Carlsbad, wrote, "It is a hard thing when a woman has no money of her own and her husband tells her every minute that she is ungrateful for his benefactions to her and the child. You cannot imagine how brutish Kugelmann is and how shameless."[11] Marx wrote, "he torments the poor woman, who is in all respects his superior, in the most revolting manner."[12] The twelve-year friendship with Ludwig Kugelmann was irreparably ruptured. We don't know how this affected his relation with Gertrude. Karl Marx and family remained at least on good terms with her brother, Max Oppenheim, who they visited in Prague in 1876.

"It is a hard thing when a woman has no money of her own." This is the proletarian condition, not having money. Without access to land, or subsistence, it is a hard thing. It is this experience which makes the chapters "immediately readable."

These are the chapters which tended to be neglected in the *Das Kapital* debates of the last quarter of the last century.[13] The big issues of Marx's theory were expressed as the problem of the state, or the problem of consciousness. There was value theory and state theory. Or, they were expressed as a problem of alternative economics. Rarely were they expressed as class struggle and never as communism.[14] These chapters were brushed aside as mere illustrations of the heavy theory, or scorned as English history in a world whose history had long passed little England by. These commentators are like the explorer whose stories from Peru made such an impression on Marx during the bad weather on the North Sea. They derive nourishment from the placenta— Althusser swallowing meconium, Rosdolsky sucking the amniotic fluids.

For E.P. Thompson *Capital* remained "a study of the logic of capital, not capitalism, and the social and political dimensions of the history, the wrath, and the understanding of the class struggle arise from a region independent of the closed system of economic logic." Thus he can agree with Louis Althusser that "history" is introduced to provide exemplification and "illustration" for a structure of theory which is not derived from this discipline."[15] Theory—structure—discipline: these are not the terms of Marx the proletarian revolutionist.

This is what the Frau Kugelmann chapters require us to question: the book is not a closed field of mental mechanics. It is not a logic machine. In trying to say that it was, Thompson gets weird. "*Capital* was—and probably had to be—a product of theoretical misceganation [*sic*]." Did he imagine that history is white and theory is black, or did he imagine it the other way around? "But misceganation of this order is no more possible in theory than in the animal kingdom, for we cannot leap across the fixity of categories of species." Are the Kugelmann chapters white or Negro? Are the five gates African or European? "Miscegenation" was a neologism invented by two New York journalists in 1864, in order to bring together into a single abstraction a host of biological and aesthetic objections to interracial sexual union. The term was a brilliant piece of racist disinformation; it was the keystone in a pamphlet designed to destroy Abraham Lincoln's reelection, and the term quickly caught on. The Emancipation Proclamation was called the "Miscegenation Proclamation." Lincoln was reelected but the racist term and the assumptions behind it have remained current from Louis Agassiz to Jared Diamond.[16] Could Thompson have thought of any metaphor that might weaken his argument more?

This is an odd way of conceptualizing the work in the years of the Thirteenth Amendment (1865) and Fourteenth Amendment (1868). Over the gate to the shorter working day Marx wrote, "Labour in a white skin cannot emancipate itself where in the black it is branded." "Miscegenation" was invented as the International Workingmen's Association was formed.

If expropriation is primary, what is secondary? This takes us to the other four gates which are: the extension of the working day, the division of the laborers, the mechanization of work, and the composition of reproduction. Extension, fractionation, mechanization, and composition: these are the four gates. Each describes means of exploitation. The fifth gate is expropriation. Expropriation is prior to exploitation, yet the two are interdependent. Expropriation not only prepares the ground so to speak, it intensifies exploitation, so together I call them X^2.

The five gates refer to the longest chapters of *Das Kapital*. Extension refers to chapter X on "The Working Day." This is the most well-known chapter. It was often published separately as a pamphlet. It was first translated into England by the German railway workers in St. Louis. Indeed, Marx was totally aware of the eight-hour agitation in the U.S. and the impact this chapter might have. It is an epitome of the whole book: it begins with the development of the length of working time from the transformation of the commons, and it ends with the transformation of the abolition of slavery into the eight-hour day movement "that ran with the seven-leagued boots of the locomotive from the Atlantic to the Pacific, from New England to California." "Labour cannot emancipate itself in the white skin where in the black it is branded." Fractionation refers to chapter XIV "The Division of Labour and Manufacture." Here is where we find brilliant dialectical history of the labor process itself and how the class struggle is inherent to capitalist change. Mechanization refers to chapter XV called "Machinery and Modern Industry." This gives an account of the Luddites, Factory Acts. The north German peasant magic of the seven league boots found their proletarian power in the most recorded song of American history. Here from the Ohio penitentiary:[17]

> John Henry said to the Captain,
> A man ain't nothing but a man,
> And before I'll let your steam drill beat me down,
> Die with a hammer in my hand,
> Die with a hammer in my hand.

Chapter 25 is called "The General Law of Capitalist Accumulation" and it describes the two parts of the working class, the paid and the unpaid. Capitalism is about the appropriation of surplus value, that is, the unpaid labors of the working class. John Henry was a convict who helped to build the Chesapeake and Ohio railroad after 1868 driving through the Appalachian mountains with his hammer. He was unpaid. In 1867 a civil engineer noted that the hand-drilling of holes in the rock was the bottleneck in the construction of railway tunnels. Rocking and rolling were the terms expressing the relation between the hammerman and the shaker holding the drill.

Primary accumulation must be seen in relation to the organization (the organs) and exploitation of the body of the working class in its every frown and limb, its brains and skin, its guts and womb. Put this way, we see why Marx's study of the working class in these Kugelmann chapters put such supreme importance on public health and children's employment.

Returning to the fifth gate, the gate of expropriation or of primary accumulation, the author's clauses follow like claps of thunder in the heavens. "This integument is burst asunder. The knell of capitalist private property sounds. The expropriators are expropriated." "Capitalist production begets, with the inexorability of a law of Nature, its own negation. It is the negation of the negation." The noise from above are F-16s, the Garden of Eden is the desiccated marshlands between the Tigris and Euphrates.

Expropriation intensifies exploitation: X^2 has been our experience. The working day is increased, the working year is reduced as holidays are removed, as weekends are shot, the working life-time is increased as retirement is postponed and social security devalued. The mechanization of material and immaterial labor (as it is called) intensifies all other forms of labor. The composition of the "working class" is strained by the worldwide feminization of poverty and a Niagara of refugees—from Palestine, Mexico, Nigeria, India—talking to each other by cell-phone and laptop.

Primitive accumulation, like primitive communism, seems unrealistic or at least non-contemporary. The word "primitive" supplies us with some anthropological distance. Primitive accumulation happened long ago; primitive communism happened far away. This distance however is illusory. In our era of so-called "globalization" and incessant war accumulation is worldwide and violent.

The essence of Marxism is the class struggle. The resolution of that struggle is communism. One is in our face, and the other is not far away. Each of the gates I have described may be opened to that "fair field full of folk," to use the phrase of English utopian dream. "The history of all hitherto existing society is the history of class struggle," begins the *Manifesto* of 1848. In later editions Engels added the footnote that at the time they knew little about "primitive communism."[18] This too must be called primary communism.

Ithaca
2007

The "UK"

CHAPTER SIX

Ned Ludd & Queen Mab:
Machine-Breaking, Romanticism, and
the Several Commons of 1811–12

No General but Ludd
Means the Poor Any Good
—Anonymous, 1811–12

I

The economic term "constant capital" denotes both natural resources and machines, or Nature and Technology, as means for the exploitation of *variable capital*, the term for the working class when it is waged or unwaged, or labor-power either employed or unemployed.[1]

The *system* of capitalism begins to collapse when labor-power expresses itself as the power of the people and attacks the machines of its degradation and resumes responsibility for the earth. We may do this in the name of democracy or popular sovereignty, or we may do this in the name of human dignity and survival. Both are now required. The 2011 natural disasters of earthquake, tsunami, tornado, and fire are inseparable from the artificial catastrophes of global warming and the nuclear meltdown.

The popular mobilization in Cairo, the Tahrir Square commons, raised hopes of the oppressed struggling for rights they never had. In Madison, Wisconsin, the workers took over the state capitol struggling for rights they were about to lose. The Fukushima disaster gave the whole world a jolt. The Occupation of Wall Street takes the system at its most abstract (banks) and exclusive (private property) and grounds it concretely and in common thus prefiguring the future in the present.

Everyone knows now that technology has brought us to an impasse, and everyone knows now that everything has to be looked at globally, though these commonplaces were not so generally known two hundred years ago when the world and the heavens were in uproar and the people in the name of "Ned Ludd" took up the hammer of redress to smash machines. The origin of the industrial *system* contains the seed of its demise, once we apply to it our hammers and our imagination which also appeared, fairy-like, two hundred years ago.

In 1811 it appeared to many that cosmic forces were at play. A great comet was visible for most of the year, 260 days, seen first in March, most visible in October, and faded by January 1812. Its tail was 25 degrees long. It was interpreted as an omen all over the world.

July 5, 1811, is Independence Day in Venezuela. Independence was led by Francisco de Miranda and Simón Bolívar. An earthquake shattered much in March 1812. Bolívar said, "If nature opposes us, we shall fight against her and force her to obey." The leaders of the bourgeois revolution were prepared to conquer nature.

December 16, 1811, a terrific earthquake shook the grounds of the central Mississippi River valley, and there were others in January and February. The earthquake brought justice to a murder committed by Thomas Jefferson's nephews who in Kentucky axed a slave, chopped up his body, and sought to burn the parts, until the earthquake caused the chimney to collapse smothering the fire leaving the body parts visible to others.[2] Among the Creek, indigenous people of the American south, the Red Stick prophets had begun to urge young braves to follow Tecumseh and prepare themselves for the war path. Tecumseh and his brother Tenskwatawa welcomed the association with the earthquake.

Meanwhile in England Anna Laetitia Barbauld published a volume, a poem, titled "Eighteen Hundred and Eleven." Generally known for introducing big letters and wide margins to help children read, she saw history with two eyes, chronology and geography, which provided her with prophetic power. The war, famine, rapine, disease of the year brought catastrophe and the eruption of subterranean forces. "Ruin, as with an earthquake shock, is here," she warned.

Frank Peel in 1878 provided the first primary, printed source of authentic memories of the Luddites. On the first page he compared the comet to "a flaming sword."[3] Only a few years before the Luddites William Blake wrote a hymn against the mechanized factory, "these dark Satanic Mills," in which he vowed,

> I will not Cease from mental Fight
> Nor shall my Sword sleep in my hand
> Till we have built Jerusalem
> In England's green and pleasant Land.

Had the sleeping sword awakened? Were the followers of Ned Ludd, like the comet in the sky, wielding cosmic justice and do they still? If so, it was not as Blake imagined because Jerusalem, a city of strife and division, is no longer the egalitarian utopia of the Protestant millennium. An ecological rather than the protestant nationalist note must now conclude this stirring and beautiful hymn.

> I will not Cease from mental Fight
> Nor shall my Sword sleep in my hand
> Till we occupy the Commons
> To green and chill our baked Lands.

On the bicentennial of the Luddite direct actions on behalf of commonality, the chthonic powers beneath the earth and the cosmic spectacle above it accompanied the revolt against the machine. The romantic poets responded to this relationship in two ways. First, they broadened our view from the local to the revolutionary macrocosm. Second, they helped make it possible to see machine-breaking as a means of defending the commons.

II

The Luddites were machine-breakers of the north of England who differed from tool-breakers of the past or of other countries by giving themselves a mythological name, Ned Ludd, or Captain Ludd. The Luddites were active in three areas of the English textile industry: i) the West Riding of Yorkshire where the croppers (those who shear, or crop, the nap of the cloth) were threatened by the gig-mill or shearing machine, ii) Nottinghamshire and adjacent parts of the midlands where the stockingers (those who weave stockings) were being made redundant by the framework-knitting machine, and iii) Lancashire where the cotton weavers were losing employment because of the application of the steam-engine to the hand-loom. This area has been called "the Luddite triangle." The main Luddite resistance took place in 1811 and 1812.

Both the general tactic of machine-breaking and its specific most famous case of Luddism, may indeed be "collective bargaining by riot," to use the phrase of E.J. Hobsbawm, but there was more to them than that.[4] "I am seeking to rescue the poor stockinger, the Luddite cropper, the 'obsolete' hand-loom weaver, the 'utopian' artisan, and even the deluded follower of Joanna Southcott from the enormous condescension of posterity," wrote E.P. Thompson in *The Making of the English Working Class* (1963). The first three figures (stockinger, cropper, weaver) are the three crafts corresponding to the three regions of Luddism and to three machines that were undermining them. To Thompson three of these five examples were machine-breakers, suggesting an identification between them and the class of all working people. The prefigurative power of a chronologically specific tactic found expression as myth, and since myth may transcend the time and place of its birth, Ned Ludd continues to wield his hammer centuries later.

Such mythological figures, like the porter in *Macbeth*, open the gates to history from below. English history is replete with them—Robin Hood, Piers Ploughman, Lady Skimmington, Captain Swing for example—and so is Irish history especially in this period (1811–12) when Captain Knockabout or Captain Rock joined Ned Ludd as anonymous, avenging avatars who meted out justice that was otherwise denied.

The world was being enclosed, life was being closed off, people shut in. In 1795, before he was silenced by government, the English Jacobin, John Thelwall, referred to "the inclosing system" which he defined as "that system of enclosure by which the rich monopolize to themselves the estates, rights, and possessions of the poor."[5]

Certainly the system of enclosure applied to land where enclosure became commodification. In 1790 there were 25 Parliamentary enclosure acts, and in 1811 there were 133. England began to become a country of fences, stone walls, ditches, and hedges. To Barbauld, writing in "Eighteen Hundred and Eleven," "stricter bounds the cultured fields divide." The result on one side was high rents and Jane Austen and on the other dispossession, hunger, and John Clare, the Northamptonshire agricultural laborer and poet of the commons, who wrote, "vile enclosure came and made a parish slave of me."

The household became part of the system of enclosure. The genders were separated by the doctrine of the two spheres, the private sphere for women and the public sphere for men. "The confines of the home were the boundaries of her kingdom," writes Linda Colley. The wife ceased to have a legal persona or existence.[6] The cult of prolific maternity was to supply cannon-fodder for empire. The "population explosion" was partly an achievement of this confinement or lying-in.

The division of labor in the arts and crafts enabled them to become part of the system of enclosure as the factory replaced the workshop. The resulting dehumanization was anticipated in Adam Smith's *Wealth of Nations*: "In the progress of the division of labor, the employment . . . of the great body of the people, comes to be confined to a few very simple operations, frequently to one or two. The man whose whole life is spent in performing a few simple operations . . . generally becomes as stupid and ignorant as it is possible for a human creature to become."[7]

The infrastructures of transportation belong to the enclosing system. Rivers were canalized and high dock walls enclosed the traffic of ports from Liverpool to London. The result was criminalization. In punishment it was an age of vast prison construction behind immense walls of granite. Lord Byron in defending the Luddites asked the legislators, "Can you commit a whole country to their own prisons?"

War itself assisted the system of enclosure. The soldiers were separated from the civilian population by the replacement of billeting by barracks. More than two hundred barracks were constructed between 1799 and the end of the war in 1815. It was said in India that if the Moghuls built mosques and tombs the British built jails and barracks.[8] Even "Albion's fatal tree" or the three-mile procession of the condemned from the city of London to the Tyburn gallows was subject to enclosure at Newgate prison.

In cultural expressions, too, we find several forms of closure, such as the dictionaries and grammars of language, the censorship of press and speech, and the silencing of Thelwall, who spent the rest of his life relieving stammerers by teaching "elocution." Thomas Spence attempted to combat it by spelling reform but to no avail. The result contributed to that social and cultural apartheid between the upper class and the common people. Indeed the word "common" became a slur.

The enclosure of handicraft started with the domestic system of the merchants putting out raw materials to the craftsman and the craftswoman working at home where the round of tasks in garden, field, and loom were industriously mixed. Then, manufactures or the separate workshop, brought all the workers together. The factory added machines and power. Enclosure depends on the separation of industry from agriculture, the factory from the land. The two processes were carried forward together. Enclosure destroyed both.

These enclosures took place in an era of world war and total war. In 1811–12, "an event took place," Tolstoy will say in *War and Peace*, "opposed to human reason and to human nature. Millions of men perpetrated against one another such innumerable crimes, frauds, treacheries, thefts, forgeries, issues of false money, burglaries, incendiarisms, and murders as in whole centuries are not recorded in the annals of all the law courts of the world, but which those who committed them did not at the time regard as being crimes."[9] As far as Britain was concerned this was a new phase in the long counterrevolution against liberty, equality, and fraternity and an opportunity to control the commerce of the Atlantic, Indian, and Pacific oceans. Its war economy and its industrialization went hand in hand: the smoke of the factory and the smoke of cannon, the hapless soldier's cry and the orphan's cry, vast fortunes and the fortunes of war, war and the machine morphed politically into the military-industrial complex.

The Americans still sing before sporting events a national anthem referring to the "rockets' red glare." Rockets were fired at Fort McHenry in Baltimore during the war of 1812. Rocketry was the advanced military technology of the day, originating in India at the battle of Seringapatam in 1799 and carefully studied by Robert Emmet in the insurrection of 1803. During this total war hundreds of thousands of soldiers put boots on the ground, boots made of hides from cattle fed in the pastures of Ireland or the pampas of Argentina. Pick any thread of this tapestry, pull it, and, yes, the historian unravels the cruelties and crimes of the era, but look more carefully and there is another story which sticks to the hand. It is the story of preservation, resistance, kindness to strangers, a seat at the table. This was the commons, and so it was with the Luddites.

David Noble's "In Defense of Luddism" (1993) like E.J. Hobsbawm's essay four decades earlier stressed the solidarity resulting from exercising power "at the point of production."[10] "The habit of solidarity, which is the foundation of effective trade unionism, takes time to learn," wrote Hobsbawm, and nothing does it better, than bringing production to a halt by machine-breaking or "to go out Ludding." By Noble's time in the late twentieth century the trade unions were cooperating in the introduction of automation. Since the permanence of capitalism can seem to rest on the inevitability of technological change, Noble called us to regain our inherently insurrectionary power with the reprise of Ned Ludd. More is at stake, however, than the "point of production." That point depends on reproduction, or the community of the producers.

When we speak of the destruction of "community" we must remember that this entailed complex kin patterns, forms of mutuality, and customs held in common. There is a material basis to community; together they constitute a commons. In both cases land and tools became commodities (they could be bought and sold) and the commodities became constant capital (a tangible means to increase of labor exploitation). In this way expropriation (X) and exploitation (X^1) became not separate stages of capitalism, as $X + X^1$, but an intensifying dynamic operating on one another simultaneously, as X^2. The expropriation from the commons and the mechanization of labor worked upon each other as in a feedback loop.

III

We can introduce "the commons" by pulling an Irish thread—Ireland so close to England geographically, so distant otherwise. In 1811 from Ulster William Carleton set out for Munster in search of a teacher to teach him the classics of Greece and Rome. Irish people, poor or not, venerated classical learning. "Such was the respect held for those who appeared to be anxious to acquire education, that . . . I was not permitted to pay a farthing for either bed or board in the roadside houses of entertainment where I stopped." Eventually he found a teacher whose brother had just returned from the Iberian Peninsula with a Portuguese wife. They will eat potatoes.

In the Peninsula, however, the British Army ate bread. The army bought grain from Malta where Egyptian wheat was unloaded. This was a major change in the international grain trade. Muhammad Ali routed the mameluk leadership at a feast in Cairo in March 1811, the first step in centralizing power in Egypt. The second step was the reorientation of the grain exports away from Ottoman markets via sea trade protected by the British Navy to meet needs of the British Army.[11] However other characteristics of "primitive accumulation" had commenced, the expropriation of charity and religiously endowed lands, centralization of taxes and tributes, and the privatization of lands, intensification of irrigation corvées, or forced labor on canals. In Upper Egypt lands were "held communally and assigned to individual cultivators annually" but in the fertile delta of lower Egypt boundaries were easily established.[12]

So here's a change in Egypt: grain for a new, large market, which causes reduction in subsistence farming and removal of several forms of commoning. While these changes might help feed armies in the Iberian Peninsula, they could not feed the hungry bellies of England during this winter of shortages. George Mellor, the Yorkshire Luddite who was to hang in 1813, was a veteran of the British campaign in Egypt.

Scarcity was answered by the renewal of the moral economy in England and the persistence of "agrarian outrages" in Ireland against tithes, taxes, cesses, and high prices of land. Land for cattle grazing left the people hungry for land for food, which was available only by the system of conacre—a half acre, or potato patch, leased from sowing to harvest, rent paid by labor. These were the conditions for a flourishing legal subculture, or "the clear notion of a code of laws quite separate from that represented by government." The Rockites defended this legal subculture against law administered by Castle and court.

Here are a few examples of Irish anonymous letters from the Luddite years of 1811 and 1812. To a curate of Ardcolm, near Wexford, a letter writer advised him "to study Divinity and not oppression especially as you being well paid for it." A second warned, "Any person who will persevere in oppression let them expect nothing but emediate [sic] execution." A third warned against a ship owner from sailing away from County Down with a load of potatoes who might receive a visit from Captain Slasher or Captain Firebrand, on behalf of "poor indigint peasants who lies fettered under the yoke of tyranny." Captain Knockabout might visit to cause the rents to fall.[13]

While studying the fourth book of Virgil's *Aeneid* and admiring Defoe's *History of the Devil*, William Carleton came upon a wedding dance upon the greensward and under the influence of poteen and a red-haired fellow who was "seldom absent in fair or market from a fight," a Catholic prayer-book was pressed into his hand, and he was given the words and signs of a Ribbonman swearing allegiance to an independent Ireland, to mutuality in defense against Orangemen, and to noncooperation with the courts.[14] This was part of the Irish Catholic "underground" with links to an older, commoning economy of land and labor.

IV

In pulling an Irish thread, we incidentally came across several types of commons, including the knowledge commons supported by Irish hospitality and the very old agrarian commons of the Upper Nile as well as the Nile delta. Notions of community and of commons were central to the Luddites.

> We will never lay down Arms [till] The House of Commons passes an Act to put down all Machinery hurtful to Commonality, and repeal that to hang Frame Breakers. But We. We petition no more—that won't do—fighting must.
>
> Signed by the General of the Army of Redressers
> Ned Ludd Clerk
> Redressers for ever. Amen

This was the conclusion to a long letter sent to Mr. Smith, a shearing-frame holder, in Hill End, Yorkshire, and made public on March 9, 1812. The letter warned that 2,782 people in Huddersfield alone were ready to destroy machines and burn the buildings of the frame holders. Furthermore the army of redressers came not only from Manchester, Halifax, Sheffield, Bradford, and Oldham, but the weavers of Glasgow were ready to join, and "the Papists in Ireland are rising to a Man." In addition "we hope for the assistance of the French Emperor in shaking off the Yoke of the Rottenest, Wickedest, and most Tyrannous Government that ever existed."[15]

Following the defeat of the Irish rebellion of '98 and its aftershocks including the Act of Union (1801), the Despard conspiracy (1802), and Emmet's revolt (1803) thousands of Irish immigrants fled for meager employment opportunities in Lancashire and the West Riding of Yorkshire. It was a crucial migratory movement to the textile factories whose spinners in 1811 struck demanding equal pay between the country and the city. Thirty thousand were thrown out of work; the factories were attacked. Despite their defeat in two or three years John Doherty of co. Donegal who himself had begun work as a child in a Belfast spinning mill would become one of the most successful trade union leaders of the era.[16]

The atmosphere of the time as felt by the gentry is described by Charlotte Brontë in her novel *Shirley* (1849) and by Emily Brontë in her novel *Wuthering*

Heights (1847). The empty landscape and ominous turbulent weather which open *Wuthering Heights* indicate the terror and fear of the Other (Irish, Gypsy, proletarian). It is a shadowy representation of the actuality when the people of the north prepared for civil war by practicing military evolutions upon the moors by the light of the moon.

"Machinery hurtful to Commonality." This is the phrase that introduces our theme, the mixture of communism and commons against which the machine and enclosure were launched in all its dehumanizing consequences.[17] For those triplets of evil which Martin Luther King called militarism, racism, and materialism and which Milton personified as demons, Moloch, Belial, and Mammon were let loose upon the world's common, "hurtful to the commonality." Veritably, this was hell on earth.

Percy Bysshe Shelley was thrown out of Oxford for atheism in March 1811 and searching for a commune of equality he began a lifelong quest, at first in the north of England, witnessing the extreme economic conditions of Lancashire and Yorkshire and tramping the commons, "over the cold and beautiful upland pastures" of the Lake District, and then, second, by a political intervention in Ireland where he went on February 12, 1812, staying until April 4. Shelley's poetic, political, and philosophical changes occurred at the peak of the Luddite disturbances.

At the same time as Ned Ludd sent his letter on behalf of the commonality, Shelley, returning from political agitation in Ireland, composed a broadside to post on the walls of public buildings, *A Declaration of Rights* of thirty-one articles. Shelley sealed a copy in a bottle and lobbed it into the Bristol Channel, and launched another copy as "heavenly medicine" in a hot air balloon. The aristocratic whimsy of a blithe spirit? Yes, and something in addition, namely, wave and wind as media of communication. At Oxford in the spring of 1811 Shelley witnessed James Sadler, the aeronaut, ascend in a hot air balloon. Man could fly over Africa and "virtually emancipate every slave," thought Shelley. The thought was not as far-fetched as it might seem. In 1812 Sadler attempted to fly from Dublin to Liverpool in a hot air balloon.[18] After the first and second articles declaring popular sovereignty and the right of resistance, the third read,

III. Government is devised for the security of rights. The rights of man are liberty and an equal participation of the commonage of Nature.

The function of the state is to ensure equality in the commons. But what is that? He elaborated somewhat this notion of "commonage." In the twenty-sixth article he does this negatively by opposing the monopoly, hoarding, or hogging of the earth, and incidentally suggests that the justification for such imbalance may originate from the church or ancestors.

XXVI. Those who believe that Heaven is, what earth has been, a monopoly in the hands of favored few, would do well to reconsider their opinion; if they find that it came from their priest or their grandmother, they could not do better than reject it.

The twenty-eighth article connects the contradiction between wealth and poverty.

XXVIII. No man has a right to monopolize more than he can enjoy; what the rich give to the poor, whilst millions are starving, is not a perfect favor, but an imperfect right.

What do the Luddite's "commonality" and Shelley's "commonage" have to do with each other besides coevality and etymology? They are not just similar words from the same time: they refer to a human discussion of political economy and privatizing on one hand, and on the other, communism and the commons.

Does communism belong to the field of politics while "the commons" belongs to the field of economics? Is communism a theory contrived by intellectuals and utopians while the practices of commoning are widespread, unlettered, and unrecognized? Certainly the Luddites combined both, a politics of revolutionary insurrection with clear influences from the revolutionary traditions of Ireland, France, and the 1790s, and a local defense of ancient right and custom which were threatened by privatization, machinery, and enclosure. Is the commons just an aggregate sum to be arithmetically equally divided into aliquot parts? The view which presents the commons as a matter of equal social division is largely the idea of dreamers and intellectuals and as such it is scorned by cynics and realists. The idea certainly is found among the *philosophes* of the Enlightenment, such as Rousseau, Mably, Morelly, or Volney.

The difference between Ludd's "commonality" and Shelley's "commonage" may be the difference between experience and aspiration. If so, in the England of the time the connection between them, tenuous though it was in 1811, was vigorously preserved by Thomas Spence. Spence, the London coiner of political tokens, the radical hymn singer, the pavement chalker, and "unfee'd advocate of the disinherited seed of Adam," mixed the English strand of communism with "figurative descriptions of the Millenium, New Jerusalem, or future Golden Age." He appealed, like Shelley, to Volney's *Ruins*, and, unlike Shelley, to the Old Testament jubilee. If Shelley was often on the run, Spence was frequently imprisoned. Spence took inspiration from the mutineers of the Royal Navy in 1797, from the United Irish people in the rebellion of 1798, and from the resistance of indigenous people in America. His concept of true justice was based on equality in land the accomplishment of which constituted his "plan." He believed oppression could come to an end with some "rich Confiscations." Malcolm Chase calls Spence "one of the most sophisticated theoreticians of revolutionary radicalism," though his views could be extremely succinct: one of Spence's political coins summed them up, "War or Land."[19]

In 1811 a small society of Spenceans was formed in London, meeting on a neighborhood basis in the free and easy manner. Maurice Margarot returned to England from Australia whence he had been punitively transported in 1793 and joined the society. He also advocated "the Confiscation and Sale of all great estates." Attending the funeral of Thomas Spence in September 1814 was Robert Charles Fair who was converted to this cause of the commons by reading Shelley's *Queen Mab*. E.P. Thompson found it quite possible that Spencean disciples could be found among the strong and traveled characters of Yorkshire Luddites.

The views of another utopian socialist, we know, were definitely present in the discussions taking place in the cropper's shed. There George Mellor in 1812 heard the view of Robert Owen "that the whole framework of society was out of joint, and that the nations and governments of the earth required a thorough remodeling." The Luddites may have been hungry, pinched, and wretched; some may have clung stubbornly to the commons of a traditional, even a Tudor, economy; yet they were not out of touch with the intellectual work required of political change, or dismissive of the erudition that can help it. The argument that the nations and governments of the earth required remodeling was advanced by a man whose father, also a cropper, kept a bed in the workshop where he sat up for many a night compiling a Greek lexicon![20] I'm not arguing that all Luddites studied utopian socialism or Greek, but some did, and others listened to them.

V

In traveling in the north Shelley gained some experience of the poverty, exploitation, and military repression from which the people suffered. Extreme economic conditions and solidifying class identities were new in comparison to the 1790s. On Christmas Day 1811 he wrote to his friend Elizabeth Hitchener, "I have been led into reasonings which make me *hate* more and more the existing establishment of every kind." He anticipates the bursting of the storm when "the oppressed take furious vengeance on the oppressors."[21] "Shall I not get into Prison," he asked in a letter, "that his Majesty will provide me a lodging in consideration of the zeal which I evince for the bettering of his subjects." Shelley began to plan a long poem eventually to become *Queen Mab*, which he thought he might be able to publish in Dublin.

Before departing the north of England he wrote a factual, narrative poem, "A Tale of Society as It Is," about a widow whose son was pressed into the army,

> For seven years did this poor woman live
> In unparticipated solitude.
> Thou might have seen her in the desert rude
> Picking the scattered remnants of its wood.
> If human, thou might'st there have learned to grieve.

It's the theme found in also in Wordsworth's *Prelude* and one might think little had changed from then until 1939 when George Orwell observed the Moroccan women carrying wood thinking that they were of a different race entirely.[22] These men were passing through, and in not talking with the women they were unable to discover the custom of estovers. They do not see the commons; the commons is not a natural resource exclusive of human relations with it. Like language itself, the commons increases in wealth by use.

The colonial Atlantic begins a short balloon ride away. Shelley wrote *An Address to the Irish People*. "Oh! Ireland! Thou emerald of the ocean, whose sons are generous and brave, whose daughters are honorable and frank and fair, thou art the isle on whose green shores I have desired to see the standard of liberty erected—a flag of fire—a beacon at which the world shall light the torch of Freedom!" As he wrote, "I consider the State of Ireland as constituting a part of a great crisis in opinions." "It is horrible that the lower classes must waste their lives and liberty to furnish means for their oppressors to oppress them yet more terribly. It is horrible that the poor must give in taxes what would save them and their families from hunger and cold; it is still more horrible that they should do this to furnish further means of their own abjectness and misery."[23]

The title of the poem *Queen Mab* is significant. Shelley was a strong believer in the intervention of spirit in the history of the world (past and to come), and Queen Mab was such a spirit—a fairy, capable of flight, and the sender of dreams. In those warring, repressive, and hungry times Shelley made supernatural appeal. For another thing Mab had a powerful association with the earth. She was a major figure in Irish legend as Maeve (or Mebh) going back at least to the eighth and ninth centuries, a female warrior deity magically associated with the land.

In England Queen Mab was associated with the tiny, entomological world of leaves and soil before the earth had become a homogeneous rent-making machine.[24] In America Charles Brockden Brown in his 1799 novel *Edgar Huntly* (a favorite of Shelley) named Queen Mab an ancient Delaware indigenous woman who intransigently refused to budge from her ancestral lands despite the overwhelming encroachment of the white settlers. Thus, Shelley's title appealed to the magical sublime of first, the colonial, second, the indigenous, and third, the agrarian. *Queen Mab* was a direct allusion to a power figure in Irish history at a time when Ireland had ceased to exist as a sovereign political entity and to the enchanted landscape of pre-enclosed England at a time of brutal privatization.

It was a communist poem in a mystical way because its grip on the actualities of the expropriation of the commons was occasional. To Thelwall's list of estates, rights and possessions of the poor enclosed by the rich, Shelley added another dimension. He sensed that the expropriations in England passing under the name of "improvement" and recognized by historians as "agrarian patriotism" were part of a worldwide devastation. "Rule of law" meant "freedom of contract" and "private property" in Nottinghamshire or elsewhere that English power went. For instance, when Thomas Stamford Raffles invaded and governed Java in 1811 he introduced a system of land rent which threatened the common rights of *sikep* villagers, discouraged cotton exports, and curtailed common rights in the teak forests, as well as fulfilling the prophecy of 1805, "the beginning of the ruin of the land of Java."[25]

VI

No sooner had Shelley arrived in Ireland than he was reading in an American newspaper about Hidalgo and Morelos and the struggle the year before for Mexican independence. In "To the Republicans of North America" he wrote,

> Brothers! Between you and me
> Whirlwinds sweep and billows roar:
> Yet in spirit oft I see
> On this wild and winding shore
> Freedom's bloodless banners wave

He called on Cotopaxi, an Ecuadorean volcano, to act as the roaring tocsin of worldwide liberty and then for the waves and winds of the ocean to bear its news to Europe. Anna Laetitia Barbauld ended her poem "Eighteen Hundred and Eleven" by also attributing prophetic power to another Ecuadorean volcano, Chimborazo, bidding America to rise.

And rise America did, but not without struggle, only its enclosures were conquest of Indian lands and its Luddites were insurrectionary slaves. The destruction of farm implements by those working them on American plantations belongs to the story of Luddism, not just because they too were tool-breakers, but they were part of the Atlantic recomposition of textile labor-power. They grew the cotton that was spun and woven in Lancashire.

The story of the plantation slaves has been separated from the story of the Luddites. Whether separation was owing to misleading distinctions between wage and slave labor or to artificial national or racial differences is unclear.

A South Carolina planter wrote in 1855, "The wear and tear of plantation tools is harassing to every planter who does not have a good mechanic at his nod and beck every day in the year. Our plows are broken, our hoes are lost, our harnesses need repairing, and large demands are made of the blacksmith, the carpenter, the tanner, and the harnessmaker." Eugene Genovese adds, "The implements used on the plantation were therefore generally much too heavy for efficient use. The "nigger hoe," often found in relatively advanced Virginia, weighed much more than the "Yankee hoe," which slaves broke easily. Those used in the Southwest weighed almost three times as much as those manufactured in the North for Northern use." A Louisiana editor wrote in 1849, "They break and destroy more farming utensils, ruin more carts, break more gates, spoil more cattle and horses and commit more waste than five times the number of white laborers do."[26]

We are not used to such juxtapositions; economic history is generally conducted by presupposing general exchange value rather than particular use-value. Its language tends to be abstract. We consider "capital" or we consider "property" in our debates about Luddism, and behind them other abstractions such as "technology" or "law." Yet these machines used or consumed cotton and wool, the one grown on the plantation, the other raised in the pastures. Who covered themselves with the woolen blankets? Who wore the cotton clothes? These are the questions of use-value. They lead the mind more easily to the human story and to the human struggle. The soldiers and the sailors wore the clothes, people in Latin America especially after 1808 used the blankets. There is a violence in abstraction which hides the negotiation of uses inherent in commoning.

The history of Louisiana between 1803 and 1812 is instructive. In the former year it was purchased by the United States; in the latter it became the eighteenth U.S. state. In each case slave rebellion preceded the change. Spain had ceded Louisiana to France in 1800, the same year that Thomas Jefferson was elected president and Gabriel Prosser led an ambitious revolt of Virginia slaves. Jefferson's policy was to civilize the wilderness, where "civilize" meant surveyed, saleable public lands—or the treatment of the earth as commodity and constant capital—and where "wilderness" meant the communal possession and use by the Choctaw, Chickasaw, and Creek people. His policy was both conquest and privatization. Moreover, he doubled the land area of the United States in 1803 by the purchase of Louisiana territories from Napoleon who used the money to finance a failed invasion of San Domingue and the reinstallation of the slave regime. The Louisiana Purchase provided the conditions for a dual economy of sugar in New Orleans and cotton from Georgia to Natchez, Mississippi, an economy based on the cotton gin (1793) and a surge of enslaved labor from Africa. These developments were fiercely resisted. As suggested in the archaeology of language where the settler qualified every plan with the expression "if the Creeks don't rise" similar to the devotional expression "in-shalla."

The Creeks were divided between accommodationists and warriors. The accommodationists accepted the loom and the hoe as the technological entrance to a future of assimilation. The warriors were called Red Sticks led by Peter McQueen and Alexander McGillivray, inspired by the Shawnee warrior, Tecumseh, opposed the commerce and new forms of property, and destroyed the loom and bolts of cloth of accommodationists.[27]

Meanwhile, the slaves on the sugar plantations rose in revolt. An army of two to five hundred young men from Kongo, Cuba, Kentucky, Senegambia, Virginia, maroon and mulatto, assembled on a rainy night in January 1811 and marched down the Mississippi River to New Orleans determined to kill the whites and establish a black republic. Inspired by both Haiti and Hidalgo, this was the largest revolt of slaves in U.S. history. The "plantation tool [was] transmuted into an icon of violent insurrection," writes its historian. Armed with hoes, axes, and machetes they were totally outgunned and suffered a brutal massacre. More than a hundred bodies were dismembered and skulls displayed on poles up and down the Mississippi.[28] This took place in one of the richest commons of the world, the Mississippi River delta, which yet was the target of U.S. expansionism, as surveyors, missionaries, squatters, and the militia invaded.

"My soul has grown deep like the rivers," mourned Langston Hughes, the African American poet of the underdog and common life. The indigenous people fought for a commons resisting the commodification of their mother Earth as real estate. The slaves rose against the plantation which from one point of view vied with Haiti in the export of sugar, and from another point of view was as near a death camp as could be imagined in the nineteenth century.

The results of the defeats of Creeks and slaves were twofold. First, the resistance of slaves and indigenous people was criminalized, and to accomplish this intensified applications of force—both a local militia and a federal military were relocated to the plantation south. Second, an alliance between federal authority and the state planters, between bureaucrats and slavocrats, was made whose militarization and racialization became pillars of the U.S. regime. In 1812 Louisiana became the eighteenth U.S. state. No defeat of the people's struggle is ever totally complete. The struggle continued in cultural forms from the delta blues of the 1930s to the *Pogo* comics of the 1950s, the swamps and bayous became the habitat of autonomous communities. These results had parallels among the Luddites of 1811–12. Cultural memory preserved a pantheon of mythological avatars of the history of the common people.

VII

When Napoleon invaded Portugal and Spain in 1808 and installed his brother as king, the Spanish king fled, the empire began to crumble, and it lost its constitutional center, impelling a crisis between creoles and peninsulars in the Latin American colonies which became the context of the first wars of independence. Other class and ethnic forces found the opening to express their grievances and to fight for redress.

Francisco de Miranda, the Atlantic revolutionary, the "Precursor," left London and arrived in Caracas on December 10, 1811, bringing a pamphlet from Jeremy Bentham (*Constitutional Legislation: On the Evils of Change*), and formed the Patriotic Club open to men and women, blacks and Indians. English authorities in March 1811 continued to advise him, "nothing will become more important than the establishment of a regular and effective police for the protection of persons and property," wrote Vansittart, the chancellor of the exchequer, to Generalissimo Miranda.[29]

In addition to the royalists and the creoles a third force emerged in Venezuela. On the one hand the *llaneros* of the south, a mixture of African, European, and Indian fighting to retain pastoral hunting, and on the other hand in the towns "the *pardos*, blacks and slaves fought for their own liberation." This was an "*insurrección de otra especie*," called the pardocracy, or government by the blacks and slaves. They participated in the "popular assemblies" and occasionally revolted independently as in June 1812. In November 1811 the *pardos* invaded the town council of Cartagena forcing it to sign a declaration of independence.[30] Bolívar's Cartagena Manifesto of December 1812 blamed the failure of this first republic upon "certain worthy visionaries who, conceiving in their minds some ethereal republic, have sought to attain political perfection, assuming the perfectibility of the human race."[31] This was the spirit which Shelley expressed and which led to his expulsion over and over again. In England the visionaries were Godwin, Spence, Volney, and Shelley.

Perhaps too it was the spirit which is found among the Indians of Mexico who in the Hidalgo revolt allied with the Virgin of Guadalupe. The Mexican War of Independence commenced on September 16, 1810, when Miguel Hidalgo uttered the Grito de Dolores and the Indians and mestizos mobilized against the King and for the redistribution of land. Hidalgo was fiercely egalitarian having grown up with Indian workers on his father's land and speaking several indigenous languages. He read Rousseau.[32] He encouraged the illegal cultivation of olive groves and vine. His program of land reform was printed on December 1810. It decreed the return of land *á las comunidades de los naturales, para que enterándolas en la caja nacional, se entreguen á los referidos naturales las tierras para su cultivo.* Hidalgo's army was large, and it took advantage of the tumultos, or riots, mutinies, and commotions which expressed village goals, and it assaulted property including "the wanton destruction of mining machinery."[33] These opposed encroachments on communal and pueblo land by the market-driven haciendas; Oscar Lewis states, "The system of communal landholding has remained practically intact through both the Aztec and Spanish conquests," and Brian Hamnett describes some of the encroachments, "Villagers bitterly resented hacienda efforts to curb their customary practices of chopping wood, burning charcoal, tapping maguey, prickly pear, gathering wild lettuce, or grazing their few animals on lands hitherto utilized by estate owners."[34] Hidalgo was defeated in 1811.

VIII

Tecumseh (1768–1813) confronted Governor Harrison in August 1810 with his famous speech about the commons when he said that the Indians considered "their lands as common property of the whole"—the basis of confederation. Denouncing land cessions, he exclaimed to Governor Harrison in Indiana, "Sell a country! Why not sell the air, the great sea, as well as the earth? Did not the Great Spirit make them all for the use of his children?" When Harrison, the future president, said that the claim was "preposterous" Tecumseh rose in a flash of temper from the ground, (Indians preferred to sit on the ground, or as Tecumseh explained, "to repose on the bosom of their mother") and the future president drew his sword. Blood was not spilt that day, but the line had once again been drawn between Native American commoning, and Euro-American privatizing. The association of indigenous American practices and the development of European ideas of communism go back at least to Thomas More's *Utopia* (1516). Was America a new world or was it, as the Greek etymology of "utopia" suggests, a "no place" similar to the *terra nullius* of legal Latin lingo. A year later in 1811 Tecumseh's brother, Tenskwatawa, or the Prophet, was defeated at the Battle of Tippecanoe and the granaries destroyed.[35] After this atrocity Tecumseh went on a three-thousand-mile, six-month journey to the south. There expropriation occurred by means of money as credit and debt became the leverage of land losses. In October 1811 he delivered a war speech to the Creeks in his attempt to renew a federation of the indigenous people against their destruction. Tecumseh's speech was described by a fourteen-year-old, John Hunter, "such language, such gestures, and such feeling and fullness of soul contending for utterance, were exhibited by this untutored native of the forest in the central wilds of America, as no audience, I am persuaded, either in ancient or modern times ever before witnessed."

Hunter lived with the Osage until he was nineteen in 1816. Later he published his memoirs with its appetizing description of prolific commons. "The squaws raise for the consumption of their families, corn, tobacco, pumpkins, squashes, melons, gourds, beans, peas, and, with a few years past, potatoes in small quantities. They collect hazel nuts, hickory nuts, walnuts, chestnuts, pecan nuts, grass, or ground nuts, various kinds of acorns, wild liquorice, sweet myrrh, or anise root, and Pash-e-quak, a large bulbous root somewhat resembling the sweet potato in form, and very similar to the chestnut in flavour, though more juicy." "They also collect, in their seasons, crab and may apples, Osage oranges, three or four kinds of plums, strawberries, gooseberries, whortleberries, black and dew-berries, and a great variety of grapes."

The economy of these resources is described too. "All their various products, as well as those of the chase, are, in general, distributed in proportion to the members of each family concerned in their acquirement; though sometimes no distribution takes place, but all draw, as they want, from the supplying source, as a common reservoir, till it is exhausted." "Whenever a scarcity prevails, they reciprocally lend, or rather share with each other, their respective stores, till they are all exhausted. When the case is otherwise, the wants of such individuals are regarded with comparative indifference; though their families share in the stock, become otherwise common from the public exigency."[36]

These then were the major eruptions in America at the time of Ned Ludd. Not all had equal participation in the commonage of nature, though those without it were fighting to *attain* it as surely as those in England with some access to the commonality were fighting to *retain* it.

IX

While E.P. Thompson's indispensable chapter on the Luddites stresses the Irish in Lancashire it otherwise rigorously keeps the focus upon the English context with two rhetorical exceptions when he compares their clandestine organization to extra-English, non-Anglo themes. Once it is to America (the authorities "were more powerless to uncover trade union lodges than Pizzarro's freebooters were to uncover golden chalices in the villages of Peru") and once to Wales ("there is a tract of secret history, buried like the Great Plain of Gwaelod beneath the sea.").[37] This secret history, he says, necessitates on the part of the historian some "constructive speculation." His figures of speech can help us if we treat them not as figures but suggestions, because they enable us to expand the range by adding to the insular lens an Atlantic optic. What was quietly underground in one part of the world may erupt in fury in another part. We have begun to do this with America. Now, Wales.

The Plain of Gwaelod is subterranean, lying beneath the shallow seas in the Bay of Cardigan, north Wales. According to Welsh legend, as modified by Thomas Love Peacock's novel *The Misfortunes of Elphin* (1829), once upon a time in the sixth century the plain consisted of extensive, fertile, level land which provided prosperity to the Welsh kingdom of the day, and attracted traders from as far away as Phoenicia and Carthage. The people built an embankment to protect the land from tide and sea, but the watchman one night fell asleep drunk and the sea overran the plain which thereafter remained, like Atlantis, a source of mythic past prosperity if not an actual Golden Age, but not before the Welsh bards had carried its wisdom to King Arthur at Avalon.

Shelley was part of something similar, for an extensive reclamation project by building a new embankment in the estuary near Portmadoc. Large numbers of laborers were mobilized. Shelley, back from Ireland, was searching for a new place to set up his commune and found one at Tan-yr-allt not far from Tremadoc. It was not long before he became involved with the project leader and the hundreds workers whose cooperative labors were constructing such extensive infrastructure. The natural conditions of labor were dangerous and so too were its social conditions.

Shelley explained this in one of the prose notes to *Queen Mab* in which he argues in favor of vegetarianism by showing that the cultivation of meat a) requires far more land than the growing of grain and garden produce, and b) that cattle, sheep, and stock raising always entails commerce and is thus, in the long sweep of history, a source of aristocracy which is built on the ruin of "all that is good in chivalry and republicanism." Lasting happiness is unobtainable as long as incentives to avarice and ambition are available to the few. "The use of animal flesh and fermented liquors directly militates with this equality of the rights of man." Surplus labor could be removed only with a sober, subsistence economy. At this point Shelley provides a footnote within the footnote.

> It has come under the author's experience that some of the workmen on an embankment in North Wales, who, in consequence of the inability of the proprietor to pay them, seldom received their wages, have supported large families by cultivating small spots of sterile ground by moonlight.

The resort to commoning was in default of wages and occurred upon sterile ground at Portmadoc where "one of the most advanced community and commercial experiments of the period" was taking place.[38] Shelley antagonized the local landlord, a Tory and an aristocrat with estates in Ireland who organized and disciplined the labor, a man named Leeson. An assassin attempted to take Shelley's life. Perhaps with Home Office connivance Leeson or his agent arranged the attack which happened a few months before the January 1813 execution of fourteen Yorkshire Luddites. Shelley sought safety in Killarney Lakes, back in Ireland. As a class renegade throwing his lot with the commonality, he was not cowardly. In Wales meanwhile an Englishman in 1815 attempted to develop land south of Portmadoc as a hunting estate for visiting gentry but Welsh rural people violently resisted and the unenclosed common on Mynydd Bach whose open pasture and stands of conifer and copses of oak and beech persisted into the twentieth century.[39]

Queen Mab, conceived in 1811, privately published 1813, and frequently pirated thereafter, became the Bible of the working class for the next two generations. Its targets were organized religion, political tyranny, war, commerce, marriage, and prostitution. "Queen Mab is no less than an attempt to state the basis for an entire philosophy of life, an active and militant view of man confronting his society and his universe." Like T.S. Eliot's "The Waste Land," the poem is fenced in with footnotes though Queen Mab's are about, we might say, the commons rather than the waste. It contains six prose essays: on the labor theory of value, on necessity in the moral and material universe, on atheism, on Christianity, on free love and vegetarianism. Like the political economists he accepts the labor theory of value, "There is no real wealth but the labour of man," though unlike the political economist he did not reckon either wealth or labor numerically or financially.

Queen Mab recuperates the radical discussions of the 1790s with heavy influence from William Godwin's theoretical anarchism and Constantin Volney's eloquent fable of the destruction of the commons in human history. With Godwin he finds that the tyrannical principle of power permeates all institutions. With Volney he finds that the human past contains within it the potential of fulfillment of the dream of liberté, égalité, and fraternité.

> Let the axe
> Strike at the root, the poison-tree will fall.

War is the business of kings and priests and statesmen. They conceal their selfishness with three words, God, Hell, and Heaven. To Shelley the machine encouraged slavishness:

> Power, like a desolating pestilence,
> Pollutes whate'er it touches; and obedience
> Bane of all genius, virtue, freedom, truth,
> Makes slaves of men, and, of the human frame,
> A mechanized automaton. (iii, 175–180)

Slavery and the machine produce the person as automaton. Maxine Berg, a contemporary historian of technological change, finds that historians have been reluctant to explore the relation between Luddism and the intellectual disputes over technological change, despite the fact, we might add, that the most brilliant political economist of the day, David Ricardo, changed his mind about machinery between the first publication in 1817 of *On Principles of Political Economy and Taxation* and its third edition in 1821 agreeing that it is "often very injurious to the interests of the class of labourers."[40]

To Shelley the machine is far from being a substitute for labor, the machine was a model for what the labor was to become.

> A task of cold and brutal drudgery;
> Hardened to hope, insensible to fear,
> Scarce living pulleys of a dead machine,
> Meer wheels of work and articles of trade
> That grace the proud and noisy pomp of wealth! (v, 74–79)

Priests, kings, and statesmen desolate society with war, sophistry, and commerce. These translated easily into the triplets of Martin Luther King Jr., or the demons of Milton. "The sordid lust of self" prevailed, "All things are sold," wrote Shelley. He anticipates a day when poverty and wealth, disease, war, and fame shall pass and Man shall stand among the creatures as "An equal amidst equals": woman and man equal and free: palaces ruins: prisons children's playgrounds. "Learn to make others happy," he advised. Shelley also takes the commodity form of wealth and says that trade or commerce ("the propensity to truck, barter, and exchange") is not inherent in human nature. The commons appears as universal benevolence or human virtue.

> A brighter morn awaits the human day,
> When every transfer of earth's natural gifts
> Shall be a commerce of good words and works;
> When poverty and wealth, the thirst of fame,
> The fear of infamy, disease and woe,
> War with its million horrors, and fierce hell
> Shall live but in the memory of Time. (v, 251ff)

X

I have placed the beginning of the Luddite risings of two hundred years ago in a worldwide perspective by referring to capitalist incursions at the same time upon traditional practices of commoning in Ireland, North Africa, South America, the Caribbean, and North America. Indonesia or India could be added. Certainly, the expropriations were resisted with the means at hand which included the tools of production. The redressers who were thus expropriated came to constitute, ideally if anachronistically, an *international* proletariat. This is most clear when considering the international textile industry, for its global division of labor propelled class developments from the cotton plantation to the Lancashire factory, but it is also true of the division of labor in the international food economy which increasingly relied on sugar. The real connections which paralleled the ideal ones occurred at sea. The proletariat from the expropriated commons of the world had an actual existence in the seafaring communities of the world's ports, hence we call it, without anachronism, the *terraqueous* proletariat. What was to prevent its revolutionary actualization for they surely were aware of the many roads not taken? An answer was provided by the Ratcliffe Highway murders which initiated processes of terror, xenophobia, and criminalization.

The Ratcliffe Highway Murders took place on the nights of December 7 and 19, 1811. The servant of the Marrs family had been sent out to buy oysters for a late Saturday night dinner and returned having to knock repeatedly at the door, the first sign that a homicidal extermination had taken place in the linen-draper's house. Marr, his wife, their infant, and an apprentice had been brutally murdered by means of a maul and a ships carpenter's chisel. No property was taken. Less than two weeks later around the corner on New Gravel Lane in the same docker's neighborhood of Wapping, Mr. and Mrs. Williamson and a maidservant were similarly bloodily murdered.[41]

A terrifying frenzy became intense and extensive. The "passionate enthusiasm" of the crowd, a "frenzied movement of mixed horror and exaltation," "a sublime sort of magnetic contagion," spread through the metropolis and the country. Shelley in the Lake District must have known of it because he was in dialogue there with Robert Southey who wrote from Keswick, three hundred miles away, that the murder mingled horror and insecurity. It brought a stigma "on the land we live in." "The national character is disgraced." We shall see that it became a moment of chauvinism.

Among the many reactions I'd like to consider two essays by Thomas de Quincey, "On Murder as Considered One of the Fine Arts" and "The Knocking at the Gate in *Macbeth*," because they lead us to the major themes of modern life, despite their obscure perversity. He writes of the murderer, "there must be raging some great storm of passion,—jealousy, ambition, vengeance, hatred,—which will create a hell within him; and into this hell we are to look." Assuredly, we accept that this is true, that the individual was in a grip of a great storm of passion. Yet the power of this individual passion can be best understood if we see that it is aligned with powerful *social* forces that were specific to the economics of the location. Hell was both within and without, subjective and social. De Quincey's second essay refers to a rare moment in Shakespearean tragedy when an important experience is represented by a low character providing the view from below.

The action at the beginning of Act II, scene iii, had reached a pitch of terror and tension in the murder of Duncan, when the knocking begins at the gate. To de Quincey, the porter's speech in *Macbeth* represents "the reestablishment of the goings-on of the world." The murder is insulated from "the ordinary tide and succession of human affairs." The knocking at the gate returns us to "the world of ordinary life." But it doesn't do this, or if it does it returns us to specifically *English* ordinary life. What the porter's speech actually reveals are several of the permanent antagonisms of English modernity, the moral economy and the criminalized wage, which for centuries were either ignored totally or expressed in slang, low speech, or cant. Let us look more closely.

The porter, hung over and slowly making his way to the door, mutters and compares himself to the porter of hell, not the homicidal introspective hell but a working-class, cynical hell damning it all. He doesn't have time to let in "all professions that go the primrose way to the everlasting bonfire," but two must be mentioned.

> Knock, knock, knock! Who's there in the name of Beelzebub? Here's a farmer that hanged himself on the expectation of plenty: come in time; have napkins enough about you; here you'll sweat for't.

This is a reference to the disappearing of the moral economy of the time, circa 1606–7, as well as 1812 when in April Hannah Smith, fifty-four years old, overturned a cart of potatoes in Manchester at the end of several days of a food rioting. The cavalry suppressed the people and she was apprehended for "highway robbery," nevertheless the prices of potatoes, butter, and milk came down. She was hanged in May 1812. A casualty to the "moral economy" whose complex market regulations expressed the ancient theme that none should profit at the expense of another's want.[42]

> Knock, knock, knock! Who's there? Faith, here's an old English tailor come hither for stealing out of a French hose: come in, tailor; here you may roast your goose.

Before electricity the smoothing iron, called the "goose," was kept on a fire. The reference is to the criminalization of the tailor's perquisites in the remnants of the cloth he cut called cabbage and stored in the "taylor's repository for his stolen goods" whose cant term was "Hell."[43] If the porter's view of life is "ordinary," this ordinary life is hell.

The "hell" within the murderer is also the "hell" of criminalized customs of the docks. For twenty years powerful commercial interests from Caribbean sugar planters to London ship owners, from Thames warehousemen to the West India interest, worked with the Home Office to devise means to destroy the customary compensation which the sailors, lumpers, and dockworkers enjoyed as customs in common. John Harriott wrote, "we succeeded by our joint efforts in bringing into reasonable order some thousands of men who had long considered plunder as a privilege." The slippage from custom to perquisite to privilege to plunder was the slide along the slippery slope of criminalization. The coalheaver took two or three bushels of coal. "Custom was their invariable plea," wrote Harriott.[44] Of the lumpers who unloaded the West India vessels one witness testified to Parliament, "they could not subsist without (what they are pleased to Term) Perquisites."[45] A Parliamentary committee of 1823 asked a ship owner, "Therefore, this, which used to be called plunderage, was at least in a considerable degree, a mode of paying wages?" and the ship owner replied, "It was certainly an understood thing."[46]

They lived in a dockside community where subsistence depended on such customs. Patrick Colquhoun labeled them "crime," convincing the propertied public and Parliament as well. This was an upside-down world Shelley described where opulence and luxury of the few were purchased by the disease, penury, and crime of the many. "The worm is in thy core," wrote Anna Barbauld, "Crime walks thy streets, Fraud earns her unblest bread." The density of habitation, collective living arrangements, inns, boarding houses, pawn shops, slop shops, second hand shops, old iron shops, receiving kens, fences, brothels, constituted an urban economic structure of opacity which Patrick Colquhoun was determined to destroy.

Two policies were followed to accomplish this end. William Tatham, a political economist of inland navigation, contrasted the care given to the *centrifugal* tendencies of overseas commerce with the neglect of *centripetal* facilities of the amazing transfer of unbounded wealth.[47] In other words England's strength in its navy contrasted with weakness in its police. Police could not easily be introduced as it had to overcome more than a century's opposition after the experience of Oliver Cromwell's military dictatorship and the consequent hostility to a standing army. Furthermore police were associated with France, the national enemy, and French dictatorship. Thus the introduction of a police force into England had to be protracted beginning at the end of the eighteenth century with small or niche forces (Bow Street patrol, Thames River police) and broadening from Irish police experience in the early nineteenth century into England. Peel's Peace Preservation Act of 1814, a police act, the result of the property panic after the Ratcliffe Highway murders, was another such step. The second policy against the underground economy of the waterfront was an investment of constant capital in dockside infrastructure, colossal building projects accomplished in the first decade of the century which at once destroyed dockers' neighborhoods and created titantic enclosures of walls, locks, and canals. In fact, the first Ratcliffe Highway murders occurred across the road from such a commercial fortress.

XI

Conventional historiography, even labor history, has not included these struggles which are still stigmatized by the discourse of criminality, or de Quincey's "world of ordinary life." Over ten years beginning in 1803, "almost the entire paternalist code was swept away."[48] The regulations regarding the woolen trade were suspended and then in 1809 repealed. In 1813 the apprenticeship clauses of 5 Eliz. I c.4 were repealed. The clauses which had permitted magistrates to set minimum wages were abolished. During the same period the last common law means of price-fixing were destroyed and laws against forestalling and regrating (two forms of profiteering—keeping goods from sale, buying in order to sell respectively) were not renewed.

The forces of order looked for a kind of catharsis to purge the property holders of their fears. The murders produced a firestorm of chauvinism: Germans, Danes, Indians, Portuguese, and finally Irish were suspected, and a roundup of forty to fifty people quickly ensued.

John Williams, a sailor who had been discharged two months earlier in October 1811, widely believed to have been Irishman from co. Down was apprehended. Williams lodged at the Pear Tree in Old Wapping. He had once sailed with Marr and with William Ablass, a.k.a. "Long Billy," born in Danzig. They sailed from Rio de Janeiro to Demarara, Surinam, where the crew mutinied. John Williams was committed to Coldbath Fields and widely believed to have been scapegoated.[49]

Divine Service on Christmas Day in Greenwich was interrupted by the alarm drum beating to arms. River fencibles (soldiers liable for defensive service only) repaired to their post to do their duty. Was it another assassin or had the French invaded? A large party of Irish had been drinking and fell into faction fighting. People were afraid to go out of doors. Five hundred Shadwell householders met on Christmas Day to arm themselves and form volunteer associations.

John Williams was found dead in his prison, an apparent suicide. His body delivered to Shadwell magistrates who, with approval of the Home Office, mounted it on a cart, in full open display, and paraded it on New Year's Eve in the neighborhood in front of ten thousand people before driving a stake through its heart beneath the paving stones of Old Gravel Lane, a "salutary example to the lower orders." The corpse of the sailor, John Williams, was subject to public, theatrical, and ritualized humiliation. It was a savage moment in the history of English law comparable to the dismemberment and humiliation in 1806 of Jean-Jacques Dessalines, the black ruler of Haiti. Richard Ryder was the Home Secretary, a reactionary and feeble man. Like Spencer Perceval, the prime minister, who always wore black, Ryder was an evangelical.

Richard Brinsley Sheridan, the Irish playwright and member of Parliament, said "they fed the worst appetites of the mob in the unseemly exhibition of the dead body to the multitude." In the midst of public hysteria the prime minister, Perceval, spoke admitting frankly that the murders were not solved and joined the clamor for more police. He was assassinated on May 11, 1812. Sheridan spoke out against English xenophobia. "The prejudice of the hour would have him an Irishman." They were made to cross themselves as corroboration. "It was nothing but an Irish murder and could have been done only by Irishmen! Beastly as this prejudice was, the Shadwell magistrates were not ashamed to act up to it in all the meanness and bigotry of its indignant spirit, viewing the murder in no less a light than that of a Popish plot."

The murders were quickly brought within a counterrevolutionary agenda. *The Newgate Calendar* conjectured that he was a veteran of the 1798 rebellion. "In the dreadful paths of rebellion probably it was that he was first tempted to imbrew his hands in the blood of his fellow creatures," and its terrible scenes of midnight murder."[50] Modern historians of the murder call Williams's arrest "a blatant example of racialism and anti-Catholicism."[51] A letter to the Hunts's *The Examiner* (January 9, 1812) expressed the view that "to keep the natives of Ireland ignorant and barbarous at home and to calumniate them to the rest of Europe was the object of every succeeding chief governor of that country." More was involved. The terraqueous humanity of the East End of the London docks was further terrorized and divided by religion, by ethnicity, by property, by country of origin.

The procession was led by the constable, the collector of taxes, a coal merchant, and the "superintendant of Lascars in the East India Company's service." This was rough street theatre of nationalism and class discipline. Lascars comprised 60 percent of the merchant service in 1814. They were seamen hired in Bengal to sail East India ships back to Britain. They were often kidnapped, mistreated on the six months voyage, paid between one sixth and one seventh the rate of the European sailor, and abandoned naked, cold, and destitute once the ship arrived on the Thames and delivered of its cargo. One thousand four hundred and three lascars arrived in 1810, and one hundred died within the year. A missionary sent among them in 1813 declared them "senseless worshippers of dumb idols" and "practically and abominably wicked." There was a depot for them on Ratcliffe Highway where they were overcrowded, underfed, and often punished. The East India Company's medical attendant said such reports came only "from the discontented and criminal."[52] And yet it was entirely likely that such a lascar provided Thomas Spence with his knowledge of Buddhism which he printed in *The Giant Killer*, the newspaper he had begun to publish just before his death in 1814.

Wapping imports as well as the commodities of empire—its "goods" to use the hypocritical term—also the people, and sometimes, like the crew of the *Roxburgh Castle*, according to Captain Hutchinson they could be "very bad."[53] Williams enlisted on the East Indiaman, *Roxburgh Castle*, bound to the Brazils, in August 1810 and fourteen months later discharged in Wapping. Detained a long time at Rio where the captain warned Williams that if he ever were to go on land he was bound to be hanged. The ship then proceeded to Demerara, where the crew mutinied, to be put down by Captain Kennedy of the naval brig *Forester*. He had been in Rio de Janeiro aboard the ship *Roxburgh Castle* at a time when the Royal Navy was actively exploiting the opening left by the collapse of the Spanish empire and in patrolling ships to enforce the ban on the slave trade. Captain Kennedy was a severe officer who wielded the lash with exceptional enthusiasm.[54] Three mutinous sailors were confined in Surinam, including William Ablass, a.k.a. "Long Billy," a leader of the mutiny, and drinking partner of Williams in Wapping.

The English had taken over the colony from the Dutch in 1803 and by 1811 sugar was replacing cotton and coffee as the export crop and John Gladstone was establishing his enormous interests. Guyanese slaves had shifted one hundred million tons of earth with their long-handled shovels creating what the Dutch called *polders*, or land reclaimed from the sea, and what Walter Rodney called "a tremendous contribution to the *humanization* of the Guyanese coastal landscape." With sugar came steam-powered mills which "saved" labor in the mill and intensified it in the fields. Hence, more slaves.

With steam and slavery came spiritual uplift whose mind-forged manacles were forged in mandatory chapel. In 1810 a law was passed against obeah, an Afro-Caribbean religious practice criminalized as witchcraft or sorcery. In 1811 John Wray, the missionary, wrote a Christian catechism of obedience, and against theft, waste, and negligence, which parallels the repressive injunctions of Patrick Colquhoun and John Harriott against customary takings on the river Thames. In the same year the government issued regulations for religious instruction (registration of instructors, location of chapels, noninterference with hours of toil, confinement to estate, etc.) which when reissued in 1823 helped to spark the great slave rebellion.[55] In 1811 Carmichael, the English governor, made English the language of rule and named the principle town for the new regent, Georgetown, as that was the year George III was declared irrevocably mad and the regency begun. In Trinidad that year it was prophesied that before long "white men will be burning in hell."[56]

The movement to village autonomy that began after the slave revolts of 1823 produced a democratic, proud community of ex-slaves which the London *Times* was to call "little bands of Socialists."[57] Machine-breaking was not unknown. Ken Robertson, my fellow worker in Toledo, Ohio, tells the story of Mr. Samuels who lost his hand to a mechanical coconut shredder and in response four men from his twin village, Golden Grove and Nabaclis, "set fire to the pumping station in the wee small hours of one wretched unforgettable morning."[58]

XII

It was the sailors of the world who manned the most expensive of machines, the deep-water sailing ship. Commerce and globalization depended on them. They mutinied and were notoriously answered with terror. John Williams was confined within the same cells of Coldbath Fields prison that fifteen years earlier had held the mutineers of the *Nore*, whose red flag, "floating republic," and direct action were inspirational to Thomas Spence, Walt Whitman, and Herman Melville as well as to innumerable sailors as far away as Cape of Good Hope or Bengal.[59] A few short years after the mutiny William Wordsworth, in the preface (1802) to *Lyrical Ballads* wrote, "the Poet binds together by passion and knowledge the vast empire of human society as it is spread over the whole earth, and over all time," forgetting to add that, howsoever such binding may take place (what passions? whose knowledge?), it could not be done without the sailor.

Hell is an element that recurs. Not long after the assassination of Perceval in May 1812 Ryder, still home secretary, received this letter from Manchester Luddites (without benefit of spell-check),[60]

> Theirfore you may Prepaire to go to the Divel to Bee Secraterry for Mr Perceval theire for there are fire Ships Making to saile by land as well as by Warter that will not faile to Destroy all the Obnoctious in the both Houses as you have been a great Deal of pains to Destroy Chiefe part of the Country it is know your turn to fall. The Remedy for you is Shor Destruction Without Detection—prepaire for thy Departure and Recommend the same to thy friends
>
> Your Hble sert &c
>
> Luddites

Thus, from Blake's satanic mills to the Luddite's damnation of the prime minister and home secretary, from Shakespeare's porter to Milton's demons, from Shelley's hell of war to de Quincy's hell of murder, the material structures of modern English history—commercial agriculture, enclosures, the criminalized artisan, the factory, and the machine—were likened to the place of burning fires and eternal torment.

Queen Mab does not belong to that infernal tradition. The widening gulf between rich and poor is deplored and denounced in language of both tenderness and wrath that does not rely on the myths of the Inferno. Influenced by Godwin and Volney, Shelley nevertheless appeals to a metaphysics of his own which owes something to local, folk, and nonmonotheistic spirits. Inasmuch as hell is underground the two traditions overlap with the Ecuadorean volcanoes, the Mississippi valley earthquake, the plain of Gwaelod, and the coal mines.

The application of steam power required extraction of coal by digging more deeply which the steam engine also enabled. The miner is described in *Queen Mab*:

> . . . yon squalid form,
> Leaner than fleshless misery, that wastes
> A sunless life in the unwholesome mine,
> Drags out in labour a protracted death
> To glut their grandeur. (iii, 12ff)

On May 24, 1812, in Sunderland took place the great Felling colliery disaster when ninety-two were killed, twenty younger than fourteen and one boy eight years old. This inspired Davy's invention of the safety lamp whose construction he brilliantly described in an inexpensive publication, "with the hope of presenting a permanent record of this important subject to the practical miner, and of enabling the friends of humanity to estimate and apply those resources of science, by which a great and permanently existing evil may be subdued."[61] Humphrey Davy had lectured to packed theatres in Dublin the year before; in 1812 William Godwin took his fourteen-year-old daughter, Mary, to listen to Davy lecture in London.[62] In *Frankenstein* (1817) Mary depicts the monster pathetically listening outside the window of a lonely mountain cottage to a peasant family reading aloud Volney's *Ruins* and how it came to be that the commons was lost and mankind was divided between rich and poor. The hunted subaltern product of scientific progress cocks his ear to the social effects of economic development, enclosure and class separation, or X^2.

In *Queen Mab* Shelley expresses the philosophy of Necessitarianism, a doctrine of the powerful. "History, politics, morals, criticism, all grounds of reasonings, all principles of science, alike assume the truth of the doctrine of Necessity." These are the assumptions of power, inevitability, necessity, fate. Shelley continues, "No farmer carrying his corn to market doubts the sale of it at the market price. The master of a manufactory no more doubts that he can produce the human labor necessary of his purposes than his machinery will act as they have been accustomed to act." Shelley is conscious of convulsive events in Manchester, and alludes to both permanent antagonisms of modernity, the moral economy and Luddism. He was not a determinist or a fatalist, and nor were the Luddites.

Looking back two hundred years from the vantage point of 2011 it is easier to see that the proletariat was not insular or particular to England. It had suffered traumatic loss as we have seen in a few of the myriad commons of 1811 such as the Irish knowledge commons, the agrarian commons of the Nile, the open fields of England enclosed by Acts of Parliament, the Mississippi Delta commons, the Creek-Chickasaw-Cherokee commons, the *llaneros* and *pardos* of Venezuela, the Mexican *comunidades de los naturales*, the eloquently expressed nut-and-berry commons of the Great Lakes, the customs of the *sikep* villagers of Java, the subsistence commons of Welsh gardeners, the commons of the street along the urban waterfront, the lascars crammed in dark spaces far from home, and the Guyanese slaves building commons and community—and these losses were accomplished by terrifying machines— the man-of-war, the steam engine, the cotton gin—which therefore were not seen as "improvement," "development," or "progress" but as hell itself.

The steam engine of Lancashire in 1811–12 differed from the steam engine of Fukushima of 2011 in the source of power. But otherwise, is Fukushima but a scaling up of the machine opposed by the Luddites? Of course not, because hammers would not bring redress, only radioactive contamination. Yet the technologies and science of both machines were products of war in the nineteenth and twentieth centuries respectively. They both have "augmented the general inquietude of man," to quote John Charnock, an engineer of the men-of-war of the Napoleonic period.[63] He referred to these engines as being "the grand promoters of those horrid scenes of slaughter and desolation which, during so many ages, have disgraced the universe."

The imaginative faculty can be political. There was a poiesis of the Luddites and the commons alike which have enabled us to gather Atlantic evidence from 1811–12. Japanese experience has given us Godzilla, a subterranean, terraqueous, and monstrous power, while English experience has given us Ned Ludd, a secular myth of insurrectionary convenience. The war machine and the machines of war, that military-industrial complex, arise from attempts to destroy the world's commons by means of X^2. The only effective antagonist must be the world's commoners with sufficient imagination to see in volcanic eruption, earthquake, and the comet's path the auguries of planetary change and the remodeling of the earth's nations and governments.

London
2011

CHAPTER SEVEN

Foreword to E.P. Thompson's
William Morris: Romantic to Revolutionary

I

Given the overall pollution of the seas, the land, the atmosphere, as well as the geological layers beneath the seas, the world, considered as a chemical organization, is undergoing an inversion. Dangerous gases derived from beneath the seas are being consumed on earth and elevated into the atmosphere with dire consequences for the biological organization of the world. As Rebecca Solnit points out, it is "the world turned upside down," although that is not what is commonly meant by the phrase, which was always egalitarian and anti-imperial.[1] Formerly it described spiritual and political revolutions; St. Paul was accused of 'turning the world upside down' when he preached universally to all—Greeks, Jews, men, women—in Thessalonica (Acts 17:6) and it was the name of the tune played at Cornwallis's surrender at Yorktown which achieved American independence ("all men are created equal").

As egalitarian and anti-imperial, E.P. Thompson and William Morris were both communists, and we need communists now as never before. But what does the term mean? I shall try to provide an approach that relies on "the commons," its cognate.

As a founder of an anti-capitalist, revolutionary, working-class organization Morris had to come up with definitions suitable for a political programme: "Well, what I mean by Socialism is a condition of society in which there would be neither rich nor poor, neither master nor master's man, neither idle nor overworked, neither brain-sick brain workers, nor heart-sick hand workers, in a word, in which all men would be living in equality of condition, and would manage their affairs unwastefully, and with the full consciousness that harm to one would mean harm to all—the realization at last of the meaning of the word COMMONWEALTH."[2] Most of the elements of this definition—that there may be several types of societies, that the prevailing society is based on the classes rich and poor, that equality is an attainable condition, that overwork and alienation of labor violate human solidarity—are derived from the struggles of the early Industrial Revolution as we have come to know them thanks to E.P. Thompson's narrative, *The Making of the English Working Class* (1963). The only point that is distinctly that of Morris is the demand for "unwaste." This is what makes his communism green.

We sense the green again when Morris loses his temper: "It is a shoddy age. Shoddy is king. From the statesman to the shoemaker all is shoddy" he exclaimed to a reporter. "Then you do not admire the common-sense John Bull, Mr. Morris?" "John Bull is a *stupid, unpractical oaf*," Morris replied.[3] At a calmer moment he said, "Apart from the desire to produce beautiful things, the leading passion of my life has been and is hatred of modern civilization."[4] That hatred stems from a repugnance of all that was squalid, stupid, dull, and hateful in capitalism and it led to its repudiation root and branch. Morris's anti-capitalism was nurtured by his study of the romantic poets and to show this is one of Thompson's achievements.

Morris possessed "a deep love of the earth and life on it, and a passion for the history of the past of mankind. Think of it! Was it all to end in a counting-house on the top of a cinder-heap . . . ?" The question has become more urgent, the counting houses have become skyscrapers, the cinder-heap has become mounds of coal ash, piles of tailings, poisonous slurry, vast oil spills, buried beryllium, et cetera. Morris says—think of it! Indeed, that is our order of the day. Or, more simply, towards the end of his life he provided a familiar meaning whose very modesty conceals what is most revolutionary in it, namely, the suggestion that the future is already immanently in the present: "We are living in an epoch where there is combat between commercialism, or the system of reckless waste, and communism, or the system of neighbourly common sense."[5]

Thompson as a stalwart member of the Communist Party of Great Britain did not have the same pressure as a founder to devise comprehensive definitions. His problem was the opposite. He joined a Party that had already attained victory in one country, the USSR, so that any definition was bound to include *raison d'état*, far from neighborly common sense. As a founder of the New Left, Thompson grafted on to the old what was new, namely, "socialist humanism," which however never took lasting hold. Morris had an aesthetic practice as poet and crafts worker wherein the relation between revolutionary communism and the commons found manifold expressions. For Thompson, the relation found private, familial expression, and it infused his writing as an historian and peacenik. Thompson's lasting political achievement was in the movement against nuclear weapons.

The periods of Morris's writings at the end of the nineteenth century and the middle of the twentieth century when Thompson wrote about Morris were characterized by a planetary transition in the sources of energy driving economic development, from coal to petroleum to nuclear. These changes are largely absent in the writings of Thompson as they are from the commentators on Morris. I do not wish to "reduce" the thought of either man to the material and energy basis of the societies they lived in (the reduction of the ideological superstructure to the material base was the Marxist error Thompson criticized most). Morris was a craftsman of many and several materials, Thompson was an innovative and skilled historian; both were historical materialists. If we are to restore notions of the commons to revolutionary communism then we need to understand the materiality of history.

As communists they were both opposed to the capitalist mode of production but they wrote little about it per se. Since capital requires the separation of the worker from the means of production and subsistence, and since the most important such means is land, commoning must logically be the answer to the ills of a class-riven society. Not only is the commons an answer or therapeutic cure (as it were), it was the previously existing condition, because the original expropriation was from the commons. Morris was aware of this, and so was Thompson, who expressed it differently. Thus, historically speaking, capitalism is merely the middle, an interlude one might hopefully say, between the old commons of the past and the true communism of the future. Our language reflects the change in the degradation of the meaning of "commoner" from a person with access to the earthly commons to the undistinguished, ignoble mass, with the implicit understanding that he or she had nothing to call his or her own.

II

William Morris was born in 1834 in "the ordinary bourgeois style of comfort," financed by a father who was a bill-broker in the City of London, one of the 250 richest men in England as a result of speculation in copper mining.[6] He lived in Walthamstow near Epping Forest with its knobbly, majestic hornbeams. He loved to read. At Oxford University he fell under the spell of the critics of Victorian society, Thomas Carlyle and John Ruskin. He began to write poetry and decided to become an architect. In 1861 he founded a firm with Rossetti and Burne-Jones producing decorative arts, such as carpets, chintzes, stained glass, carvings, wallpaper, thus realizing his ideal of handicraft and leading to the Arts and Crafts movement. His floral style remains familiar after so many years. In 1871 and again in 1873 he went to Iceland and translated its sagas. He started Anti-Scrape, or the Society for the Protection of Ancient Buildings, preservation work that would lead to the National Trust. He was treasurer of the Eastern Question Association opposing war in the Balkans. He founded the Socialist League in 1884. He founded the Kelmscott Press in 1891, which published sixty-six volumes. He died in 1896.

Edward Thompson was born in 1924, the second son of Edward Thompson senior (1886–1946), a lapsed Methodist missionary in India, a poet and historian, veteran of the murderous Mesopotamian campaign, and liberal ally of the Indian movement of independence. Edward Thompson's mother, Theodosia Jessup, was an American Presbyterian missionary, associated with the American College in Beirut. Their first son, Frank, was brilliant classics student, who joined the Communist Party in 1939 and then signed up for war. His brother, Edward, followed in 1942 joining the Communist Party and going to war. Frank was killed in Bulgaria in dubious circumstances in 1944, an episode in the transition from the anti-fascist alliance to the Cold War.[7] Returning to university and then to adult education in Leeds, Edward began his work on *Morris* publishing some of it in 1951 and his major study in 1955, the year before he left the CPGB (Communist Party of Great Britain), or the Old Left, and helped to found the New Left and work with its ally the CND (Campaign for Nuclear Disarmament). For two decades in the 1960s and 1970s he practiced as an historian taking further academic positions at the University of Warwick and in the U.S. In the 1980s he returned again to the peace movement and became a founder of END or European Nuclear Disarmament taking up themes of 1945, themes inevitably poised between the hope of the Welfare State and the terror of Hiroshima. He died in 1993.

Morris of the nineteenth century and Thompson of the twentieth century were serious scholars and voluminous writers. Morris wrote more than half a dozen fantasy romances whose mood was dreamy, gothic, and "medievalist"; he wrote two socialist classics, *The Dream of John Ball* and *News from Nowhere*; he wrote poetry and songs; for years he wrote weekly for *The Commonweal*, the socialist newspaper he financed and edited. Thompson wrote a novel and poetry; he wrote campaigning political essays; he wrote influential history books such as *The Making of the English Working Class* (1963), *Whigs and Hunters* (1975), and *Customs in Common* (1995). They were both prodigious agitators who wrote, spoke, and endured countless tedious committee meetings. Actually Morris joined the Social Democratic Federation in 1883 and left it in 1884 to form the Socialist League, which had an influential run until 1890 when he was removed by anarchists, so Morris went on to form the Hammersmith Socialist League. Thompson, too, had a six-year career from expulsion from the Communist Party in 1956 to departure from the *New Left Review* in 1962. They both were English. They both too were Marxists, if we treat that term problematically, as we treat "England," as a label. Finally, they were both craftsmen. "The poet loves words, the painter loves paints: the historian loves getting to the bottom of everything in the sources themselves."[8]

III

This edition of *William Morris: Romantic to Revolutionary* was published in 1977 considerably revised from the first edition of 1955 and with the addition of a fifty-page postscript. The first edition itself was the result of many years of work some of which had appeared four years earlier in the leftist literary journal *Arena*. So we have three dates in the evolution of Thompson's Morris, 1951, 1955, and 1977. Actually, the relationship begins earlier.

In January 1944 Frank wrote Edward, two brothers now two soldiers in armies defeating fascism, about *News from Nowhere* as an example of "the most passionate possible idealism."[9] "Until we are conscious shapers of our own destiny there can be no balanced coherent goodness or beauty." When the troops returned they were determined to shape their own destiny. *News from Nowhere* helped shape the outlook of Jack Dash, a London docker, and fierce rank-and-file leader of the dockers—port-wide, nation-wide, and world-wide—whose strike of 1947 was the beginning of postwar industrial turmoil.[10]

Morris remained with Thompson his whole life. He told an American interviewer, "[after the war] I was teaching as much literature as history. I thought, how do I, first of all, raise with an adult class, many of them in the labour movement—discuss with them the significance of literature to their lives? And I started reading Morris. I was seized by Morris. I thought, why is this man thought to be an old fuddy-duddy? He is right in with us still." Thompson concluded that Morris was "the first creative artist of major stature in the history of the world to take his stand, consciously and without the shadow of a compromise, with the revolutionary working class." "The Morris/Marx argument has worked inside me ever since. When, in 1956, my disagreements with orthodox Marxism became fully articulate, I fell back on modes of perception which I'd learned in those years of close company with Morris, and I found, perhaps, the will to go on arguing from the pressure of Morris behind me."[11] And perhaps it was a way of keeping faith with the passionate idealism of his brother. Thompson did not drop Morris's unequivocal assertion of allegiance to "the revolutionary working class" from his 1977 edition. Thompson himself elaborated on it in his history *The Making of the English Working Class* (1963) if not in his current politics, for both terms had been perversely compromised by Cold War discourse.

The textual evolution of Thompson's biography of Morris stems from this idealism of 1944. I shall comment on each of these texts, the *Arena* articles of 1951, the first edition of 1955 published by the Communist Party publishing house Lawrence and Wishart, and the excisions and excursus of the second edition of 1977. Before doing this, however, we have to step back before the war to the 1930s when unemployment and fascism necessitated such idealism.

In 1934 Stanley Baldwin inaugurated the Morris centenary at the Victoria and Albert Museum. An iron and steel magnate, leader of the Tory Party, and already twice prime minister, he was to lead the country again as prime minister in 1935–7. Edward Burne-Jones, Morris's oldest friend, was Baldwin's uncle. As a child Baldwin was "a great pet of Morris and Burne-Jones." In fact Morris was in love with Baldwin's mother's sister. Baldwin's discourse was sentimental and pompous: "to me, England is the country, and the country is England." He evoked "the tinkle of the hammer on the anvil in the country smithy" or "the last load at night of hay being drawn down a lane," or "the wild anemones in the woods in April." In 1935 he spoke of that "dear, dear land of ours." And "the level evening sun over an English meadow." To Baldwin, William Morris was an innocent, child-like craftsman whose legacy was artsy-craftsy nationalism.[12] The plutocrat ignored the fact that Morris was a communist revolutionary.

Hardly were the honeyed words out of the Tory mouth than R. Page Arnot, the Scottish conscientious objector and a founder of the CPGB in 1920, responded with a sixpenny pamphlet in defence of Morris, the revolutionary.[13] All political persuasions claim Morris from the Labour Party, which only inhales "this fragrance of the Garden of England" to the fascists who claimed Morris because he was "imbued with the Viking spirit." *The Dream of John Ball* (1886–7) is "one of the greatest imaginative books of the world," said Arnot. Why so? Morris was studying *Das Kapital* when he wrote it. Arnot summarised the whole Morris, artist and revolutionary, in two points: "first, art must perish unless it be a people's art; secondly, that the worker must be an artist and the artist be a worker."

For May Day 1936 Jack Lindsay, editor of *Left Review*, published a long poem called "not english?" The ragged thief, the soldier, the sailor, the cotters, peasants, Anabaptists, Levellers, miners, and weavers, are not English according to ruling-class definitions. Lindsay set about a working-class definition of England.

> Stand out one of the men who are not english,
> come, William Morris,
> you that preached armed revolt to the workers and said
> of the men who died for us in the Commune of Paris:
> *We honour them as the foundation-stone*
> *of the new world that is to be. . . .*
>
> though we have plucked hazelnuts of autumn,
> making faces at the squirrel, to kiss between laughter,
> that was not our land, we were trespassers,

the field of toil was our allotted life,
beyond it we might not stir though blossom-scents
left tender trails leading to the heart of summer

This is what Edward, his brother Frank, the young students, read and which inspired them. Edward in conversation used to summarize the problem with the two-word interrogation whose simplicity, obviously, came from the distillation of years if not decades of thinking and talk: "whose England?" he'd ask. We also ask, *what* is England—an imagined community or hazel-nuts? From this problem came an agenda too—the insurrectionary commune, woodland common rights, internationalism. The urban insurrection of the Paris Commune (1871) abolished night work and destroyed the guillotine, putting an end to the inhuman instrument of terror. What is the nature of the commons? Is it a natural commons that is free for all? Is it a regulated agrarian commons where only recognized commoners may gather hazel-nuts or avail their pigs of forest pannage? Is it "public" ownership regulated by government? The contradiction points to the subtitle of the Morris biography: romantic to revolutionary.

IV

The Cold War played out domestically within the labor movement, within electoral politics, within ideology, and it showed itself in the international contest between the USA and the USSR. As a corollary to it was the transformation of leadership from Europe to America as the leading force of imperialism, as Portugal, the Netherlands, France, and Britain faced insistent demands of independence from their colonies. The matrix which undergirded these domestic and international conflicts was the world organization of the base commodity, petroleum, and the consequent reorganization of economic infrastructures.

The struggle against the industrial worker was presented as the supersession of coal. The labor of this change shifted to the new oil producing states, and while the European and American workers of the railway industry and the coal industry were defeated only by protracted struggle, for their struggles had achieved the social wage of the New Deal and the Welfare State, their power would be out-flanked by geo-political and technological means rather than assaulted directly.[14]

Suffice to say that in England the coal industry was nationalized in 1946, electricity in 1947, railways in 1948, and iron and steel in 1951, "culminating in the constitution of the world's first universal welfare state."[15] In the United States the powerful coal miners faced intense mechanization associated with the Bituminous Coal Agreement of 1950. The railway networks changed from coal to diesel and the limited access, interstate federal highway system began in 1956, long lobbied by the auto industry, providing the infrastructure for the trucking industry and automobile civilization. The European Coal and Steel Community formed in 1951 subordinating French and German coal production to a supranational "higher authority" becoming the forerunner of the Common Market and then the Europe Union. The Trans-Arabian Pipe Line, or Tapline, opened in 1950 linking the Persian Gulf oil fields to the Mediterranean at the port of Sidon in Lebanon. It loaded almost a thousand tankers a year.[16] Israel obtained independence in 1948 and a million Palestinians were expelled on al-Nakba, or the Day of Catastrophe. As an additional measure of security in the geopolitical environment for the pipeline the CIA organized a coup in Syria in 1949.

These, then, are a few of the global effects of the petroleum economy driving industrial production and the Keynesian economies. They reverberated in and out of the Communist Parties. The Stalinist theory, as a rulers' theory, obscured "the theory of class struggle in the process of production itself." There capitalism developed a theory (Taylorism) and a practice (Fordism) which became the bureaucratic basis in production of what C.L.R. James called in 1950 "state capitalism." He emphasized "continuous flow" and observed that it required "advanced planning for production, operating and control." Domination by the machine and promotion of consumerism became the hallmarks of the 1950s as compensation for tyranny and terror in production.[17]

Petroleum became the hidden basis not only of economies. The materials of daily life changed to plastics, whose principle feedstock became petroleum. Culturally, in 1941 *Plastic Man* appeared as a crime-fighting comic book, and in 1944 Disney Productions produced a Donald Duck cartoon "The Plastics Inventor."[18] After the war, in the United States plastics became the modern material of daily life, while in the UK plastics were associated with vulgarity and insincerity. Encouraged by the Arts Council, the BBC, and the Council of Industrial Design all still under the sway of the arts-and-crafts aesthetic, the high priests of elitism, such as T.S. Eliot or Evelyn Waugh, bemoaned the plastics of mass culture as did the tribunes of plebeian England, Richard Hoggart or George Orwell for whom plastics symbolized all that was false, American, and shoddy. Dustin Hoffman in the 1968 film *The Graduate* is advised by a family friend, "I just want to say one word to you . . . Plastics. There's a great future in plastics." To the *soixante-huitards* this was a supreme moment of hilarity. The laugh concluded a formless, ersatz era that had begun in 1951 with the publication of *The Catcher in the Rye*, which made the word "phony" the semantic signature of a generation's cultural opposition.

T.S. Eliot on the one hand, a proper church-and-king conservative, published *Notes towards the Definition of Culture* in 1948, while Raymond Williams, on the other hand, began work in 1950 on *Culture and Society* which was very much a product of these times and an answer to Eliot though it didn't appear until 1958. *Arena* was a literary and political magazine started on May Day 1949, and like *Our Time*, *Circus*, or the "Key Poets," one of the leftist literary initiatives not quite completely under the political direction of the CPGB and therefore expressive of what Thompson later would call "pre-mature revisionism."[19] *The Daily Worker* attacked it as too intellectual, and the Party would order it to become an instrument of socialist realism after which it died. It published Neruda and Pasternak. Here in the spring of 1951 Thompson published "The Murder of William Morris" and then in the summer "William Morris and the Moral Issues To-day" especially for a Party conference called "The U.S.A. Threat to British Culture." Indeed, as the Communists said, culture is "a weapon in the struggle" and Thompson's contribution was a belligerent intervention in the cultural wars of the period.

Moral nihilism is how Arthur Miller saw the years after Hitler's death. The dissenting intellectual and artist became the consenting intellectual and artist. In 1949: Peekskill riot against Paul Robeson, NATO formed, USSR drops A-bomb, Chinese revolution succeeds, Berlin airlift ends, Greek Civil War ends, War Department changes its name to Defense Department. In June, Orwell's *Nineteen Eighty-Four* was published. The year before Bernard Baruch, the financier, used the term "cold war" to refer to the contest between the USA and the USSR, and Walter Lippmann published a book with it as the title.[20] Intellectually speaking, this is when, as Thompson later said, "Vitalities shrivelled up and books lost their leaves." Established in 1947 the CIA created concepts of "the necessary lie" and "plausible deniability."

The God That Failed (1949) was "as much a product of intelligence as it was a work of the intelligentsia." The Congress of Cultural Freedom founded in 1950 was the centerpiece of the CIA's covert cultural campaign; it organized exhibitions, subsidized publishing houses and orchestras, and funded journals and magazines, notably *Encounter* (1953–1990). The British Society for Cultural Freedom was founded in January 1951 with Isaiah Berlin, T.S. Eliot, Richard Crossman, and at the same time the American Committee for Cultural Freedom was founded in New York, led by Sidney Hook.[21] "The CIA was in effect acting as America's Ministry of Culture," dispersing money through the foundations of the robber barons, Ford, Rockefeller, Carnegie. The postwar atmosphere indeed became poisonous and the attack was deliberate, secret, and well-funded. Doris Lessing arrived in London in 1949, a young communist with a two-year-old. She remembered the scene—"no cafés. No good restaurants . . . Everyone was indoors by ten"—and she remembered the mood, "The war still lingered, not only in the bombed places but in people's minds and behaviour. Any conversation tended to drift towards the war, like an animal licking a sore place."[22] For Thompson the emotional wounds of the period at the end of the war included the death of his beloved brother, the death of his father in 1946, and the unprecedented human destruction of the nuclear bombing of Hiroshima and Nagasaki.

Thompson's essays of 1951 were punches thrown in the second round of the contest for Morris. Furthermore he wrote within a distinctive culture of English communists which systematically organised its cultural life around various ethnicities (Irish, Cypriot, Jewish, Welsh), and the arts—music, folk songs, theatre, poetry, and—what concerned Thompson particularly—history. Another founder of the CPGB in 1920 was the scholar Dona Torr.[23] She began a discussion group among British Communists before the war, and then following the war, she helped establish the Communist Party History Group, which was both one of the Party's most creative cultural groups and influential in twentieth-century historiography.[24] Thompson described his gratitude to Dona Torr in the preface to his Morris. "She has repeatedly laid aside her own work in order to answer my enquiries or to read drafts of my material, until I felt that parts of the book were less my own than a collaboration in which her guiding ideas have the main part. It has been a privilege to be associated with a communist scholar so versatile, so distinguished, and so generous with her gifts." He preserved this generous tribute in the 1977 edition.

"Let us . . . [pay] even more attention to our own history and cultural achievements, and by bringing our almost forgotten revolutionary traditions once again before the people." This was a project of the 1930s "red culture" and it was this culture which Thompson was seeking to renew. It was under attack, and Thompson attacked back. He provided a scathing critique of a biography by Lloyd Eric Grey called *William Morris, Prophet of England's New Order* (London: Faber, 1949) not only for "the disintegration of the elementary standards of bourgeois scholarship"—wandering in and out of quotation marks, paraphrase, and commentary—but for its inability to notice "the integrating factor which bound together all Morris's mature thought and activities—Marxism, with all that it implies of depth and breadth." Grey was brought to task for claiming that Morris became disillusioned towards the end of his life with revolutionary socialism, and for arguing that Morris's critique was "moral" and "visionary" rather than "economic." This was the binary—"the Marx/Morris argument" he also called it—which worked in him like a dynamo.

"Lloyd Eric Grey" was actually a pseudonym for an American academic named Eshleman whose biography had originally begun as a Princeton Ph.D.

in the 1930s before being published in America in 1940 under the title, *A Victorian Rebel* (New York: Scribner's, 1940). He took the meat out of Morris, leaving a mild milquetoast socialism, "a doctrine of give and take—of sportsmanship and of fellowship." His book reviews for the *New York Times* during the 1930s reveal a noncommittal, liberal man of the American cultural élite, but I have found no evidence that Eshleman worked for the American government or was paid by it (he died in 1949). The animus of Thompson's fury was partly driven by the policy of the CP.

He began his attempt to "take the moral offensive firmly in our own hands" against the threat of American culture whose targets included comic books and chewing gum.[25] Both his Morris essays attacked U.S. academia. In his second *Arena* essay, "William Morris and the Moral Issues To-Day," he lambastes American academia with an appalling anecdote. He met a New England English Literature professor who failed in the chaos of the postwar to profit from fresh meat, i.e., getting some of his buddies to put up some capital, chucking Shakespeare, renting a warehouse and an abattoir, buying "some first class American refrigerating equipment," and returning to the Near East where he used to teach. "Boy, I could have set up a chain of slaughter-houses throughout the Holy Land! My God, I could *have cleaned up.*"

V

William Morris: Romantic to Revolutionary was first published in 1955. At the beginning of 1956 Krushchev gave his "secret speech" denouncing Stalin but in October of that year Soviet tanks rumbled onto the streets of Budapest suppressing a revolt of the workers' councils. Between these events Thompson and his comrade John Saville began a discussion in three issues of *The Reasoner.* Thompson had to make his mind up about the moralism that he'd been explor-ing through the study of Morris. He wrote in the third and last number of *The Reasoner.*[26] The "subordination of the moral and imaginative faculties to political and administrative authority is wrong; the elimination of moral criteria from political judgment is wrong; the fear of independent thought, the deliberate encouragement of anti-intellectual trends among the people is wrong; the mechanical personification of unconscious social forces, the belit-tling of the conscious process of intellectual and spiritual conflict, all this is wrong."[27] He was expelled from the Party. It was a moment of personal liber-ation too. He described "a psychological structure among Communist intel-lectuals from the mid-1930s to the late 1940s which left us all lacking in self-confidence when confronted by the intrusion of 'the Party.'"[28]

It was not merely fortuitous that the questioning of the CPGB represented by *The Reasoner* and less directly by *William Morris* the year before, occurred as the students and workers of Hungary rose up against domination by the USSR forming as they did so councils of direct democracy. The Budapest students struck on October 23, 1956. A week earlier, on October 17, Queen Elizabeth II opened the first ever nuclear energy plant commercially providing electricity. It was at Calder Hall, Sellafield, Cumbria on the coast of the Irish Sea. Otherwise electricity in England was provided thanks to the aid of tens of thousands of coal miners who, as we have seen, had the power to install the Welfare State and might change society even further. Ever since President Eisenhower gave his "Atoms for Peace" speech at the UN in 1953, the peaceful use of nuclear energy sparked as many fanciful dreams of cheap energy without the interruptions of either oil politics or industrial disputes. The response in England was the Campaign for Nuclear Disarmament whose famous peace symbol signaled a taboo upon nuclear bombs but not nuclear energy. Although the New Left was defined by its relation to the Aldermaston marches (1958) against nuclear weapons, it was unable to organize against nuclear energy as such. The base commodity was directly linked to the war machine. Nuclear war was averted, but Three Mile Island (1979) and Chernobyl (1986) were down the road.

His subtitle raises questions. What is a romantic? What is a revolutionary? Is the former all ideal and imagination, while the latter is all reality and science? The English romantic movement among poets corresponded with both counter-revolution and intensity in the enclosure movement. The agrarian commons and the subsistence it provided were fast disappearing. Although Thompson will make this the theme of one of his most important history books, *Customs in Common*, he did not in the 1950s tie it to the Romantic poets. Thompson claims that Morris's greatness is found in the "moral realism" that infused especially *News from Nowhere* (1890) and *A Dream of John Ball* (1886).

The biography belonged to the year when the nonwhite people of the world met in Bandung, Indonesia, searching for a third way that was neither capitalist nor communist. Rosa Parks took a seat at the front of the bus in Montgomery, Alabama. The French historian Alfred Sauvy coined the term "the Third World" in 1952 to reflect the reality that neither the capitalist West nor the Soviet East comprised geographically Latin America, South Asia, the Middle East, Africa, and Oceania. His usage referred to the Third Estate, the commoners of France who, before and during the French Revolution opposed priests and nobles who composed the First and Second Estate. Sauvy wrote, "Like the third estate, the Third World is nothing, and wants to be something." Allen Ginsberg read "Howl" that year, seeking a rhapsodic, hip liaison with people of color against "Moloch whose love is endless oil and stone." Although Thompson's biography was a powerful contribution to the search for indigenous radical roots in England it was also part of the global stirring of the moral capacities of humankind whose most bitter outrage perhaps was that greeting the American explosion of the H-bomb, code name Bravo, on the Bikini atoll in 1954, which poisoned the Japanese fishermen aboard the *Lucky Dragon* and inspired *Godzilla*.

VI

Comparing the *Arena* articles with the two biographical texts of 1955 and 1977 yields interesting results. The second one is shorter, less dogmatic, less strident, without "Stalinist pieties," as he said. But there was more to it than that. To John Goode "The disappearance of Shelley from the book is remarkable."[29] The suppression and emasculation of Shelley within the teaching of literature was one of the Cold War projects. Shelley remained true to the principles proclaimed with the dawn of modern history—*liberté, égalité, fraternité*—even after darkness descended on the day with the guillotine. Liberty, equality, and fraternity had distinct and definite meanings in Ireland, Haiti, the United States, and England that were not confined to Francophilia. "The revolt of definite social forces championing definite human values in the face of definite tyranny" was not yet transmuted into the indefinite idealism of imaginative aspiration against the definite reality of nineteenth-century life. In his tremendous sonnet "England in 1819," precise wrath is directed to every part of the political and cultural superstructure. The agent of historical change—the working class in England—had been defeated at Peterloo and was present in Shelley's poetry, not in its historical reality, but only as a "Phantom." Morris had to find this real history again, that is, the social agency of revolutionary change, from where Shelley had left it off. Morris explained, "what romance means is the capacity for a true conception of history, a power of making the past part of the present." Morris presented a copy of Shelley's poems to the reading room of the Socialist League.[30]

To Perry Anderson the differences between editions fall under his consideration of utopianism and strategies. Thompson wrote of "the whole problem of the subordination of the imaginative utopian faculties within the later Marxist tradition: its lack of a moral self-consciousness or even a vocabulary of desire, its inability to project any images of the future, or even its tendency to fall back in lieu of these upon the Utilitarian's earthly paradise—the maximization of economic growth." To this Anderson objected that the discussion of desire was obscurantist and irrational. Moreover, Anderson "described the historical conditions for Morris's utopianism" to be his rich inheritance from his father which released him from drudgery and enabled him to acquire his cornucopia of craft skills. Yes, Morris was a creature of a bourgeois upbringing and he had money. This is true. Yet history impinges on biography in additional ways. The historical conditions for his utopian book, *News from Nowhere*, included the new unionism of unskilled workers, the great dock strike of 1889, and the proliferation of organizational initiatives like the Fabians, the Scottish Labour Party, and the Irish Land League.

For Anderson the first edition was informed "by a fierce polemic against reformism that is notably mitigated in the second." He quotes from an 1886 lecture anticipating civil war. Those who believed in piece-meal change underestimated the structural unity of capitalism; those who believed in the reform of the system did not understand its ability to beguile its opponents while simultaneously swindling them. Morris's opposition to meliorists, reformists, palliativists, was often expressed. Anderson is convinced that these writings comprise "the *first frontal engagement with reformism in the history of Marxism.*"

Morris believed that revolution, or the "great change" or "the clearing of misery," could not be attained without armed struggle. Anderson fusses because Thompson does not assess "his changing conceptions of the means to attack and destroy the bourgeois State." Morris develops the scenarios of dual power (council, assembly, congregation) in the chapter in *News from Nowhere* called "How the Change Came." Parliament became a dung market. But where does that power reside? To Anderson it is the state and the law, likewise with Thompson. They neglect the economy, from the points of production to the organization of reproduction, from the base commodity to the division of labor.

"Thompson's work is haunted by political or intellectual junctures that failed to occur—historical rendez-vous that were missed, to our enduring loss: romantic poets and radical workers at the start of the nineteenth century, Engels and Morris at the end of it, libertarian and labor movements today."[31] The junction between Morris and Engels was made and it was via "the commons" in its European form. Engels had published an essay on "The Mark" as an appendix to *Socialism: Utopian and Scientific* (1880), written particularly for English and German comrades who did not know the history of these commoning forms of land tenure (*Gehferschaften* and *Loosgter*). The commoners practiced the jubilee and a land distribution system based on periodical assignments by lot. In describing the pigs, the mushrooms, the turf, the wood, the unwritten customs, the mark regulations, the berries, the heaths, the forests, lakes, ponds, hunting grounds, fishing pools, he has quite forgotten his polemic against the economics professors (which is what inspired his tract) and he relished an imaginative reconstruction of a pre-commodity world, the "mark," and its indigenous inhabitants. "Without the use of the mark, there can be no cattle for the small peasant; without cattle, no manure; without manure, no agriculture." That is the living commons. In 1888 William Morris wrote *A Tale of the House of the Wolfings and All the Kindreds of the Mark*, which is a historical fantasy of tribes (he says "kindreds") of northern Europe facing invasions from Rome. The Wolfings practice a simple direct democracy. They combine cattle and corn cultures. They maintain equality between the genders. The "mark" may not be the complete intellectual juncture between Engels and Morris that Anderson believed Thompson longed for! Yet it was part of the international debate about common property of the late nineteenth century which we find in Wallace on Malaysia or Cushing on the Pueblo or, indeed, Marx on the *mir*.[32]

VII

The 1977 edition omits a significant part of the chapter concerning "The Last Years of the Socialist League." If we examine this omission closely we can wend our way to a central issue to both thinkers, the relation between the actual reality of commons and the revolutionary ideal of communism. "Under the Elm Tree," first published in *Commonweal*, July 6, 1889, finds Morris lying on a strip of roadside green, near a riverbank, surrounded by wild flowers and meditating upon the landscape and England.

The structure of the essay moves from contemplation of the flowers, observation of the freedom of the fish and birds, to a meditation on history and the armed defense by Alfred the Great of this particular countryside, then to conversation with the agricultural workers and their struggle, to a conclusion advocating socialism, abolition of the class division between rich and poor, and the abolition of the geographic division between town and country. Thompson is right to call it "wayward" inasmuch as it begins by the side of the road, the verge, where so much of the conflict takes place between commodity civilization with its turnpikes and "the King's highways" and subsistence culture, the byways and lanes.

You think you know what's coming—centuries of the pastoral have prepared us, and hundreds of cameras have filmed the vision—green lawn, ancient elms, white people in white dress, leisured innocence, and a recent scholar, Michelle Weinroth, falls for it. She observes that the Communist Party accepted this pastoral ideal: "their propagandist efforts could neither escape nor eclipse a traditional Englishness, figuratively crystallized in the sensuality of the countryside where [here she quotes "Under the Elm Tree"] 'the fields and hedges . . . are as it were one huge nosegay . . . redolent of bean-flowers and clover and sweet hay and elder blossom.' This fragrant bucolic place cradled the tender affections of their mainstream public and was thus a source of powerful rhetoric."[33] I am not going to dispute whether or not the CPGB was able to escape "a traditional Englishness figuratively crystallized in the sensuality of the countryside," but I shall say that there is nothing like this in Morris!

What Morris actually sees is war. Hollywood and English Lit have not prepared us for this. There is first the heroism that he sees in Ashdown. This was the site of a battle in 671 when a young Alfred helped defeat the Danes, or Vikings, advancing up the Thames Valley. The victorious soldiers cut turf from the slope of a chalk hill in these Berkshire Downs so that the white showed through the green in the figure of a horse. Scholars date the "White Horse" to the late Iron Age, but in Morris's day it was part of the iconography constituting the history of the Anglo-Saxon nation.[34] The Saxons were led by Alfred, "the sole man of genius who ever held an official position among the English," admitted Morris (at least there was one!). On another occasion Alfred fled battle and took refuge in a peasant's cottage where the woman scolded him because while she was out fetching water, he allowed the cakes to burn in the oven! His is a legend of royalty and domesticity, a fable worthy of Lao Tzu.[35] This is the history Morris loved and wrote, history from below.

Thompson comments that the flooding sense of "the earth and the growth of it and the life of it" which pervaded *News from Nowhere* was returning. In the first edition he has some paragraphs describing "the most unusual piece of socialist 'propaganda' ever written" "with its deliberate waywardness, its intermingling of Socialist homily and of the leisurely lyricism of the Oxfordshire countryside!"[36] Yes, as a homily it expounds chapter six of the Book of Matthew. For those from a Christian culture, and Thompson certainly was, Morris begins by considering "the birds of the air" and "the lilies of the field." The aura of this "commons" is a mix of nature and divinity.

"It opens with the conventional summer scene of the poet" Thompson says, and quotes,

> Midsummer in the country—here you may walk between the fields and hedges that are as it were one huge nosegay for you redolent of bean-flowers and clover and sweet hay and elder-blossom. . . . The river down yonder . . . barred across here and there with the pearly white-flowered water-weeds, every yard of its banks a treasure of delicate design, mead-owsweet and dewberry, and comfrey and bed-straw.

Next, the scene is placed within the lengthening perspective of man's history: "the country people of the day did verily fight for the peace and loveliness of this very country where I lie, and coming back from their victory scored the image of the White Horse as a token of their valour, and, who knows? Perhaps as an example for their descendants to follow." This last thought is the key to both Morris and Thompson. It is not one of teleological determinism but of exemplary suggestion. Thompson continues with Morris picturing the socialist future, of "friends working for friends on land which [is] theirs," when "if . . . a new Ashdown had to be fought (against *capitalist* robbers this time) the new White Horse would look down on the home of men as wise as the starlings, in their *equality*, and so perhaps as happy." Interweaving the beauty of nature and the struggle of man, past, present and future, and employing the eye of the craftsman and the poet, the whole is a tour de force. And yet, so quiet and mellow is the tone that the excellence of the artist's handiwork passes almost without notice. Certainly, in his respite from intense political activity, Morris was re-opening old veins of feeling."[37] Thompson is moved to ask whether Morris is losing interest in socialism? But why should acute observation of birds, fish, and flowers dull interest in socialism? Thompson wonders whether Morris found propaganda and creativity incompatible? But why should this be a contradiction?

Thompson's formulations are abstract: for example, "The beauty of nature and the struggle of man." Morris is much more particular. Thompson speaks of "nature" and this is where the trouble lies. What is evoked depends on the commons. Morris stops and talks to the workers in the field about money. Thompson's omits the conversations with the agricultural workers. Morris employs the ear of the socialist and historian, as well as the eye of the craftsman and poet, and it is the ear that saves the essay from becoming another pretty picture. It is neither conventional nor a scene.

The transition in the essay from the birds and fish to human beings was via a four-footed creature, a shambling and ungainly cart-horse, and he saw other animals, male and female, two-footed, ungraceful, unbeautiful, and thirsty! Could they be the same creature as those depicted in the Sistine Chapel and the Parthenon frieze? Beauty and these labourers are contrasted, and beauty is associated with gods or heroes. Could they be the same creature? He starts the conversation, "Mr So-and-so (the farmer) is late in sending his men into the hayfield." Yes, the older men and the women bred in the village are past working, and the young men want more wages. They learn, one at a time, that, yes, they can refuse 9s a week. However, they find no farmer willing to pay 10s. Such is the fatuity of the phrase "free wage labour." These are the stories of "unsupported strikes."

Morris laments the ugliness of exploitation and the squalor of the landscape which is artificialized in the most groveling commercialism. The agricultural system of landlord, farmer, laborer produces parsimony and dullness, just as the excitement of intellectual life in the city produces the slum. The essay moves from impressionistic natural observation through working-class oral testimony to an exposition of the systemic structure of capitalism in both town and country. In a mere four and a half pages, Morris creates powerful effects alluding to the deepest well-springs of his culture—the harvest,

Christianity, animal life, classical and Renaissance artistic ideals—all this while lying on the side of the road!

VIII

The strike for "the dockers' tanner" closing the imperial Port of London occurred one month after the essay was published. If it reverberated on the other side of the world in Australia, surely it did so up the river in Hammersmith. Indeed Morris returned to the place (the upper Thames valley) and the occasion (the hay harvest) to provide the concluding chapters to *News from Nowhere* which appeared in *Commonweal* from January to October 1890 while the memory under the elm tree of the farm laborers was still fresh. But now, men and women are equal, money, prisons, formal education, the state are no more. The countryside is no longer polluted. Men, women, children gather in colorful tents "with their holiday mood on, so to say," for the haysel, or hay harvest, up the river Thames, with description of elms, blackbirds, cuckoo, clover, the gleaming riverbank, the wild roses. And a scene preceding the haymaker's feast of returning home and seduction: "She led me to the door, murmuring little above her breath as she did so, 'The earth and the growth of it and the life of it! If I could but say or show how I love it!'" Morris has imagined past and future as one—equality, love, a feast—at one of the most ancient human activities. It is the opposite to the dull squalor of "Under the Elm Tree."

Internationally, harvesting was being mechanized. In fact, it was the strike by the iron molders who made the mechanical reaper in Chicago that set in train the well-known events of the Haymarket bombing, the kangaroo trials, and the state murders the protesting of which was the occasion of "Bloody Sunday" at Trafalgar Square. Morris was not enamored by machines. One of the characters in *News from Nowhere* says that "only slaves and slave-holders could live solely by setting machines going."

> Clara broke in here, flushing a little as she spoke: "Was not their mistake once more bred of the life of slavery that they had been living?—a life which was always looking upon everything, except mankind, animate and inanimate—'nature,' as people used to call it—as one thing, and mankind as another. It was natural to people thinking in this way, that they should try to make 'nature' their slave, since they thought 'nature' was something outside them."

Terry Eagleton has pointed out that "coulter" (the cutting blade immediately in front of the plough share) shares a cognate with "culture."[38] There is a strong relationship between subsistence food production, or cultivation, and other forms of human creativity, and this relationship is reflected semantically in such words as agriculture (*ager* = field), horticulture (*hortus* = garden), and viticulture (*vitis* = vine), and that in all of these cases culture is an activity rather than a thing.

The revival of the socialist movement in the UK during the 1880s was initiated by discussions of land. The Land and Labour League (which Marx had praised) demanded land nationalization and the settlement of the unemployed on unused land. Alfred Russel Wallace published his *Land Nationalization* in 1882.The Irish Land League led the tenantry in the land wars of 1879–82 (boycott, "outrages") under the slogan "the land for the people" and encouraged a revival of communal custom and the Brehon law. The expropriated crofters of the Scottish Highlands provided the energy of the Scottish Land and Labour League. In a different kind of land struggle, the Labour Emancipation League of the East End of London (1883) led the fight for public places of speech and propaganda which led to the struggles to assemble at Trafalgar Square of 1886 and 1887. In fact on "Bloody Sunday" November 13, 1887, Morris lectured on "The Society of the Future" anticipating the extinction both of asceticism and luxury. He noted "the common people have forgotten what a field or a flower is like."[39] Easy to do, we hasten to add, when the places where they might flourish become forbidden behind enclosing boundaries of fence or hedge.

So Morris was unequivocal about land. "The Communist asserts in the first place that the resources of nature, mainly the land and those other things which can only be used for the reproduction of wealth and which are the effect of social work, should not be owned in severalty, but by the whole community for the benefit of the whole." Again, with a choice of words whose etymology sums up the transition from nature to capital, "The resources of nature, therefore, and the wealth used for the production of further wealth, the *plant* and *stock* in short, should be communized [emphasis added]." Here stock equals inventory and plant equals factory. To Morris, "communism" was a verb; it signified conscious human activity, at a social level in a cooperative spirit to attain human equality. To communize is to convert the reified products of the land, the live *stock*, the cattle herds, the kine of the pastoral economy or the grasses, the grains, and botanical *plants* of the agricultural, once again into means of attaining practical equality, rather than the ancient means of class division. "The communization of the means of industry would speedily be followed by the communization of its product."

IX

I don't know why Thompson excluded "Under the Elm Tree" from his second edition. Was it because it was too close to his own childhood experiences? He referred to these once. While living with him I broke off the tedium of desk-work to lend a hand to a neighboring farmer harvesting hay in a field adjoining Wick Episcopi. Unused to such labor, I did not last long. Thompson heard about it, and I prepared myself for some ribbing. Instead, he smiled, and I seem to recall him referring to something similar in his own youth. Or, perhaps, war was still fresh in his mind, a "new Ashdown . . . against capitalist robbers," and his own battle losses. Thompson and Morris kept Jesus stories well below the surface of their writing, yet the sufficiency of the natural commons as described in the Book of Matthew, chapter six ("behold the birds of the air," "consider the lilies of the field") depend on living in righteousness: "Ye cannot serve God and mammon."

Thompson and Morris were walkers, not outdoorsmen as Americans understand as a sport, but as habit, a restorative. To Americans, the flower is the sign of the wild, as in, for example, "Sunflower Sutra," Allen Ginsberg's contrast with industrial petro-waste. Similarly, it may take on anti-imperial connotations. In 1965 Allen Ginsberg coined "flower power," as an expression of anti-war nonviolence. By 1967 hippies, or "flower children," wrapped army induction centers in daisy chains. "The cry of 'Flower Power' echoes through the land," said Abbie Hoffman. "We shall not wilt."

But if you look at the flowers not as wild, or scenery, or symbol but as resources, you find uses for them which could be significant to laborers on 9s. a week. Richard Mabey, in the great compendium of late twentieth-century popular knowledge, *Flora Britannica* organized by Common Ground, notes that despite the Puritan's suppression of sport and village festivals which generally accompanied the enclosure movement, plants remain essential to the rituals and mystical gestures of the seasons—holly at the solstice, kisses under mistletoe, red poppies for the war dead, et cetera. Inherently sexual, the spirit of vegetation, precedes commerce. Mabey suggests that the grass roots of vernacular relationships with nature should be taken every bit as seriously as the folklore of less developed areas. They "may yet be the best bridge across the gulfs between science and subjective feelings, and between ourselves and other species." Wild flowers belong to an ecology and can no more be understood in isolation than can land, factories, workshops, or mines be understood in isolation from the subjectivity of human uses and desires or the objectivity of the social division of labor. We can list the flowers Morris names in his essay with some of their uses.

Bean-flowers—many escape the garden and are naturalized in wastes and rubbish tips.
Clover—children learn that the white flower can be pulled and sucked for a bead of honey and that the four leaf, or five-leaf clover brings luck.

Elder—roots so easily and grows so quickly that in the era of enclosures it was called "an immediate fence." When its freshly-opened umbels are fried in butter you have elder-flower fritters. Malodorous and works as a charm against warts, vermin, and the Devil.

Meadowsweet—contained an ingredient used as a remedy for chills and rheumatism which was isolated in 1899 as acetylsalicylic acid and which the pharmaceutical company Bayer called aspirin after its botanical name, *Spiraea ulmaria*.

Dewberry—a common bramble in hedge banks, a fleshy indehiscent fruit, succulent in jams and pies. Berrying going back thousands of years one of the universal acts of foraging to survive through industrialization.

Comfrey—found near streams and damp roadsides played a part in the sympathetic medicine of the doctrine of signatures as a poultice for bruises as it contains allantoin, which heals connective tissue. In Yorkshire coal miners applied it to their knees after a day of crawling underground.

Thompson admired the country crafts, the wheelwright's shop, pig-keeping, and the songs. He wrote a foreword to one of Roy Palmer's collection of folk ballads; he wrote a foreword to George Sturt's beautiful work of social history, *The Wheelwright's Shop* (1923, 1992), which was recommended to him in 1939 as a school boy as an introduction to "the organic community." Sturt was a writerly kind of craftsman, and a socialist contributor to Morris's *Commonweal*. Sturt was a listener and observer who found philosophy at "the point of production" which yielded up its insights only after hands-on attention. Thompson also wrote an introduction to the second edition of M.K. Ashby's memoire of her father, *Joseph Ashby of Tysoe, 1859–1919: A Study of English Village Life* (1974). If Sturt was the Wittgenstein of the village, Miss Ashby was its Wollstonecraft. Although Tysoe was a post-enclosure village, the struggle for allotments is described with precise artistry and emotional subtlety. It ceased to be "a sound co-operative village of freemen, free to get a living, free to say yea and nay in their own affairs." The hedge became sanctified; "it carved up the hills and valleys absurdly" pushing out the hawthorn "one of the loveliest of smaller trees."[40] The children could no longer roam, threading by balk and headland, from one village to another, instead they were carted off to the cotton factory. The poor become pauperized, the paupers become degraded, forced to creep and cringe, taking to drink and "foolishness of outlook."

The young Joseph Ashby learned that "under the wide acreage of grass and corn and woods which he saw daily, there was a ghostly, ancient tessellated pavement made of the events and thoughts and associations of other times." The intertwining of history and morality occurred from the bottom up. Joseph searches "new forms of communal land-holding relevant to the English countryside." Thompson calls it a vestigial communal democracy, and compares it to the "participatory democracy" which we in SDS (Students for a Democratic Society) named. This relationship between knowledge of the flowers and freedom to roam in recently enclosed land was often exercised by Edward Carpenter (1844–1929), the socialist, gay liberationist, and reformer was trained from childhood to observe the wild flowers of the Sussex Downs—red clover, pink centaury, dwarf-broom, and yellow lotus. And wherever he went from the Alps to the Himalayas he looked for them.[41] Thompson's powerful conceptual contribution to the discussion of food and land was made in 1972 with his article on the "moral economy." It put food, not profit, as the agrarian priority. It is not a great distance of thought to go from "moral realism" to "moral economy." The concept, like the practice, arose "from below."

Edward loved wild flowers. Walking with him in Worcestershire or Wales he'd stop and talk about them as they appeared on the path. I lived upstairs in 1972–73 at Wick Episcopi, which had a grand staircase at the end of the flagstoned hall on the ground floor. At the time Reg, the paperhanger, was exactly aligning a Morris print on its walls leaving his ladder, his glue pots, and paper rolls strewn about. Here I saw Edward slowly mounting the stairs brooding with papers in his hand or steadily carrying a vase of flowers to an upstairs room, passing as he did so the emerging Morris design.

His father and brother, Frank, wrote one another about them, these soldiers, the father from Mesopotamia in the Great War, the brother from Syria and Persia during the Anti-Fascist War. It was a distinct aesthetic that was a signal across the world to one another in the midst of war. This was part of the patrimony of this family of writers, scholars, and soldiers. Wild flowers were one of the links between father and sons.

Edward's father was chaplain to Indian and Leicestershire forces to the catastrophe of the Mesopotamian campaign of 1916. He did not want to fight ("I feel ashamed about the war"), so he did hospital duty and kept a diary. "The poppies were a larger sort than those in the wheat fields, and of a very glorious crimson. In among the grasses were yellow coltsfoot; among the pebbles were sowthistle, mignonette, pink bindweed, and great patches of storksbill. Many noted the beauty of those flowers, a scene so un-Mesopotamian in its brightness." Melancholically he wrote, "among us were those who would not drink of this wine again till they drank it new in their Father's Kingdom."[42] His is a sacred and a nationalist view. Dorothy Thompson wrote me, "I think wild flowers were one of Edward's close links with his much-loved father. Edward senior used to take him on flower walks in Oxfordshire."

In May 1942 Frank Thompson describes the wild roses, hawthorn, and garden freesia, honeysuckle of Nablus and Jenin. During the desert campaign Frank Thompson saw the goosewort, stitchwort, groundsel and ground ivy." He describes the Libyan desert's flowers—"dwarf toadflax, purple stock, small marigolds, red and yellow ranunculus, and even small blue irises." We see him in Cairo going around to florists looking for the name of morning-glories in French, Greek, or Arabic. When in the spring he expressed homesickness, he thinks of blackthorn which more than any other flower symbolizes "the peculiar loveliness of the English spring." In January 1944 Frank writes Edward, "the English countryside is still the only one that really moves me."

Frank Thompson was among the first to land on Sicily in 1943. He and his comrades were under heavy mortar fire. "I could see that all the men were badly shaken. With a vague feeling that it was up to me to rally morale, I said the first thing that came into my head. 'Blackberries, by Jove! How delicious! It's years since I had a meal of blackberries!' I picked a few. The men stared at me a little oddly and then picked some themselves. . . . The wadi almost reeked with thyme and mint and the nearby lemon-groves."[43] Fragrance, appetite, picking: these stave off traumatic reactions under fire.

In one of his last letters Frank wrote, "the question of building a new communal ethic is one of the most important that we have to elaborate. My own list of priorities is as follows.

> 1. *People* and everything to do with people, their habits, their loves and hates, their arts and languages. Everything of importance revolves around *people*.
> 2. *Animals and flowers.* These bring me a constant undercurrent of joy. Just now I'm reveling in plum blossom and young lambs and the first leaves on the briar roses. One doesn't need any more than these. These are enough for a hundred life-times."[44]

Lives were at stake. Parenting, brotherhood, sanity, health, communal ethics: these were some of the values triggered by encounters with non-commodified botanical species, not to mention the pleasures of recognition, the delight in color, or the tokens of love. Morris helps us to see this and to see it in Thompson. On the other hand, Thompson helps us to understand the expropriation, the loss, and the contest for such a world. The building of a new communal ethic required the sensibility aroused by the vestiges preserved from the expropriation of the commons.

Morris was active in Anti-Scrape, or the Society for the Preservation of Ancient Buildings, also the Commons Preservation Society, and the National

Footpaths Preservation Society. Morris was a street fighter, he was muscular, and admired traditional soldierly virtues such as courage, fortitude, solidarity, dynamic stoicism. He presents thriving organic systems, extensive living thickness, powerful tangles of hedgerow or meadow array, floral and vegetal motifs, chunky clusters of hawthorn blossom. Morris was fascinated by illuminated representations of wodehouses, or wild men, in costumes of green like "vegetable man." The wodehouse was naked, a satyr, faun, ivy-covered man, or savage. Morris was interested in the deep "past characterized by communal tribal living." His design work structured around issues in 1870s that in the next decade will be articulated in class terms. The tree of life in *Sigurd the Volsung* (1876) is symbol of connectedness of all life, and the ritual of the earth-yoke cutting away the greensward represents this integration.[45]

Morris's coffin was borne in an open hay-cart "festooned with willow-boughs, alder, and bulrushes."[46] The church itself was decorated with ears of oats and barley, pumpkins, carrots, and sheaves of corn. "For three miles or more, the road lay through the country he had loved so well and described so often, between hedges glorious with the berries and russet leaves of the guelder rose, hips and haws and dark elder berries."[47] Thompson lived in the English midlands for some years, Wick Episcopi, and here was a large tulip tree with wild cyclamen round its base. The original plants had come from Palestine before the war. "Edward's coffin had a large pile of them on it."

John Gerard wrote in his *Herbal* (1597), which Morris studied as a child— "it is reported to me by men of good credit, that cyclamen or sow-bread groweth upon the mountains of Wales; on the hills of Lincolnshire and in Somerset-Shire. Being beaten and made up into trochisches, or little flat cakes, it is reputed to be a good amorous medicine to make one love, if it be inwardly taken." More than aesthetics, more than pastoral nationalism, more than the Christian sacred, knowledge of wild flowers helped the expression of emotion and the renewal of subjectivity.

X

I have been arguing in this introduction that both Thompson and Morris possessed strong attachments to what I can only call "the commons." The waste or the margins or the roadside was a rough-and-ready commons which nourished Morris's roots and designs and dyes and which helped inspire Thompson by releasing him from the Stalinist and utilitarian grip of the CPGB without falling as an apostate into the septic system of the CIA and its fragrant out-houses in academia. For Morris this showed itself aesthetically, for Thompson it usually found private expression. These attachments were restorative. Earlier in quoting Jack Lindsay's poem, "not english?" I referred to a contradiction. How is it possible that the earth can be at once beautiful and a source of exploitation? It is this which both Morris and Thompson sought to resolve for one or the other must cease. G.D.H. Cole concluded that Morris "helps to keep the cause sweet" but this is to forget the cinder-heap.[48]

When the anarchists ejected Morris from the editorial control of *Commonweal* at the meeting May 1890 we learn that "As the room thickened with tobacco smoke and revolutionary bluster, he busied his hands with flower-patterns and lettering on his agenda paper, in the end flinging himself back in his chair growling, "Mr. Chairman, can't we get on with the business. I want my TEA!"[49] The next issue contained another installment of *News from Nowhere*. I don't know whether that agenda paper has survived among the archives of Morrisiana, or the flower patterns he drew on it. What is clear is that his urge to make floral designs was never far away, even in such times of maximum sectarian stress. Thompson did not doodle in this way, but he had immense admiration for the floral observations which the Spitalfields weavers revealed in their patterns.

In 1896 he designed the last of his wallpapers called "Compton." It is a sinuous, swirling, several layered, combination of flower blossoms, leaves, and stems in an energetic and mysterious interplay of light and dark. A red tulip blossom is the largest shape, and it is accompanied by three different pink blossoms against a background of willow leaves in deepening shades of green. There is an impression of both brilliance and depth, like spattered sunlight through the tall trees upon the forest floor. I do not think that the colors (red, pink, green) were intended as political allegory though in light of Morris's subsequent influences on the revolutionary, reformist, and environmental movements it is tempting to see them that way. "In wilderness is the preservation of the world," wrote Thoreau towards the end of his life.[50]

Weinroth quotes part of Marx to the effect that society offers consolatory "imaginary flowers." This is the "false consciousness." To give up illusions is to give up the conditions that require illusions. She might have continued the quotation, "Criticism has plucked the imaginary flowers on the chain not in order that man shall continue to bear that chain without fantasy or consolation but so that he shall throw off the chain and pluck the living flower."[51]

William Morris gave a lecture on communism in 1893 towards the end of his life at the Hammersmith Socialist Society. He started, "If our ideas of a new Society are anything more than a dream, these three qualities must animate the due effective majority of the working people; and then, I say, the thing will be done." The three qualities wanting to attain practical equality were the "intelligence enough to conceive, courage enough to will, power enough to compel."

The strength of Thompson's biography is that it takes you right into the political developments of Morris's life as an activist. Therefore, it must go to the working class, and hence to the mode of production. Thompson may not have written about the material changes of social life at the time he was writing, but he was assuredly aware of them at the time Morris was living. "What was the hinge that Labour depended upon at present?" Morris asked. "Coal-mining," he answered.

The Glasgow branch of the Socialist League in 1887 declared, "When the Miners resolve to demand an advance, let it be understood that, should it not be conceded, every riveter would lay down his hammer, every joiner his plane, every mason his trowel. Let it be known that every railway guard, porter, signalman, and driver folded his arms; that every baker refused to make his dough, every cook refused to make dinner, and every maid refused to wait at table."

Miners and socialists spoke from the same platform on Glasgow green in 1887. Hundreds, sometimes thousands, attended socialist meetings. In Scotland Morris spoke on a cinder-tip at night to a crowd which gave him good heart ("the thing is taking hold") before traveling to Newcastle, arriving April 10, where he marched six miles to meeting-field to address thousands of men and women from the surrounding pit villages. "They worked hard day in, day out, without any hope whatever. Their work was to work to live, in order that they might live to work. (Hear, hear, and 'Shame'.) That was not the life of men. That was the life of machines." "They must rebel or be slaves."[52]

If there was to be a general strike, he warned, they must expect "that the masters of society would attack them violently, he meant with hot shot, cold steel, and the rest of it. It was not that the master could attack them by themselves. It was only the masters with a certain instrument, and what was that instrument? A part of the working classes themselves." He saw half a dozen policemen in the crowd and began to tease them to the crowd's delight for the bright buttons, white gloves, red livery of their uniforms. "When these instruments, the soldiers and the sailors, came against them and saw that they were in earnest, and saw that they were many—they all knew the sufferings of the workers—what would happen? They would not dare obey their masters." He wished them not to stop at shorter hours or more wages. "He wished that the men might have a life of refinement and education and all those things which made what some people called a gentleman, but what he called a man." At this the crowd burst into cheers.[53]

Morris went on to catch the Newcastle train to take him to Ryton Willows, a recreation ground by the river Tyne. This was "a piece of rough heathy ground . . . under the bank by which the railway runs: it is a pretty place and the evening was lovely." It was Easter and there were lots of folks on the swings, playing cricket, "dancing & the like." Morris thought it was "a queer place for a serious Socialist meeting" but he felt "lectury" and spoke until the dusk fell and the stars came out. The people stood and listened, and "when we were done gave three cheers for the Socialists." The green, the heath, a meeting-field, a riverbank by the railway: these were places to assemble or to play, the common places of that time during the era of coal.

Ann Arbor
2011

CHAPTER EIGHT

Preface to the Korean Edition
of *The Magna Carta Manifesto*

OF THE ARISTOCRATIC AND STYLISH SIX MITFORD SISTERS, JESSICA PROVIDES US WITH the Lazy Interpretation of Magna Carta beloved by sluggards everywhere. As a lovely communist (two of her sisters were fascists) she was disowned by her family and fell from the social peaks of English aristocracy to the Dickensian depths of the Rotherhithe docks in London in 1939. Unable to pay the rent she and her husband lived in fear of the process-server who they avoided by going in disguises which the process server soon came to recognize. "Esmond had a theory that it was illegal and in some way a violation of Magna Carta to serve process on people in bed."[1] So they stayed in bed all day and then all night, and again all the next day, and all the next night under the covers, before deciding to immigrate to America. (Tom Paine, too, thought that independent America was a realization of Magna Carta).

Once we stop smiling, we see the wisdom of rest. William Morris's wonderful utopian novel, *News from Nowhere*, is called in its subtitle "An Epoch of Rest" and the story actually begins in bed! The Bible solemnly orders that the earth itself be given a rest every seven years. This of course made sense agronomically at the time to prevent soil exhaustion. And it makes sense today more than ever because earth, air, water, and fire, formerly common, are utterly exhausted by the world's privatizers who call their exploitation "business." But business is the opposite of rest.

The subtitle of this book, *Liberties and Commons for All*, expresses two aspects of the ancient English Charters of Liberty; first is the restraint on political power of the King, second is the protection of subsistence in the commons. The former are legal issues—rule of law, trial by jury, prohibition of torture, habeas corpus; the latter are economic principles—neighborhood, subsistence, commons, reparations, and travel. How have they fared since the book was published? A worldwide crushing financial crisis of austerity has been met with new demands in the Occupy Wall Street movement and anti-capitalist mobilizations in Greece, Spain, Egypt, and a renewed push-back against nuclear power. Can Magna Carta and its sister companion, the Charter of the Forest, contribute to these discussions? How to put the commons into the constitution, and the constitution into the commons? Can the centuries of human wisdom found in these Charters help the people of Jeju Island preserve the last pristine commons on earth from the inevitable destruction entailed by the construction of a U.S. naval base in its bid for Pacific hegemony?

The book was conceived at a time of the systematic devaluation of the working class of the world. The USA gloated in its imagined omnipotence and one after another destroyed the internal restraints on that power, and eliminated the external restraints with endless global wars. War provided the shock for devaluation and enclosure. From nurses and doctors health care was turned over to insurance profiteers; from carpenters and masons housing or shelter was turned over to bankers; from gardeners and farmers food was turned over to genetic engineers; and from librarians and scholars knowledge was turned over to machine operators. Work was as much alienated drudgery as ever, only now as "jobs" became a desperate social desideratum to have one was to be privileged. "Jobbery" once was scorned as corrupt careerism second only to stockbrokers in vile repute, instead it has thoughtlessly become the ultimate good. Prison has become a mass experience. They have combined to destroy self-respect, creativity, wellness, clearness of thought, probity of mind, and actual usefulness. They undermine integrity, and reenslave mind, body, and soul.

The Gwangju People's Uprising of May 1980 occupied a central city square, renaming it Democracy Square. Some commentators stress three aspects of that uprising, the struggle for truth, the transcendence of secular life, and the creation of a historical community. George Katsiaficas compares it to the Paris Commune.[2] One might also compare it to the Commons Rebellion of 1381 in England both for those three aspects and for the occupation of central urban spaces, and for the miracle of mobilization, accomplished at least in the thirteenth and fourteenth centuries by "murmuring."

Knowledge of previous struggles for justice is transmitted in many ways through the law and extra-legally. Among the latter are commemorations, such as July Fourth commemorating the Declaration of Independence of the thirteen American colonies in 1776 or Fourteenth of July commemorating the storming of the Bastille and the beginning of the French Revolution in 1789. The commemoration itself may become an occasion to renew the struggle of the past in the present of the events it commemorates, though this is dangerous. Nostalgia or official piety is the safer course. "All men are created equal" sounds good, as does *liberté, égalité, et fraternité* though the actual process of equalization, actual real equality, entails a perilous, though necessary, historical course of redistribution, confiscation, and leveling.

The spectre of the commons has haunted the long arch of British history. The leader of the Commons Rebellion of 1381 was Wat Tyler who forced the King to negotiate the return of expropriated commons. He was massacred on June 15, 1381. The fact that June 15 was the date when King John was forced by civil war to succumb to limitations on his power in Magna Carta in 1215 was not mentioned by the chroniclers of 1381. The archive of human knowledge is controlled by the rulers. This is not to argue that the class war of the Commons Rebellion of 1381 and the civil war leading to the armistice of Magna Carta in 1215 were either the same issues or led by the same social forces. In the latter the barons and nobility were enjoined to restrain the King, while in the former this was left to the commons. Yet both acted for the commonweal, or the common good as we might say.

The concept of the commonweal emerged after the Commons Rebellion of 1381 whose insurgents included craftsmen, proletarians, and vagabonds in addition to the peasants who were the most numerous and fundamental. Ever since the semantic field of the "commons" includes this association with rebellion. David Rollison shows that "weal" derives from the Anglo-Saxon term *wele* itself meaning wellness, welfare, or well-being.[3] Riches, or the accumulation of commodities, undermines well-being, as all the world's religions once taught. At best, properties can be instruments for the attainment of wellness; at worst, they impeded it.

The English State in its sixteenth century depended on the centralized monarchy and established religion to oppose the commons. Thomas Elyot, Renaissance humanist, clerked for the King's Council and did business for Star Chamber. He wrote *The Book Named the Governor* (1531) and dedicated it to King Henry VIII and it was published by the King's printer. It went through eight editions in the sixteenth century. Its second paragraph is an argument against communism.

People have mistaken "republic" for a "commonweal." The English word, "republic" derives from two Latin words, *res publica*, which means things belonging to the populous, or the public, which is to be distinguished from the *plebeia*, or common people. *Plebs* is Latin for English commonality and *plebeii* is commoners. *Res plebeia* thus should be translated as the "commonweal." Those who make this mistake, claims Elyot, do so "that every thing should be to all men in common." "If there should be a common weale, either the commoners only must be wealthy and the gentle and noble men needy and miserable, or else excluding gentility, all men must be of one degree and sort, and a new name provided." He feared the Biblical text requiring Christians "to have all things in common."

Why was the argument against commons conducted on philological or semantic grounds? It had to do with the control of language, and thus the control of understanding, as Latin was giving way to the vernacular English during the period of the formation of a national market in commodities (traffic). The clerical, or priestly, caste was losing its monopoly on political discourse. It no longer was the exclusive voice of the nation. Latin was the software code, as it were, of what they called "the republic of letters." Those letters, as Marx wrote, were "letters of blood and fire," that is the expropriation of the commons.

They did not want the subject to be generalized from local practices, nor did they want the struggles against expropriation to be linked as they had been at the time of the Commons Rebellion of 1381, any more than do the powers-that-be want the struggle at Gwangju or Jeju Island generalized. Whispering and "murmuring" were means of communication among the people who were wise enough to express themselves just short of the coherent articulation that rulers could understand, and yet all the more ominous for that. The ruling class wished to exclude such voices and thus to control the human archive upon which the human story is based.

Thomas More, the same King's loyal servant, was late in delivering the manuscript of *Utopia* (1516) to his printer and made excuses by blaming his wife, his children, and his servants. Written and published in Latin it was not translated into English until 1551. The translator, Raphe Robinson, rendered More's Latin excuse for not having the time for writing, "For when I am come home, I must common with my wife, chat with my children, and talk with my servants."[4] Common with his wife! Communism was not a dream! Utopia was not nowhere, it was right here at home! So much is implied with this translation. It occurred just after Kett's Rebellion in Norfolk, the largest effort in that century to preserve English commoning. In 1563, the English monarchy established the famous thirty-nine articles of the Church of England. Preached from every pulpit, studied by every child, from that century on, the penultimate, Article 38, flatly stated, "The Riches and Goods of Christians are not common." The control of the pulpit was as jealously guarded by the state as the internet is against WikiLeaks.

In the following century another effort to secure the commons and gain access to the pulpit, led by Levellers and Diggers in the English Revolution, gave the ruling class a lasting fright. Between 1551 and 1684 commoning had considerably diminished, with the defeat of many rebellions, riots, and revolution. The patriarchy was unable to common. The domestic system of production was also diminished as the workshop or manufacture advanced as a separate establishment from the family. The attack on women proceeded with multiple burnings and torture.[5] So it should not surprise us that Gilbert Burnet, the complacent defender of the Whig Establishment after the restoration of monarchy should translate *Utopia* anew in which commoning between husband and wife has disappeared to be replaced by "discourse."

In the USA neither aspect of Magna Carta has flourished, despite important attempts. The African American T. Thomas Fortune wrote in 1880s in the depths of the Jim Crow segregation of the American south installing slavery under another name, "that land is common property, the property of the whole people." He too reached deep into the human past, "The fires of revolution are incorporated into the Magna Carta of our liberties, and no human power can avert the awful eruption which will eventually burst upon us as Mount Vesuvius burst forth upon Herculaneum and Pompeii. It is too late for America to be wise in time. 'The die is cast.'"[6]

Franklin Roosevelt sought to be wise in the crisis of capitalism during the 1930s, and to cast the dice again. At his third inauguration as President in January 1941 he reminded America that "the democratic aspiration is no mere recent phase in human history . . . it blazed anew in the Middle Ages. It was written in Magna Carta." In the context of the Four Freedoms, and the explanation of Freedom from Want was provided by the commoner and proletarian, Carlos Bulosan.[7] Bulosan had worked the succulent cornucopia of mother earth: in the orange groves, flower fields, asparagus rows, winter peas, vineyards, Wyoming beets, plant cauliflower, picked hops, lemon farms—but working as a proletarian he suffered beatings, gambling, prostitution, drugs, homelessness. As for the commons, this became a memory of family life in the Philippines.

> We are the desires of anonymous men everywhere,
> Who impregnate the wide earth's lustrous wealth
> With a gleaming florescence; we are the new thoughts
> And the new foundations, the new verdure of the mind;
> We are the new hope new joy life everywhere
> If you want to know what we are—
> WE ARE REVOLUTION

Woody Guthrie, the Oklahoma dust-bowl balladeer, worked his whole life for that time "when there shall be no want among you, because you'll own everything in common. . . . That's what the Bible says. Common means all of us. This is old Commonism."[8]

Magna Carta continues to play a part in litigation. For example, Michael O'Shea, a glass-cutter in Waterford, Ireland, went fishing in the River Blackwater. The twelfth duke of Devonshire, owner of Lismore Castle, convicted him of trespassing and illegal fishing. O'Shea defended himself citing Magna Carta which permitted common fishing on navigable, tidal rivers.[9] Another example occurred in December 2007 when with the encouragement of the Bristol Radical History Group the local Commoners Association of the Forest of Dean, in England, cited the Charter of the Forest to support their claim to graze sheep in the forest. Three years later the Tory government introduced the Public Bodies Bill to the House of Lords which would have allowed the government to sell the British forests. A local newspaper, *The Forester*, sprang into action October 2010. An organization was formed, Hands Off Our Forest. The local conservative Member of Parliament, Mark Harper, was mobbed at the Forest of Dean and had to be rescued by the police. He escaped the fury of the commoners with egg on his face. Hundreds of thousands protested, and prevented the sales. The Tory government in a humiliating climb-down withdrew the legislation three months later.

In October 2009 Elinor Ostrom won the Nobel Prize for Economics, the first woman to have received the award. She showed that people can manage common resources like forests, fisheries, or pastures without allocation by market pricing or government direction. She did this at a time when mathematical modeling dominated the methodology of economics. Her methodology instead required talking directly to the producers such as the Indonesian fisherman or the Maine lobsterman.[10]

The commons is both a social relationship and a material thing; it is neither a commodity nor exclusively a "resource." This double meaning was expressed clearly in the two definitions provided in Dr. Samuel Johnson's English *Dictionary* of 1755. A commons might refer to "an open ground equally used by many persons," or to "one of the common people, a man of low rank, of mean condition."[11] The commons belongs in an actual landscape, then the two meanings become clear.

In April 2010 the World People's Conference on Climate Change published the Universal Declaration of the Rights of Mother Earth. It was issued from Cochabamba, Bolivia, a significant location for two reasons because first, led by the indigenous people, the international effort to privatize its water, was roundly defeated, and second these were the Aymara and Quechua people whose labors at the silver mountain at Potosí produced the silver of the monetary system at the birth of capitalism, basically turning the mountain of silver into a monumental genocidal coffin. What was ripped out of the earth became fetishized tokens organizing the global division of labor and the exploitation and oppression of peoples. People with such a history know what it means to declare "we are all part of Mother Earth, an indivisible, living community of interrelated and interdependent beings with a common destiny." The Cochabamba declaration includes for all beings rights of life, respect, water, air, health, and in a remarkable unintended hearkening to the past, "every being has the right to *well-being*. . . . The pursuit of human *well-being* contributes to the *well-being* of Mother Earth, now and in the future." The common *wele* again.

Christopher Caudwell, the English intellectual who died fighting fascists in Spain, and Hugh MacDiarmid, the Scottish communist from the same era, both liked to quote, "Communism becomes an empty phrase, a mere façade, and the Communist a mere bluffer, if he has not worked over in his consciousness the whole inheritance of human knowledge."[12] Wow! Unless we continually make this part of our life's practice, this working over in our consciousness of the whole inheritance of human knowledge, we easily become dupes of the façade of the public relations industry which hides its cynical malevolence, or we are duped by the emptiness of corporate media with its charming spectacles, or we are conned by the basic bluffing of privatized commercial schooling which passes technique as wisdom. If we are to rework the whole inheritance of human knowledge, and give the world a rest and ourselves a break, we must do so east and west, north and south, commoning.

Ann Arbor
2012

CHAPTER NINE

Enclosures from the Bottom Up

Some man or other must present Wall. And let him have some plaster, or some loam, or some rough-cast about him, to signify Wall, and let him hold his fingers thus, and through that cranny shall Pyramus and Thisby whisper.
—Bottom the Weaver, in *A Midsummer Night's Dream*

Enclosure, like *capital*, is a term that is physically precise, even technical (hedge, fence, wall), and expressive of concepts of unfreedom (incarceration, imprisonment, immurement). In our time it has been an important interpretative idea for understanding neoliberalism, the historical suppression of women as in Silvia Federici, the carceral archipelago as in Michel Foucault's great confinement, or capitalist amassment as in David Harvey's accumulation by dispossession.[1] In our time it has also been an important empirical *fact*. On the one hand, the fall of the Berlin Wall marked the beginning of the current moment; on the other hand, the vain security fence between Mexico and the United States, and the hideous gigantism of the Israeli wall immuring Palestine, also define the current moment.

The "English enclosure movement" has belonged to that series of concrete universals—like the slave trade, the witch burnings, the Irish famine, or the genocide of Native Americans—that has defined the crime of modernism, limited in time and place but also immanent with the possibility of recurrence. Raj Patel writes, "Over the past thirty years the accelerating pace of enclosures, and the increasing scale of the theft, have brought our planet to the edge of destruction."[2] Yet enclosure's antonym—the commons—also carries with it a promising but unspecified sense of an alternative. Philosophically, too, the concept has stood close to the center of our times, as in Michael Hardt and Antonio Negri's recent book *Commonwealth*.[3] Enclosure indicates private property and capital: it seems to promise both individual ownership and social productivity, but in fact the concept of enclosure is inseparable from terror and the destruction of independence and community. Take the cowboy, for instance:

Next to his way with a horse, a cowboy was proudest of his independence. He worked for other men, but they owned nothing of him except
his time. He was a free soul. He could ride from the Rio Grande to the
Powder River and seldom see a fence. He could start that ride with five
dollars in his pocket and have three left when he finished, if that was the
way he wanted to travel. Money did not rule him.[4]

The cowboy novelist Elmer Kelton wrote these lines about the 1883
Canadian River cowboy strike in Texas. The cowboy's independence has
been perverted into the egotistical individualism of American manhood by
Hollywood, which figures him as a gunslinger and the "Indian" as a killer.
We lose sight of the cowboy as a worker in the continental meat trade that,
as Alexander Cockburn has shown, lies at the base of social and ecological
changes that have taken place in North America since the sixteenth-century
conquest.[5] The "roast beef of old England" also depended on a cattle trade
whose geography connected Scotland and the meat markets of Smithfield in
London. But the drovers did not acquire that cultural ideological subjectivity
that the American cowboy did. Why? The symbol of independence was the
commoner, the yeoman—a tougher, more enduring breed. But this figure
also defined independence in relation to fencelessness. If not the open range,
then the open field; if not barbed wire, then the thorn hedge.

The enclosure of the commons has reappeared in the twenty-first century
owing to four developments at the end of the twentieth century. First was the
uprising in Chiapas led in 1994 by the Zapatistas in opposition to the repeal of
Article 27 of the Mexican Constitution that provided for *ejidos*, or common
lands, attached to each village. The renewed discourse of the commons
formed part of the struggle of indigenous people against the privatization
of land. A process of "new enclosures," however, took place in Africa and
Indonesia.[6] If the cowboy novelist implied a relation between the fence and
money, Pramoedya Toer draws attention to the relation between crime and
the fence, or the criminal and the indigenous, using the example of Buru
Island under the Suharto regime in Indonesia:

> But the Buru interior was not empty; there were native people living off
> that piece of earth long before the arrival of political prisoners forced
> them to leave their land and huts behind. Then, as the prisoners converted
> the savanna into fields, the native people watched their hunting grounds
> shrink in size. Even the area's original place names were stolen from them
> and they, too, were calling the area "Unit 10." With ten large barracks
> planted in their soil and five hundred prisoners settled on their land,

what other choice did they have? But the strangest thing of all was when the prisoners began to build fences, erecting borders where no boundaries had ever been. The native people had no word for "fence"—the concept was completely foreign to their culture. They didn't recognize such manmade limitations on land-use rights.[7]

A second development of the late twentieth century bringing about a discussion of enclosure and the commons was the development of the Internet and the World Wide Web as a knowledge commons. The privatization of intellectual property was challenged at the "battle of Seattle" in 1999. A third process was the pollution of the planet's waters and the poisoning of its atmosphere. Finally, a fourth factor in this renewed discourse was the collapse of the USSR and of the communist countries of eastern Europe, which made it easier to discuss the commons without automatically being suspected of ideological intercourse with the national enemy.

As each of these examples referred either to "enclosures" or to "the commons," interest in the classic case of enclosures, namely England, was renewed. In England, though, the scholarly discourse of enclosures had changed from accumulation to culture. Raymond Williams surveys English literature via the country and the city, from the aristocratic pastoral of the fanatical sixteenth century to the industrial energy workers in D.H. Lawrence's persistent dream. He is careful to limn enclosure as but one of several forces in the development of capitalism.[8] Enclosure was a visible social fact, and the sense of social collapse and melancholia found in authors like Oliver Goldsmith, George Crabbe, William Cowper, John Clare, and William Cobbett was a response to it.

Yet the process of enclosure had been ongoing in England since the thirteenth century before reaching one peak during the fifteenth and sixteenth centuries and then another during the eighteenth and nineteenth centuries. The extension of cultivated land and the concentration of ownership in the hands of a minority went together. We can call this the "great arc" of English history. As late as the end of the seventeenth century, for instance, Gregory King estimated that there were twenty million acres of pasture, meadow, forest, heath, moor, mountain, and barren land in a country of thirty-seven million acres.[9] Even if common rights were exercised in only half of these, it means that in 1688 one quarter of the total area of England and Wales was common land. Between 1725 and 1825 nearly four thousand enclosure acts appropriated more than six million acres of land, about a quarter of cultivated acreage, to the politically dominant landowners. The Parliamentary enclosure made the process more documented and more public. It got rid of open-field villages and common rights and contributed to the late eighteenth century's crisis of poverty. In the 1690s the proportion of landless laborers to occupiers was 5:3; by 1831 it was 5:2. Violent alterations in condition affected many thousands. Arthur Young, at first an aggressive advocate of enclosure, changed his mind in the early years of the nineteenth century, often quoting a poor man who said, "All I know is, I had a cow and Parliament took it away from me." The acts were part of the legalized seizure of land by representatives of the beneficiary class. As J.M. Neeson has summarized, "Much of England was still open in 1700; but most of it was enclosed by 1840."[10] E.P. Thompson called it a plain enough case of class robbery.[11]

On the wastes, cottagers and squatters lost marginal independence. Many villages were lost, and airplane surveys alone detect their traces.[12] Indeed, the first impression that visitors often have when flying into Heathrow is the predominance of green fields and hedges on the ground. This is a post-enclosure feature of the landscape. Hundreds of miles of quickset hedge symbolize barriers between people and land. A visitor who takes a train to the Midlands will perhaps see earthworks in the land resembling the rolling swells of a surf before the waves break. This is the ridge-and-furrow pattern caused by the long practice of strip farming on the open-field system. In the eighteenth century the network of great houses or neoclassical mansions was formed establishing strong points of the rural ruling class. This, along with colonial expansion, constituted the architecture of enclosure.

The General Inclosure Act of 1845 declared that the health, comfort, and convenience of local inhabitants needed to be taken into consideration during enclosure, and commissioners could set aside an area "for the purpose of exercise and recreation for the inhabitants of the neighbourhood." This act envisioned the great London parks. The Common Lands Census of 1873–74 showed that only 2.5 million acres of common land remained in England. The 1955 Royal Commission on Common Lands introduced a third legal party in addition to the landlord and the commoners, namely, the public. Although this recognized "a universal right of public access on common land," the public significantly does not manage the land, as commoners used to do.

★ ★ ★

In 2009 Elinor Ostrom was awarded the Nobel Prize in Economics, the first woman to have received this honor. She won it for her work on the governance of the commons.[13] There is an important association to be made between Ostrom's status as a woman and the development of agrarian common rights, as Neeson has demonstrated.[14] In an early case of enclosure—that of Otmoor, Oxfordshire, to which we shall return—Alexander

Croke, a gentleman and Otmoor's encloser, bitterly attacked the commoners' theory of the origins of their rights, which they argued stemmed from some queen (perhaps Elizabeth I) who had granted as much land as she could ride around while an oak sheaf was burning. Such, Croke wrote, are "those improbable and ridiculous old women's tales which are current in many places and impose upon the credulity of the vulgar."[15] This is the kind of comment that it would be unwise to dismiss hastily because, while the disdainful view of its author is unconcealed, one cannot help wondering how the force of humble women could have made such a powerful impression on a man whose property and status were so much greater than theirs. When V.I. Lenin referred to "honeyed grandmothers' tales," it was not specifically to common rights but to the idealization of the pure air of peasant life.[16] Old wives' tales, honeyed grandmothers' tales, old women's tales: clearly the storytelling abilities of women were accorded, backhandedly, an acknowledgment by this kind of condescension.

In her work, Ostrom has been deeply critical of Garret Hardin, the biologist who in 1968 published his famous essay "The Tragedy of the Commons" in *Science*.[17] His was a brutal argument with an inhuman conclusion: "Freedom to breed will bring ruin to all." Hardin here alludes to Jeremy Bentham's utilitarianism, Adam Smith's invisible hand, Thomas Malthus's population theory, and Charles Darwin's theory of natural selection to buttress his arguments with the thinkers of the nineteenth-century English establishment. The influence of his article did not arise from such authorities but rather stemmed from its striking tone, which combined the somber and the terrifying with the simple and jejune. The article began with nuclear war and rapidly proceeded to tic-tac-toe as an example of strategic thinking, or "thinking about the unthinkable," in the phrase of the day. His was capitalist thinking, and his class markers were made with remarkable candor: "But what is good? To one person it is wilderness, to another it is ski lodges for thousands. To one it is estuaries to nourish ducks for hunters to shoot; to another it is factory land." These are the activities of the factory owner, not of the factory worker. The crux of his argument is expressed in a few paragraphs:

> The tragedy of the commons develops in this way. Picture a pasture open to all. It is to be expected that each herdsman will try to keep as many cattle as possible in the commons. Such an arrangement may work reasonably satisfactorily for centuries because tribal wars, poaching, and disease keep the numbers of both man and beast well below the carrying capacity of the land. Finally, however, comes the day of reckoning, that is, the day when the long-desired goal of social stability becomes a

reality. At this point, the inherent logic of the commons remorselessly generates tragedy.

As a rational being, each herdsman seeks to maximize his gain. Explicitly or implicitly, more or less consciously, he asks, "What is the utility to me of adding one more animal to my herd?" This utility has one negative and one positive component. . . .

Adding together the component partial utilities, the rational herdsman concludes that the only sensible course for him to pursue is to add another animal to his herd. And another. . . . But this is the conclusion reached by each and every rational herdsman sharing a commons. Therein is the tragedy. Each man is locked into a system that compels him to increase his herd without limit—in a world that is limited. Ruin is the destination toward which all men rush, each pursuing his own best interest in a society that believes in the freedom of the commons. Freedom in a commons brings ruin to all.

Three times Hardin refers to the "rational" herdsman; it is a fantasy. What he most likely means is the selfish herdsman or the lonely herdsman, because, in history, the commons is always governed. The pinder, the hayward, or some other officer elected by the commoners will impound that cow, or will fine that greedy shepherd who puts more than his share onto the commons. This idea forms the basis of Ostrom's intervention. For Hardin, the world is governed by "dog eat dog," not "one and all." For Ostrom, by contrast, the problem is not the commons per se; it is the *governance* of the commons.

Let us return to the Otmoor case quoting Bernard Reaney, its historian:

The commoners turned out their geese, cattle, horses, pigs and sheep to graze on the moor. Peat was dug for fuel, and old women scraped up the cow-dung to earn a pittance by its sale. The moor provided a plentiful supply of osiers, which enabled the craft of basket-making to thrive in the village. In addition to feed for poultry, grazing for cattle, and fuel for the winter, there was also good ducking and fishing, and a profusion of rabbits and wild birds which could furnish an important part of the diet of the poor. . . . Thus the essential elements of a peasant subsistence economy were provided. The presence of fuel, game, and land for grazing cattle, enabled the Otmoor townspeople to live independently if precariously.[18]

The communal regulations did not permit sheep on the moor from May 1 through October 18 under pain of a three shillings four pence fine. A fine of four pence was given to anyone who put a pig on the moor that was not secured with a ring. Four pence was also the fine for keeping a horse, mare, or colt that was not branded. Each town had its own brand reserved by those known as the "moormen." No hog or pig could be kept between Christmas and April 1. Digging for peat was forbidden on highways and otherwise the pit had to be filled in. And so on. No rational herdsmen here!

Hardin's combination of fake scientism, faux mathematics, and the invocation of a global holocaust to justify a conclusion of coercive demographic policy was itself a highly ideological response with important precedents. Hardin admitted that his argument was adopted from that of "a mathematical amateur named William Forster Lloyd (1794–1852)." It is true that Lloyd was a mathematician of no particular note—Greek had been his specialty—but this is not to suggest that he was an insignificant figure in the firmament of the establishment. Lloyd was a professor of political economy at Oxford, a member of Christ Church College, and a vicar in the Church of England. His brother, Charles, died in 1829 as the bishop of Oxford and a member of the House of Lords. Charles was a close friend, and the former tutor, of Robert Peel, the home secretary and founder of the London police, the "bobbies" or "peelers."

At Michaelmas term in September 1832, three years after Charles's death, William Lloyd delivered *Two Lectures on the Checks to Population*.[19] He was a Malthusian, believing that the increase of food could not keep up with the increase in population. To Malthus (1766–1834), population may have preventive or positive checks. The former reduces births, the latter increases deaths. It is a peculiar jargon.

Why think of death as positive? Like Malthus, Lloyd opposed "having all things common." He made pithy observations such as "systems of equality, with a community of labour and of goods, are highly unfavourable" (17), and "a state of perfect equality by its effect in lowering the standard of desire and almost reducing it to the satisfaction of the natural necessities would bring back society to ignorance and barbarism," and "under a community of goods, there is a want of appropriation to each person of the consequences of his own conduct" (28). Furthermore, Lloyd had his own jargon and spoke of "the amount of existences repressed." He was frightened by the "contagion" of the French Revolution (9). He believed that the diminution of fecundity and the extinction of life would enhance the means of subsistence. He had a fantasy of the American woodsman living in the wild (8), that harbinger of Hollywood and Marlboro cigarette ads.

Lloyd regarded marriage as a commons productive of common property: "Marriage is a present good. The difficulties attending the maintenance of a family are future. But in a community of goods, where the children are maintained at public tables, or where each family takes according to its necessities out of the common stock, these difficulties are removed from the individual. They spread themselves, and overflow the whole surface of society, and press equally on every part" (21). The "prudent man determines his conduct by the comparison of the present pleasure with his share of the future ill, and the present sacrifice with his share of the future benefit. This share, in the multitude of a large society, becomes evanescent; and hence, in the absence of any countervailing weight, the conduct of each person is determined by the consideration of the present alone." Here is the precursor to Hardin's selfish herdsman. "While it exists in a considerable degree of force in the present condition of the labouring classes in this country, it seems nevertheless, as to its veering on those classes, in a great measure to have escaped observation." Like Hardin, Lloyd is obsessed, if not by nuclear war, then by overpopulation and "the parallel cases of inclosed grounds and commons" (30). And like Hardin, the herd is the metaphor for population. "Why are the cattle on a common so puny and stunted? Why is the common itself so bare-worn, and cropped so differently from the adjoining inclosures . . . ? The common reasons for the establishment of private property in land are deduced from the necessity of offering to individuals sufficient motives for cultivating the ground" (30). Lloyd was fond of Malthus's metaphor—"At nature's mighty feast, to use an expression of Mr. Malthus, there should be no free sittings" (60)—and made one of his own: "To a plank in the sea which cannot support all, all have not an equal right" (75). Thus Hardin acknowledged his predecessor, the Christ Church College professor at Oxford.

As Hardin sent off his essay in 1968, he would not have known that in Oxford at the same time the legendary new left historian Raphael Samuel, wrapped in his duffel coat (de rigueur in the Campaign for Nuclear Disarmament) and tossing the hair out of his eyes, went tramping about villages in the vicinity talking to the elderly with two of his students from Ruskin College, the young London-Irish historian Reaney and the glamorous women's libber Sally Alexander. They and their colleagues such as David Morgan, the "cow man," were to tell a new history and to forge new tools for finding it. Ruskin was founded in 1899 to provide "educational opportunities for the working-class men." Noah Ablett, a south Wales coal miner, attended Ruskin and led a student strike there in 1908 *against* teaching the marginal utility theory of William Stanley Jevons (1835–82) and *for* teaching Karl Marx's labor theory of value. The motto of the strike was taken from John Ruskin, "I can promise to be candid but not impartial," and its slogan was "Oxford, city of dreaming spires / And bleeding liars." With that as its backdrop, the History Workshop responded to and helped create the freedoms of "the sixties." Little did they know that the conversations they were having would develop into a potent scholarly clue to Hardin's rage expressed in California. Samuel was the founder of the History Workshop movement. "Dig Where You Stand" was its slogan. Accordingly, the first pamphlets concerned Oxfordshire. Those walks with his students resulted in the History Workshop Pamphlet No. 3, Reaney's *The Class Struggle in Nineteenth Century Oxfordshire*, which enables us to now turn our attention directly to the enclosure of Otmoor.

A few miles from Oxford University are four thousand acres of lowland moor, Otmoor. It was inundated every winter. Otmoor people had a funny walk, "a slouch," which evidently helped them get through the mud puddles, the ditches, and inches of water covering the ground. They were said to have webbed feet. Otmoor's marshy hollows were called "pills," and one of the soggy pieces of land was called "Splosh." Commoners had their own language, most evident in the poetry of John Clare (1793–1864), himself a laboring commoner. A distinct epistemology informed the minds of the commoners working the land. This was not the genius loci but a different ecology. Indeed, John Barrel has commented on the semantics of Clare's geography. "We have come across . . . 'balks,' 'fallows,' 'furlongs,' 'furrows,' 'eddings,' 'lands'; and in addition, 'ground' which Clare almost always uses of an enclosed piece of land, usually meadow-land; 'close,' an enclosed field, usually for pasturing cattle and distinct from the 'plain,' which refers almost always to open land, usually under grass; and finally 'nook,' a particularly angular corner of a field."[20]

In Clare's autobiography, written in the early 1820s, he describes how as a child he walked across Emmonsailes Heath and got lost. "So I eagerly wanderd on & rambled along the furze the whole day till I got out of my knowledge when the very wild flowers seemd to forget me & I imagind they were the inhabitants of a new countrys the very sun seemd to be a new one & shining in a different quarter of the sky."[21] This points to an epistemology and an orientation dependent on the unenclosed. In his book *Remains*, published in London in 1824, Robert Bloomfield remembers Tom Paine going for a walk with his sister "to Fakenham Wood, in search of nuts; and being by themselves, they wandered out of their knowledge, and knew not the way out again."[22] They got lost. Clare puts more into the phrase than just not knowing how to get back. The sun was in a different place in the sky, and the wild flowers forgot him. The loss of the common meant the loss of his whole world. Since we are on the verge of losing ours (clearly, we have gone out of *our* knowledge) we might pay those commoners more mind.

Richard Mabey has written of the need for common ground and a place for nature in Britain's future.[23] Common ground, he explains, is a system of land tenure, not a type of land, in which one party may own the land but others are entitled to various rights in it such as grazing or cutting firewood. This is a very old system that predates the Norman Conquest of 1066. "It is now generally accepted that the rights that began to be defined in the eleventh century represented the relics of a much wider network of unrecorded 'customary practice' (amounting probably to the communal ownership of land) which was largely destroyed by political and military force during the Norman Conquest."[24] Mabey has identified four major types of common rights: pasture, estovers, pannage, and turbary. But there were many others (piscary, housebote, shack, ploughbote) depending on uses or resources (gorse, bracken, chalk, gravel, clay, rushes, reeds, nuts, and herbs). These customary rights might provide fuel, meat, milk, tools, housing, and medicines.[25] Rights were matched to a comprehensive range of rules and controls designed to prevent overconsumption and to reward intricacy, ingenuity, and thrift. It was vital to the community that commons be maintained and harvested to keep resources self-renewing. Epping Forest pollards could not be felled because, while they were the property of the landowner, the commoners had rights to lops and tops. In Selborne Woods, where the commoners had pasture and pannage, the landowner could not replant trees unless they were beech, whose mast was necessary for the pigs. Thirteen cherry balls each with a different name were distributed by lot for harvest rights in Pixey and Yarnton Meads in Oxfordshire. The order in which they were withdrawn from a bag determined the strips in the meadow from which each commoner could take hay that summer.

Mabey admits that if such a system were re-adopted, a "state of impenetrable muddle" could prevail.[26] But how did such a muddle first come about? The tidy reasoner may pull out his or her hair, but this "state of impenetrable muddle" was also a source of power. Why did it take seven or eight centuries to enclose England when in Russia it took one generation and in Iraq it took just over a century through the force of intermittent bombing? Neeson helps us answer the question because she describes the various forms of resistance to enclosure that included petitioning, spreading false rumors, attacking property, foot-dragging, mischief, anonymous threatening poems, grumbling, playing football, breaking the squire's gates, fence breaking, wood stealing, and so forth. She states, "The sense of loss, the sense of *robbery* could last forever as the bitter inheritance of the rural poor."[27]

★ ★ ★

The seven towns around Otmoor were Charlton, Fencot and Murcot, Oddington, Beckley, Horton, Studley, and Noke. They were small; Noke had fewer than a hundred inhabitants, while Beckley had 370 in 1831. The Moor Court at Beckley in 1687 defined the relation of the towns to the moor as they had been defined in the Domesday Book: "That ye Comon of Ot more shall belong to none but ye Inhabitants of ye seven Townes belonging to Otmore for commoning any manner of Cattle there." Commons were of three kinds. First, the common or open fields of each village, which rotated year to year. Second, common rights on them. Town wastes provided a third type, in this case, Otmoor. The only gentleman residing in the area was Croke, and it was he who indefatigably fought to enclose the moor for more than fifty years.

John and Barbara Hammond also have described the protracted struggle to enclose Otmoor.[28] It began with the proposal in 1801 by the Duke of Marlborough to drain and allot enclosures of over four thousand acres in Otmoor. When, according to law, notices were affixed on the parish church doors announcing the proposal, they were taken down "by a Mob at each place." The next application was made in 1815. Again it was found impracticable to affix the notices "owing to large Mobs, armed with every description of offensive weapons." The humbler people began to bestir themselves. No records of any manor enjoying rights of common could be found; "the custom of usage without stint, in fact, pointed to some grant before the memory of man." The bill was passed despite these discoveries, which "made it unlikely that any lord of the manor had ever had absolute right of soil." The enclosers had Atlantic experience. Croke had been employed by the government in 1801 as a judge in a vice admiralty court in Nova Scotia, attaining a reputation as a narrow-minded Tory. He argued that only proprietors, those who owned their own house, had common right, while "the poor, as such, had no right to the common whatever."[29]

In 1830 the dam that had been part of the drainage effort broke, and the farmers took the law into their own hands and cut the embankments. Twenty-two farmers were indicted and acquitted. This made a profound impression on the cottagers, and for a week parties of enthusiasts paraded the moor and cut down its fences. One of Croke's sons appeared with a pistol, but the moormen wrested it from him and gave him a thrashing. Assembling by the light of the full moon, blackening their faces, and dressing in women's clothing, the commoners stepped forth to destroy the fences, the hedges, the bridges, the gates—every part of the infrastructure of enclosure.

The high sheriff, the Oxfordshire militia, and Lord Churchill's Yeomanry Cavalry were summoned. Yet the inhabitants were not overawed. They determined to perambulate the bounds of Otmoor in full force, in accordance with old custom. On Monday, September 6, five hundred men, women, and children assembled from the Otmoor towns, and they were joined by five hundred more from elsewhere. The commoners of Otmoor decided they would "perambulate the whole circumpherence of Otmoor, in the manner which they state it was customary for them in former times to do, and that abandoning their nocturnal sallies, they would in open daylight go possessioning and demolishing every fence which obstructed their course. . . . Armed with reap-hooks, hatchets, bill-hooks, and duckets, they marched in order round the seven-mile-long boundary of Otmoor, destroying all the fences on their way."[30] A reap-hook is a sickle that everybody knows from the Soviet symbol of the hammer and sickle. A bill-hook resembles a sickle except that it has a long handle instead of a short one and is used for lopping tree branches or pruning hedges. (I don't know what a ducket is, and the *Oxford English Dictionary* is of no help with that particular knowledge.) Armed with these various tools, a thousand people went a-possessioning, covering the moor in an impressive display of power and self-respect. Wheelwrights, hatters, and hay dealers, along with slaters, shoemakers, bakers, tailors, butchers, basketmakers, masons, plumbers, and grooms—the full panoply of village artisans were evident. The commoners were organized. A flyer signed by the "King of Otmoor" and "given at our court of Otmoor" called on the commoners to assemble—and assemble they did from the seven villages and from the entire vicinity.

There were retaliatory efforts, of course. Sixty or seventy commoners were seized by the cavalry, and forty-four were sent to Oxford jail under the escort of the yeomanry. But the protests also happened to take place on the day of Saint Giles's Fair. The streets were crowded with folk. When the cry was raised, "Otmoor forever," the crowds took it up and hurled brickbats, sticks, and stones from every direction. All forty-four prisoners escaped. Many thousands were present, and the two dozen soldiers had no heart for the job and fled. A bill of indictment was found against two persons for riot, but the jury unanimously recommended mercy.

> The law locks up the man or woman
> Who steals the goose from off the common
> But leaves the greater villain loose
> Who steals the common from the goose.

James Boyle has tracked these lines to 1821, tacked as a handbill in Plaistow as a caution to prevent support for the intended enclosure of Hainault or Waltham Forest.[31] Called a *jeu d'ésprit* or a naive epigram, its very ease may cause us to overlook two themes of utmost importance, namely, incarceration and reparations. It was the powerful Lord Abingdon who openly opposed Croke's first attempt to get a parliamentary act enclosing Otmoor. A leading eighteenth-century Whig, though not a resident, Abingdon argued that hundreds of families would lose their subsistence that depended on "the Right which they now enjoy, of breeding and raising geese upon the Moor."[32]

* * *

Sally Alexander organized the first Women's Liberation Conference in England, which met in February 1970 at Ruskin College. "A completely new kind of movement had broken to the surface," Sheila Rowbotham writes.[33] One wonders whether her organizing power was inspired by her historical discoveries. Earlier that year she had published the second History Workshop Pamphlet, *St. Giles's Fair, 1830–1914: Popular Culture and the Industrial Revolution in Nineteenth Century Oxford*. Samuel hoped that "it may make some contribution to undermining confidence in the ways in which history is now taught."[34] Alexander, herself a descendant of show people, combined local sources and oral histories in the form of the memories of traveling showmen; these two types of sources comprised "an authentic popular history." The fair held caravan shows, puppet booths, fantoccini performances, games of chance, toys for children, gingerbread stalls, and much else besides. Alexander's pamphlet begins with an astonishing typographical yawp from the Oxford Board of Health issued on September 1, 1832, warning of cholera (which it calls "the Indian Disease"),

ST. GILES'S FAIR
CAUTION AND REMONSTRANCE
To all Drunkards and Revellers, and to the thought-
less and imprudent of both Sexes

It recommends abstention from intemperance and imprudence:

Beware of late and long sittings, dancings, revellings, surfeitings, and such like. Beware of mixed, crowded, and unknown Companies in the distempered atmospheres of Booths, Show Rooms, and Canvas or Boarded Apartments. Infection lurks a lolling time in Stone and Brick Buildings; it is impossible to say how long it may continue in the materials of Wooden, Woollen, and Hempen inclosures. . . . Let all beware who think no cost too great for the purchase of present pleasure—Death smites with it surest and swiftest arrows the licentious and intemperate—the rash, foolhardy, and imprudent.

Both Lloyd, the professor of political economy, and the Oxford Board of Health were comfortable blaming the poor and their counterculture (one could say based on the evidence of Alexander), and both predicted death to the working people. The laboring classes, they averred, were incapable of planning beyond the morrow. Alexander concludes that "one of the most compelling features of the fairground is its feeling of anarchic possibility. The everyday niceties of dignity and status are lost in the jostle of the crowd." She also writes, "the fair offered a release from normal constraints" and that "there was always the possibility of sexual adventure. . . . In place of drabness, splendour; in place of work, self-expression; in place of hierarchy, equality; in place of the quotidian, the wonderful; in place of restraint, freedom."[35]

The cattle resumed their grazing. The inhabitants of the seven towns appointed a herdsman. A few weeks later Captain Swing riots broke out in Oxfordshire, taking the spanner to the steam-powered threshing machines. Philip Green was a chimney sweeper and an Oxfordshire leader of anti-enclosure and anti-mechanization. He was "an old man of wars" and was "not afraid": "They had been oppressed long enough and we will bear it no longer, great changes were taking place in other parts of the world, and there must be a change here—there was plenty of money in the country if it was equally distributed—the rich have had their say long enough, and now it is our turn. The machines must come down and every man ought to have 2/- a day."[36]

If wages were not raised, Green predicted, commoners would unite to "break all the machines in the Neighbourhood and stop the Labourers from work." As Croke, the encloser, was an Atlantic figure, so Green, a commoner and a sailor, was conscious of world affairs. Such sailors as he would have paid special attention to the Nat Turner revolt of 1831 in Virginia or to the huge Christmas revolt of twenty thousand slaves led by Sam Sharpe in Jamaica during the same year.

The Enclosure Act was fifteen years old in 1830. For two more years Otmoor would remain in rebellion. As Reaney summarizes, "Otmoor was kept under more or less permanent occupation."[37] A detachment of Coldstream Guards was dispatched to the area. In August 1831 the Home Office sent some London policemen. The church door riots of September 1831 demonstrated the ability of locals to organize an attack during which notices of the financial rates to pay for the work of enclosure were removed. The police officer attempting to put up the notice was stoned as he fled to the clergyman's house. "Damn the body snatchers" was the cry. What did it mean?

It was widely believed that the authorities were complicit in "burking," the grim practice of kidnapping and suffocating people, especially young people, and selling their bodies to medical schools. The practice takes its name from an Edinburgh resurrection man, William Burke, who was hanged in 1829. In 1831, five hundred medical students in London would have needed three bodies apiece for their anatomical training, about fifteen hundred cadavers a year. Seven resurrection gangs of body snatchers flourished in London at the time, and one man, John Bishop, sold between five hundred and a thousand over the course of his career. The poet Thomas Hood expressed popular anxiety,

> The body-snatchers they have come
> And made a snatch of me.
> It's very hard them kind of men
> Won't let a body be.

The year 1831 also saw the foundation of the Metropolitan Police in London, where more than a thousand uniformed and armed men patrolled the streets. They were hated and believed by many to be unconstitutional, in violation of the prohibition of a standing army. The taking of land and the taking of bodies were thus closely associated, and it is not difficult to see why. Indeed, a few months after the described incident in Otmoor, three burkers were arrested in London for the murder of an Italian boy.[38] As the horror of the deed rapidly spread, the police were widely believed to be in league with the surgeons of many of London's distinguished medical colleges.

The commoners turned out on the moor whenever there was a full moon and pulled down the fences. In January 1832 a local magistrate wrote Lord Melbourne that "all the towns in the neighbourhood of Otmoor are more or less infected with the feelings of the most violent, and cannot at all be depended on. . . . The mood in the villages was one of open defiance of the law." The constabulary was helpless and more soldiers were dispatched. "Any force which Government may send down should not remain for a length of time together, but that to avoid the possibility of an undue connexion between the people and the Military, a succession of troops should be observed."[39] This was the way revolutions were prevented: no fraternization.

★　★　★

Marx was quite aware that his work of political economy "summons as foes into the field of battle the most violent, mean and malignant passions of the human breast, the Furies of private interest."[40] Marx wrote in the preface to the first edition of *Das Kapital* that "the English Established Church will more readily pardon an attack on 38 of its 39 articles than on 1/39th of its income."[41] It is not clear whether or not Marx had reviewed the text of the Thirty-Nine Articles established under Elizabeth I during what have been called the "religious" wars of the sixteenth century. The thirty-eighth article in fact reads, "the riches and Goods of Christians are not common, as touching the right, title, and possession of the same, as certain Anabaptists do falsely boast."[42]

Anti-communism thus formed an essential part of the doctrine of the English establishment.

At the time Marx was writing, the portals of power opened only to the propertied and to the communicants of the Church of England. There is a long association in English history between religion and enclosure going back, as William Cobbett (1763–1834) best described, to the Protestant Reformation.[43] To Marx this separation of people from the land—he called it original or primary or primitive accumulation—played "the same part as original sin in theology."[44] The red cloth of the magistrate and the black cassock of the priest combined in Oxford to enclose Otmoor. Four clergymen of the Church of England—the curate of Beckley, the rector of Oddington, and the vicars of Charlton and Noke—were strong supporters of enclosure. Two of them became commissioners of the enclosure, which actually took away land from seventeen hundred people and reassigned it to seventy-eight. Much of the land went to clergymen and to three of the Oxford colleges, Balliol, Oriel, and Magdalen.[45]

Lloyd, besides being a professor, was also a clergyman of the Church of England. Without having traced his personal property relations or those of his Oxford college to the struggles over the Otmoor Enclosure Act, it nevertheless seems clear that his arguments responded to the struggles of the common people, those nocturnal and those occurring by daylight, those protracted and those immediate, those urban and those rural. Like Malthus before him and Hardin after him, he was an encloser, not a commoner. Just as Malthus was interested in "positive checks," so Lloyd was interested in "existences repressed." It was a murderous response from a criminal ruling class to a desperate attempt by the common people to protect and extend the means of their subsistence. The same knee-jerk reaction came from the biologist Hardin.

★ ★ ★

The expropriation of the commons in Iraq, one of the oldest in the world, was exercised on the people of the reeds. Their marshes were drained under Saddam Hussein and the American occupation. Likewise, in Afghanistan commoning the land was an ancient practice that Mountstuart Elphinstone in 1814 compared to Tacitus's account of the Germanic commons. To Marx's letters of blood and fire we must now add the bomb and the drone as means of expropriation. We now set these parallels of expropriation and war against Livy's cynicism: "The Senate, they declared, deliberately tormented the commons with military service and got their throats cut whenever they could, keeping them employed in foreign parts for fear lest, if they enjoyed a quiet life at home, they might begin to think of forbidden things—liberty, farms of their own to cultivate, the division of the public domain, the right of voting as their consciences dictated."[46]

★ ★ ★

In the 1920s Otmoor became a bombing range.

★ ★ ★

Bottom-up history requires that we pay attention to the cranny in the wall, as Bottom the Weaver expressed it in *A Midsummer Night's Dream*. We must attend not to the completeness of the wall but to its chinks. The story of Pyramus and Thisbe, after all, takes place in a setting that now comprises Iraq. What was long ago and far away has come home. John Berger has observed that "the Wall is the front line of what, long ago, was called the Class War."[47] Lest we forget, the Bristol Radical History Group has renewed the History Workshop tradition in many ways, not least in its pamphlet series, and two of these publications concern enclosures and resistance to them.[48] They bring to life again the real history on the ground when the concrete is the enemy of the abstract and when the historian, or people's remembrancer, is a cultural worker serving the people in struggle.

Ann Arbor
Fall 2012

CHAPTER TEN

Wat Tyler Day: The Anglo Juneteenth

JUNETEENTH IN AMERICAN HISTORY WAS THE DAY WHEN NEWS OF THE EMANCIPATION Proclamation finally reached Texas, June 19, 1865, two and a half years late, and it makes me think about a similar day in English history, June 15, a temporary emancipation.

It is the anniversary of Magna Carta sworn to by King John on June 15, 1215. It is also the anniversary of another charter, this one proposed by Wat Tyler, a leader of the Peasants' Revolt until he was assassinated on June 15, 1381. The English people expressed a preference that June 15 be made a national day to remember Magna Carta, though—who knows?—some may have been thinking of Wat Tyler and the great uprising against bondage and the poll tax. The Peasants' Revolt helps us to remember the actual commons and its agents, the real commoners, which is why June 15 may be celebrated for Magna Carta but it should be named for Wat Tyler.

I had been meeting all night long in Bristol (UK) with an economist, an aerospace engineer, a philosopher, and an anthropologist. We were attempting to draft a manifesto for the twenty-first century, manifesting the commons. Who were we, white men, to speak for all? Self-doubt crept into our deliberations. Was it some mixture of egotism, "whiteness," and academic vanity which threatened what was best in our dreams and aspirations? We had trouble with "class" and "the commons" and it didn't occur that we might speak, if not *for* others, then *with* others.

Surely this kind of muddle had happened before. My comrades were not inclined to follow me into the long-gone past. So in the morning I took the train through the west Midlands to Worcester to visit the sometime Communist, the generous and hospitable Dorothy Thompson, widow of E.P. Thompson. She is a distinguished scholar of Chartism, and here's a song from the Chartist years (1830s):

> For Tyler of old,
> A heart-chorus bold,
> Let Labour's children sing

Dorothy and Edward, people's remembrancers, always brought the past truthfully into the present to help us in a thousand ways. The train passed the Malvern Hills in whose shadow I used to live back in 1971 with Edward and Dorothy. I remember walking up the Malvern Hills on a sunny June day with some friends including an Italian comrade. On attaining the summit we gazed to the west upon "England's green and pleasant land" (Hereford and Shropshire) and when I asked the revolutionary visitor (a partisan of *Lotta Continua*, a theorist of *Potere Operaia*) what it was that he saw in this lovely landscape, he startled me with the simplicity of his answer: "Money."

It is an answer that a man of the Malverns, William Langland, author of *Piers Plowman*, would have perfectly understood for not only did his allegorical satire of the 1370s denounce clerical fraudulence and legal chicanery, but he took particular aim at King Penny. Adult head taxes were imposed to finance wars against France, and such a poll tax of one groat per adult (a groat being four pence) began to be collected just before the rising in June 1381. William Langland came to London where he lived in poverty with his wife, Kit. Educated as a cleric he made his living by keeping vigil, reciting orisons, and saying prayers for rich folks. Otherwise, he held out his begging bowl, unfit for work bending over in the fields on account of his height (he said).

There are fifty-seven surviving manuscript versions of the poem, seventeen of them produced before 1400. Preceding the age of print by more than a century the poem was meant to be recited, and it was talked about enough that the name, "Piers Plowman," was taken up by the insurgents in the great Peasants' Revolt of 1381. Like the English Bible of John Wycliffe which was translated at approximately at the same time, Lollards passed manuscripts around, mumbling or muttering the contents. Plebeian utterance has always been a problem to ruling-class ears, especially then when the former was English and the latter either Latin or Norman-French. Their muttering wasn't quite intelligible, and evidently sounded something like . . . la, la, la . . . anyway that's how these Christians got their name as Lollards.

William Langland spoke with optimistic confidence about the commons. "For human intelligence is like water, air, and fire—it cannot be bought or sold. These four things the Father of Heaven made to be shared on earth in common. They are Truth's treasures, free for the use of all honest men, and no one can add to them or diminish them without God's will."

Communism may be theoretical (ideal) or practical (customary). It is the ideal of "having all things in common"—aye, the phrase appears in John Wycliffe's English translation of the Bible (Acts 2:44). Wycliffe had argued this in a treatise of 1374.[1] It is theoretical and we contrast it with the actual. When the actual is threatened or destroyed, as in the 1380s, again in the 1540s, the

1640s and 1790s, or in our era, then people are reminded of the other, the one that consists of dreams, theories, ideals, hopes, fantasies, utopias, theologies, and we can imagine realistically, as Massimo De Angelis has put it, the beginning of history. In the Cold War social democrats distinguished themselves from communists by, among other things, contrasting sensible workers with impractical intellectuals. This bifurcation affected Norman Cohn who in 1957 argued that the artisans and peasants were concerned "with limited realistic objectives" while priests such as John Ball or scholars such as John Wycliffe promoted a "doctrine" or "phantasy of an egalitarian State of Nature."

"The rising of the commons is one of the most portentous phenomena to be found in the whole of our history," wrote the Victorian historian, professor, and bishop Stubbs in his *Constitutional History of England*. What did he mean? "Portentous" means both awesome and significant for the future; both an omen and ominous. He was writing after the Paris Commune of 1871. Was he fearful of urban insurrection? Of a London commune? Of communism?

Langland helps us understand the social forces producing this most portentous phenomenon. *Piers Plowman* begins:

> And on a May morning, on Malvern Hills,
> There befell me as by magic a marvelous thing . . .
> A fair field full of folk I found between them
> Of human beings of all sorts, the high and the low,
> Working and wandering as the world requires.

The prologue commences with themes of hierarchy and class composition. Those who work and those who wander. We used to begin the work of class composition with the antagonism of town and country symbolized by the hammer and sickle: under what circumstances will peasants ally with the workers of the towns? But the tension which Langland asks us to examine is between work and wandering. Work consisted of forms of bondage and the workers were named variously thralls, rustics, churls, villeins, slaves, and serfs. They were forced to work. More than half of the population consisted of small-holders, divided roughly between those who owned plough teams and those who had to hire themselves out to live. The problems of his society concerned the price and terms of labor-power. The transition from wage inflation to vagrancy or social mobility was the moral panic of 1360s.

England's population was reduced by the Bubonic Plague of 1347–1350 (one in three perished), its wealth was depleted by three crippling poll taxes, the Hundred Years War against France began to bleed the country white, and England was led by the unpopular the Duke of Lancaster, John of Gaunt. The Statute of Labourers (1351) obliged workers to work at low wages on pain of imprisonment. The rates were as follows: one penny a day for weeding or hay making, reapers two pence a day, mowers five pence a day, tilers threepence a day and their boys a penny and a half, same with thatchers, and none with food or drink. A fourteenth-century labor statute mandated that all "artificers and craftsmen as well as servants and apprentices who are not of great account" were to be forced to serve in harvest at cutting, gathering and bringing in the corn. Imprisonment, likewise, awaited those who "under color of pity or alms" give anything to "sturdy beggars" or "to cherish them in their sloth." The verb, "to cherish," gives us pause. In the Middle Ages the mendicant was holy.

The country peasants and the town craftsmen rose to defend their commons against tax collectors and cunning lawyers. The combination of military disasters and war taxation converted anxiety to action. A tax man molested Wat Tyler's daughter. This incident was at the center of the 1790s accounts of the rising by Thomas Paine, Robert Southey, and William Blake. Tom Paine (1737–1809) included an important footnote on Wat Tyler in the second part of *Rights of Man* published in February 1792. It falls in the chapter "Ways and Means," at first glance an unlikely subject except that to Paine Tyler was a successful rebel against taxes. The people in Tyler's day "certainly were a people who would not be imposed upon" in contrast especially to the gigantic increase in taxes since "the rage for foreign wars and foreign dominion" took over the kingdom after 1688. Tyler is thus an anti-war, anti-imperialist forebear. In addition Tyler illustrates the long reach of despotism, the tax-gatherer's indecent examination of his daughter provided further example of unrestrained power. Tyler lifted his hammer and brought it down upon the tax man's head, bringing all "the neighbourhood discontents to an issue." Paine was answered by royal proclamation banning the book as subversive and him an outlaw. As for "the people," answered Burke, Paine's antagonist, they were "wild beasts," "a disbanded race of deserters and vagabonds," and John Ball was a "patriarch of sedition."[2]

William Blake (1757–1827) twice depicted Wat Tyler, once during revolutionary time and again afterwards. The first time was a commission from Joseph Johnson, the publisher in 1797 as an illustration to accompany Charles Allen's *New and Improved History of England* (1798), and the second time was twenty years later in 1819. The first is called "Wat Tyler and the Tax-gatherer." It shows the tax man dead on the ground, Tyler's daughter fleeing the scene her arms raised in fright, her head turned back in horror, her dress flowing in the speed of her flight, and a young, athletic Wat Tyler straddling the corpse, his arms partially raised and elbows held back, the hammer in his hand, and his head looking down shocked at the deed. If Southey is the apostate, Blake is the poet. While Southey renounced his adherence to the ideals of revolution, Blake deepened his.

The second depiction of Wat Tyler is a drawing in pencil of Tyler's neck and head. It is entitled "Wat Tyler by Wm. Blake from his spectre as in the act of striking the Tax Gatherer on the head, October 1819." It was one of his "Visionary Heads." These were the result of an interesting séance/experiments which he conducted with the astrologer, John Varley. Between midnight and the very early morning, three or four o'clock, they awaited the appearance in the darkness. He sketched the visions of the dead such as Socrates, Herod, Mohammad, Voltaire—and Wat Tyler. The drawing is certainly an arresting image, some stubble on the chin, clear-eyed, a mouth apart not in horror but in articulate anger, the eyes are clear and focused, the eyebrows elegant, the neck strong, the curling hair like flames. This is Orc, the fiery figure of revolutionary days.[3]

The tension between mobility and stability was taut within the commons. Piers plowman is the figure for stability; his is the hand on the plow, he keeps his eye on the prize, the straight furrow. He follows daily labor; he rolls with the rhythms of the seasons. Geoffrey Chaucer was in London during the Peasants' Revolt but he lay low from authorities and insurgents alike biding his time until he published his *Canterbury Tales* of life on the road. The figure of mobility is the vagabond, the person who lolls, idles, or loiters, the one who rests at ease. It overlaps with the Lollard, the semi-monastic cleric who was derided on the one hand as heretical, on the other hand, who cares for the sick. The "gyrovage" was the wandering monk, who strolled from monastery to monastery sleeping rough, who brought the religious into everyday life—a hippie. John Ball was such a mendicant, a lay hermit, scorned as a drifter, a layabout, a good-for-nothing. Dobson calls him part of "the ecclesiastical proletariat," William Morris called him a "hedge priest." François Villon is perhaps most well-known of the type, honored by hippies and beatniks alike. John Ball's letters were broadsides, attached to public places. The surviving letters were found "in the garment of a man about to be hanged."

Who were we in 2008 to speak for all? In 1381 we are at the birth of bourgeois individualism, the modern ego, and the civil name. For baptism, confession, marriage, one name was enough. But for "civil society"—taxation, military service, inheritance of property—another was added. What was a man? What was a person? This question was at the center of the revolt. John Ball preached on the riddle with its cunning avowal of equality and its subtle subversion of episcopacy,

> When Adam delved and Eve span
> Who was then the gentleman?

Edmund Burke wrote that the phrase "is fully equal to all the modern dissertations on the equality of mankind; and it has one advantage over them—it is in rhyme."[4] Even this was not to last however, because three years later Robert Southey (1774–1843), believing that Wat Tyler was one of his ancestors, wrote a dramatic poem in three acts called *Wat Tyler*, and it was all in rhyming couplets like,

> England is growne to such a passe of late,
> That rich men triumph to see the poore beg at their gate.
> But I am able by good scripture before you to prove,
> That God doth not this dealing allow nor love,
> But when Adam delved and Eve span,
> Who was then a Gentleman.

Fully a play of its time with references to the language of the American Declaration of Independence ("your sacred, your inalienable freedom,"), with the naïveté of the aristocratic pastoral, with fascination with electricity ("The electric truth shall run from man to man"), its combination of "long withholden rights" with solar energy ("shines not the sun with equal ray on [all]"), and with the revolutionary simplicity of its communism,

> But merrily with the world it went,
> When men eat berries of the hawthorne tree,
> And thou helpe me, I'll helpe thee,
> And make division equally,
> Of each mans goods indifferently,

He did not publish it, and as an apostate against the revolutionary beliefs of *égalité* he joined the ranks of counter-revolution and was rewarded as poet laureate. In 1817 his enemies published his *Wat Tyler* to Southey's acute embarrassment.

Piers Plowman offers us some continuities in the problem of naming, and we might read this in relation to identities. Perhaps it is just a technical problem of clandestinity or the avoidance of surveillance. It is also a problem of experience. Work was the central experience of the fourteenth century. This is the period of the stabilization of the English surname in its modern form, a heritable paternal addition, by it rights of tenant and free were claimed through time, as the copy holder, and through them access to common rights, or customs of the manor as surnames were introduced for purposes of taxation and patrilinear inheritance.

John Ball, the vagrant priest, and Wat Tyler, a tile-maker, were well-known leaders of the revolt. John Ball sent a letter to the commons of Essex, followed by a poem. The letter warns the craftsmen to be wary of city tricks, to stand united, to hold faith with the plowman, to rebuke ruling-class thieves, and to follow the lead of the true man "and all his fellows":

> John Schep, sometime Saint Mary's priest of York, and now of Colchester, greeteth well John Nameless, and John the Miller, and John Carter, and biddeth them that they beware of guile in borough, and stand together in God's name, and biddeth Piers Plowman go to his work, and chastise well Hob the Robber, and take with you John Trueman, and all his fellows, and no more.[5]

We come now to the second part of the letter, the poem which begins with a menacing riddle, includes a watchword, continues with a caution, and overall amounts to a combination of performance discourse, a short creed, and revolutionary prayer.

> John the Miller hath ground small, small, small;
> The King's son of heaven shall pay for all.
> Beware or ye be woe,
> Know your friend from your foe,
> Have enough, and say ho!
> And do well and better, and flee sin,
> And seek peace and hold you therein,
> And pray for John Trueman and all his fellows.

The miller operated the most advanced machine of the day, the water-mill, in rarer cases, wind-mills. More to the point, the peasantry or the commoners had to take their grain to him and he abused his position. In this case, a time of scarcity, the miller grinds small by weight not fineness. The substance of nurture, the staff of life, has been reduced and human substance diminished. The King's son of heaven, Jesus, pays for all by his sacrifice: His mercy is so embracing that in the harrowing of hell he will grant life even to the condemned, as in the account of *Piers Plowman*.

Revolutionary strategy is found in the gnomic letters sent by the priest John Ball. Jack the Miller said,

> Look thy mill go aright, with the four sails, and the post stand in steadfastness. With right and with might, with skill and with will, let might keep right, and skill go before will and right before might, then goeth our mill aright. And if might go before right, and will before skill, then is our mill mis-adight [unprepared].[6]

The machine is taken as the force of the collective.

Shepherd, carter, miller, plowman are preceded by John Nameless. Anonymity is prized. Anonymity was politically essential, as it certainly was to "William Langland" the "author" of the poem whose excoriation of the clergy exposed him to considerable punishment, if they could find him. Anonymity is however incomplete: what is expressed is also a collectivity opposed to the process of individuation and expropriation.

People are named for types or occupations. But what of the new identity that emerges in the struggle for justice? The victory of the commons must bring with it new kinds of human beings. What kind? The Middle English word, "kynde," perhaps is a clue because it denotes both benevolence, the nature of something, and law. To be unkind is to be unnatural, cruel, and lonely or devoid of the company of others of your class. This concerns class composition, and meaning of "kynde," as in human kind, or mankind. It also means benevolence, or solidarity. Philosophically, we might conclude that the notion of commoning is one that neither rests on natural law as we associate with, let us say, the Enlightenment nor with agrarian customs made evident by social history but with a third ground, namely, the law of "kynde." Proletarian cladistics differs from gender and racial taxonomies by class-based ethics and activist mutuality. Cohn quotes *Dialogue of Dives and Pauper*, a source from early in the fourteenth century, "by the lawe of kynde and by Goddes lawe all thynge is common."[7] The notion of "kynde" is related to ours of "class."

E.P. Thompson (1924–1993) structured *The Making of the English Working Class* in three parts—thesis (the eighteenth-century free-born Englishman), antithesis (the exploitation of the Industrial Revolution), and synthesis (working-class consciousness). The third part begins with a motto from Hazlitt's essay, "The people are not apt . . . to volunteer a rebellion for the theatrical éclat of the thing."

William Hazlitt (1778–1830) wrote "What Is the People?" in 1817. It was a brave essay written in starving times. The title and the year are significant. Not "who is the people?" but "what is the people"? The interest of the people consists of "common and equal rights" in contrast to the privileges of the great and powerful. He asks, "What is it that the wealth of thousands is composed of? The tears, the sweat, and blood of millions." "Where are we to find the intellect of the people? Why, all the intellect that ever was is theirs." What actions can the people take? How can history move? "The people do not rise up till they are trod down." He brings the Bible, Shakespeare, Milton to support his thesis of *vox populi vox dei*. Excessive irritation and disgust with the government arises from a sudden and violent stretch of power departing from spirit and form of government, or by blind and willful adherence to old abuses when the state of manners has rendered them odious and ridiculous.

America is an example of the former, France of the latter. Wat Tyler is a case in point. Yes, he was defeated but the grievances he fought against were removed a few years later.

Persons of indeterminate status between fictive and actual, whose power lay partly in being unnamed, or unnameable. Anne Middleton calls them confected names and improvised identities. The miller and the carter were essential to an agrarian civilization. These are appeals not to the margin of society but to the center of the social division of labor. They link the settled and the mobile, the worker and the wanderer, the "good subject" and the "vagabond."

There have been many such "confected" figures in English social history. John Trueman, Piers Plowman, John Carter, and Wat Tyler are such insurgents from the fourteenth century. In the sixteenth century, Lord Pity, Lord Poverty, or Captain Charity led risings. Lady Skimmington did so in the seventeenth century. In the nineteenth century Captain Ludd, the brave hero of the handicraftsmen, or Captain Swing the mysterious incendiary who led the agricultural laborers, were both doomed by the steam engines of the Industrial Revolution. And hovering over the arch of these centuries like a green arbor is the person of Robin Hood—elusive, ecological, avenging, beautiful, and just.

Country people marched on London, one contingent from Essex and another from Kent. The city workers enabled the country people to enter the city by opening the gates and clearing the bridge. Certainly there was sympathy between the 'prentices and crafts people of London and the incoming insurgents who after several days sleeping in the open, hungry and thirsty, were ready for hospitality. Among their first deeds, comparable to the liberation of defendants in the American fugitive slave cases, was the opening of the prisons. This was habeas corpus in action. The commoners wanted to get rid of the lawyers, and often in connection with the excarceration of the prisons the crowds searched out legal documentation of their oppressions and destroyed them in the bonfires of the rising. Some of the rebels believed "that the land could not be fully free until the lawyers had been killed." The Kentish commons opened the Marshalsea prison in Southwark on Wednesday. On Thursday they freed the prisoners of the Fleet. Then they broke open Westminster prison and freed the prisoners, and proceeded by way of Holborn to break open Newgate prison.

The Kentish and Essex rebels met in London on Thursday, June 13, 1381, the feast of Corpus Christi. Midsummer traditionally is the beginning of harvest time, the most labor-intensive time of year. Exceptional seasonal mobility. The festival of Corpus Christi in the Christian calendar was a new feast, proclaimed by the Pope in 1317, with the Eucharistic host held high. With the formation of Corpus Christi fraternities in 1350s came elaborate processions taking place out doors. "The element of disorder, the excitement of a populous event, perco-lated and erupted in a variety of ways," says its historian Rubin.

The central ritual of the Christian is the miracle of the mass or commun-ion celebrating the last supper of Jesus with his disciples. He held up bread saying, eat this as a symbol / as remembrance / as my body. The peasantry might easily construe this mystery the other way around, not as a priestly mystery of consumption (transubstantiating bread into body) but as a collective action of production when mowing, plowing, weeding, harrowing, reaping, harvesting, binding, threshing, carting, milling, and kneading works the body into bread.

Keeping body and soul together was a cooperative labor and visible to all. Strip-farming in open-field agriculture required intensive ad hoc coopera-tion, to share the plow, coordinate of grazing, to use of balklands, to distrib-ute wastes, above all, to glean. Bylaws were "by common consent," and relied on customs older than feudalism. When the communities, the neighborhood, brought out from the fields by the tocsin marched through the highways and byways they elevated the bread high stuck on the tines of a long-handled pitchfork. Harvest home was a solemn, sacred moment of triumph or defeat.

On Thursday they called for "a charter to free them from all manner of serfdom." On Friday the commons met just outside the City walls on the road to Essex at a place of play, a ludic location, between city and country where sports and games were held. Henry Knighton, an early chronicler, wrote of the Mile End meeting on Friday. "The king, for the sake of peace and because of the circumstances at the time, granted the commons, at their petition, a charter under his great seal—declaring that all men in the realm of England should be free and of free condition; they and their heirs should be forever released from the yoke of servitude and villeinage." The King ordered thirty clerks to start writing preparatory for royal sigillation. Parchment charters were drawn up for Essex, Kent, Norfolk, Suffolk, and Hertford on this pattern: "Richard, by the grace of God, king of England and France, and lord of Ireland, to all his bailiffs and faithful men to whom these present letters come, greet-ings. Know that by our special grace we have manumitted all our liegemen, subjects, and others of the country of Hertford; and we have freed and quitted each of them from bondage by the present letters."

At the Mile End meeting Cohn argues there was "nothing at all to hint at any impending miraculous restoration of an egalitarian State of Nature." Perhaps not in capital letters but nature was fully present otherwise, in demands of common right and customary access to forests, rivers, and pasture land. Millennarian eschatology or "miracles" did not seem to be part of the expression in word or deed of the revolt whose causes, course, and conse-quences were this-worldly.

So we arrive at Saturday, June 15, 1381. The chronicler, Thomas Walsingham of St. Albans, says that charters written the day before were unacceptable to Tyler. Tyler, Jack Straw, and John Ball "had assembled their company to common together in a place called Smithfield" outside Lud's gate where only the day before a huge cattle market was held. Now two-footed creatures crowded the scene and one (Tyler) separated himself from his "kynde" and approached the King. Wat Tyler at Smithfield

> half bent his knee and took the king by the hand, shaking his arm force-fully and roughly, saying to him "Brother, be of good comfort and joyful, for you shall have, in the fortnight that is to come, forty thousand more commons than you have at present, and we shall be good companions." And the king said, "Why will you not go back to your own country?" But the other answered, with a great oath, that neither he nor his fellows would leave until they had got their charter as they wished to have it with the inclusion of certain points.[8]

It was at these points that the ideal and the actual intersected. Let us look more closely.

Two accounts of the Smithfield meeting describe specific demands. The *Anonimalle Chronicle* says that Wat asked that there should be no law except for the law of Winchester (which substituted mutilation for hanging as punishment for serious felonies, and asserted rights as sokemen including exemption from military service) and that henceforward there should be no outlawry in any process of law, and that no lord should have lordship in future, but it should be divided among all men, except for the king's own lordship. He also asked that the goods of Holy Church should not remain in the hands of the religious, nor of parsons and vicars, and other churchmen; but that clergy already in possession should have a sufficient sustenance and the rest of their goods should be divided among the people of the parish. And he demanded that there should be no more villeins in England but that all men should be free and of one condition. To this the king gave an easy answer, and said that Wat should have all that he could fairly grant, reserving only for himself the regality of his crown.[9] This account contains the principle of redistribution of wealth, reparation, but not of commons. Henry Knighton supplies a second account which refers specifically to the rural commons. "The rebels petitioned the king that all preserves of water, parks, and woods should be made common to all: so that throughout the kingdom the poor as well as the rich should be free to take game in water, fish ponds, woods and forests as well as to hunt hares in the fields—and to do these and many other things without impediment."[10] This is the key.

Ernest Jones (1819–1869), a leader of the English Chartist movement of the 1840s and a colleague of the communists, Marx and Engels, was alone among radical interpreters of the Smithfield encounter in calling attention to this demand.[11] After 1848 Jones was imprisoned for two years under sickening conditions. In Jones's account the king asked, "What do the people want?" Tyler responded, according to the Chartist, "What you have granted the men of Essex; and, in addition, our natural rights in wood, waste, and water, fish and game." Of all the contemporary chroniclers, Knighton was perhaps the best eyewitness. Tyler did not base the demand on "natural right" but upon the common.

Despite the fact that John Ball clearly warned against the "guile in the borough," Walworth knocked him in the gutter with his baselard, stabbing him unawares. Ever since the dagger has been part of the City of London coat-of-arms or crest, the urban bourgeoisie coming to power on the backs of the Peasants' Revolt. He perished "while his hands and feet quivered for some time. Then an enormous wailing broke out." Wat Tyler was assassinated by William Walworth, Lord Mayor, who made his money from the Flemish sex workers in the Southwark brothels.[12] London, the famed haunt of the international bourgeoisie, has its crested origin in a pander, an assassin, and sex-trafficker.

No wonder that Paine called him "a cowardly assassin," while Burke praised Walworth's "spirited exertion." James Northcote (1746–1831) exhibited a huge canvas (nine feet tall and more than twelve feet wide) of the death of Wat Tyler at the Royal Academy in 1787 depicting the violence at the Smithfield meeting.[13] Commissioned by a London alderman it was displayed while the memory was still fresh of the Gordon riots of 1780 which opened the London prisons, threatened the Bank, and destroyed property.[14] The inverted pose of Tyler and the rearing horses depict the upside down, unnatural world of the rebel. The title expressed the municipal priorities, "Sir William Walworth, mayor of London, A.D. 1381, in the presence of Richard II then 15 years old, kills Wat Tyler, at the head of the insurgents, who are appeased by the heroic speech of the king."

Lordship depended on extraction of surplus from the peasantry. The serf was obliged to give boons, corvées, or days of labor to the lord. The abolition of lordship was an abolition of surplus labor, and thus the basis of surplus-value. Not only would feudalism fall but capitalism could have no basis. That is the significance of the charter proposed by Wat Tyler. But, it might be asked, how could people live? While the class-consciousness is direct and blunt, these common peasants seek a justice that is accomplished with moderation, peace, and fleeing from sin. Central to the author's outlook is the affinity between divinity and necessity. To Langland the theory of the commons derives from that relationship.

At the beginning of *Piers Plowman* a fair lady wakes the sleeping author that the Tower on the hill represents Truth who "commanded the earth to provide wool and linen and food, enough for everyone to live in comfort and moderation. And of his goodness he ordained three things in common, which are all that your body requires: clothing to protect you from cold, food to keep you from want, and drink when you are thirsty."

The *manuscript* versions thus appeared during the first great peasants revolt in defense of their commons. The *printed* version of the poem appeared two centuries later in 1550 at the time of the huge revolts of the commons against enclosures, known as Kett's Rebellion in the east and the Prayer Book Rebellion in the west. It was published by Robert Crowley, the commonwealth man, whose diatribes against greed, enclosure, and egotism retain their force.

"Need, who knows no law and is indebted to no one. For to keep alive, there are three things which Need takes without asking. The first is food; for if men refuse to give him any, and he has no money, nothing to pawn, and no one to guarantee him, then he seizes it for himself. And there he commits no sin, even if he uses deceit to get it. He can take clothing in the same way, provided he has no better payment to offer; Need is always ready to bail a man out of prison for that. And thirdly, if his tongue is parched, the law of his nature ["the lawe of kynde"] compels him to drink at every ditch rather than die of thirst. So in great necessity, Need may help himself, without consulting Conscience or the Cardinal Virtues—provided he keep the Spirit of Moderation." Crowley occasionally inserts printed comments in the margin, such as:

> What liberti
> need
> giveth

Need resembles divinity in humility, and he quotes Matthew 8:20, "Foxes have their holes, the birds their roosts; but the Son of Man has nowhere to lay his head." The same chapter warns against treating this theology of hunger, cold, and thirst with the pagan doctrine of communism spouted by Envy and propounded by Seneca "that all things on this earth should be held in common." William Langland was not a doctrinaire communist because as *doctrine* the notion of commons arises from either immoderate envy or academic pride. Yet ever since you find such ideal commoning or leveling every century or two. A play about the revolt, *Jack Straw*, was performed in 1593.

> . . . all mankind are equal, is most true;
> Ye came as helpless infants to the world:
> Ye feel alike the infirmities of nature;

And at last moulder into common clay.
Why then these vain distinctions!—bears not the earth
Food in abundance?—must your granaries
O'erflow with plenty, while the poor man starves?

Tom Paine concluded his concise account of the rising, "If the Barons merited a monument to be erected in Runnymede, Tyler merits one in Smithfield." In London today there is no blue plaque attached at Smithfield, or at Mile End, or Southwark to remember this medieval worker who called the King "brother" and called for emancipation from serfdom. As for John Ball, he was drawn, hanged, and quartered at St. Alban's on July 13, 1381, his body parts sent for exhibition to four towns of the kingdom.

Although the rebels conceived of themselves as a mysterious *Magna Societas* no evidence has yet come to light expressing consciousness that they linked themselves to Magna Carta. Magna Carta succeeded because the ascendant classes after civil war formed a historical bloc of forces which provided a basis of intra-ruling-class resolution. They killed the poll tax, and not even Margaret Thatcher could bring it back. Her "community charge" was defeated at the Battle of Trafalgar Square in 1990. From our perspective Magna Carta can hardly be called a success, and the Peasants' Revolt appears to have been, if not the "historically unnecessary catastrophe" which Dobson avers, then it was the portent which Stubbs named, a portent whose promise is unfulfilled.

What about all that scribbling at Mile End and Smithfield, all those charters, all that emancipation? The king's fingers were crossed. "Miserable and detested men, who have sought to be your lord's equals, you are not worthy to live. You were and are serfs, and you will remain in bondage not as before, but incomparably viler. For as long as we live, we shall do our utmost with all faculties at our disposal to suppress you, so that the rigor of your servitude will serve as an example to posterity. Both now and in the future people like yourselves will always have your misery before your eyes like a mirror, so that you will be cursed by them and they will fear to do as you have done." Certainly that is part of the story. Yet the mole stirred.

William Morris (1834–1896) turned the focus from the episodes of violence either by Wat Tyler or against him, and instead meditates upon the writings of John Ball. The project is a philosophical and political encounter with the ideas half a millennium earlier.[15] And like Thompson's *Making of the English Working Class*, the *Dream* is structured dialectically in three. *A Dream of John Ball* begins with the word (a sermon), continues with the deed (a battle), and concludes with (again) the word (conversation).

The year began with "Black Monday" when "an immense mass of poverty stricken humanity" marched through the genteel club land of Pall Mall smashing shop windows. Morris published *A Dream of John Ball* between November 1886 and February 1887 in *Commonweal*, the newspaper of his Socialist League. It was an extraordinarily creative, open-minded time for Morris: politically, he had just founded the Socialist League; intellectually, he was learning from both Karl Marx and Peter Kropotkin; artistically, he was bringing together the arts-and-crafts with his notions of a socialist transformation of labor. Kropotkin, the Russian anarchist, came out often to the Coach House for Sunday lectures and supper, regaling the table with a fable of the encounter between the Russians and the "Redskins" of California. Morris read the Br'er Rabbit fables to his family in the context of *John Ball*. In the summer he lectured in Dublin. He could be often found wandering the streets of the East End, an habitué of its International Club where he held forth with fiery invective, eyes shining, head back.[16] He aspired to an expression of ideas which could actually *move*. That is the significance of John Ball's sermon.

In the *Dream* Morris is transported back to June 1381 and the company of the Kentish rebels, a few days after they had delivered John Ball from the Archbishop's prison in Canterbury. What was the thing they fought for? Most immediately they had fought for the deliverance of John Ball from prison. Upon release he preached upon the famous couplet about Adam and Eve. John Ball expounds an earthly doctrine of fellowship as Heaven and the lack of fellowship as Hell. "It is for him that is lonely or in prison to dream of fellowship, but for him that is of a fellowship to do and not to dream." He rouses the people to action. Listening to this Morris is moved: "I pondered all these things, and how men fight and lose the battle, and the thing that they fought for comes about in spite of their defeat, and when it comes turns out not to be what they meant, and other men have to fight for what they meant under another name." Frederick Engels, after the defeat of communism in 1848, turned to history and wrote *The Peasant War in Germany* (1850) concluding of medieval peasant wars generally that their "anticipation of communism nurtured by fantasy became in reality an anticipation of modern bourgeois conditions." In 1886 Morris is pondering theories of change—liberation theology, Marxism, anarchism, and he is intervening in that debate, thinking about how theories come and go; about conceptions of what human beings may become.

The opening of the prisons, the emancipation from serfdom, and the resumption of commoning (actual and ideal) went hand in hand.

Ann Arbor
2008

REFERENCES

Ault, Warren O. "By-Laws by Common Consent." *Speculum* 29, no. 2 (April 1954): 378–94.

Cohn, Norman. *The Pursuit of the Millennium*. London: Secker & Warburg, 1957.

De Angelis, Massimo. *The Beginning of History: Value Struggles and Global Capital*. London: Pluto, 2007.

Dobson, R.B. *The Peasants' Revolt of 1381*. London: Macmillan, 1970.

Gooch, Steve. *Will Wat? If Not, What Will?* London: Pluto Press, 1975.

Hilton, Rodney H., and H. Fagan. *The English Rising of 1381*. London: Lawrence and Wishart, 1950.

Hutton, Ronald. *The Rise and Fall of Merry England: The Ritual Year, 1400–1700*. Oxford: Oxford University Press, 1994.

Hyde, Lewis. *The Gift*. New York: Vintage, 2007.

Justice, Stephen. *Writing and Rebellion: England in 1381*. Berkeley: University of California Press, 1994.

Langland, William. *Piers Plowman*. Norton Critical Edition. Translated by E. Talbot Donaldson and edited by Elizabeth Robertson and Stephen H.A. Shepherd. New York: Norton, 2006.

———. *Piers the Ploughman*. Translated by J.F. Goodridge. New York: Penguin, 1959.

The Life and Death of Jack Straw. London: Danter, 1593. Reprinted by Tudor Facsimile Texts, edited by John S. Farmer. London, 1911.

McKisack, May. *The Fourteenth Century, 1307–1399*. Oxford: Clarendon Press, 1959.

Middleton, Anne. "William Langland's 'Kynde Name': Authorial Signature and Social Identity in Late Fourteenth Century England." In *Literary Practice and Social Change in Britain, 1380–1530*, edited by Lee Patterson. Berkeley: University of California Press, 1989.

———. "Acts of Vagrancy: The C Version 'Autobiography' of the Statute of 1388." In *Written Work: Langland, Labor, and Authorship*, edited by Steven Justice and Kathryn Kerby-Fulton. Philaelphia: University of Pennsylvania Press, 1997.

Morris, William. *The Dream of John Ball* (1886–1887). The Collected Works of William Morris. London: Routledge, 1992.

Oman, Charles. *The Great Revolt of 1381* Oxford: Clarendon Press, 1906.

Paine, Thomas. *Rights of Man* (1791–1792). In *Collected Writings*. New York: Library of America, 1995.

Rubin, Miri. *Corpus Christi: The Eucharist in Late Medieval Culture*. Cambridge: Cambridge University Press, 1991.

Savage, Charlie. *Takeover: The Return of the Imperial Presidency and the Subversion of American Democracy*. New York: Little, Brown and Company, 2008.

The "USA"

CHAPTER ELEVEN

Introduction to Thomas Paine

"WHERE LIBERTY IS, THERE IS MY COUNTRY," DECLARED BENJAMIN FRANKLIN, TO WHICH Thomas Paine replied, "Where is not liberty, there is mine." Tom Paine was a worker and commoner. He spoke and wrote from a particular experience, that of an English artisan at the onset of industrialization. He was, too, a planetary revolutionary—indeed, he helped give meaning to the term—and as such his writing is hugely significant for the twenty-first century. If we were to compare him to any contemporary figure, it would be Che Guevara. He asserted aspiration, possibility, the unheard of. He breathed the warmth of human agency to frigid hierarchies of power. The phrase "world revolutionary" might have several meanings—a sailor of the seven seas, a scientist of the universal mind, a *philosophe* in the republic of letters, a journeyman on the move. Rachel Corrie in Palestine, Ben Linder in Nicaragua, Brad Will in Oaxaca, those from the USA who step forth onto the world stage at places of maximum hope in the class struggle, express his spirit. As with Guevara or José Martí, he too struggled within the belly of the beast. He likened the British Empire to Jonah's whale.

"These are the times that try men's souls," he wrote.[1] His own soul was divided; so has been his legacy. "The Age of Paine" (as John Adams called it) was contradictory, like any other individual or historical age. While he gave voice to the age, he would bend, if not kneel, to power. Power and Empire have claimed him as one of their own. He has been quoted by American presidents, from Ronald Reagan to Barack Obama (who would not name him).[2] A prevailing view is that he was only an American patriot (the Nation), another that he was chiefly a citizen (the Republic). He defended private property and wrote on behalf of banking. His pamphlet *Common Sense* elucidated and called for revolution in America; *Rights of Man* defended revolution in England and France, constituting it upon popular sovereignty. As a patriot, as a citizen, as a populist, was Paine not an adjunct to the bourgeois revolution? We must take a fresh look.

If Paine was these things, he was also an outlaw, a traitor, an alien, a felon. He died forlorn, his funeral in 1809 attended by a Frenchwoman, her two sons, some Irishmen, and two African Americans. In relation to power, Paine's life and thought was also divided. He took part in three attempts at revolution: in America and France it succeeded while in Britain it failed. He was a class-conscious man, sensitive to the differences of power and money. He wrote and spoke for the common people. You see this in his first major writing, which is about the central capitalist relation, the wage; you see it also in his last major writing, which is about commoning. *The Case of the Officers of Excise* denounced the relations of money and wages, while *Agrarian Justice* called for social reparations for class injustice. It is between these two major concerns that we place Paine's concepts of revolution and constitution.

Paine lived during times of "industrial revolution," "commercial expansion," "urbanization," and "population growth." Behind these sclerotic phrases, so characteristic of the ideology of the Cold War, were the Atlantic-wide transformations of the class relations of capitalism whose legacy endures to this day. The factory proletariat propelled the machines of industry; the slave plantation of the West Indies and the plundered indigenous peoples provided the commerce; the young, the unemployed, and the criminalized peopled the towns; the separate public and domestic spheres of women's endeavor reproduced the population on an enlarged scale. The working class was thus composed of waged artisans, criminalized unemployed, unwaged domestic workers as mothers and wives, slaves, and the indigenous and colonized.

We tend to think of communism and capitalism as incompatible, but Paine did not think in such terms which were still, to quote his great antagonist Edmund Burke, "in the gristle," that is, not yet well-defined or full-bodied. In preparing this introduction I have found fresh evidence of commoning (and its continuity in English history) whose significance has been neglected in Paine scholarship. I have found it in the landscape of Paine's childhood and formative years, his ancestry, and his experience. This evidence shows us that Paine came from, and belonged to, a long English anti-capitalist tradition; moreover, it helps us understand the tasks of "revolution" and "constitution" in the twenty-first century.

Landscape and Commons

Thomas Paine was born in 1737 in a small corner of East Anglia: Thetford, a small town in the flint-rich, sandy-heathed Brecklands. His mother, Francis Cocke, was an Anglican and the daughter of an attorney; Joseph, his father, was a stay-maker (or corset-maker), the owner of a small-holding, and a Quaker. Together they formed a domestic compromise between Established religion and historic Dissent, the two forces (Anglican and Puritan) that collided during the English Revolution (1640–60). As a Quaker, Joseph was "no respecter of persons," that is, he believed in equality, exactly what Voltaire admired in the Quakers. Yet, for Thomas, his baptism, his marriage, and his funeral were all occasions of religious carpings and cavils.

The landscape of Tom Paine's childhood world was the product of apparent capitalist triumph. The countryside had been enclosed, privatized; the country's bodies were bound, and the people's voices gagged by, in Blake's eloquent phrase, "mind-forged manacles." In consequence, Paine as an individual suffered from a kind of social trauma which repressed historical memory. This memory began to find release in 1774 when, at the age of thirty-seven and by all conventional standards a failure in both love and money, he left England for North America, where he found his voice in an extraordinary revolutionary career.

The Brecklands was beautiful with heartsease, cypress spurge, spiked speedwell, grape hyacinth, wild asparagus, and the blue of viper's bugloss which provided spectacular color, "surpassing in splendor anything that can be imagined," in the opinion of Paine's contemporary, the scientific botanist Carl Linnaeus.[3] Engrossment, emparkment and enclosure had been at work for many centuries, and a map of the deserted villages of Norfolk shows a decided concentration in the Brecklands.[4] But the region had been producing "loose and wandering people" since the sixteenth century. Perhaps this explains why the region became "a symbol of liberty," in Oliver Rackham's words, or why the gentry was afflicted with ericophobia, or fear of the heath.[5] The soil was too sandy for the "improvement" that Norfolk was famous for among eighteenth-century agribusinessmen. The heather and bracken in the great sweeps of sandy landscape provided raw materials of domestic life—fuel, fodder, thatch, and the ingredients of rural medicine. If enclosure and engrossment could not make the sandy desolation into fenced fields of agribusiness, then the emparkment and warrening would restrict the ecology into a partial hunting preserve for the privileged.

The Duke of Grafton, who ruled Thetford from his estate at Euston, north of London, led the enclosure movement in the Brecklands during the 1780s. He had brought into cultivation extensive acreage that had previously been rough grazing common lands. He was a founding member of the Board of Agriculture in 1793. He ran a renowned stables and kennels, and the views landscaped by Capability Brown at Euston were admired by the ladies of England. This cold, sullen and profligate contemporary of Paine was basically the ruler of Thetford. He managed to pass the Thetford Enclosure Act of 1804, in the process privatizing 5,616 acres and denying public access to 80 percent of the borough.

A couple of months after Thomas was born, his father was made "free" of the town, that is, he joined its oligarchy. The accompanying privileges, though, were disappointing, and "amounted to little more than the right of pastur-age on the commons."[6] At about the same time, the great Norfolk historian Francis Blomefield records that a sturgeon was taken in the paper-mill pond, seven feet long, and weighing thirteen stone ten pounds. The fact is that, while the birds of the air and the fish of the sea were thought to be God's creatures, their habitat was fast being privatized, and such creatures were deliberately bred in a type of semi-domesticated animal husbandry in the fish ponds and dovecotes and deer parks of the enclosing gentry. Around Thetford rabbits were bred in the thousands, and woe betide the poacher who violated "free warren," as the landlord's exclusive right was paradoxically termed.

Rabbits had come to England with William the Conqueror.[7] The early eighteenth century had seen an increase in commercial warrens providing fare to the London food markets and fur for felt-hat manufacture. After the First World War, a local farm worker said, "They'd let you take a rabbit or two, for instance. Before 1914, if you'd caught a rabbit, my God, the world would have come to an end."[8] Poaching had become a serious criminal offense. Its criminalization was an especially humiliating form of destroying the subsistence commons, and Paine had no doubt where the blame for it lay. Writing in 1792, he got straight to the point: "Had there been a house of farmers [and not a House of Lords], there had been no game laws." Indeed, in one of the first acts of the independent USA, an alliance of backwoods-men, artisans and militiamen provided in the Pennsylvania Constitution of 1776 the right to fowl and hunt on their own land and "on all other lands . . . not enclosed."

The Brecks was renowned for more than its warrens. Then as now, it is the name for the flint-strewn open fields, locally known as the Wilderness. At its heart is Grime's Graves, the Neolithic flint-mining galleries of five millen-nia past. The sound of the flint knappers' clear, precise tapping—quartering, flaking, and knapping are the stages of ever-finer shaping of flints—filled the village of Brandon five miles from Thetford. Paine's prose is like this quartz; hard, crystalline, and perdurable, it has a glass-like, glittering sheen: "The palaces of kings are built on the ruins of the bowers of paradise."

The comparison can be taken a step further. Flint had been essential to the arms industry since Neolithic times, used for arrowheads, axes and spear points, and in Paine's era, for guns. When the flint was struck against steel (the frissen) a spark was emitted that ignited the powder in the pan, whose explosion propelled the bullet down the smooth-bored musket, the Brown Bess of the American Revolution.

"From a small spark, kindled in America, a flame has arisen not to be extinguished."[9] Literally so, inasmuch as the British used black flints, which the Americans also preferred. When a shortage of flints hobbled effective fire-power in 1776, early in the war, the Second Continental Congress received a huge correspondence regarding flints. The Americans discovered black flints at Ticonderoga and sent 30,000 specimens to Washington.[10] The shot heard round the world was detonated by Brecks flint, while flint and steel were the technics of the imperial hunt. Paine writes in *Common Sense* that "Freedom hath been hunted round the globe. Asia and Africa have long expelled her. Europe regards her like a stranger, and England hath given her warning to depart."[11] Brecklands flints are scattered about the planet today, the scat of empire.

Brecks Rebels

Born a few miles east of Thetford, Francis Blomefield went to the same school as Paine, and published the first volumes of his history around the time of Paine's birth. A transcriber of church memorials, a genealogist of lords of manors, a describer of coats-of-arms, Blomefield was not a remembrancer of popular memory, yet he acknowledged a long tradition of rebellion. Like Paine, Blomefield drew upon a common store of local knowledge. Andy Wood has shown the shared tradition of popular revolt from the fourteenth century onwards, revealing continuities in leadership and organization, in similar patterns of regional involvement, and finally, in the very consciousness of the continuity.[12] The Peasants' Revolt of 1381, Kett's Rebellion of 1549, and the English Revolution of 1649 were part of social memory, as they were steps in the long commodification of land, until England could be bought and sold.

Blomefield writes of the Revolt of 1381, when the peasants rose for equal-ity and the commons: "these were the outrageous doings of this county . . . the people of Thetford, Lyn, and Yarmouth, assembled together, and came and rested before Norwich, and as they came, caused every man to rise with them." Tom Paine knew this story well and tells it in *Rights of Man*, albeit very differently to Blomefield. Blomefield retrojected the charged political term "Levellers" from the eighteenth century back to 1381, adding historical depth to his condemnation of the actual Levellers, the radical republican movement of the English Civil War that was brutally suppressed by Oliver Cromwell.

About two centuries before Thomas Paine, the second camp of Kett's 1549 rebellion organized operations at Brandon and Thetford, stopping traffic on the river Ouse. This "camping time" or "commotion time" was, as Blomefield told it, class war: "They openly declared great hatred against all gentlemen, whom they maliciously accused of covetousness, pride, extortion, and oppres-sion, practiced against their tenants and the common people, and having thor-oughly imbibed the wicked notions of the ancient levellers, they begin to put in execution their vile designs."[13]

About a century before Paine's birth, the vicar of Santon Downham, a Brecks village once totally buried beneath shifting sands, kept a diary from 1625 to 1642. In it he criticized a Mr. Paine of Riddlesworth, six miles east of Thetford, when noting that "men be disposed to speake the worst of State bisnesses and to nourish discountente, as if there were a false carriage in all these things, which if it were so what would a false hearte rather see than an insurrection? A way whereunto these men prepare."[14]

Paine's mother's ancestor, George Charles Cocke, was a Puritan, a supporter of Oliver Cromwell, a Parliamentarian, a law reformer, a seques-trator of royalist livings, and a Commonwealth judge. Two years after Charles I was beheaded in 1649, Cocke published *English Law or a Summary Survey of the Household of God on Earth.*

English Law evinces the class-consciousness of revolutionary times: justice, it stated, would be served by turning out all the rich men and setting "the plough-man to be their Lord." In the 1640s the Levellers claimed "that the Land was theirs originally," not the property of the descendants of the Norman conquerors. Cocke defined Levellers as those advocating the "forcible taking away the property of rich men" and distinguished at least six kinds of level-ling. Those effected by individual suits at law were one kind. A second held that all estates should be cast into a common stock and divided equally on the grounds "that the poor had an interest in the Commonwealth as well as the rich." A third called for "a perpetual community" of goods against the insa-tiable thirst for riches to be governed by virtuous magistrates, thus avoiding "indiscrete agitations" and "perturbations of state." A fourth was Christian communism, "as one Family." A fifth was unregulated "when the flood-gates of Liberty were broken up." A sixth "of equity and righteousness" would be based "on proportionate justice" or progressive taxation.

Cocke finds Levelling part of Satan's work, the snake in the garden, but it is not difficult to see allusions to actual rural movements of the time by Ranters, Levellers, and Diggers. The Diggers, in the theory and practice of Gerrard Winstanley, based their practice on the actuality of commoning, an argument which Cocke attempted to dismiss by asserting that "commons were the tenant's rights originally not the poor's." In a subsequent work Cocke argued that custom, a form of commoning if not communism, is not to be admitted as law unless they be "reasonable."[15] We are used to think-ing of the relation between the radical demands of the 1640s and of the 1790s in terms of voting and the franchise, because that was the theme at the Putney Debates, the Levellers' celebrated gathering at Putney Church in 1649. The debate about subsistence and levelling in the 1790s is the debate of the 1640s continued—the several methods of wealth redistribution, the links with religion, the fear of disorder, the relation between custom and the commons.

In 1740, when Paine was a toddler, dearth threatened starvation, so the people took appropriate measures, posting notices on baker's doors in Norwich to force down the price of bread: "Wheat at Sixteen Shillings a Comb [a dry measure of 4 bushels]." This was the heralded *taxation populaire* of French social history and the "moral economy" of English. The people assembled at the sound of horns, a hostile witness reported, "purposing to visit the Gentlemen and Farmers in the neighboring villages, in order to extort Money, Strong Ale, &c. from them. At many places, where the Generosity of People answer'd not to their Expectation, 'tis said they shew'd their Resentment by treading down the Corn in the Fields." This method of price regulation persisted in Brandon when in 1816 two hundred women and boys shouted "Cheap bread, a Cheap Loaf and Provisions Cheaper" and a woman submitted the demands on a paper, "Bread or Blood in Brandon this day." Despite the threat of dragoons the women kept the price down.[16]

Thomas Paine of Thetford belonged to an unbroken tradition of rebellion.

The Worker

In the early 1960s, when jets were replacing ocean liners as the preferred mode of transportation for academics, professor W.W. Rostow compared the changes in mid-eighteenth-century capitalism to an airplane takeoff. Agriculture products, exports, imports, banking, manufactures and population suddenly boomed, flying into the clear blue skies of "self-sustaining economic growth." Adam Smith's genius in *The Wealth of Nations* was to note that these changes originated in that despised, neglected arena, the division of labor in production. The botanical specimens, the zoological order, the mineral layers underground, as well as human manufactured products, had become, or were rapidly becoming, commodities. Both raw materials and tools of production could be exchanged with one another, and against money. This glory—the market—is the precondition of capitalism, whose essence was and remains the exploitation of labor, because labor too became commodified in the marriage market, the slave auction and the labor market of wages.

In the twentieth century people of color, women, and indigenous people were at the center of struggles against ideologies which attained their modern form during Paine's lifetime. The ideologies propounding white supremacy, the separate spheres of patriarchy, and the stadial inevitability of the extinction of indigenous people helped to produce the structures of modernity. The global South, feminism and deep time are notions in the twenty-first century which were achieved only through these struggles.

As a worker, Tom Paine gained experience in exploitation in the sexual markets, in military expeditions, and in revenue collection. As a corset-maker he witnessed the spirit of vanity; as a sailor aboard a privateer he absorbed the spirit of plunder; and as an officer in the Excise he suffered from the spirit of fraud. One craft produced garments of erotic allure, the other prowled in military adventures, and the last sunk him directly in the corruptions of the mercantilist state. Each might be said to serve a social function of modernity: state-sanctioned marriage, imperialist war, and state taxation.

Paine's introduction to corset-making came in 1750, when he was removed from Thetford Grammar School at the age of thirteen and apprenticed to his father. Over the next seven years Thomas Paine learned to make corsets. Historians have described him simply as an "artisan" and inquired no further; his enemies in the 1790s made fun of him as a corset-maker in a way both snobbish and misogynist. Originally a garment with protective and orthopedic purposes, the corset had become by the mid-seventeenth century a garment to mold a woman's body, flattening the stomach, straightening the back, in conformity with ruling concepts of female beauty and with upper-class deportment (*épaulement* is the ballet term). From around 1650, whale fins—boiled, cut, split, and sliced—replaced wood and steel as the "stays," the elements of rigidity in the manufacture of the corset, or "little body." A hundred years later, when Paine took up the craft, the corset had been altered to give prominence to the breasts. Radiating traverse strips for the stays were added to the traditional pattern of stiffening and molding, emphasizing curves.[17]

A contemporary situated the trade in the Atlantic economy, comparing the body to enclosures of land and treating it as a commodity. "They discover to us indeed a Sample of what we wish to purchase, yet serve as a Fence to keep us at an awful Distance. They encourage the Consumption of our Manufactures in a prodigious Degree, and the great Demand we have for Whale-Bone renders them truly beneficial to our Allies the Dutch; in short, they are a public good."[18] The market was enlarging, servant-maids accepted the cast-off corsets of their employers as one of their perquisites, and the corset ceased to be the exclusive dress of the upper class. With the expansion of the market came the division of labor. Men did the fitting, the cutting of the whale fin, and the insertion of the stays into the heavy linen or canvas, which had been stitched by women. An apprentice boy in stay-making had to learn servility, to command his temper, to hold his tongue, and to be "very polite."

As Paine took up the craft, the corset became the model for the essence of beauty. In his 1753 *Analysis of Beauty* the English painter William Hogarth argued that the serpentine "line of beauty" was the foundation of aesthetics, illustrating his argument with successive images of the corset in profile.[19]

The focus was less on the waist than the bosom (in his description of the line of beauty he did not even include the waist). In 1758 in the tenth edition of his popular *Systema Naturae*, Carl Linnaeus defined mammals as possessing mammary glands—yet hair, the three bones of the ear, or the four-chambered heart would have distinguished mammals from other classes of animals just as well, if not better. In fact, Linnaeus had another agenda. In 1752 he wrote against wet-nursing, the practice of putting out infants to nurses of "inferior" social class—peasants, indigenous people, or Africans, who, it was believed, caused an excess of infant mortality. This was part of a larger state-sponsored policy to restructure child care and women's lives according to an ideal of domesticity for the demographic purpose of producing a healthy, growing population.[20] The veneration of the breast as an ideal of aesthetic beauty and as the scientific criterion for placing *Homo sapiens* within the animal kingdom served this political purpose.[21]

Having finished his apprenticeship, Paine the artisan abandoned his craft. In 1757 he went to sea for six months aboard a privateer, *The King of Prussia*. A study of his sea voyages, linking England, America and France, awaits its historian. Months at sea can bring a person to another conception of the terraqueous world; indeed, Paine worked with people from around the world on board ship. In *Rights of Man* he protested the torture of sailors and their impressment. As early as 1745 the New England sailors were being compared to the Levellers; two years later Sam Adams wrote that the crowds of sailors opposing impressment "embodied the fundamental rights of man." "All Men are by nature on a Level," he explained, "born with an equal Share of Freedom."[22] They assert the right of resistance to oppression and they assert an axiomatic egalitarianism which Paine summarizes in *Common Sense*: "Mankind being originally equals in the order of creation."[23]

Following his spell at sea, Paine returned to England in 1758. For the next sixteen years he worked variously as a stay-maker, school teacher, occasional Methodist preacher, tobacconist, and then as an officer in the Excise Service, moving from Thetford to Diss, London, Dover, Margate, and Lewes. He was twice married: his first wife died in childbirth, and his second marriage ended amicably in divorce. These were years of intellectual formation without political expression; he began thinking and studying in earnest. In London he attended scientific lectures, learning techniques of inquiry, investigation, imagination, truth, error. At the Headstrong Club, which met at the White Hart Inn in the Sussex town of Lewes, he practiced declamation and debate on behalf of justice, liberty, and rights. These became elements of his writing style. In *Rights of Man* he would praise his own writing for its plain talk, in contrast to Edmund Burke's vapors, romances, complexities.

There is a tendency to say that plain talk arises from plain people, but this need not be the case. Paine's style, straightforward as it may seem, avoids many of the speech communities around him: the slang of the street, the jargon of the trade, the cant of concealment, the dialects of East Anglia, the commoner's nomenclature, Gaelic, the vehicular languages or pidgin talk of the wharf or the ship's deck are not present directly in his writing. Paine laughs at Burke's argument that hereditary leadership is necessarily wise leadership: "To use a sailor's phrase, he *has swabbed the deck*, and scarcely left a name legible in the list of Kings."[24] Here, Paine's sense of decorum in eighteenth-century prose requires that he consciously introduces the sailor's language. However, when all is said and done, the source of Paine's eloquence was emancipatory. As John Thelwall, closest of the 1790s radicals to the project of Paine, expressed it: "even the popular language of Thomas Paine would not have provoked any very alarming discussion, if the general condition of mankind had not predisposed them to exclaim—We are wretched!—Let us enquire the cause!"[25]

The Case of the Officers of Excise, Paine's first pamphlet, was published in 1772–73; its reasoned arrangement, clarity of address, and collective origins would remain characteristic of his subsequent writings. A petition to the members of Britain's Parliament, it was not published for the general public until 1793. In London, Paine gave a copy to the Irish writer Oliver Goldsmith, author of gentle satires on commercial society and privatization of land (his acclaimed poem "The Deserted Village" had just been published in 1770). Paine's pamphlet is an argument about the wage. As such, it is one of the few of its kind in eighteenth-century England, even though the wage defines the central relationship of capitalism, because it conceals paid from unpaid labor. Writing on behalf of his fellow workers, he provides a variety of arguments in favor of more pay.

His first argument was economic. A £50 annual salary for an Excise officer sounds like a lot, but, Paine noted, it amounts actually to one shilling, ninepence farthing a day: taxes, charity and sitting expenses, horse-keeping and house rent, must all be deducted from the gross amount. Moreover, that amount does not take into account "the excessive price of all necessaries of life." The flexibility of money and the deceptions of the wage removed customary forms of compensation. "There are no perquisites or advantages in the least annexed to the employment," such as the "cabbage" or accompanying benefits Paine would have enjoyed as a stay-maker in the tailoring trades. The absence of such perquisites introduced the problem of dishonesty and crime. Wages, Paine stated, had replaced commoning.

This takes us to his second argument, based on religion. He quotes an ancient Hebrew wise man, Agur, who was against class division between rich and poor. The rich person's temptation was to become proud; for the poor, it was to steal.[26] For both, estrangement of the spirit is the result. "There is a great gulf fixed" is the scripture of implacable class division. Lazarus the beggar was in heaven and the rich man Dives was in hell—forever!

Paine's third argument is philosophical. "A very little degree of that dangerous kind of philosophy, which is the almost certain effect of involuntary poverty, will teach men to believe that to starve is more criminal than to steal." "The bread of deceit is a bread of bitterness; but alas! How few in times of want and hardship are capable of thinking so: objects appear under new colors and in shapes not naturally their own; hunger sucks in the deception and necessity reconciles it to conscience." The sharpness of want overcomes the tenderness of conscience. He concludes on a literary note: "But poverty, like grief, has an incurable deafness, which never hears; the oration loses all its edge; and 'To be, or not to be' becomes the only question."

Paine observed, based on bitter experience, that the office of the Excise men, "removes them far from all their natural friends and relations" and the occasional assistance "which even the poorest among the poor enjoys. Most poor mechanics, or even common laborers, have some relations or friends, who, either out of benevolence or pride, keep their children from nakedness, supply them occasionally with perhaps half a hog, a load of wood, a chaldron of coals." Paine refers to actual commoning, as opposed to the theoretical variety. As ever, "the commons" is best understood not as abstract justice but as fulfillment of actual need.[27] The criminalization of customary practices in commoning was backed up by the gallows. Firsthand experience had taught Paine the evils of wage-slavery.

The Death Penalty

Right outside the door of Paine's family home in Thetford, on Gallows Hill, the pitiable wretches ("examples of their country's laws") swung in the strong winds that blew in from the North Sea. The Lent Assizes met in Thetford, and the young Paine was a regular witness to the operation of state terror. A month after he was born three men swung: a former ship's carpenter for stealing money and goods to the value of 20 shillings; "a poor stupid Creature"[28] who stole a bushel of wheat from a barn and a woman's purse on the highway; and John Painter, a warrener and family man, who stole a parcel of tea but protested his innocence to the end. All were heinous offenses to a regime of property. By the age of eight the lad had absorbed the diction of the gallows. When his pet bird died he composed the lines

Here lies the body of John Crow,
Who once was high but now is low;

Ye brother Crows take warning all
For as you rise, so must you fall.

The year he began his apprenticeship a woman was burned to death at the stake in Ely only ten miles away. It was a barbaric society. As Paine would later write, "Every place has its Bastille, and every Bastille its despot." He knew whereof he spoke: his father's Quaker meetinghouse stood next to the town gaol.

Paine's birthday, January 29, 1737, was a significant date: one associated with regicide. January 29 is the eve of the anniversary of Charles I's beheading in 1649, an act which ushered in the English Revolution. In England republicans of every stripe remembered the day, as did monarchists who called Charles a martyr. Two years before Paine's birth, the last meeting of the Calves' Head Club took place. A secret gathering held annually to commemorate the death of monarchy and all that it stood for, the Club had met to toast "the worthy patriots who killed the tyrant" secretly after the Restoration; its meetings were discontinued after 1735 when the London house where the assorted republicans were dining was smashed and destroyed by the mob.

Later, in America, Paine reminds his erstwhile countrymen of their past. In his *Crisis Papers* issued during the American Revolution Paine called for revolution in the mother country: "England is unsettled. Take heed! Remember the times of Charles the first!" "Your present King and Ministry will be the ruin of you; and you had better risk a revolution and call a Congress than be thus led on from madness to despair, and from despair to ruin. America has set you the example, and may you follow it and be free."[29]

Regicide was never far from his mind, especially around his birthday.[30] Though a revolutionary opposing the puppet-show of sovereignty, the abject wretchedness of despotism, and the warmaking essential to monarchy, he was also opposed to capital punishment. He never advocated the assassination of George III. In France he refused to vote for the execution of Louis XVI, remembering the example of Charles I whose execution created a royalist party where there had been none before. Alone in Paris in 1794, the fifty-six-year-old Paine was cast into prison, escaping the guillotine only by an amazing accident. The cell doors along the prison corridor of those to be guillotined were chalked the night before, but Paine's door was not yet closed. Swung open against the wall, in the dim light it was chalked on the wrong side. When closed at the end of the evening it displayed the unchalked side the following morning, when the executioners came calling. The angel of death had passed him by.

In the nineteenth century the anniversary of the regicide, January 30, was no longer much observed. On the other hand, the birthday of Tom Paine,

January 29, became the occasion for banquets, drinks, and celebrations by American reformers from William Lloyd Garrison in the nineteenth century to C. Wright Mills in the twentieth.

Revolution and Constutitution

In November 1774 Paine arrived in Philadelphia so sick that he had to be carried off the ship. He found "the disposition of the people such, that they might have been led by a thread and governed by a reed."[31] His metaphor was taken literally, the reed and thread of the former corset-maker becoming the means to stiffen the backbone of the disenchanted, in preparation for the revolutionary break.

His first articles written in Philadelphia were on India, the focus for British imperialism, and against slavery. Britain has, he stated, done little but "rip up the bowels of whole countries for what she could get;—like Alexander she has made war her sport, and inflicted misery for prodigality's sake. The blood of India is not yet repaid, nor the wretchedness of Africa yet requited. Of late she has enlarged her list of national cruelties by her butcherly destruction of the Caribbs of St. Vincent's." The reduction of India was "an extermination of mankind," and England's "cruelties in the East-Indies will never, never be forgotten."[32]

Fourteen months after arriving in the New World, Paine published *Common Sense*, with its themes of unity, independence, and equality. To attain them the government of Great Britain must be overthrown by force. Already he defends the "rights of all Mankind." Indeed for Paine, the rights of mankind and of the free and independent state of America were inseparable. Fully aware of proletarian energies (sailors, emigrants, servants, slaves, journeymen), Paine reminded his readers that the country "is every day tottering on the brink of commotion and disturbance." He warns that "the mind of the multitude is left at random." Another kind of line is being drawn, a class line, and it gives ominous meaning to one of his most powerful images: "the least fracture now will be like a name engraved with the point of a pin on the tender rind of a young oak; the wound will enlarge with the tree, and posterity read it in full grown characters." He sees society in two parts. The male and the female are divisions of nature, he says; the good and the bad are the divisions of heaven, but the class division between rich and poor parallels the division of king and subject.

The shock and power of the pamphlet arises from its ridicule of kingship—"the principal ruffian of some restless gang"—and of English kings in particular, starting with William the Conqueror in 1066, "a French bastard landing with an armed banditti . . . a very paltry rascally original." Paine made the high and mighty look not only human but criminal. This was no carnival, turning the world upside down as a temporary joke or relief: he was in earnest, and so were his propertied and less courageous backers like Benjamin Rush. The pride of kings has laid "the world in blood and ashes." The crime of king-ship was a crime of despotic rule going back to the origins of states and classes.

The people's war, Paine asserts, will be fought with the people's means. Soldiers will elect their own officers. Even the mobilization of munitions procurement was based on the organization of the domestic kitchen. At the time he was drafting *Common Sense* he was also showing "the practicality of a Salt-Petre Association for voluntarily supplying the public Magazines with Gun-powder." By conducting experiments using saucepans and soup bowls to extract from the soils of the stable, barn, and cellar, a treasure could be collected which "to a free people [is] more valuable than the mines of Peru or Mexico," namely potassium nitrate.[33] To Paine, then, revolution was a practical matter, and its means (popular mobilization) were closely related to its purposes (popular sovereignty). Revolution was also a cosmic force, its principles in consonance with those of the universe. In this respect it can be compared to the south Andean notion of *pachakuti*. In the Quechua and Aymara languages, *pacha* means earth or cosmos, *kuti* means a turning over. It combines sacred and profane notions. Both the Bolivian and the Zapatista movements are based upon the re-membering of a past mutilated by coloni-alism. Paine frequently referred to the planet earth and its revolution around the sun. Here "Revolution" concerns recurrence as well the restoration of balance in a world that is otherwise out of whack.

While in London in 1758 Paine had bought a pair of globes, one terrestrial, the other celestial. He took lessons on their use from the Scottish astronomer and mechanic James Ferguson. Paine's six months at sea had contributed to his knowledge of the stars. He knew the difference between the rotation of the earth and the revolution of the earth, and never wrote far from his globes, or far from their science.

Thomas Paine thought globally; America was his Archimedean point. He was of that English generation of mechanics and artisans whose inven-tions transformed the material infrastructure and industrialized labor. Paine himself dreamt up, invented and modeled a single-spanned, iron bridge, and tried to realize it across the Schuylkill, the Thames, and the Seine. In *Crisis* no. 8 (February 26, 1780) he wrote that "Natural philosophy, mathematics and astronomy, carry the mind from the country to the creation, and give it a fitness suited to the extent." This ability to think both locally and globally was evident throughout his prose, for example in his 1772 *The Case of the Officers of Excise*: "The rich, in ease and affluence, may think I have drawn an unnatural portrait, but could they descend to the cold regions of want, the circle of polar poverty, they would find their opinions changing with the climate." In *Crisis* no. 5 (March 21, 1778) he writes: "Had it not been for America there had been no such thing as freedom left throughout the whole universe." His passion for America left him reaching for superlatives: "the sun never shined on a cause of greater worth," "a new method of thinking hath arisen," "posterity . . . will be affected to the end of time," "we have it in our power to begin the world over again." "Contemplating a subject that embraces with equatorial magnitude the whole region of humanity," he writes, "blends the individual, the nation, and the world." This is revolutionary scaling.

"Counter-revolution," like the "United States of America," was a phrase or neologism invented by Paine. He did not find a place for himself in post-revolutionary America, or during its counter-revolution, so he returned to England. George Washington needed his pen during the American Revolution in 1776–83, but abandoned Paine to the guillotine during the French Revolution in 1793–94. Paine called Washington "an apostate or an impostor,"[34] the choice of term depending on whether it was felt that Washington had either abandoned good principles—or that he ever had any in the first place.

The great debate about the French Revolution, and revolution generally, began, paradoxically, with an Irishman (Burke) creating the conservative style and arguments, and an Englishman (Paine) responding with the fresh eloquence of the radical. The first round in the debate was Dr. Richard Price's sermon, "Discourse on the Love of Country," on November 4, 1789, the anniversary of the Compromise of 1688. Price was a Welsh Dissenter and philosopher, a friend of Benjamin Franklin, and an advocate of American Independence. He upheld liberty of conscience, resistance to abusive power, and the rights to choose our own governors, cashier them for misconduct, and frame government for ourselves. Round two was Edmund Burke's *Reflections on the Revolution in France*, published in November 1790. In lurid, erudite, extravagant, hyperbolic writing it denounced the French Revolution. George III said "every gentleman should read it." Infamously Burke called the people "the swinish multitude" and drew the class line against people such as Paine: "The occupation of an hair-dresser, or of a working tallow-chandler, cannot be a matter of honor to any person."

Paine the corset-maker did not take the bait. Round three came with Paine's *Rights of Man*, Part One of which was finished on his fifty-fourth birthday, January 29, 1791. Priced at 3 shillings, it became a publishing phenomenon. It defended the French Revolution, linking it to the American Revolution and to ideas of popular sovereignty. To this day it provides a readable introduction to the events of French Revolution, laying out the main arguments against monarchy and hereditary rule; it created, too, a new style of writing that was accessible to the population as a whole. It made kingship appear ridiculous, and Burke pompous and irrelevant. In February 1792 Paine issued Part Two of *Rights of Man*. In it, Paine's class hostility was vivid ("All monarchical governments are military. War is their trade, plunder and revenue their objects."), the meaning of constitution clear ("a constitution is not an act of a government, but of a people constituting government"), and his internationalism universal ("My country is the world, and my religion is to do good").[35] What made Part Two so dangerous to the existing capitalist regime in Britain was its forthright translation of equality in economic terms, and its overall tone of democratic confidence. "The graceful pride of truth knows no extremes, and preserves, in every latitude of life, the right-angled character of man."[36]

The British government fought back against Paine's book, and against widespread dissent, with every weapon at its disposal. A proclamation against "wicked and seditious writing" was issued; the book police patrolled every nook and cranny; spies dogged Paine's every step; a loose word at a tavern became the basis of prosecution; the government hired scurrilous writers and bought mobs; Paine was burnt in effigy. In December 1792 he was outlawed, but by that time he had fled England to take the seat in the French Assembly to which he had recently been elected.

Hannah Arendt recognized the importance of the several meanings the constitution has had in American life. Thomas Paine developed two of them: the acts by which a people constitute themselves as a body politic; and a written document. The awe or blind worship towards it may thus be either a revolutionary event of self-determination or a kind of totem with institutional backing of law and jurisprudence. To Paine, "the continual use of the word Constitution in the English Parliament, shows there is none; and that the whole is merely a form of government without a Constitution, and constituting itself with what powers it pleases."[37] To worship the constitution may be to cherish the potentialities of democratic action and not at all the somnolence of sanctimonious idolatry. It is vain to govern beyond the grave, each generation must "begin the world over again." In the twenty-first century it is obvious that the acts of constitution must focus on housing, health, water, and food.

"My country is the world, and my religion is to do good" he wrote in *Rights of Man*. On November 4, 1791, in London, celebrating the anniversary of the English Revolution of 1688 and replying to speeches in his honor, he proposed "The Revolution of the World," a toast that echoed throughout the world, and down centuries. To name but a few examples: eighteenth-century Ireland, nineteenth-century India, and twentieth-century Indonesia.

Paine had a huge impact on Ireland and many close links with it. The Belfast volunteers toasted Thomas Paine in 1791: "May his principles of common sense establish the rights of man." In that year alone ten thousand copies of *Rights of Man* were distributed throughout the country, replacing the Psalter and the prayer book in Cork. Wolfe Tone called the book "the Koran of Belfast." In Ulster the British assessed the situation, Brigadier General Knox writing the Duke of Abercorn: "There is great alarm here as to the state of the country. The north is certainly inoculated by Paine, who persuades every man to think himself a legislator and to throw off all respect for his superiors." After the United Irish were proscribed, some went to America, others to Paris. There in 1793, Lord Edward Fitzgerald, who cast away his title in exchange for Citizen Edward, lodged with Paine, saying "there is a simplicity of manner, a goodness of heart, and strength of mind in him, that I never knew a man before possess." Paine's American publisher was an Irishman who promoted Irish invasion plans. On a personal level Paine's trajectory followed that of these revolutions, suffering defeat with the counter-revolution. With the failure of the French invasion of Ireland Paine drank away his sorrows with the Irish exile, Napper Tandy. Before leaving for America Paine met the brilliant young Irish revolutionary, Robert Emmet, whose speech in the dock in 1803 was memorized by the young Abraham Lincoln. Reportedly, Paine was Lincoln's favorite author.[38]

In India, the key figure in the dissemination of Paine's work was Henry Louis Vivian Derozio (1809–31), appointed lecturer in 1828 at the secular Hindu College in Calcutta. He urged his students to read *Rights of Man* and *The Age of Reason*, parts of which were translated into Bengali. An American publisher exported a thousand copies into Calcutta.[39] Derozio's students were inspired and radicalized, breaking caste taboos by (for example) eating with one another, irrespective of caste. Derozio caused a backlash by conservative Hindus, and was discharged in 1831. His students were on the vanguard of cultural nationalism. Derozians adhered to the motto, "He who will not reason is a bigot, he who cannot reason is a fool, and he who does not reason is a slave."

In 1945 the national liberation fighters in Indonesia addressed K'tut Tantri, "We, the guerrilla fighters of Java Timor, know only too well the suffering and torture that you have been subjected to by the Japanese, just as we know how the Dutch persecuted you for so many years." Formerly Muriel Pearson, K'tut Tantri was born on the Isle of Man, and was a Hollywood painter and Bohemian hotelier in Bali who refused to knuckle down under Dutch imperialism, and who refused to flee from the Japanese invasion. After her release from prison at the end of the Second World War, the anti-imperialist guerrillas stated that "It is our great hope that K'tut Tantri will join the Indonesian Revolution, and become to us the Mrs. Thomas Paine of Indonesia." Left between "laughter and tears," she made her choice and became an important courier, journalist, and broadcaster as "Surabaya Sue," speechwriter to Sukarno in the Indonesian war of independence, which she actively compared to the American Revolution of 1776. Like Paine, she was British by birth, fled her country of origin, was controversial, an independence fighter, was labeled extremist by her enemies, and narrowly escaped execution. Like him, too, the USA turned against her, denying her a passport in 1949, the same year that the FBI ordered the removal from public libraries of Howard Fast's influential wartime biographical novel, *Citizen Tom Paine*, as well as his one-volume selection of Paine's *Works*.[40]

The Commons Again

"Government does not consist in a contrast between prisons and palaces, between poverty and pomp; it is not instituted to rob the needy of his mite, and increase the wretchedness of the wretched,"[41] Paine wrote in *Rights of Man*, though in 1792 this is exactly what the British government was doing. Consequently, it was a period of intense, exciting revival of debate about commoning as a practice and communism as a theory. William Godwin's *An Inquiry into Political Justice* (1791) was an overintellectualized promotion of communism, while James Pilkington's *The Doctrine of Equality of Rank* (1795) was published in a year of dearth and high grain prices, and Thomas Spence's tracts also found fertile ground.

Paine had lived in London during the debates of 1772 for the repeal of the laws against forestalling, the practice of withholding grain from the market to force prices up—this was a classic moment in the attempt to defeat the "moral economy" and replace it with *laissez-faire*. During the American war Paine sat on the price-fixing committees, established in Philadelphia, against war profiteering. During this aggressive formation of capitalist *laissez-faire*, William Ogilvie in *Essay on the Right of Property in Land* (1781) argued that the commons and wastes should be distributed to the poor, while James Murray's *Sermons to Asses* (1768) renewed the redistribution theory of jubilee, and Richard Price's *Observations on Reversionary Payments* (1771) opposed enclosure.

Three global forces of the time made these debates urgent. One was the invasion of the Ohio valley and the robbery of the lands, forests, and waters of the Iroquois. This was done in the name of civilization and inevitability. The second was the enclosure acts in England, passed in the name of progress and improvement in the period 1760 to 1830. The third was the 1793 Permanent Settlement in Bengal, which privatized and commodified the land. "The life of an Indian is a continual holiday, compared with the poor of Europe; and on the other hand, it appears to be abject when compared to the rich," Paine writes in *Agrarian Justice*. "Civilization therefore, or that which is so called, has operated two ways, to make one part of society more affluent, and the other more wretched, than would have been the lot of either in a natural state."[42]

The English edition of *Agrarian Justice* appeared in 1797. Its publication was provoked by a sermon delivered by Richard Watson, the Bishop of Llandaff, whose "Apology for the Bible in a Series of Letters, Addressed to Thomas Paine," was written in answer to Paine's *The Age of Reason*. "It is wrong to say God made rich and poor," Watson sniffed; "He made only male and female; and He gave them the earth for their inheritance." It does not surprise us that William Blake, the London artisan poet, damned Watson as "a State trickster" with "cloven foot." But at a time when an international campaign was attempting to smear Paine as an atheist, it is interesting to find Blake, the Christian antinomian, writing in his defense: "To defend the Bible in this year 1798 would cost a man his life." Blake believed that Paine's "Energetic Genius" led him to perform miracles: "Is it a greater miracle to feed five thousand men with five loaves than to overthrow all the armies of Europe with a small pamphlet?"[43]

The Duke of Grafton's successful efforts at land privatizations no doubt encouraged the same in his neighbor Lord Cornwallis, formerly commander of British armies in America, who returned to his Suffolk estates to lick his wounds following the British surrender to the American revolutionary forces at Yorktown in 1781. Cornwallis instigated the "Great Gleaning Case" of 1788, in which the court in *Steel v. Houghton* (Mary Houghton, an agricultural laborer, gleaned on his lands in Timworth, a few miles south of Thetford) declared unequivocally against the law of Moses and centuries of customary practice by declaring that "no person has, at common law, a right to glean in the harvest field."[44] It was such criminalizing of customary access to the means of production and subsistence that played a decisive role in the creation of the proletariat. Paine returned to England in September 1787 and journeyed to Thetford to visit his mother. One doubts that he crossed paths with Cornwallis, though one easily pictures him (it was harvest time), if not passing Mary Houghton at Timworth, then encountering other crowds of gleaners singing on the way to and from the fields.

In war Paine did not conceal his class fury. He warned the British in New York, "as you do so shall you be done by," reminding them that "there is not a Nobleman's country seat but may be laid in ashes by a single person." Moreover, the ships on the Thames, the East India House, and the Bank, "neither are nor can be secure from this sort of destruction."[45] He records a deep experience, as old as human agriculture itself, in Part Two of *Rights of Man*. He is explaining the meaning of the phrase "the landed interest." The phrase conceals the class relationship: who does the work, who takes the product. The landed interest are the aristocrats and their "pillar," the House of Lords. But Paine reminds us:

> Were that pillar to sink into the earth, the same landed property would continue, and the same ploughing, sowing, and reaping would go on. The aristocracy are not the farmers who work the land, and raise the produce, but are the mere consumers of the rent; and when compared to the active world are the drones, a seraglio of males, who neither collected the honey nor form the hive, but exist only for lazy enjoyment.[46]

He knew whereof he spoke. That is the context for Paine's tremendous description:

> Every individual, high or low, is interested in the fruits of the earth; men, women, and children, of all ages and degrees, will turn out to assist the farmer, rather than the harvest should not be got in; and they will not act thus by any other property. It is the only one for which the common prayer of mankind is put up, and the only one that can never fail from want of means. It is the interest, not of the policy, but of the existence of man, and when it ceases, he must cease to be.[47]

From the first word to the last, the existence of the individual is, at bottom, a collective labor of the whole. Here, society is not an abstraction of market relations; it is an actual and mighty phenomenon of collective human labor. We hear in this passage, not the signs of the utilitarianism to come, but the divine theology of the labor theory of Winstanley. The harvest was the central event of the year. The diction is that of English Protestantism ("fruits of the earth"): the repetition of distinctions of rank ("high or low," "all . . . degrees"); the invocation of and allusion to the central prayer of Christianity ("give us this day our daily bread"). Doubtless as a youth Paine entered into harvest labor. *Homo faber*, Thomas Paine was a man of the hammer and the scythe, as well as needle and thread. He continued his joke against Edmund Burke about "swabbing the deck" clean of monarchs to include aristocracy: Burke, he said, "has mowed down and thinned the House of Peers, with a scythe as formidable as Death and Time."[48]

Two hundred years later an East Anglian harvester explained the centrality of harvest in the lives of the working:

> There was still no money about. People seemed to live without it. They also lived without the Church. I'm sorry about this but it is true . . . The holy time was the harvest. "Tell me your harvest bargain," the farmer

said to the harvesters. So the men chose a harvest lord who told the farmer how much they wanted to get the harvest in . . . We reaped by hand. You could count thirty mowers in the same field, each followed by his partner, who did the sheaving . . . The lord sat atop of the last load to leave the field and then the women and children came to glean the stubble . . . we all went shouting home. Shouting in the empty fields— I don't know why. But that's what we did. We'd shout so loud that the boys in the next village would shout back.[49]

Blake, some two centuries before, had heard something similar and in 1797 added an instrumental arrangement:

They took [the sheaves] into the wide barns with loud rejoicings & triumph
Of flute & harp & drum & trumpet horn & clarion[50]

The composers of the nineteenth and twentieth centuries continued to tramp the fields at harvest time listening to the people's songs.

The strongest expression of the theme of the commons comes in Paine's short 1795 pamphlet *Agrarian Justice, Opposed to Agrarian Law and to Agrarian Monopoly*. Recent scholarship has tended to downplay its importance, discrediting socialist theories. In 1970 Gwyn Williams noted that it is often overlooked that the pamphlet was a response to Babeuf's *Conspiracy of Equals*. Twenty years on Gregory Claeys noted that it was still the most neglected of Paine's major works.[51] Written in the winter of 1795–96 and published in 1797, *Agrarian Justice* had a well-defined polemical and political context as well as a disastrous economic and social one. 1795 was a year of starvation in England and France alike, and of desperate responses: food rioting was widespread. State-driven political and military violence was rampant, prison construction flourished, and regional army barracks were built.

The pamphlet's political context was, more generally, the French Revolution, and in particular the Babeuf conspiracy, which was uncovered in May 1796; its leaders were guillotined a year later. Babeuf is traditionally held to have been the founder of modern communism, uniting the urban insurrectionary coup with the theory of Agrarian Law that landed property should be equal to all. Paine opposed the attempt at insurrection, while John Adams had articulated his fears of Agrarian Law in 1776. In France, to advocate it was punishable by death.

John Thelwall compared the "gigantic mind of Thomas Paine" to Licinius and Gracchus, authors of the agrarian law of ancient Rome.[52] In *Agrarian Justice*, Paine develops the argument that "all individuals have legitimate birthrights in a certain species of property."[53] Here is where he distinguishes natural from artificial property, personal property from capital. Paine asks us to consider the Indians of North America, because among them "those spectacles of human misery which poverty and want present to our eyes in all the towns and streets in Europe" do not exist.[54] Poverty, he deduces, is manmade, created by civilization. Paine relies on his own empirical encounters with American Indians. In 1777 he led a diplomatic delegation to Easton, Pennsylvania, to meet with scores of members of the Six Nations of the Iroquois Confederacy led by Chief Last Night. The earth is "the common property of the human race," he writes.[55] Its cultivation without indemnification has created poverty and wretchedness. The landed interest took the property of the dispossessed, partly by "the agrarian law of the sword."[56]

"The present state of civilization is as odious as it is unjust. It is the reverse of what it ought to be, and it is necessary that a revolution should be made in it. The contrast of affluence and wretchedness continually meeting and offending the eye, is like dead and living bodies chained together."[57] This was a common scene in the slave trade and one which Paine probably witnessed first hand, in the epidemic which ravaged the cargo of indentured servants carried in the ship bringing him to America in 1774. "Uncivilization," as he called it, produced such atrocities. "When, in countries that are called civilized, we see age going to the workhouse and youth to the gallows, something must be wrong in the system of government." He finds that the number of poor people actually increases with the advance of so-called civilization; they are becoming "an hereditary race."

Paine proposed, as a solution, that the state distribute a lump sum to everyone on their twenty-first birthday, enough to buy a cow and a few acres, in other words enough to live on, a subsistence. He also advocates a similar sum being granted to everyone on reaching retirement, on their fiftieth birthday, such subventions to be paid from an inheritance tax. In *Rights of Man*, Paine had defended himself against the charge of levelling. Nevertheless, in *Agrarian Justice*, he observed that a

> revolution in the state of civilization is the necessary companion of revolutions in the system of government . . . Despotic government supports itself by abject civilization, in which debasement of the human mind, and wretchedness in the mass of the people, are the chief criterions. Such governments consider man merely as an animal; that the exercise of intellectual faculty is not his privilege; *that he has nothing to do with the laws but to obey them*; and they politically depend more upon breaking the spirit of the people by poverty, than they fear enraging it by desperation.[58]

This is a decisive insight: poverty is deliberately created for political purposes.

While Paine advocated the household production of gunpowder, another contrasting style of innovation was practiced by the British war machine, which produced gunpowder at its arsenal in Walthamstow, east London. Before becoming the Divine who attacked Paine on behalf of class society, Richard Watson was a professor of chemistry, and it will not surprise us to find that he was a colleague and correspondent of Cornwallis. In 1787 he found a way of improving the manufacture of gunpowder so that a cannon ball weighing 68 lbs could be fired 273 feet instead of the usual 172. This innovation was worth more than £100,000 a year. Let us listen at a royal levee to Watson's obsequious mewlings, "On my saying that I ought to be ashamed of myself inasmuch as it was a scandal in a Christian bishop to instruct men in the mode of destroying mankind, the king answered, 'let not that afflict your conscience, for the quicker the conflict, the less the slaughter.'"[59] Unpacking this simple anecdote, we see that hideous modern combination where science and religion promote the state and war. Such a murderous knot of fake spirituality and murderous technology is the essence of modern savagery leading directly to, for instance, the twentieth-century bombings from Guernica to the Enola Gay. Against it, Thomas Paine took up his pen to slice through the horrid knot, again and again and again. The war machine with its miniature companion, the death penalty, brutalized human beings as conquest and criminalization expanded the regime of expropriated property. "War is the art of conquering at home."

Paine concluded the second part of *Rights of Man* as follows: "It is now towards the middle of February," he says. "Were I to take a turn into the country, the trees would present a leafless winterly appearance. As people are apt to pluck twigs as they walk along, I perhaps might do the same, and by chance might observe, that a *single bud* on that twig had begun to swell."[60] This gentle sentence is the key to Paine: notice how in the logic and the grammar of it the author follows the reader. Furthermore, the sentence expresses the first step in reaching an accurate conclusion about the real world, the scientific method begins with the making of an observation. Then comes the second step, reasoning.

> I should reason very unnaturally, or rather not reason at all, to suppose *this* was the *only* bud in England which had this appearance. Instead of deciding thus, I should instantly conclude, that the same appearance was beginning, or about to begin, everywhere; and though the vegetable sleep will continue longer on some trees and plants than on others, and though

some of them may not *blossom* for two or three years, all will be in leaf in the summer, except those which are *rotten*.[61]

Nations and individuals are his matter. Some people can flower—that is, learn, flourish, speak, and act—some quicker than others, some not at all. Likewise, some nations can throw off despotism. "What pace the political summer may keep with the natural, no human foresight can determine. It is, however, not difficult to perceive that the spring is begun."[62] The essential point, popular sovereignty, is introduced at last as an adjective and the seasons or the summer, the turning of the earth on its axis towards the sun, is the real world of us all—"the political summer." The paragraph ends with the powerful word "spring," here as one of the seasons, and as we now think about it as one of the stages in revolutionary transformation. But spring is also a verb, a very active one, sudden, a leap. And this is what revolutionaries do—they jump and they surprise, here, there, all over. They do it together, and nowadays we do it by commoning.

Paine guides us; he helps us think. But we do the thinking. The only thing in the passage which might give us pause—it is two centuries old—is that we live in post-enclosure time: our country, our world, is closed, shut up. His had not yet been, or not completely. So we pause . . . and remember, as he wrote in *Rights of Man*, "the greatest forces that can be brought into the field of revolutions, are reason and common interest."[63]

Thetford–Oaxaca–Detroit
February 2009

CHAPTER TWELVE

Meandering at the Crossroads of Communism and the Commons

THE STORY BEGINS AT BLUE MOUNTAIN LAKE IN THE ADIRONDACKS WHEN, AT A GATH-ering of cultural workers for the commons and through no wish of their own, Peter and George Caffentzis were asked to speak about violence and the commons. Accordingly, following dinner after what had been a chilly October day, they settled into armchairs by the fire and explained to the gathering that way back in the day (history) the commons was taken away by blood and fire and that, furthermore, as we all basically knew, it was still violently happening which ever way you happened to look. Indeed, this violent taking-away, or "expropriation," was the beginning of proletarianization and thus of capitalism itself!

George added that he thought that there was a difference between the commons and "the tradition of communism" which began in the 1840s. Peter (that's me) wasn't so sure about that, thinking that it was earlier, and that in any case there was considerable overlap. He said something about Cincinnati and promised to get back to everyone. So, making good on that promise, here's what I had in mind.

Not far from Blue Mountain Lake, on the western side of those ancient mountains, is Whitestown, NY, known to you already perhaps as the location of the Oneida commune where property was once communistically shared. But that particular utopia wasn't established until 1848, after our story had well begun.[1] Our story continues with two brothers, Augustus and John Otis Wattles, who left the Oneida Institute, a Presbyterian outfit, in 1833 and 1836 respectively. Their destination was "the gateway to the west," Cincinnati, the fastest growing city in North America at the time, a.k.a. Porkopolis, a meat market in more senses than one, where people slaughtered swine and hunted man, woman, child.

Augustus moved to attend the Lane Seminary in Cincinnati whose president was Harriet Beecher Stowe's father. Augustus helped form the Lane Seminary Rebels, ultra evangelical abolitionists, and he helped start the Ohio Anti-Slavery Society. Sabbath services, night school. Lyceum and library, day and night school offering courses on topics such as sewing or salvation. In the next two decades he founded twenty-five schools in Ohio for African American children.

John worked as a tutor in Augustus schools for blacks.[2] "Colors are more vivid; odors more delicate, flowers more beautiful, and music more thrilling when tested by the senses of J.O.W. than by those of ordinary men—he transcended transcendentalism." John believed in diet reform, women's rights, abolition, and communal living. John attempted to build several utopian communities where "all things were held in common," and of them I'll tell you in due course.

Before that, however, a little etymology, and a trip to Paris.

"*Common* has an extraordinary range of meaning in English, and several of its particular meanings are inseparable from a still active social history," says the twentieth-century critic Raymond Williams.[3] The root word is *"communis*, Latin, derived alternatively, from *com-*, Latin—together, and *munis*, Latin—under obligation, and from *com-* and *unus*, Latin—one." It thus points to either "a specific group or to the generality of mankind." What is striking is the absence of the material or economic meanings which are so pervasive in local and agrarian history and from there into law.[4] We tend to think of the commons in relation to a specific place—John Clare on Northamptonshire, UK, or Lewis Henry Morgan on western New York, or Luke Gibbons on co. Kerry, Ireland—while communism concerns "the generality of mankind." In the actuality of commoning the place of children and the activities of women were more open, less enclosed, than in the subsequent regimes of private property.

Karl Marx himself wrote that such expropriations of commons were what first sparked his interest in economics or material questions, referring to the criminalization of a commoning practice in the Moselle River valley near Trier (where he was born).[5] In his day the vineyard workers fueled their winter stoves by customary takings of forest estovers (windfalls, dead wood, and such). Growing up, Marx knew something about this since his parents owned some vines themselves. This wood however was criminalized at the behest of the timber companies, and the young Marx was shocked into philosophical outrage which he expressed in a series of articles for the *Rheinische Zeitung*.[6] But the loss of the actual commons of his neighbors did not lead directly to the politics of communism. In his case nearly a decade intervened.

Marx remained a city man, Berlin, Brussels, Paris, London, and the urban proletariat became his subject of study and his hope for the future. The urban proletariat were commoners without a commons, their customs having been criminalized. The conjunction of the struggle to retain common rights with the urban struggle expressed in the food or subsistence riot became one of the factors of the revolutionary insurrections which annually punctuated the French Revolution. When this conjuncture takes place in conditions of cultural or racial oppression, as it has in Ireland, the preconditions of communism arise. This conjuncture has also given us, via the Irishman Bronterre O'Brien's translation of Buonarroti's *History of Babeuf's Conspiracy for Equality* (1836) the very powerful concept, the moral economy.[7]

"More than any other movement within the revolutionary tradition, communism was born with a name," writes a scholar.[8] This begs the question assuming as it does the relative novelty of the practice of cooperation and sharing in the use of land, means of production, and means of subsistence when it was precisely this novelty which the recovery of commoning challenged. Conversely, it correctly implies that commoning did not have a name. We find this over and over again. Part of the power of *The Communist Manifesto* was that it conflated both the revolutionary future of communism (the spectre haunting Europe) and the hidden obviousness, the invisible given, of the commons in the present. The hobgoblin (as "spectre" was first translated) belonged to a folk discourse that presupposed the commons.

The communist tradition is said to have started with Marx and Engels in *The Communist Manifesto* published in 1848. *The Oxford English Dictionary* quotes the first English translation (Helen MacFarlane's) of Marx and Engels's *The Communist Manifesto*. "It is not the abolition of property generally which distinguishes Communism; it is the abolition of Bourgeois property . . . In this sense, indeed, the Communists might resume their whole Theory in that single expression—The abolition of private property."

In March 1840 a conservative German newspaper wrote, "The Communists have in view nothing less than a leveling of society—substituting for the presently existing order of things the absurd, immoral and impossible utopia of a community of goods." In Lyons after the suppression of the revolt of 1834 a secret Society of Flowers survived which is sometimes called the first communist society. After the failure in 1839 of the revolt in Paris of August Blanqui another greenish name sprouted for the communists, and the Society of the Seasons was created.[9]

The actual appearance of the word, at least in English, occurred in 1840. The *OED* as its earliest recording in English of "communism" quotes Goodwyn Barmby writing in *The Apostle* in 1848. "I also conversed [in 1840] with some of the most advanced minds of the French metropolis, and there, in the company of some of the disciples of Babeuf, then called Equalitarians, I first pronounced the word Communism, which has since . . . acquired that worldwide reputation."

Who was Goodwyn Barmby? We know that at the age of sixteen he harangued the expropriated agricultural laborers of Suffolk against the New Poor Law. Then at the age of twenty with a letter from Robert Owen he crossed the English Channel to Paris to establish "regular communication between the socialists of Great Britain and France," calling himself a "friend of socialism in France, in England, and the world."[10] He reported that people were "on fire with the word" and he eagerly seized upon it himself.

I want to make three comments about this first use of "communism" in English. First of all, in opposition to the nationalism of the day or that patriotism which is the refuge of scoundrels, we note that communism right from the start was worldwide. He proposed an International Association that summer. In 1841 he formed the Central Communist Propaganda Society, later called the Communist Church. It had five branches including ones in London, Merthyr Tydfil in Wales and Strabane in Ireland. He corresponded with French, American, and Venezuelan communists or potential communists. Barmby was affected by the orientalism of the day and proposed that the best place to site the first utopia would be in Syria.[11] He toured the industrial midlands of England.

(Though Peter, your author here, received his advanced training as a social historian in Coventry at the University of Warwick and though he studied with one of the most knowledgeable of twentieth century English communists,[12] he never did hear tell of Goodwyn Barmby's 1845 tour into Warwick or his speech in Coventry on "Societary Science and the Communitive Life." What might he have missed? Barmby's *Book of Platonopolis* offers a clue containing as it does forty-four "societarian wants" for humanity and many scientific projects for the future, including a steam-driven automobile. Each community would have its own baptistery or hydropathic center complete with frigidary, calidary, tepidary, and frictionary for cold, hot, warm bathing followed by vigorous exercise.)

The second comment I wish to make concerns "the most advanced minds" of Paris. Readers understood that communism arose in the context of revolution. Parisian thought was advanced only in the context of a theory of the progress of history. Barmby's theory was this. History evolved through four stages. First, paradisation which was pastoral, clannish, and nestled in the Vale of Arcady. Second, barbarization, which was both feudal and municipal. Third was monopolism or civilization, and communization was to be the last. It too would go through four stages, first, the club or lodging house, second, the common production and consumption center, then the city, and finally the world. We note, incidentally, that he treats communism actively, as a verb, something which William Morris also would do at the end of the century.

A communist banquet was held on July 1, 1840, for one thousand artisans in Paris, and speaker after speaker extolled the "explosive impact" of communism. Albert Laponneraye and Théodore Dézamy, the organizers of the event, were "the true founders of modern communism."[13] Dézamy asked the "unhappy proletarians to reenter into the gyre of the egalitarian church, outside of which there can be no salvation." When another communist banquet was planned at the Institute of Childhood to celebrate the secular marriage ceremony of leading communists the government prohibited it. At its beginning communism was associated with both spirituality and reproduction. Barmby was in touch with William Weitling, the tailor and revolutionary, who also visited Paris and who also sought the followers of Babeuf. Weitling was active in the League of the Just which later became the Communist League which commissioned *The Communist Manifesto*.

The revolutionary egalitarians, François-Noël Babeuf and Restif de la Bretonne, were progenitors of modern communism during the French Revolution of 1789 which we celebrate on Bastille Day. Babeuf was a commoner from Picardy who became a proletarian canal navvy or ditch digger (hence, the first line of his autobiography, "I was born in the mud"). Babeuf, like Marx, had experience with the violence of commons expropriation, and like Marx, Babeuf became a communist revolutionary. In the trajectory of their biographies from commons to communism it was the crucible of international revolution which effected the transition.

Babeuf crossed paths with James Rutledge in May 1790 in Paris. Rutledge, a "citizen of the universe" as he called himself and an Anglo-Irishman, he petitioned for agrarian laws with "no ownership of property."[14] Perhaps it was a result of this encounter that led Babeuf to change his name to Gracchus indicating his utter revolutionary identification with the ancient Roman brother who advocated equality and the "agrarian law."

Babeuf publicized the radical feminist Confédération des Dames. He was secretary of Franco-Haitian Claude Fournier. Babeuf was imprisoned for six months when he wrote about his "co-athlete," as he called the carpenter's son, *A New History of the Life of Jesus Christ*. Accused of fomenting civil war, he said the war already existed of the rich against the poor. In November 1795 he published his *Plebeian Manifesto* calling for a total upheaval or *bouleversement total*. "Dying of Hunger, Dying of Cold" was the title of a popular song he wrote. In 1796 he placarded Paris with a poster beginning, "Nature has given to every man the right to the enjoyment of an equal share in all property." He was beheaded by the guillotine in May 1797.[15]

Restif de la Bretonne was called "Jean-Jacques des Halles," or the "Rousseau of the gutter." In 1785 he reviewed a book describing a communal experiment in Marseilles whose author, Victor d'Hupay, was the first to describe himself as a communist, and who later wrote a *Republican Koran*. He was inspired by Restif's *Le Paysan perverti*. In this private property is limited to clothing and furniture. Civilization had perverted the peasant whose philosophical community could be restored based on "the principles of the New World." America, the religious Moravians, and the *philosophe* Mably were the sources of communism. By Restif 1793 begins to use communism to describe common ownership. Restif's *Philosophie de Monsieur Nicolas* of 1796 spoke much about "communists." He attacked U.S. republicanism as being "nominal" only.

This ends our short trip to Paris. We can propose some short ruminated contrasting commons and communism. Commoning practices persist among workers and peasants, communism consists of the generalization of such practices. A historic role of the bourgeois state was to criminalize the commons; an aspiration of the communists was to overthrow the bourgeois state. Evidence of the commons will often appear anecdotal or as folklore or as "crime," just a small story, a minor transgression; evidence of commons may appear incidentally to some other, major theme; evidence of customary commons may appear particular to locale or craft, and belonging thus to trade or local histories, not "grand narratives." Evidence of communism, on the other hand, is provided by journalists, philosophers, economists, and controversialists, and grandiosely aspires to become the narrative to end narratives!

Goodwyn Barmby returned to England in 1841 as a feminist, a vegetarian, and a communist. He began to publish *The Promethean or Communitarian Apostle* ("the reign of the critic is over, the rule of the poet commences"). In its pages he urged, "Unitedly let the genii embrace communism, unitedly let the capacities apostolise for Communisation." In 1843 he started a Communitorium, named for Thomas More, the Moreville Communitorium where "persons desirous of progress upon universal principles are received in affection and intelligent fellowship."

The third comment on Barmby arises only after we cultural workers for the commons dispersed from Blue Mountain and after we had completed our farewell water ceremony led by the two soul sisters of Climbing PoeTree, we paddled our canoes into the lake on a night of the full moon. Yes, after that spiritual, therapeutical, and comical experience, I received intelligence from an International Commons gathering held in Berlin a month later, to the effect that evidently a faction had arisen and a tendency was described, of "religious revolutionary commoners." This certainly throws light on our story, because religion was a big part of communism!

"I believe . . . that the divine is communism, that the demoniac is individualism," testified Barmby. In France, England, and Germany this association of communism with religion was widespread. Propagandists exploited the tendency to identify communism with communion. Jesus was "the sublime egalitarian" whose first communion was the type of future communist banquets. Barmby wrote communist hymns and prayers. He demanded the restoration of the monastic lands confiscated by Henry VIII, not as monasteries of the past but as communisteries of the future.

Besides catching the fire of "communism" in Paris in 1840, Barmby also married in the same year, Catherine, a high-minded bohemian woman, who became his ardent helpmeet. She too was communist as we infer from her view expressed in 1844 that the female franchise "would be in vain" unless accompanied by opposition to private property. Women were active in the Communist Church. Barbara Taylor, the historian of socialism and feminism in this period, paints an affecting picture of the couple pushing a cart through the rainy streets of London (they had founded a communist group in Poplar, East London) and hawking their pamphlets to passers-by.

On returning from Paris she declaimed, "The mission of woman is discovered by Communism: will she hesitate to perform it: The grass is growing, sorrow is accumulating—waves are rushing, the world is warring—life and death, soul and body, are in the conflict, the saviour is in the hearts of the redeemed, and prophet is the inspired one, WOMAN LEARN THY MISSION! DO IT! AND FEAR NOT!—the world is saved."[16] They observed that "The Free Woman who shall give the womanly tone to the entire globe is not yet manifested." He wrote, "In fine, to be a true communist, or Socialist, the man must possess the woman-power as well as the man-power, and the woman must possess the man-power as well as the woman-power. Both must be equilibriated beings." Catherine proposed autonomous woman's societies in every city, town, and village.

Thomas Frost, his Chartist publisher, broke away and founded the *Communist Journal* to rival the Barmby's *Communist Chronicle*. Barmby claimed that copyright had been infringed and forbade its further use in a document sealed with Masonic symbols in green wax, "green being the sacred colour of the Communist Church."[17] With such backsliding into egotistical privatization we can get back to the Wattles brothers and Porkopolis. In 1847 Goodwyn Barmby was approached by John O. Wattles of Cincinnati, editor of the *Herald of Progression* and founder of a communist church of his own.[18] Wattles proposed to put "the wheat and corn of the west into the hands of the people of your country and keep it out of the hands of speculators." Here is the crux of this story, where the commons and communism intersect. It was a violent and heroic crossroads, literally and figuratively. Our story must stop its aimless meandering and begin to march with purpose.

"There had been a long Atlantic roll reverberating throughout the decade of the 1840s," writes the historian of English utopian experiments.[19] Could the New World with the commercial abundance of the Ohio Valley, come, as Tom Paine trumpeted in the earlier revolutionary generation, to the rescue of the Old World suffering during the "Hungry Forties" with millions starving especially in Ireland? In particular, could the communism of one side of the Atlantic help preserve that on the other side? Barmby and Wattles could not accomplish this alone, or independent of the powerful energies of the huge class forces at work.

Babeuf explained at his trial that the class war had begun already; it did not need him to start it. The same thought must be applied to the American Civil War, namely, from the standpoint of the enslaved workers the war of freedom had begun much earlier than 1860. Battles for freedom were fought night and day along the Ohio River valley. That is the reason that the freedom train was an *Underground* Railroad. Cincinnati was the train station. And here the most influential freedom story of the nineteenth century began.

Harriet Beecher Stowe was all ears at her father's Lane Seminary in 1838. Ripley, Ohio, was about fifty miles up river from Cincinnati. The river was the great thoroughfare from east to west; it was also the boundary between the slave states and the free states. It was both barrier and passage. One of the Rankin boys of Ripley told the incredible, nearly unbelievable story of the runaway slave woman who carried her baby across the river from Kentucky at night upon the slushy ice floes, falling into the freezing water, throwing her child on to firmer ice ahead of her, swimming, stumbling, running, falling, getting up again, with her pursuers and their barking dogs within earshot behind.[20] As young Rankin recounted the ordeal, Harriet Stowe absorbed every word, and thus Eliza was born the heroic figure of *Uncle Tom's Cabin* published in 1850, the book that more than any other turned world opinion against slavery.

In 1841 Augustus Wattles and his wife, Susan, bought 160 acres in Mercer County, Ohio, where they developed a manual labor school for black boys. It also contained, as he wrote, "Large farms under fence and cultivation. . . . Nearly every settler is a member of the Teetotal pledge, and *lawing* is almost unknown among them."[21] The community included twenty-one emancipated slaves. Seeking a location far away from commodity commerce, settler cupidity, and white racism, they settled in Mercer County where (as it happens) some fifty years earlier, November 4, 1791, the United States suffered the first of many defeats, the Battle of Wabash River, or St. Clair's Defeat. Here Little Turtle of the Miami Indians and Blue Jacket of the Shawnee led the confederation of indigenous people (including the Pottawatomie and Delaware) in wiping out the militia and regulars of General St. Clair, the first war fought by the USA and the first defeat of U.S. imperialism. The victory was temporary and the Battle of Fallen Timbers in 1794 put an end to effective armed resistance by the Indian confederation yet indigenous ideas of alternative economies and having "all things in common" persisted. The individual settler with his whiskey, Bible, and musket or the collective Indian horticulturalist with tomahawk and calumet were the stereotyped options.

Johann Georg Kohl, a German émigré from the revolution of 1848 sailed to Philadelphia and then spent six months in northern Michigan living with the Ojibway, whose "natural generosity develops into a species of communism," he wrote.[22] Lewis Henry Morgan published *League of the Ho-de-no-sau-nee, or Iroquois* in 1851 his study of the Seneca, Mohawk, Cayuga, Oneida, and Onondaga. He addressed the Grand Council of the Seneca in 1844. He was adopted by the Seneca in 1847 for fighting against the Ogden Land Co. in 1842. "The law of hospitality as administered by the American aborigines, tended to the final equalization of subsistence." "Its explanation must be sought in the ownership of lands in common, the distribution of their products to households consisting of a number of families, and the practice of communism in living in the household." Thus by the 1850s communism had become a term of art in anthropology or ethnography.[23]

After a decade Augustus Wattles lost his community to benefactors among the Philadelphia Quakers, and it became the Emlen Institute.[24] Homeless, he wrote in Biblical language, "Now I must wander in sheep skins and goat skins again and seek the caverns and dens of the earth." Augustus moved to small farm in Clermont County on the Ohio River. The town of Utopia is on Route 52 in this county on the Ohio River, founded in 1844 for French Fourierists. In 1845 his brother John asked him to join a utopian community.

In 1842 John Otis Wattles helped form Society for Universal Inquiry and Reform to eradicate government, capitalism, and coercive relationships. In 1844 he purchased land in Champaign County [or Logan County, sources differ], Ohio, to build Prairie Home, a community based on cooperative labor and common property. Its members ate at a common table. After six months it failed ("the selfish element was predominant"). Despite this failure I imagine that the vicinity retained enough of its reformist vibrations to influence later inhabitants. To the south lay the town of Yellow Springs, founded in 1825 by followers of the English socialist Robert Owen. It became a busy part of the Underground Railroad, and by 1851 the Antioch College was formed there. Celebrated alumni such as Stephen Jay Gould, Coretta Scott King, Harry Cleaver, and George Caffentzis renewed its anti-racist, anti-capitalist traditions, though I do not know that they knew of John Otis Wattles or the communism of the Prairie Home. The mole burrows deep.

John Wattles and his wife Edith moved to Cincinnati where he published the reform paper, *Herald of Progression*. In 1846 established a utopian community on the Ohio River called Excelsior and it was presumably from this one that he made his offer to Goodwyn Barmby, to ship grain without speculation, as one communist church to another communist church. However, tragedy struck in December 1847 when the Excelsior Community was washed away by floods with the loss of seventeen lives.

The Wattles brothers were conductors on the Underground Railroad, they were educators, and they were utopians who believed in having all things in common. The force behind them was the freedom struggle of the emancipating slaves, just as the force behind Goodwyn Barmby was the struggle for subsistence and the Charter by the factory workers of England.

The black population of Cincinnati lived on the border between slave and free and in constant danger of kidnapping. Its economy depended on good commercial relations with the slaveholders across the river. Native Americans came south down the river Miami, African Americans came north across the Ohio, settlers from Virginia came from the east, and settlers from New York via Pennsylvania also came from the east. Its population was heterogeneous. The location of white riots against African Americans in 1829, 1836, and 1841. The black community had churches, barbershops, schools, and a few commercial enterprises. It helped slaves off the steamboats, or across the river, concealing them in town. Residential patterns were dense and, perforce, cooperative. Many of the emancipated slaves had been purchased by friends, family, or kin. John Wattles canvassed black population finding that about one fifth were self-emancipated, i.e., purchased themselves.[25] As with the notorious pass laws of South African apartheid, papers had to be shown. Like the shack-dwellers of South Africa in other respects the community learned to fight collectively for water, security, roof. But that is not all. Everybody sang. At the Union Baptist Church and Bethel A.M.E. a white visitor reported, "Such hearty singing!— sometimes too fast, sometimes too slow, but to my ear music, because it was soul not cold science. . . . I went home happy, for I had not fed on husks."

John Mercer Langston (1829–1897) was in the vanguard of African American struggle in radical anti-slavery politics. He recruited soldiers in the black regiments during the Civil War and was an inspector of the Freedmen's Bureau after the Civil War. He was U.S. Minister to Haiti for eight years. His father was white and his mother was part Native American and part black, the child of an emancipated slave. Orphaned, he moved to Cincinnati in 1840. The Ohio Constitution of 1802 denied blacks the franchise. Large-scale riots engulfed the city in 1829 and 1836, expelling blacks and destroying an abolitionist press. Lower cost of living after depression of 1837 and "a near-barter economy."

The Baptist minister preached in 1837, "Ethiopia shall soon stretch forth her hand to God is the declaration of infinite goodness and wisdom. It must take place, and will doubtless be effected by human agency; and who so proper as educated colored people to be the heralds of the gospel, and teachers of science and civilization to their benighted brethren in all lands." This preacher did not teach Karl Marx directly. However, the human agency in whose power he never for a moment doubted, would lead to the American Civil War which, as Marx never doubted, was a leap in human emancipation.

When the black abolitionist Martin Delany visited in 1848, he noted of the teaching in the African American schools of Cincinnati, "They don't capitalize i," which he took to be a severe criticism whereas we, remembering it as a transcendental age, might give an inclusive meaning to the practice—unselfishness, a sign of the common!

John Langston attended the August 1 celebrations in 1841 commemorating the abolition of slavery in the British West Indies. A riot began on September 1 as city officials refused to intervene against white mobs, with bank closings, unstable economic conditions, and a press which blamed the abolitionist movement and the refusal to cooperate with the Fugitive Slave Law. City Blacks defended themselves with arms successfully at first, but the combination of martial law and mob law prevailed. It was most severe urban outbreak against blacks in antebellum America. John ran through the backyards, over fences, across bridges, evading the police to protect his brother. Thrilled by courage of black defenders, and thrilled too by news of Cinque and the mutiny aboard the slave ship *Amistad*. He lived with family and boarders of seventeen persons.

In school he wrote an essay on Alfred the Great, the beloved monarch of British history and the only one they call great. "I think if the colored people study like King Alfred they will soon do away with the evil of slavery." He would have identified with Alfred, who to fight another day had to flee a military rout and seek refuge in a poor woman's house where, legend has it, while she went to the well to fetch water, he—such a klutz in the kitchen!— let the cakes burn in the oven. From Alfred the Great to those dispersed after Hurricane Katrina the refuge from disaster depends on the kindness of strangers. It is how commons are renewed and class solidarity is maintained, starting in the kitchen.

The African American community began an educational mutual aid society in 1836. It was a cooperative effort to educate the black youth, to educate its members, and others unable to afford school including orphaned and the destitute. "The Education Society is proof," argues Nikki Taylor, "that African Americans in Cincinnati were community-conscious; they had moved beyond seeing education merely as a means of individual uplift, but as a means of racial uplift and community empowerment."[26] John Gains—stevedore, steamship steward, and provisions shop-owner on the riverfront—was Cincinnati's foremost African American antebellum intellectual, who publicly spoke against the race riot of 1841 and gave the August First address in 1849. His leadership is a direct experience of the formative power of the Cincinnati community.

These urban conditions can be compared to the plantation as a historical setting of African American oppression, but characterized by architectural density, educational mutuality, self-defense, "criminality" and gambling and dealing. To call it "the community" is to be true to American usage. To call it commoning, however, calls attention to the proletarian experience of violent loss shared wherever capitalism seeks self-development by taking away subsistence, the violent expropriation of the common. This urban mass of commoners without commons was a problem to Marx too, and the vexed question of the political and economic composition of the working class, which he posed variously as proletarian and lumpenproletarian.[27]

To conclude. If the English origin of the word "communism" is to be found among the revolutionary workers of Paris, an American origin, at least of the communist communities of Ohio, arose in association with the militant movement against slavery. Certainly, it had become a *proletarian* experience, a term I use with its *class* meaning. That the English semantics and the American politics were connected in correspondence between Barmby and Wattles is surely only a single thread within the worldwide struggle. Reflecting on Indian and African American experience from the standpoint of the composition of the working class, forced migration became the policy towards the former as in the Trail of Tears, while forced immobility became the policy for the latter as in the Fugitive Slave Law.

In the 1840s, then, "communism" was the new name to express the revolutionary aspirations of proletarians. It pointed to the future, as in "historic tasks." In contrast, the "commons" belonged to the past, perhaps to the feudal era, when it was the last-ditch defense against extinction. Now in the twenty-first century the semantics of the two terms seems to be reversed, with communism belonging to the past of Stalinism, industrialization of agriculture, and militarism, while the commons belongs to an international debate about the planetary future of land, water, and subsistence for all. What is sorely needed in this debate so far is allegiance to the actual movements of the common people who have been enclosed and foreclosed but are beginning to disclose an alternative, open future.

In that debate we need realism and imagination. Marx writes in the well-trodden paths of section four of chapter one, of *Das Kapital*, "The Fetishism of Commodities," and as we join him in that familiar walk, he appeals to our imagination, "Let us finally imagine, for a change, an association of free men, working with the means of production held in common and expending their many different forms of labor-power in full self-awareness as one single social labor force."

After 1848 Barmby lost his revolutionary restlessness, closed the doors of his Communist Church, and became a Unitarian. So we can leave him serenely soaking in the gradated temperatures of his tubs of hydropathy. Karl Marx was only temporarily upset by the upheavals of 1848 and betook himself and family to London and to the bracing waters of political economy and the poverty-given agonies of boils. John Otis Wattles, meanwhile, moved to Illinois and attempted communal living again in Lake Zurich, and then again moved to West Point, Indiana, and finally to Kansas where he and Edith, his wife, with Augustus and Susan, his wife, started a town, Moneka.

John was known as an "ardent advocate of spiritualism" and as "an optimist of the most pronounced type." There they provided a headquarters and safe house to hide John Brown and his men when fleeing from a posse of racist, slave-holding murderers. After the failure of John Brown's raid on Harpers Ferry in 1859 the Wattles brothers may have had a hand in failed attempts to free Brown and his comrades from jail. [28]

In Moneka at Brown's headquarters with the Wattles brothers, "There was a general buffet supper for all, white and black." Barbara Taylor emphasized something similar in England, the importance of men and women eating together. It is something which brought us together too in the Adirondacks. In conclusion, various forms of commoning, some traditional and some not, provided the proletariat with means of survival in the struggle against capitalism. Commoning is a basis of proletarian class solidarity, and we can find this before, during, and after both the semantic and the political birth of communism.

Adirondacks
December 2010

"First Nations"

CHAPTER THIRTEEN

"The Red-Crested Bird and Black Duck"—A Story of 1802: Historical Materialism, Indigenous People, and the Failed Republic

"He had heard his father say that she was a spoiled nun and that she had come out of the convent in the Alleghanies when her brother had got the money from the savages for the trinkets and the chainies. Perhaps that made her severe against Parnell."

—James Joyce, *A Portrait of the Artist as a Young Man*

Introduction

I write in the aftermath of the November 2000 U.S. election whose corrupted result has thrown a mantle of suffused silence upon the once garrulous republic.[1] More immediately, I write in the week that the indigenous people of Mexico, led by those of Chiapas, left the Forest and marched to the City where they entered the congress of the Mexican republic and made their voices heard, despite centuries of silencing. In North America we are once again revisiting under the leadership of "the people of the color of the earth" the political meaning of a republic and the lineaments of U.S. imperialism. What follows are some notes designed to help us escape the impasse of the imperialist pall of silence and to renew, if possible, the discussion of historical materialism with its *raison d'être* of equality of goods within the earthly commons.

Col. E.M. Despard, the United Irishman, was executed in February 1803 for conspiracy to topple the British Crown and empire. Though he was long regarded as adventurist, if not crazed (did he not know that revolution in France, England, and Ireland was over?), I shall bring together three texts from the years 1802–3 with a view to exploring some of the forces at play in the period (what is it that we do not know?). The texts are, one, "Lithconia," a political romance appearing in United Irish circles of Philadelphia; two, a study of the Ohio Indians by Constantin Volney, the French intellectual and ideologue; and three, some Indian stories which were published in the *Transactions of the Royal Irish Academy* by John Dunne.[2]

These will help us understand the full expanse of revolutionary discussions because, like Despard, both Dunne and Volney brought to Europe from indigenous America messages which renewed European debates at a tender point: private property. The appropriation of common lands by private proprietors was challenged, in practice by the commoners of those lands, and in theory during the French Revolution, during the United Irish rebellion of 1798, and by the indigenous people of the American Great Lakes, or the *pays d'en haut* as the region has been termed by Richard White.[3] It is White also who introduces the idea of the village republic to characterize the miscible human settlements of the middle ground autonomous from European empires or USA. In Belfast, you could read that the Indian villages of the Old Northwest (Illinois, Michigan, Ohio, Indiana) were also places of runaway slaves.[4] In Ireland Kevin Whelan in an essay on the United Irishmen and popular culture calls attention to "the republic in the village." Thus, from opposite sides of the Atlantic scholars recently have applied the expression "republic" to settings where it had not heretofore been applied, and in doing so its meaning has been enlarged.[5]

It so happens that Frederick Engels located in precisely these years the appearance of both the modern working class and the birth of socialism, though this, to be sure, in its utopian rather than "scientific" form. According to Engels, modern socialism is the direct product of the recognition of class antagonism between proprietors and non-proprietors; it also appears as the logical extension of the principles of Reason, Equality, Justice of the French Enlightenment. Against the rampant crime, prostitution and cheating of the time Engels delighted "in the stupendously grand thoughts and germs of thought that everywhere break out through their phantastic covering." Engels found the birth of the industrial working class in 1800–1802. He neglected women workers, the slaves of the plantations, and the indigenous peoples. Their unpaid labors provided essential products to capitalism. The women reproduced labor-power. The slaves produced sugar. The indigenous people preserved the "natural" products (the animals of the forest). In all three cases their labors appeared as free gifts—gifts of love, gifts of race, gifts of nature. The master narrative is merely the narrative of the masters: the mistresses, the mastered, and the masterless have a story to tell. We have a century of scholarship about African American slavery; we have the scholarship of women's history; we have the "new Indian history." None of this did Engels have or know.[6]

He does not recognize the stadialism [the theory that history can be divided into a sequence of stages, progressing forward from a state of nature to civilization] of the Scottish Enlightenment.[7] The problematic of historical stages was developed in the Scottish Enlightenment by, among others, Adam Ferguson, David Hume, William Robertson, and Adam Smith in the aftermath of the defeat of the Scottish highlanders who, according to theory, were living somewhere between the savage and the barbarian stage, and thus their defeat was inevitable and progressive. Savages, as hunters and fishers, were without property; barbarians as pastoralists and herdsmen, had moveable property; only civilization depended on real estate. As Ferguson expressed it echoing Rousseau, "He who first said, 'I will appropriate this field; I will leave it to my heirs;' did not perceive, that he was laying the foundation of civil laws and political establishments." Ferguson might have added that this same act of appropriation was that of a patriarch, or that the patrilinear succession of private property required the monogamous marriage with its Gothic opacity and subordination of women to a "separate sphere."[8]

The Lithconian Republic

Jefferson, at the head of the party of republicans, was swept into the White House in the election of 1800. He allied with the Indian-haters and secessionists of the western frontier who were in the midst of the forty year war (1772–1812) to take of the Indian lands of the old northwest. In 1801 he outlined his dream of a white continent that could not contemplate "either blot or mixture on that surface." The years 1802–3 were decisive in the formulation of his Indian policy—trade monopolized at federal factories, inevitable ties of indebtedness, surreptitious and violent alcohol dealing, the depletion of forest resources which had sustained the fur trade, introduction of patriarchal agriculture, land cessions, forced removal if incorporation was resisted, and acquisition of the whole northern continent. A recent scholar concludes, "the Jeffersonian vision of the destiny of the Americas had no place for Indians as Indians."[9]

Jefferson was a scholar as well as a land-grabber. His only publication provided a studious investigation and stratigrapahic analysis into the Indian burial mounds that used to characterize the North American human landscape.[10] He also collected Indian vocabularies as a means of investigating the origins of Indian peoples (he had twenty-two of them in 1803), though there is no evidence that he spoke any Indian language. Duplicitous, subtle, implacable, a secret land speculator, a ruthless zealot with the appearance of benevolence, his smile surely was a sign of danger. He was Chief of the Long Knives who chopped up history into fixed stages.

During the 1790s students at Yale, Dartmouth, Princeton, and William and Mary read Volney, suspected authority, and believed that ignorance, fear, poverty, and superstition were rooted in political and ecclesial authority.[11] Elihu Palmer published *Principles of Nature; or, A Development of the Moral Causes of Happiness and Misery among the Human Species* in 1801. "Reason, righteous and immortal reason, with the argument of the printing types in one hand, and the keen argument of the sword in the other, must attack the thrones and the hierarchies of the world, and level them with the dust of the earth; then the emancipated slave must be raised by the power of science into the character of an enlightened citizen."[12] American deists campaigned for freedom of conscience, abolition of slavery, emancipation of women, universal education, the end of economic privilege. Deism "solicits the acquaintance of peasants and mechanics, and draws whole nations to its standards." With class privilege threatened, Jefferson and Volney, once deists themselves, attempted to cover their tracks.

Before 1798 the United Irish were curious about the American Indians; afterwards, as exiles they had opportunity to learn from them. "I will go to the woods, but I will not kill Indians, nor keep slaves," vowed Archibald Hamilton Rowan.[13] John Binns "expected that among the people, even in the large towns, I should occasionally meet one of our red brethren with his squaw lovingly on his arm. I expected to find the white men so plain and quakerly in their dress that I had the lace ripped from my neckerchiefs, and the ruffles from my shirt." It was known in Ireland that many white men disguised themselves as Indians especially around the Great Lakes, well enough known for Waddy Cox to report it without surprise.[14]

The Temple of Reason was first edited by Dennis Driscoll, an Irish exile of '98.[15] The editor after April 1802 was John Lithgow. Taking a leaf from the book of Thomas Spence whose "Spensonia" advocated a system of common ownership of land and resources, Lithgow named his political romance "Lithconia." It was a coded intervention in an international political discussion. "Equality: A Political Romance" began to appear in *The Temple of Reason* on May 15 and thenceforth for seven numbers into the summer of 1802. The editors dedicated it to Dr. James Reynolds of co. Tyrone, the United Irish emigré who, on the occasion of George Washington leaving office, said there "ought to be a jubilee" at a time when the term referred to release from debts, return of land, and abolition of slavery—a precise program to satisfy frontiersman, Indian, and slave.

With blithe disregard of the prevailing orthodoxy, the author merely inverted the stadialist fairy tale of orthodox opinion. "The Lithconians are not a people that are progressing from a state of nature, to what is vulgarly called civilization; on the contrary, they are progressing from civil society to a state of nature, if they have not already arrived at that state: for in the history of the country, many and surprising revolutions are recorded." Its history began as "a small island in few leagues from the continent of Europe." Love, friendship and wealth are attainable for all. Prostitution is removed by the abolition of private property and the patrilinear lines of descent. "Here the laws do not make the trembling female swear to the father of her child." Dancing on the green commences every day at four o'clock. Music is the principle branch of liberal education. A printing press is open to all in every district. There is no money in the country, the lands are in common, and a few hours of labor required of all. As for children, "No such words as *mine* and *thine* are ever heard." No markets, no shopkeepers, no debtors, no creditors, no lawyers, no elections, no embezzlement, no theft. Machines are permitted; railways are widespread.[16] "The laws are not contained in huge volumes—they are written in the hearts of Lithconians," an antinomian view propounded by William Drennan.

The Temple of Reason folded on February 19, 1803, three days before Despard suffered his last, and a day after Jefferson privately wrote his extraordinary letter to Benjamin Hawkins about the Indians, "I have little doubt but that your reflections must have led you to view the various ways in which their history may terminate." The best that the Indians can do is to sell their land and become U.S. citizens. The chiefs can get rich, the men will take the plough, women give up the hoe, exceptional souls may go to college, and the whiskey keg is full for the rest.[17] The hanging and decapitation of Despard, the closing of The Temple of Reason, and the termination of Indian history (at least as imagined by President Jefferson) thus all took place within a few days of each other. This is not to say that European proletarian insurrection, or American utopian socialist discussion, or Native American resistance were crushed—no, not at all—but it is to suggest linkages among the three themes to a common project. A recent scholar dismisses the work as a "utopian socialist" tract.[18] Certainly, the authors of Lithconia did not think it was impractical: "The genuine system of property to be spoken of, as no visionary phantom, but as a *good*, which might be realized."

Tecumseh and the Commonist Project

The French Revolution went about as far as it could in the summer of 1793 when on the one hand it restored communal lands without respect to gender and inclusive of domestics and laborers, but on the other hand in March 1793 it prescribed the death penalty for whomsoever should propose an agrarian law. Although the idea of leveling distinctions based on wealth could be found in the *cahiers de doléance* of 1789, the exploration of proto-communism could not begin to be aired until after the proclamation of the republic and the execution of the King. *The Manifesto of the Equals,* intending to establish the Republic of Equality, addressed the people of France in 1796, "*The land is nobody's personal property.* Our demand is for the communal ownership of the earth's resources." Gracchus Babeuf (1760–1797) wrote of this republic, "Such a regime will sweep away iron bars, dungeon walls, and bolted doors, trials and disputations, murders, thefts and crimes of every kind; it will sweep away the judges and the judged, the jails and the gibbets—all the torments of body and agony of soul that the injustice of life engenders; it will sweep away enviousness and gnawing greed, pride, and deceit . . . ; it will remove—and how important is this!—the brooding, omnipresent fear that gnaws always and in each of us concerning our fate tomorrow, next month, next year, and in our old age; concerning the fate of our children and of our children's children."[19]

The Poor Man's Catechism in Ireland (1798) called for a return of the common land—"It is not possible that God can be pleased to see a whole nation depending on the caprice and pride of a small faction, who can deny the common property in the land to his people, or at least tell them, how much they shall eat, and what kind; and how much they shall wear, and what kind"—and in *The Cry of the Poor for Bread* John Burk wrote, "Oh! lords of manors, and other men of landed property, as you have monopolized to yourselves the land, its vegetation and its game, the fish of the rivers and the fowls of heaven . . . in the present condition of things can the laborer, who cultivates your land with the sweat of his brow, the working manufacturer, or the mechanic support himself, a wife and five or six children?" Such voices were silenced in Ireland after 1798 but not in America where in 1803 Joseph Brant, the Iroquois leader, wrote, "we have no law but that written on the heart of every rational creature by the immediate finger of the great Spirit of the universe himself. We have no prisons—we have no pompous parade of courts . . . we have no robbery under the color of law—daring wickedness here is never suffered to triumph over helpless innocence—the estates of widows and orphans are never devoured by enterprising sharpers. Our sachems, and our warriors, eat their own bread, and not the bread of wretchedness. . . . The palaces and prisons among you form a most dreadful contrast. Liberty, to a rational creature, as much exceeds property, as the light of the sun does that of the most twinkling star: but you put them on a level, to the everlasting disgrace of civilization."[20]

Tecumseh refused to enter the house of Governor W.H. Harrison in August 1810, insisting on meeting in the open air. "The earth was the most proper place for the Indians, as they liked to repose upon the bosom of their mother." Reposed, he spoke eloquently, and his words were translated in an English diction whose origins arose in the seventeenth-century transformations of land associated with enclosures and their antiperistasis. "You wish to prevent the Indians from doing as we wish them, to unite and let them consider their lands as the common property of the whole," as militants had argued for three decades.[21] "Since my residence at Tippecanoe, we have endeavored to level all distinctions, to destroy village chiefs by whom all mischiefs are done. It is they who sell the land to the Americans." "The way, the only way to stop this evil is for the red men to unite in claiming a common and equal right in the land, as it was at first, and should be now—for it was never divided, but belongs to all. No tribe has the right to sell, even to each other, much less to strangers. . . . *Sell a country! Why not sell the air, the great sea, as well as the earth?* Did not the Great Spirit make them all for the use of his children?" The resonances to the seventeenth-century revolution in England become explicit, "When Jesus Christ came upon the earth you killed Him and nailed Him to the cross. You thought He was dead, and you were mistaken. You have Shakers among you and you laugh and make light of their worship."

Tecumseh was killed in battle on the River Thames, Ontario, in 1813, but his brother, the one-eyed prophet Tenskwatawa, escaped to Canadian exile. In 1824 a young proto-ethnologist of the Indian Department sought him out to answer a government questionnaire. He was now an object of study. Stories and dreams, once so powerful, had lost their force. Nevertheless, Tenskwatawa attempted to tell a story, stories could be tested against action; but in defeat, they lose the sense of belonging to history and become timeless traits of the *sauvage,* as if the story too were dead. Volney announced the return of the *sauvage.* "These men," he wrote, "are in the actual state of wild animals." But which animals?

Turtle's Students: Volney the Apostate

Constantin-François Volney, a conscious victor of history's stages, rode no triumphal chariot—he was wrapped up in a blanket at the back of a wagon bouncing through the forest on the road from Cincinnati up to the Maumee River that General Wayne had made three years before. Riding in "a convoy of money" he feverishly clung to his portable escritoire, his pens, and ink bottles. Back at Fort Vincennes he got his ethnology from a liquor salesman and refused to leave the palisade to converse himself with the beseeching Indians. He observed in disgust an Indian stabbing his wife to death "within twenty steps of me" and assumed his reader would not wonder whether he intervened to stop it. But he had fallen ill, unable to complete his rendezvous with William Wells, the interpreter, "white Indian." His own English was shaky. He returned east, seasick on Lake Erie, his researches brought to a halt, memories of ghastly filthy settlement behind him. He was a globalizer. A savant; an ideologist, Napoleon would be his employer. He was looking for land and "at the same time correcting prejudices formed during a period of enthusiasm." He had apostacized.

His revolutionary "enthusiasm" was expressed in *Ruins; or, Meditations on the Revolutions of Empires*, published in 1791, which provided a narrative of human history without gods or magic and it placed the people at the center of hope against the cupidity and perfidy of the rulers, be they priests, soldiers, or law-givers. Furthermore, the book put the origins of civilization in the Nile, a view unaccepted by subsequent European historiography and thus the book was kept in print by pan-African publishers, while it dropped out of print by white publishers. This was the book beloved by Shelley, Percy and Mary. Mary wrote (1817) of Dr. Frankenstein who created the monster without a name. "My person was hideous and my stature gigantic. What did this mean? Who was I? What was I? When did I come? What was my destination?" Engels would recognize the dawning of class-consciousness. Is he the industrial working class at the moment of its making? Is he the racial "other" at the moment of expanding slavery? The monster escapes and at the window of a lonely mountain cottage he listens to the poor cottagers read Volney aloud, learning of the extermination of the first peoples of America, of the dispeopling of Africa and the sale of its inhabitants, and of "the division of property, of immense wealth and squalid poverty." The monster listened and wept.

Volney's tears by this time were dry. He embarked in 1795 for America to find an asylum for his declining years. Once there he decided to remain in consequence of "the facility of acquiring landed property." Volney was obsessed by property. No right of property exists among the savages, he said. "The land . . . is undivided among all the nations, and remains in common" as is still the case in parts of France, Spain, Italy, Corsica. He refers to Sir John Sinclair's *Essay on Commons and Waste Lands* and the enclosures of England and Scotland. "The abolition of these commons should every where be the first law." Agriculture, industry, and individual and national character depend on enclosure. "One of the most radical and active causes [of barbarism and savagery in Corsica] is the undivided and common state of the greater part of it's territory."[22]

He published *Tableau du climat et du sol des États-Unis d'Amérique* in 1803, which was translated into English by the novelist Charles Brown the following year. It has the warmth of an investor's report. The background is knowledge that climate and weather are to a degree affected by human action; the clearing of woods especially affected soil temperature, inland breezes, the fluctuation of seasons. Drought keeps pace with clearing.[23] The Gothic is the attitude of overwhelming forces of death, famine, war, pestilence. Charles Brockden Brown published a Gothic novel called *Edgar Huntly; or, Memoirs of a Sleep-Walker* (1801). It compares and contrasts parallel stories of an Irish immigrant, Clithero, who assassinated his landlady's brother and believed he had killed her, and a Pennsylvania Indian-killer, Edgar Huntly.

Volney has an eight-page appendix vocabulary of the language of the Miami. He had nine or ten visits in January and February 1798. "This incident furnished me with a more fortunate opportunity, than I could have expected, not only affording me an interpreter to communicate my ideas, but the mouth of a native to give me the sounds in all their purity." The collecting of words like this already objectifies and distances Little Turtle: his language is not a means of dialogue, an exchange of meanings, it is a bunch of sounds, for unilateral appropriation. The European has ideas and the Indian has sounds.

Wells describes the "middle ground," or the many whites who join the savage life—children, Canadians, "men of bad character," and libertines. The village republic is a political unit whose members originated from several tribes, ethnicities. These are not the imaginary *sauvages* of Rousseau or Chateaubriand. They are without hierarchy, order, authority. The architecture is frame and bark, its people are European and Algonquian.[24] Women would determine whether hostages were acceptable alternative to war. The village republics contained runaway slaves, too. Thus the first article of the 1785 Treaty of Fort M'Intosh provided that the Indian sachems provide three hostages until prisoners had been returned to the U.S., *white and black*. Thus the image of common children from a common mother expressed heterogeneous nature of kinship. The Indian confederacy of 1786 met at Brownstown where Brant enunciated his famous principle of Indian unity and common land as a "dish with one spoon." To Volney it was all separate, isolated dishes with many knives and forks. "They live wholly in their feelings, little in remembrance, not at all in hope." "Theirs in fact is an extreme and terrible democracy." "These men are actually in the state of wild animals and birds . . ." Which is it, actually, animals or birds?

Volney praises Turtle who "has been led by the nature of things, to discover the essential basis of the social state in the *cultivation of the earth*, and, as an immediate consequence, in *landed property*." Volney claps his hands and turns to Rousseau "who maintains that the deprivation of the social state originates from the introduction of the right of property." The true picture of savage life, Volney says, "is a state of non-compact and anarchy, in which wandering, unconnected men are moved by violent necessities." "After this let sentimental dreamers come forward and boast the goodness of the man of nature." Volney had a bad experience in the prisons of the Jacobin republic.

Will Napoleon honor the land transfers of the Revolution? Will Washington and Adams open the Ohio to the unpaid veterans who showed in the Whiskey Rebellion that instead of fighting the Indians they might fight the great landowners like Washington? Will Pitt authorize the Parliamentary enclosure acts? Will the sugar plantations of the slaves still grind amid the transfer of flags from one to another European? Was the terror of the Orange Order enough to hold back the advance of an outraged peasantry whose independence was reduced to service occupations? Will the Act of Union guarantee private property from the fairies of the night?

Turtle's Students: John Dunne the Antiquarian

John Dunne spoke at the Royal Irish Academy in May 1802, on Dawson Street, Dublin. John Dunne was a son of a native of Lurgan, co. Armagh, who became a Dissenting minister at Cooke Street, Dublin, a classmate of William Drennan, graduate of Glasgow University, and a leading member of the bar; and a member of the Irish house of commons for Randalstown, co. Antrim from 1783 to 1797 under the patronage of John O'Neill, a Whig.[25] He became a Unitarian, and like Coleridge and thousands of others of the hopeful young, he was filled with projects of changing the world. Let Archibald Hamilton Rowan introduce him further: "Disgusted by the turbulent and sanguinary scenes of civilized life at a time when his professional reputation would have seated him on the bench, he was led by a romantic wish to become acquainted with men in the savage state. Accordingly he crossed the Atlantic, and for a time conformed to the manners and customs of an Indian tribe."[26]

The guns between France and Britain were silent in May 1802. The Peace of Amiens brought a lull in the struggle between the European titans though not in the agony of the slave revolts of Guadeloupe and Saint Domingue, nor the nocturnal arson against the machines of industrial England, and the groans remained from the prisons and exile. A year earlier the first Parliament of the "United Kingdom" met: Dunne was speaking to Irishmen who had their independence taken away (the Act of Union went into effect a year earlier, January 1801), a final act against the bid for freedom launched in 1798, which was crushed with greater casualties than were visited on France by the Jacobin Terror. If the French Revolution offered a universal ethical reprise from the *ancien régime* in its slogans of possibility—*liberté, égalité, fraternité*—these same slogans had to be translated as it were into the vernacular of other countries if their universality was to be realized. In Ireland this became the project of the United Irishmen whose demands for the emancipation of Catholics and independence from England, were formulated within the effervescence of cultural nationalism—the harp restrung at the Belfast Harp Festival of 1792, the folk songs, *Éireann go brách*, and an antiquarian validation of a vernacular Gaelic civilization. Ledwich published a second edition of *Antiquities of Ireland* in 1803, as part of the response to the scholarly work of the Catholic Committee which was active in discovering and preserving Gaelic culture.

Gaelic antiquaries were assisted by Anglo-Irish liberals of the Royal Irish Academy which encouraged Celtic studies since its founding in 1785. They used the remote past to achieve social and civic parity; it proved that they were at least on the same footing as the conquerors.[27] Ledwich argued that the association of Gaelic, Catholic, and radical political views was dangerous. The project was defeated by government in London and Dublin in policies of maleficent sectarianism, military repression, and cultural regression.[28] The political diaspora to the mines of Prussia, to the factories of Lancashire and Yorkshire, to become hewers of wood and drawers of water in London, vanished in the fleet, exiled in America. Off the banks of Newfoundland near the end of his voyage of exile James Orr (1770–1816), United Irishman, sang,

> "How hideous the hold is!—Here, children are screaming,
>> There, dames faint, thro' thirst, with their babes on their knee;
> Here, down ev'ry hatch the big breakers are streaming,
>> And, there, with a crash, half the fixtures break free:
> Some court—some contend—some sit dull stories telling—
>> the mate's mad and drunk, and the tar's task'd and yelling:
> What sickness and sorrow, pervade my rude dwelling!—
>> A huge floating lazar-house, far, far at sea."

Drennan's *Letters of Orellana, an Irish Helot* (Dublin 1785), which began as a series of letters in Belfast, took its name from indigenous Americans. "The freedom of your present mutilated constitution is only to be found in the Utopia of a fanciful Frenchman, or the political reveries of a Genevan philosopher. By those wretched multitudes, I swear, who wander with their fellow bruits through the fertile pasturage of the south, by those miserable emigrants who are now ploughing a bleak and boisterous ocean—the democratic spirit of the constitution is no more!" Contrast Drennan's generosity (exiles and "fellow bruits" are within the constitutional pale) with the Irish barrister, Herman Blennerhassett, Co. Kerry, a visitor to Paris in 1790, "thoroughly read in the political writings of Voltaire, and a disciple of Rousseau," In 1798 he purchased an island in the Ohio River "lucrative in the hands of a capitalist, with forty or fifty negroes, who would engage in raising hemp or tobacco." He was explicitly praised as an Indian fighter."[29]

Dunne knew "from a thousand sources" that they hunted and fought and sported. But did they also exercise memory, invention, and fancy? Did they laugh and weep at fictitious tales? Did they conjure up "the forms of imaginary beings to divert and instruct them"? He obtains the friendship of Little Turtle who adopted him "according to their custom, in the place of a deceased friend, by whose name I was distinguished." Thus, like Lord Edward

Fitzgerald who received a Seneca name, Eghnidal, in Detroit in June 1789, John Dunne, now possessed a dual identity. "I wish I could make the Indians here speak," he lamented to the academicians. Their discourses are forcible, feeling, and expressive in tone. "The Indian lyre is unstrung," he writes alluding to the slogan of the United Irish of cultural liberation, the harp restrung. "How then can I exhibit examples of Indian speech?" Dunne spends several weeks at Niagara Falls where he is moved to compose poetry in the Algonquian language. He searches for insight into "the workings of the Indian mind." Little Turtle could extend his imitations even to animals.

The Indians are degenerating and wasting away; in half a century they will be extinguished. He hopes these stories "may furnish an additional motive to treat them with humanity." "It is a part of the destiny of an unlettered people, to write their memorials with the pen of a stranger. They have no alternative, imperfect representation, or blank oblivion—But of whom are we speaking? Who are these evanescent tribes? And in what class of created beings is posterity to place them?" He does not answer the questions; he records their answers. The Abenaki will say he is *the man of the land*; ask the Illinois, they will say he is a *real man*; ask the Algonquian speakers, they will say he is *doubly men*. The Spaniards will say *barbarian*, the Canadian will say *savage*. Ask the wise men of Europe who, though they have never even seen the smoke of an Indian village, will "dogmatize and write volumes upon their nature, powers and capacities, physical moral, and intellectual; these men will tell you they are *an inferior race of men*." "To what opinion shall we hold? What constitutes a man? What energies entitle him to rank high in his species?"

At first he compares the Indians to Homer, or rather to the precursors of Homer. The stories might have "beguiled the hours at the ships or the tents at the Scamander," the river of Troy flowing into the Hellespont where two continents meet.[30] Homer is the poet of the heroic stage of history "while the Indian is yet in his infancy, and in the gristle" (scant agriculture, poor pasturage) using a phrase of Americans that Burke employed a few years earlier, "a people who are still, as it were in the gristle not yet hardened into the bone of manhood." The transition from the woods to the farm was also an ancient figure of rhetoric of Cicero and Horace. Corresponding to the economic bases in this transition there loomed above, so to speak, a cultural superstructure of the transition from song to writing, or of speech to letters. Eloquence said Cicero, not reason, drew men from sylvan retreats to build the city. Orpheus, claimed Horace, sang men from roaming the woods to the building of the city. Dunne tells several stories. One is a racial one of envy and color change. Another is sexy but is in Latin. A third is a trickster tale. However it is the first story I want to tell.

The Red-Crested Bird and Black Duck

A man separated himself from "the society of his fellows, and took up his abode in a desert place, in a remote part of the wilderness." He hunted by day, and in the evening he imparted a portion of food to his brother whom he had imprisoned in a gloomy cave. "This unfortunate brother, from having his hair of a fiery red, infectious to the touch, was known among the men of his nation by the name of the red man."

The younger brother is the figure of dispossession in societies where primogeniture prevails such as Europe. The infectious red hair is symbolic of ethnic origin and of the Jacobin revolutionary who wore the *bonnet rouge*, or red Phrygian cap of liberty, which had made its appearance as a signifier of revolutionary militance in the early months of the French Revolution. In the contest of symbols for dominance over the head, it had replaced the crown. Indeed a "battle of the bonnets" in October 1793 pitted *républicaines* of the Club of Revolutionary Women who boldly wore the cap of liberty against the Jacobin men who feared that the demand for pistols would follow.[31] The title page of the *Transactions of the Royal Irish Academy* portrayed two women, Britannia and Liberty seated next to a pike with the *bonnet rouge* on top.

After many winters, the hunter grew lonely. He went to a village, he approached a wigwam on its perimeter, and finding a widow he presented her some deer meat for dinner. The next day he hunted and brought her a whole deer and invited her to share it with the villagers. It was given to be understood "in whispers by the women that a great hunter whom she was bound to conceal, who appeared to come from some distant country, was the providore of her bounty." His presents "excited the curiosity of the whole nation whose joint efforts scarcely equaled the success of this single hunter, notwithstanding their superior knowledge of the best hunting grounds."

Let the solitary hunter stand for the isolated individualist, the "providore" of prolific productivity, the yankee, the capitalist, the inventor, the symbol of the Industrial Revolution. At the same time the Indians had two things to sell—furs and land, and each became their undoing. Furs were traded for alcohol; land bribed away. The Indians are the first example Thomas Malthus provides in 1798 of his population thesis that "misery is the check that represses the superior power of population and keeps its effects equal to the means of subsistence." Women, children, and the old are the first to suffer, he argues, in this "rudest state of mankind," or "the first state of mankind," where hunting is "the only mode of acquiring food."[32] By 1803 this was no longer possible. The actual conditions of the forest hunt in the lands of the Ohio, Monongahela, and Wabash were of diminishing game, severe competition of hunters, red and white. In fact, in 1798 the Indians of the Ohio were in an advanced political economic relationship with imperial Europe, of considerable commodity trade, capital intensive agriculture, massive drug addiction (alcoholism), and incubative racial separations. Malthusian law is not a demographic hypothesis but an episode in a fictional narrative of termination.

The hunter expressed his desire for a wife, and the chief's brother obliged his wish to form an alliance with his sister. They married; they feasted; "thus the moons rolled away," until he returned to take her away, to "the seat of solitude." Again he passed the days hunting. She noticed that after dinner he tiptoed away carrying the tongues and marrow of the animals he killed. Not many days passed before her worry grew and against his commands, she stole away to the spot where she had seen him descend into the cavernous prison. His brother heard "the sound of her feet upon the hollow ground, roused the half torpid senses of the subterraneous inhabitant and drew forth his groans." She recognized her brother. "She learnt his story, she wept over his sufferings, she administered to his wants, her conversation like a charm gave him new existence." She induced him to clamber out into the sunshine.

The "underground" was a vivid reality to the miners of the Industrial Revolution, and it was a figure of speech of the repressive years of the first decade of the nineteenth century applied to the Luddites. We can compare him to the Irish political prisoners of St. George who will be released in June 1802, or to Michael Dwyer in the caves of Wicklow mountains. Much of the chase in *Edgar Huntly* takes place underground in mountainous caverns or caves. According to a note to the public at the beginning of the novel it is such settings of the western wilderness as well as Indian hostilities that must distinguish American lit.[33] The "underground" and the "wilderness" thus possessed both a geological or geographical presence and a construction of political imagination.

Her humanity was engaged, she separated the clotted knots of his hair, she removed the clammy concretions on his forehead. An alliance, in effect, is made between the dispossessed younger brother, the figure of the Jacobin or the United Irishman, and the woman seeking her own subsistence and longing for her own community of women's labor.

Her husband observed her hands strained with red. She sank in despair, to be roused when her husband held before him, suspended by his long red hair, the severed head of her brother. The air resounded with her screams. He fled into the moonlit forest coming at length to an ancient oak hollowed by lightning where he hurled the head with its fiery tresses. Then with wolfish yelps he began to transmogrify, "adding to his nature what alone was wanting, the shape and figure of a wolf." *Homo homini lupus.* She has lost the source of her food. His productivity still depends on murder and oppression. "Some human beings must suffer from want," Malthus concluded. "All cannot share alike the bounties of nature."

Indeed on the frontier, as far from the plantations Monticello or the merchant houses of New York or Independence Hall of Philadelphia, "murder," to quote Richard White, "gradually became the dominant American Indian policy." The *lex talionis* prevailed. Whiskey was the poor man's medium of exchange, solace, capital investment, and drug to deal to his enemies. Volney observed it with disdain, disgust, and distance. John Heckewelder, the Moravian missionary, wrote, "when the object is to murder Indians, strong liquor is the main article required; for when you have them dead drunk, you may do to them as you please." Lithconia mocked the subject: "murder was but a lean trade, though it was, of all others, the most honorable," Jonah Barrington recalled the first two questions of a young man: What family is he from? Did he ever blaze?[34] General Wayne encouraged dueling in the army of Ohio, for instance, Lieutenants Bradshaw, a gentleman physician, and Huston, a weaver, both Irishmen, killed each other in a duel.[35]

Meanwhile, the days passed in near-lifeless despair. She heard a distant sound. She listened, she was aroused, she recognized the voice of her brother calling. He was telling her where to find berries. She ascended the tree and with a cord of twisted bark drew forth the head. She placed it in her bosom and it became her counselor, providing subsistence by felling deer or caribou with a glance of his eye. "The storm was now passed over, and a better world seemed to open through the separated clouds. The wants of hunger supplied, the fears of danger banished." She only missed "the cheerful buzz of the village, the labors of the field sweetened by the converse of her companions." This is the collective labor of the commons, practiced in the Great Lakes, Ireland, England alike, prior to enclosures, clearance, or conquest. The absence of the market, the entirely incidental character of private tenures, the communal work with hoes and digging sticks is the picture of women among the Seneca people.[36]

The red man attempted to deflect her attention: "Did he show her the beauties of the wilderness, she was blind; did he warn her of the dangers of the frequented village, he spoke to the winds." He relented on condition that she hide his head from the view of all mortals. So clasping "the friendly head still closer to her bosom; and associating it with her heart," she made her way to a village. Her longing for the village was thus a return to a specific culture, the village republic of the *pays d'en haut*.

Charles Brockden Brown worked with this theme in *Edgar Huntly*, since his two protagonists, the Irish cottier and the frontier squatter, had distinct relationships to women who control the land. Clithero was beholden to Mrs.

Euphemia Lorimer, an absentee resident in Dublin, who having his parents
for tenants promoted him to steward. In contrast, Huntly's parents had taken
lands from the Delaware Indians, or Lenape people, who murdered his parents
but without regaining their land. His uncle squatted on the clan's village and
drove them into Ohio. Refusing to budge was only Old Deb or "Queen Mab,"
who maintained her sovereignty by weeding her corn and keeping compan-
ionship with three domestic wolves. Towards the end of the novel the two
themes are brought together as Clithero finds shelter in Queen Mab's mountain hut, and Huntly seeks to protect Euphemia Lorimer now resident in New
York, as her own country "contained a thousand memorials of past calamity,
and which was lapsing fast into civil broils." Queen Mab, it transpired, had
directed underground attacks to recover her people's patch of the commons,
while Mrs. Lorimer formed connections with capital appropriating wealth in
Ireland, India, and America.

In the village she joined a numerous assembly of women gambling. A
brooch, a ring, the "trinkets and chainies," were at stake. Enticed by the passion
of play, the inevitable followed: her cloak opened and the head dropped from
her bosom down a hill into a river below. As she chased after it she saw the
head transform itself into a rare bird whose dusky plumage was surmounted
by a tufted crown of red feathers, while she herself was transformed into a
black duck. Among the Miami, Dunne explains, the red-crested bird is the
forerunner of calamity, while the black-duck is so despised that its feathers are
never used for totems of war but it is only devoured as food, and then, only
in "seasons of extreme famine."

"What constitutes a man? What energies entitle him to rank high in his
species?" Who are these evanescent tribes? And in what class of created beings
is posterity to place them?" These were Dunne's questions. Volney's conclusion: "These men are actually in the state of wild animals and birds." It is a
story of mutilation and of organic, interspecies reproduction. In the context
of diminished game reserves, considerable corn production, and strategic reli-
ance on European trading items, it is unpersuasive to pass off the story as one
belonging to a society of hunters and gatherers, though certainly the nativist
revivals (Neolin in the 1760s, Handsome Lake in 1802, Tenskwatawa in 1809)
resisted the fur trade.

Gambling is the agent of corruption. Commodity exchange and the
appeal to fortune subverted the community that she had hungered for. But the
magic of the story is one of transformation and continuity: the Jacobin *sans-
culottes* and his nurturing female sister persist despite money, despite decapitation. The possibility of insurrection remains, survival even in famine is possible.
Little Turtle and his people knew famine and defeat (Battle of Fallen Timbers

1794), and the listeners to Dunne's story remembered the famine of 1800–1801 in Ireland and the assassination of Lord Edward Fitzgerald and the defeat of the Wexford Republic of 1798. We have listened to a story among the defeated.

Whose Story?

Whose story was this? Little Turtle, the Miami chief, spoke to John Dunne, the jurist of Armagh, and between them was William Wells, interpreting. When we learn that Wells was captured in 1784 as a thirteen-year-old boy by the Miami Indians, who raised him and named him Apeconit meaning "wild carrot" on account of his red hair, we realize there is another story here than the one Dunne is telling in Dublin. Further, when we learn that William Wells also married a chief's daughter, Manwangopath, or Sweet Breeze, the daughter of Little Turtle, the storyteller himself, it is clear that the story of the red-crested bird and black duck is also a complex story of a multi-ethnic family from the border country.[37] John Dunne was thus present at an intimate family gathering. It was also a political family. Little Turtle in October 1791 defeated General Harmar twice, and then in November 1791 with war whoops sounding like the ringing of a thousand bells the governor of the Northwest Territory, General Arthur St. Clair, and his army of the Federal Government of the USA succumbed to Little Turtle and the braves who followed him. The battlefield casualties were found with earth placed in their mouths; thus, did the warriors of Little Turtle try to satisfy the land-hunger of the Long Knives.

Satisfaction was short-lived. In 1794 the Indians of Ohio were decisively defeated by "Mad" Anthony Wayne at the Battle of Fallen Timbers (Toledo, Ohio), and Wells, now working for the Americans, led a team of eight translators at the 1795 Treaty of Greenville that grabbed the land that became the fat State of Ohio (1803). On the one hand, he had to make comprehensible such abstract redundancies as "the said Indians do hereby cede and relinquish forever" or racial categories like "any citizen of the United States, or any other white person or persons" and on the other hand he had to provide legal abstraction or equivocation to "to bury the hatchet" or "to collect the bones of your slain warriors [and] put them into a deep pit."[38]

The Turtle addressed President Jefferson in January 1802, translated by Wells. Jefferson preferred, despite his leadership of the Republican Party, the patriarchal family as his model of close human encounter; here he could rule, unopposed by different opinions. So, of the twenty-six paragraphs of the speech, twenty-four begin with direct address of "Father," one begins "my Father," and one begins "My Father and Brothers."

The volume of rum into the region, essential lubrication to the land cessions, doubled between 1800 and 1803.[39] "Father, When our White Brethren came to this land, our forefathers were numerous, and happy, but since their intercourse with the white people, and owing to the introduction of this fatal poison, we have become less numerous and happy." "Father, the introduction of this poison has been prohibited in our camps, but not the towns, where many of our hunters, for this poison, dispose of not only their furs, &c., but frequently of their guns and blankets and return to their families destitute."[40]

The Turtle died in 1811 at Wells's house, asking only to be taken outside to die in the orchard. Wells himself painted his face black, as was the Miami custom when facing certain death, and was killed in 1812. As his niece watched on, a warrior chopped off his head and another cut out his heart, and devoured the organ of courage. "The spirit, the true life of any animal, resided in the heart and blood of the beast."[41] Wells was an intermediary and a great translator. He once spoke in the Wabash language to a large bear he wounded. The Moravian missionary, John Heckewelder, asked him what he said. "I told him that he knew the fortune of war, that one or the other of us must have fallen; that it was his fate to be conquered, and he ought to die like a man, like a hero, and not like an old woman; that if the case had been reversed, and I had fallen into the power of my enemy, I would not have disgraced my nation as he did, but would have died with firmness and courage, as becomes a true warrior."

In 1802 he was appointed to issue treaty annuities and promote "civilization" among the Indians. He had to share authority with the factor of the Indian trading house at Fort Wayne, John Johnston, who was an Irishman. Born 1775 near Ballyshannon Co. Fermanagh, he came to USA in 1786, moved to the Alleghanies, and became a provisioner of oxen and pack horses to the Americans.[42] In 1801 as the Quakers began their work among the Miami, Johnston married a Quaker woman. Their ploughs furnished by the Society of Friends and a £100 gift from an ancient female friend from Cork. In 1802 Johnston opened the book containing the first records of the fur trade at Fort Wayne ($13,320 = deer, raccoon, bear, otter, beaver, mink, muskrat). His second marriage was to a Chippewa woman. Their daughter, Jane, married Henry Schoolcraft, a prodigious collector of Algonquian tales, who, after an evangelical conversion, became a violent critic of Indian superstition and sloth. Schoolcraft advocated Indian removal, the tales collected dust on the shelf, and the marriage fell apart.

Wells, Turtle, and Dunne understood one another. As Lord Edward Fitzgerald learned something from Joseph Brant about "the dish with one spoon"—a unified Ireland of Catholic and Protestant, so about ten years later John Dunne brought back to Dublin something about survival and transformation in a period of traumatic catastrophe. His writing style is refined, conscious of high decorum. The style of abstractions was that of universals supposedly unavailable to savages. The style of "particles" (conjunctions, prepositions and connecting adverbs) was the style expressing relations among substantives, and again was believed to characterize the superior mind of Europeans. Primitive language was concrete not abstract, emotional not reasoned, metaphorical rather than systematic.[43] It is more than an act of translation; it is a deliberate cultural decision with political implications. He writes in the prose of the authentic nation, like that of his classmate at the University of Glasgow, William Drennan. Dunne wants his listeners to pay attention to the story. To Dunne such stories in the first place prove that the Indians are of advanced mental development, contrary to the view of European philosophers. In the second place those who excel in narrative invention and embellishment have a character comparable to the minstrels of Europe. Finally, the subject, manner, image, and lesson prove them "to be the spontaneous productions of the soil."

The stadialism of Jefferson and Volney has not been transcended, though it has been refined with racial determinants in the nineteenth century and structures of rationality in the twentieth century. Johannes Fabian showed that the European travelers of the seventeenth and eighteenth centuries assumed an equivalence between "further away" and "longer ago." Darkest Africa, deepest Amazonas, dreaded Mississippi, desperate Pacific islanders were both geographic regions and stadial episodes of time. In contrast, Fabian propounded a notion of undistanced, coeval time, with a shared present.[44] As George Caffentzis has written, "Only by acknowledging that intellectual transmission is not simply a matter of diffusion from center to periphery can the stages metaphor be transcended."[45] It was Brecht who said that wisdom was passed by word of mouth, and that new transmitters passed the old stupidities. There was an active argument, an energetic discussion. The reality was contested. The complacent acceptance of multiple discourses is a sophisticated elision, if not elitist evasion, of that conflict.

In the terms of Volney and Jefferson, the red-crested bird and black duck might have evolutionist, scholarly interpretations, but they would not be part of a dialogue: the Indians were defeated at Fallen Timbers, their land was taken at the Treaty of Greenville, their stories now were groundless. To an Irish audience, in the throes of the loss of political independence, widespread famine, recurring pestilence, repression of spirit, the story had a totally different meaning. James Connolly wrote, "the sympathetic student of history . . . believes in the possibility of a people by political intuition anticipating the lessons afterwards revealed to them in the sad school of experience."[46] What Connolly meant by sympathy or intuition, Luke Gibbons finds, "These agrarian reformers were captivated by the cooperative potential of Irish agriculture, and looked to the existence of a pre-conquest Gaelic commonwealth, a form of Celtic communism, to establish a native pedigree for their coopera-tive ideals."[47] Time is allochronic, if not coeval.

If we jettison the evolutionary scheme of stadialism, does history revert to "a wild whirl of senseless deeds of violence," as Engels feared? Though the industrial proletariat was in the gristle itself, at the machine in the factory of the city, it had allies among the slaves in revolt, the indigenous people in retreat, and the commoners in resistance. Adding them surely alters the dialectics. Older cultural forms like the animal tale gathered a magical political realism. The cultural nationalism could not easily be expressed when the grounding of it was being "ceded and relinquished forever," a bird-and-duck phrase of its own. "Mutato nomine de te fabula narratur," Marx quoted Horace to explain the equivalence of the slave trade and the labor market, of Kentucky with Ireland—the names are changed but the story is told of thee.[48] Dunne helps us to understand that the allegory is a code of survival. It can be understood by an appeal to the materialist world (described in words of substantives) that is historically shared among the *res publica*—hoes, dishes, spoons, ducks, or birds.

Tivoli, New York
April 2001

CHAPTER FOURTEEN

The Commons, the Castle, the Witch, and the Lynx

ONE DAY AT CROTTORF WE EAT MOUTHWATERING STRAWBERRIES AND YOGURT FOR our lunch-time sweet.

Crottorf is the name of a castle, or *schloss*, in Westphalia, Germany. Twenty-one of us are assembled from around the world to discuss the commons. We come from India and Australia, Thailand and South Africa, Brazil, Italy, Germany, Austria, France, England, Greece, California and the Great Lakes. It is midsummer. Surrounded by green meadows and cool forests, the castle seems sprung from a German fairytale, a piece of paradise. Indeed the Italian plasterer said as much in 1661 carving onto the hallway ceiling the words,

Un pezzo del paradiso
Caduto de cielo in terra

For three days we sit in a circle, twenty-one of us, discussing, if not heaven on earth, then the commons. Somehow that term, "the commons," comes to embrace the entire social product of human beings, the countries of the world, the substances of earth, air, water, and fire, the biosphere, the electromagnetic spectrum, and outer space. Speaking passionately, choosing words carefully, stammering sometimes in frustration of inadequate expression, we demand of ourselves maximum hope in conditions of undeniable desperation. The atmosphere and the climate change, the earth and gardening, the rise of slime, the internet and software, the rich and the poor, the enclosures and foreclosures, the shack dwellers of Johannesburg, the disappeared pedestrians of Bangalore, the workers of Brazil, Frankenstein foods and genetic monsters, the totalization of the commodity form, the transformation of expropriation to exploitation, the convergence of ecological crisis and capitalist crisis, the neoliberal assault on the commons and its criminalization from the rain forest to the village: these provide some of the topics, themes, and theses of this Crottorf consultation.

I would not, could not, summarize, though Googleers will find summaries on various websites (David Bollier, onthecommons.org, Massimo De

Angelis, thecommoner.org.uk). What I remember are the refreshing inter-ludes between the bouts of intellectual intensity. They were in a different register, even a kind of dream time—strawberries, singing in the ballroom, and woodland strolls.

We set off to walk in the woods. Our host, the noted forester, Hermann Hatzfeldt, stops among the tall beeches straining to the sky from the dense underbrush, and we form a circle under their canopy to listen to his stories of the war, of wilderness and cultivation, of cat-and-mouse with elusive mush-room gatherers. The life of the forest was changing in surprising, wild ways which depart from the venerable and admired traditions of German forestry. He says that there are even reports that the lynx might return. (And it would, but not in a way I could have imagined in a million years.)

We assemble on a pathway between the drawbridge over the moat and the four-towered *schloss* for an after-lunch tour to a site less than two miles away. It takes a few minutes for all of us to gather, so I take the opportunity to read aloud a report of Handsome Lake's vision at the Strawberry Festival in western New York in 1799, two hundred and ten years earlier. These berries of midsummer, I feel, can act as jewels of remembrance.

Handsome Lake was the brother of Cornplanter, both were Seneca Indians, one of the six nations of the Iroquois League, or Haudenosaunee. He was a drunk, or an addicted victim of the white man's systemic alcohol poisoning. He reached a near-death bottom in April 1799. Then he had his first vision. Three men appeared to him, messengers, dressed in clean raiment, cheeks painted red, carrying bows and arrows in one hand, and a huckleberry bush and other kinds of berries in the other hand. They told him that the juice would provide medicine against alcohol withdrawal, and he must celebrate the strawberry feast. The red checked messengers then continued.

"They saw a jail, and within it a pair of handcuffs, a whip, and a hangman's rope; this represented the false belief of some that the laws of the white man were better than the teachings of *Gaiwiio*. They saw a church with a spire and a path leading in, but no door or window ("the house was hot") and heard a great noise of wailing and crying; this illustrated the point that it was diffi-cult for Indians to accept the confining discipline of Christianity" (Wallace, 243). The punitive regime of capitalism with its prisons, granite churches, and factories—"the great confinement" as Michel Foucault, the French philoso-pher, called the era—was rejected at a moment of its inception. Certainly that rejection is part of the significance of Handsome Lake's prophetic career.

There on the bridge between the moats I skipped ahead three years in the story of Handsome Lake, little knowing what I was leaving out, because I wanted to get to 1801 when Handsome Lake advised the Iroquois "that they should not allow their children to learn to read and write; that they might farm a little and make houses; but that they must not sell anything they raised off the ground, but give it away to one another, and to the old people in particular; in short that they must possess everything in common." (Wallace, 264). John Pierce, a Quaker, translated the speech which is why it has a familiar ring.

"Everything in common." The phrase should strike home: evictions in America, destruction of shacks in south Africa, taking down the forests in Peru, drying up the rivers, privatizing the resources of Iraq, obliterating the African village. In our world of neoliberal privatization, the phrase easily becomes a slogan if not a panacea. But in 1799? Looking at the conjuncture of the late 1790s from a nominalist perspective, the phrase looks to the past, coming as it does from the earliest translation of the English Bible (Wycliffe, 1380s). In the midst of the Atlantic revolutions (France, Haiti) the phrase also looks to the future and the true communism in the workers' movements with its eternal statement of just conditions: from each according to his or her abilities, to each according to his or her needs.

The Iroquois had long held up the mirror of commoning to European privatizing. A hundred years before Handsome Lake, Baron Lahontan who traveled among the Iroquois in the 1680s wrote, "the Nations which are not debauch'd by the Neighbourhood of the Europeans are Strangers to the Measures of Meum and Tuum [mine and thine], and to all Laws, Judges and Priests." That's the best of anarchism straight up, and as a chaser he adds, "a man must be quite blind who does not see that the Property of Goods is the only Source of all the Disorders that perplex the European Societies."

The Haudenosaunee have been on my mind for personal and political reasons. The personal reason is this. The Appalachian mill-village of Cattaraugus in western New York is my ancestral home, and my parents are buried there in Seneca ground. In respect to them I felt a kind of historical pride in bringing to Crottorf the commons of the Seneca. Then the political reason is that in the post-Marxist world the late Marx has begun to come into its own, with the *Ethnological Notebooks* so dependent on the labors of Lewis Henry Morgan whose *Ancient Society,* based on his studies of the Iroquois conducted in the 1840s, helped Marx to return to the communist themes of his youth when, also in the 1840s, he stood philosophy on its head. To him philosophy meant action.

Toward the end of his life Marx studied the Arabs, the Algerians, the Iroquois *gens*, and the Russian *mir*. Marx became convinced that "the commune is the fulcrum for social regeneration in Russia." Marx speculated in the preface to the second Russian edition of the *Communist Manifesto* that Russia's "peasant communal land-ownership may serve as the point of departure for a communist development." In one of his famous letters to Zasulich he wrote "The rural commune [in Russia] finds [capitalism in the West] in a state of crisis that will end only when the social system is eliminated through the return of modern societies to the 'archaic' type of communal property." He then quotes Morgan, "the new system will be a revival, in a superior form, of an archaic social type." Marx was impressed with the grandeur, complexity, and basic superiority of primitive society. The sense of independence and personal dignity are the qualities which moved Morgan, then Marx, as Franklin Rosemont has made clear.

Whether we conceive dialectical reasoning as the historic movement from thesis (the commons) to antithesis (privatization) to synthesis (revolution), or as the mutual interaction between theory (communism) and practice (commoning) Marx was a practitioner of both. The boy who collected berries from common lands in Trier, or the fiery young journalist who defended the peasants' estovers, or customary access to fuel in the woodlands of the Moselle Valley, was both a great theorist of proletarian revolution and an ordinary commoner with practical knowledge. His wife, Jenny, kept his body and soul together, living with the deaths of their children, with poverty, with defamation, disaffection, unceasing repression from all European authorities, and exile. Crottorf is in the same part of Germany, Westphalia, as she was from—Jenny von Westphalen.

So in her ancestral country that evening two of us bicycle into the gloaming. It is all atmosphere: the deserted roads through gentle hills, the solitude of silent cottages, a small flock of sheep, a mare peacefully grazing in the last light startled only by the squeak of a noisy bicycle brake. We climb a hill to a tower that once served as a dungeon; in fact, where witches had once been tried. We coast back to the schloss in the midsummer twilight mulling over communism and the commons.

On another day we go for another walk. Silvia Federici, the scholar of European witchcraft, learned that three witches had been destroyed several centuries ago in the hills near by. Hermann Hatzfeldt kindly proposes to lead us to the site of those crimes. The path is long and the sun is high. On a knoll overlooking neat field and forest and a village nestled within the Westphalian landscape a small red chapel stands. (Scottish ancestors on Jenny von Westphalen's mother's side had suffered violent deaths at the stake.) The red chapel was erected more than three hundred years ago in remorseful memory of a woman who had been executed as a witch at the linden tree. Though the red chapel is locked, we can see through the tiny window that there is enough room for two straw-plaited chairs—one for sitting, one for kneeling—as well as fresh flowers adorning the interior of this simple place of piety and remembrance.

The truth must be told, even at this late date. Standing under that linden tree Handsome Lake's vision did not seem so bright. Was he implicated in murder?

In February 1799 Cornplanter's daughter died. Witchcraft was suspected so he ordered three of his sons to kill the suspected witch, an old woman. On June 13, 1799, they found her working in a field and in full view of the community stabbed her to death and buried her. We do not know for a fact that Handsome Lake was part of this murder, though the circumstantial evidence does not look good. It certainly gives us pause before offering unqualified praise to Handsome Lake's version of the Seneca "commons." Tradition recounts several other witch killings between 1799 and 1801 (Wallace, 236; Mann, 321). Handsome Lake accused a mother and daughter of Cattaraugus of using witchcraft to cause a man to moon Handsome Lake and fart loudly while he spoke. The mother and daughter were bound to a tree and given twenty lashes. Female spirit workers and clan mothers opposing Handsome Lake were redefined as witches, "the slur du jour," as Professor Mann says.

Leaving to one side the dispute about the meaning of witchcraft among the Iroquois during the eighteenth century, those familiar with Silvia Federici's work in *Caliban and the Witch* will approach the subject as an aspect of the transition to capitalism. This means the expropriation of reproduction and the expropriation from land. The consequences of these forces is disempowerment of women and creation of a proletariat.

The Iroquois people had been matrilocal, matrilinear, matriarchal. In 1791 Lafitau reported that the clan mothers admonished the men, "you ought to hear and listen to what we women shall speak, for we are the owners of the land and it is ours." "The economy of the village depended on the women, who owned it collectively," writes Wallace (190). He sums up: "the prophet gave emphatic encouragement to the transformation of the Seneca economic system from a male-hunting-and-female-horticulture to a male-farming-and-female-housekeeping pattern." (281)

The four key words in Handsome Lake's first vision reflect the demographic desperation of the Iroquois—whiskey, witchcraft, love-potions, abortion. A crisis of reproduction, of the society, of the children, of men-and-women, of the culture, of the land. Al Cave writes that in Handsome Lake's visions "women were frequently portrayed as particularly offensive sinners" (213). To Handsome Lake women "bore much of the responsibility for the moral decay he found rampant among the Iroquois."

The demographic condition had deteriorated rapidly after the wars of the American Revolution. Call it genocide or call it depopulation. The former term conveys the exterminating human agency of the conquerors, the latter suggests natural, Malthusian mechanisms of social change. The raids in 1779 by Sullivan, Brodhead, Van Schaick, waging total war, destroyed Indian settlements by burning houses, cutting down apple and peach orchards, torching corn, squash, bean, and incinerating hay fields. George Washington was called "the town-destroyer." To this day the region of New York between the Genesee and Allegheny rivers is known as the burned-over district. Measles and smallpox epidemics struck subsequently. War, exposure, disease, and starvation reduced the population of the Six Nations in half. Loss of confidence was deliberately inflicted by government policy. Alcoholism, family violence, and witch-hunts were the pathological results. The dread of dispossession haunted the inhabitants of these slums in the wilderness. "Now the Dogs yelp and cry in all the houses for they are hungry." Social disaster provided the conditions for the introduction of the land market. The earth became a commodity. Here's how it happened.

Robert Morris "owned" four million acres of Iroquois country. Morris was a Liverpool immigrant who thanks to his slaving and privateering enterprises became "the financier of the American Revolution," the first to use the dollar sign, a Founding Father of the USA, and a capitalist who was so fat that when he sold his property deeds at the Treaty of Big Tree (1797) in Geneseo, New York, to English investors and the Holland Land Company, his son negotiated with the Iroquois while Robert Morris apologized for not attending in person on the grounds of his "corpulence." Gluttony was basic to the art of diplomacy and the Iroquois were kept in a state of unrelieved drunken stupor.

The clan mothers of the Iroquois appointed Red Jacket as their spokesman. A year later he spoke against the treaty: "we have injured our women & children in the sail [sic] of our country." "We now speak soberly" "we women are the true owners we work on it & it is ours" (*Sagoyewatha*, 98, 99). Evidence of the commons is found in his speeches. Red Jacket visited Washington, DC, in February 1801 at the end of the Adams administration seeking justice for the victims of U.S. soldiers who killed three horses "although it was an open common on which they were killed" (108). In 1802 Red Jacket on the sale of a stretch of land along the Niagara River reserved the beach to encamp on, wood to make fire, the river for fishing, and the use of the bridge and turnpike toll free. In June 1801 Red Jacket was accused of witchcraft by Handsome Lake.

Quakers went to Iroquois lands with Bible, plow, and good intentions prepared as it were to revolutionize both the base and the superstructure from primitive communism into full-scale capitalism. In 1797 John Chapman carried apple seeds into western Pennsylvania and Ohio so settlers could produce the cash crop, strong cider, whose political and social function was fully analogous to the poppy of Afghanistan, or cacao of the Andes. A barrel of alcohol provided the lonely settler with a poisonous gesture of welcome to Indian visitors. Thomas Jefferson in 1802 wrote Handsome Lake explaining private property. "The right to sell is one of the rights of property. To forbid you the exercise of that right would be wrong to your nation." Oh, the sly discommoner! He will familiarize these strangers to the measures of meum and tuum. Get the Indians into debt, advised this "economic hitman."

The man who made these dynamics crystal clear at the time was a parson, Thomas Malthus, and like Marx after him he drew on the Iroquois. The first edition of his *An Essay on the Principle of Population* was published anonymously in 1798. It was a critique of William Godwin's doctrinal espousal of theoretic communism and of the French revolutionary Condorcet who, while virtually peering up at the glistening blade of the guillotine, sang the possibilities of human benevolence. Malthus attacked both arguments with a bit of smarty-pants sophistry, saying that since humans increase geometrically while food increases arithmetically, organized death was inevitable. In 1803 he fattened his second edition with substantial research beginning with his dire "observations" of the American Indians including the Iroquois. His list of the checks on their population reads like the bigoted symptomology of victimization: "the insatiable fondness" for liquor, the decrease of the food supply by procuring of peltry to exchange for drink, dishonorable forms of warfare, cannibalism, degradation of women, and "a want of ardor among the men towards their [sic] women."

Produced after two years of revolutionary struggle against scarcity and near famine in England and Ireland, Malthus categorically denies to all human beings the right to subsistence. He criticizes Tom Paine's *Rights of Man* in particular and argues that in America the number of people without property is small compared to Europe. He infamously wrote, referring to the dispossessed and poor, "At nature's mighty feast there is no vacant cover for him" and explained, "the great mistress of the feast . . . wishing that all guests should have plenty, and knowing she could not provide for unlimited numbers, humanely refused to admit fresh comers when her table was already full" (book IV, chapter VI). The principle of European economics—scarcity—is personified as a woman, at the historic moment when on both sides of the Atlantic actual women were disempowered by either the Poor Laws of England or the Land Sales of Iroquoia. Malthus says "humanely refused," and we know what Hazlitt meant in saying "his tongue grows wanton in praise of famine." Genocide.

In August 1799 at the time of the Strawberry Festival Handsome Lake had a second vision. A messenger came to him and revealed the cosmic plan. The rejection of the white man's law and the white man's church was repeated.

He saw a woman so fat she could not stand up, symbolizing the white man's consumerism. He saw a chief who had sold land to the whites now forced to push huge loads of dirt in a wheelbarrow for eternity. Thus began the years of a new religion, based on nativism, evangelism, temperance, and repentance.

Handsome Lake was influenced by Henry O'Bail, son of Cornplanter, educated in Philadelphia, 1791–1796, an accomodationist if not an assimilationist. He imported European concepts of monotheism ("the Great Spirit") and dualism (heaven and hell). Handsome Lake's struggle was also a struggle against traditionalists. He opposed armed struggle, he opposed Red Jacket, he opposed the medicine societies, and he opposed the traditional religion of the clan mothers. But what was the traditional?

The land conquest, the witch killing, the nativist commons must be put in their historical context of the French Revolution. The years 1798 to 1803 saw repressive forces and events conjoin. The conjuncture of the Haitian war of independence, of the Irish rebellion, of the naval mutinies, of millennial outbursts, of trade union organizing, of massive mechanization of the human crafts, of the Alien and Sedition Acts, of the advance of the slave plantation based on cotton, of English enclosure acts (basically deeds of government robbery), and of English combination acts (prevented workers from organizing to increase wages or decrease work but not capitalists from doing so for the opposite purposes). Privatizing and profiteering were dominant values: the commodity and the market ruled supreme: the global planning of morbidity and industrialization went hand in hand. That was the historical conjuncture. During it the spirit of human liberty went underground.

We hike to the Red Chapel, but not everyone of the Crottorf commons consultation comes along. Nicola Bullard takes a gander into the woods.

She sees the lynx.

It most certainly sees her first. They observe each other before the cat casually, characteristically, sauntered silently on. Later as she tells this, people are speechless not knowing quite what to make of it.

> *and our hearts*
> *thudded and*
> *stopped*

writes Mary Oliver in *her* poem on seeing a lynx. Called a "nature poet" we could also call her a poet of the Ohio commons for her respect of the Shawnee, the Iroquois, and creatures like the lynx. For me, it was not only the heart that thudded and stopped but my research bump was alerted too. I continued my studies into the Iroquois commons with the works of my Ohio colleagues, Professor Al Cave, historian of Native Americans, and Professor Barbara

Alice Mann, scholar and exuberant polemicist on behalf of the women of the Haudenosaunee. I wanted to learn more about women and witchcraft and this led me (back) to . . . the lynx.

Handsome Lake's religion evicted Sky Woman from her central place in tradition (Mann, 336). The relationship between monotheism and commodity production, or class society, is clear in the evolution of "the great spirit" in the mid-eighteenth-century North American Indian societies adjusting to the invasion of the Europeans (Cave, *passim*). Religion grew precisely as the gentile commonality shrank. And this paralleled the attacks on women. The "women formed the spiritual backbone of the culture, acting as its prophets, healers, shamans, and seers, untangling the hair of generations" (Mann, 354). "If materialism underpins capitalism, spirituality is the core of Iroquoian communalism."

Barbara Mann surveys the anthropological and historical literature, and she issues a cautionary tale of her own to the collectors of oral tradition, for ever since the Europeans in the seventeenth century sought to make dictionaries and grammars they have been the subject of droll disinformation, comic and profane. Thomas McElwain warned his colleagues that the Haudenosaunee enjoyed some fun with the facts. For instance while collecting material for his Seneca dictionary (*Handbook of the Seneca Language*, New York State Museum and Science Service, Bulletin no. 388, 1963), the informants to the New York anthropologist Wallace Chafe, grew fatigued from going through his long list of botanical names. Entry 1228 used a word for "low blueberry bush that sounds a good deal like 'f**k off,'" but according to McElwain "the gloss for high bush blueberry . . . is the correct one for both forms." The Seneca word for the low blueberry bush points to an essential principle of the commons, the principle of limitation. Bearing that in mind, here is the story of Sky Woman and how the world began.

In the first epoch of time the people of the Sky World passed Earth, or the water world. The dog-tooth violet tree held together the top and bottom of sky. The Sky People toppled it by mistake. Sky Woman was pushed through the hole by the machinations of her husband who was jealous of her shamanic abilities. Sky Woman gripped the roots of the tree grasping the Three Sisters (corn, squash, beans) with her right hand and tobacco with her left before tumbling further on down. Loon and heron saw her falling and joined their wings to parachute her down to a safe landing. But there was no place to land.

The water animals held council agreeing that Sky Woman could not live in water. A giant tortoise volunteered his back. If only earth could be found to put on it, he would be still forever. By turns otter and muskrat plummeted to the depths of the ocean to bring back dirt. Each perished in the attempt.

When beaver tried he stirred up the ocean floor with his spatula-like tail, and surfaced successfully. The others smeared the dirt across the back of Turtle, which thus became North America, or Turtle Island.

Loon and heron near to exhaustion were able to set down Sky Woman on her new home. Sky Woman was pregnant, and gave birth to Lynx who when she grew older became the inseparable walking companion of her mother. They roamed the length and breadth of Turtle Island planting seeds wherever they went. Lynx, for instance, created potatoes, melons, and sunflowers. Sky Woman became too old but Lynx continued wandering on the four Shining Roads returning every night. One day, longing for children of her own, she was seduced by North Wind who wooed and impregnated her behind Sky Woman's back. The delivery was difficult; in fact, she died giving birth to boy twins. The twins were named Sapling and Flint. Theirs is another story. Here we just say they continued the work of creation of plants, animals, mountains, and the running waters. Barbara Mann informs us that "Sapling is honored for creating the strawberry" (33). Meanwhile Lynx was buried and became Mother Earth.

Professor Mann quotes the primary sources of the eighteenth century. In 1703 Lahontan found that the Iroquois would "choose rather to die than to kill" a lynx (I, 345). Heckewelder was with a hunting party in 1773 which refused to eat a lynx even though the hunters were starving. "Mother Earth was (and still is!) a living entity. Her Spirit was the Spirit of the Lynx, Herself" (Mann, 204). Mary Oliver again:

> we've heard,
> the lynx
> wanders like silk
> on the deep
> hillsides of snow—
> blazing,
> it lunges in trees
> as thick as castles
> as cold as iron.
> What should we say
> is the truth of the world?
> The miles alone
> in the pinched dark?
> or the push of the promise?

The particular lynx of Crottorf and the Ohio lynx which caused the poet to ask about the truth of the world are not quite the same. The poet broke the historical silence over the destruction of the Ohio commons and the trauma of the defeated Iroquois with a tone of sadness and a concept of Nature separate from human activity. The Crottorf lynx appeared in the form not of destruction but return and in the context of the restored forest. The return was in the midst of our powerful talking of a non-capitalist future partly instigated by the indigenous revolt which is no longer romantic, primitive, utopian, or surreal. We have an idea of the truth of the world and we push toward the promise of "the commons."

Putting the Iroquois and the lynx to one side, what does this mixture of coincidence and the tangled hairs of the commons amount to? What tales are *we* creating? Is the commons tribal or cosmopolitan? What values are shared by commoning in a high-tech environment and a low-tech situation? What holds together the microcosm of the urban garden and the macrocosm of the polluted stratosphere? Does it necessarily gum up the money-making machine? Does the red commons require revolutionary war while the green commons requires unpalatable compromises with NGOs? Why must the crèche be its base?

These are now the conversations of the world, "mother earth."

The actuality for the people of the Long House was the law of hospitality where none is refused. Karl Marx noted, "at twilight each day a dinner in common served to the entire body in attendance," and with the commons came gratitude. Marx noted the meal began with grace: "it was a prolonged exclamation by a single person on a high shrill note, falling down in cadences into stillness." (Marx, 172–73)

Such ends the story of the commons, the castle, the witch and the lynx.

Westphalia
August 2009

REFERENCES

Cave, Alfred A. *Prophets of the Great Spirit: Native American Revitalization Movements in Eastern North America.* Lincoln: University of Nebraska Press, 2006.

Dunayevskaya, Raya. *Rosa Luxemburg, Women's Liberation, and Marx's Philosophy of Revolution.* New Jersey: Humanities Press, 1982.

Engels, Friedrich. *The Origin of the Family, Private Property, and the State.* New York: International Publishers, 1972.

Federici, Silvia. *Caliban and the Witch.* New York: Autonomedia, 2004.

Ganter, Granville, ed. *The Collected Speeches of Sagoyewatha, or Red Jacket.* Syracuse, NY: Syracuse University Press, 2006.

Heckwelder, John. *History, Manners, and Customs of the Indian Nations Who Once Inhabited Pennsylvania and the Neighboring States.* 1820; reprinted New York: Arno Press, 1971.

Lahontan, Baron. *New Voyages to North-America,* English translation. 1735.

Malthus, T.R. *An Essay on the Principle of Population,* 2nd edition. 1803.

Mann, Barbara Alice. *Iroquoian Women: The Gantowisas.* Peter Lang: New York, 2004.

Marx, Karl. *The Ethnological Notebooks,* with an introduction by Lawrence Krader. Assen: Van Gorcum, 1972.

Oliver, Mary. *American Primitive: Poems.* Boston: Little, Brown & Co., 1983.

Pollan, Michael. *The Botany of Desire.* Random House, 2001.

Rosemont, Franklin. "Karl Marx and the Iroquois." Red Balloon Collective Pamphlet, Environmental Action Series, no. 5.

Shanin, Theodore. *The Late Marx and the Russian Road.* New York: Monthly Review, 1983.

Wallace, Anthony F.C. *The Death and Rebirth of the Seneca.* New York: Knopf, 1970.

CHAPTER FIFTEEN

The Invisibility of the Commons

DEAR KEVIN, MALAV, AND SILVIA,

I said that I would write you about "the invisibility of the commons." I just have three literary examples in mind. One's from the 1930s, another's from the 1790s, and then there's one from the 1940s.

George Orwell wrote an essay, "Marrakech," in 1939. He wrote, "People with brown skins are next door to invisible. Anyone can be sorry for the donkey with its galled back, but it is generally owing to some kind of accident if one even notices the old woman under her load of sticks." His theme is racism and invisibility, though we would add to this obvious and unexamined misogyny. "The file of old women had hobbled past the house with their firewood, and though they had registered themselves on my eyeballs I cannot truly say that I had seen them. Firewood was passing—that was how I saw it." This is the imperialist eye; it sees product, product, product, while the producer simply vanishes. Orwell testifies to this eye: gold from South Africa, tea from Ceylon, tin from Malaya, rubber from Congo, aluminum from Jamaica, on and on they march carrying the wealth of the Third World to be transmuted into the superiority of western economic "development," if not the white-skin privilege of imperialist entoptics. And still they hobble on. But where does the firewood come from? Orwell does not ask. By what right, by what custom, was the firewood gathered? What struggles had preserved this practice? Yet this is the seventh chapter of Magna Carta, the widow's estovers, meaning social stability required that the sovereign recognize her right to wood in the "reasonable common." In other words there are centuries of struggle preserving the practice, and it provides an essential principle in legal tradition. Did Orwell not know this? "One day a poor old creature," Orwell continues, "who could not have been more than four feet tall crept past me under a vast load of wood. I stopped her and put a five-sou piece (a little more than a farthing) into her hand. She answered with a shrill wail, almost a scream, which was partly gratitude but mainly surprise. I suppose that from her point of view, by taking any notice of her, I seemed almost to be violating a law of nature.

She accepted her status as an old woman, that is to say as a beast of burden."
Orwell does not talk to her, the money is in her hand. "Gratitude": how characteristic of imperialism's attitude, forever doing good deeds! Orwell projects
the racism, the misogyny, into his description, but he does not take the opportunity to talk with the commoners. Where does the wood come from? What
fires will it fuel? What children will it warm, or aged parents? Why did he not
converse with her?

That is my first example. It points to an attitude characteristic of many
who fulfill subaltern roles in the imperialist regime, the belief that they are
doing good to people who are basically beasts. This attitude can be maintained
only by refusing to engage, or to talk, with the people. "We must ever believe
a lie when we see with, not through, the eye," said William Blake.

The second is similar, and it comes from Book IX of William Wordsworth's
Prelude, the exalted autobiographical poem of English Individualism and
Romanticism which records the growth of the poet's mind in the midst of
revolution and counter-revolution. I quote from the 1805 version. It describes
an oft-quoted encounter that occurred in the summer of 1792 when he visited
Michel-Arnaud Beaupuy who participated in local political discussions in Blois,
and its provincial club Les Amis de la Constitution (Jacobins) in the transition in the national discussion which was moving the country from limited
constitutional monarchy to radical republicanism and the downfall of monarchy. Beaupuy supported the Jacobin republicans and later became a military
hero dying (1796) in defense of the Revolution. The young men rode their
horses through the beech forests of chateau country, Wordsworth dreaming
of chivalry until brought up short by Beaupuy.

> And when we chanced
> One day to meet a hunger-bitten girl,
> Who crept along fitting her languid self
> Unto a heifer's motion—by a cord
> Tied to her arm, and picking thus from the lane
> Its sustenance, while the girl with her two hands
> Was busy knitting in a heartless mood
> Of solitude—and at the sight my friend
> In agitation said, 'Tis against *that*
> Which we are fighting! I with him believed
> Devoutly that a spirit was abroad
> Which could not be withstood; that poverty,
> At least like this, would in a little time
> Be found no more; that we should see the earth

> Unthwarted in her wish to recompense
> The industrious and the lowly child of toil
> (All institutes for ever blotted out
> That legalized exclusion, empty pomp
> Abolished, sensual state and cruel power,
> Whether by edict of the one or few);
> And finally, as sum and crown of all,
> Should see the people having a strong hand
> In making their own laws—whence better days
> To all mankind.

Wordsworth's poetic transition in these lines begins with the observed image of a starving, overworked, young cow-keeper and goes to idealist hopes of the abolition of poverty and the achievement of self-government by the people. Like Orwell, the young revolutionaries do not stop to talk to the worker, and instead, mixed the warmth of pity, they came to their own grandiose conclusions without talking to the young woman.

Babeuf defended peasants, such as this young woman, from encroachments by the seigneurs, such as the countess de la Myre who exploited the *droit de voirie* (timber rights along the highways). The issue here of course is not estovers but herbage or pasturage, perhaps the central common right of all. Take it away, and you take roast beef and milk away. Both the French Revolution and the Industrial Revolution attacked customary rights in the land representing a great theft of the resources of one class—commoners— by another—privatizers. Wordsworth sees the girl as poor not as commoner. He saw dependence. Had he talked with her he might have understood her independence. Why didn't he?

The blind spot here becomes a typical element in the bourgeois vision. The bourgeois revolution, remember, is not only a sweeping away of monarchy ("empty pomp," "sensual state an cruel power"), it is a vast and massive expropriation of common lands and customs of commoning. That is the "spirit" which was "abroad." So when Beaupuy says to Wordsworth "'Tis against *that* which we are fighting" we wonder what is the *"that"* that he means? Is it the *"that"* of hunger? Is it the *"that"* of knitting furiously in order to compete with the new framework-knitting machine? Or is it the *"that"* of the commoner with her ancient, indefeasible relationship to land? *Halsbury's Laws of England* expresses it this way, "the interest which a commoner has in a common is, in the legal phrase, to eat the grass with the mouths of his cattle." Wordsworth does not explore the ambivalence. Wordsworth was in Blois that summer, not to visit with Beaupuy, but to see his lover, Annette, who was pregnant. When

Wordsworth leaves France a few month's later, he left not only the radical moment of the revolution but also his responsibilities as a father and lover.

The third example of the invisibility of the commons comes from C.L.R. James whose *Notes on Dialectics* meant much to the comrades of Detroit (the Johnson-Forest Tendency of the Fourth International) when they received it in its first form as carbon copies of a typescript sent from Reno, Nevada, in 1948. The *Notes* attempted to finish what Lenin and Trotsky started, namely the application of Hegel's dialectics, and in particular the unity of opposites, to the history of the labor movement. At every stage in its history the labor movement meets its opposite which it must overcome. This was the philosophical grounding for the critique of the notion of the revolutionary party. It jammed philosophy against history and history against philosophy in discussion of the French Revolution and the English Revolution. The *Notes* became a central document to the postwar development of small groups of Marxist revolutionaries in Europe, America, and the Caribbean which in turn welcomed the movement of Third World liberation and working-class insurgency in the First World of the period 1955–1968. And yet it too yields a blind spot. To me, studying the *Notes* years later in 1981, what was liberating was the unity in the concept of the labor movement from the 1640s (at least) to the 1940s. He apprehended this unity against the stadialist categories of bourgeois positivism (feudalism-capitalism-socialism) in inevitable progression but with ideas derived from dialectics—notion, idea, understanding, cognition, contradiction. Despite this powerful speculation, the commons was also invisible to James.

Why was James in Reno, Nevada? Like many he was there to establish residency in order to obtain a no-fault divorce, the only state in the USA where this was possible at the time. He stayed at a ranch near Reno, "the most beautiful spot you ever saw. But it belongs to an Indian tribe and is not commercialized or built-up in any way." For a time he worked as a handyman on the ranch, helping in the garden and with the irrigation. His fellow workers were sailors, cowboys, Filipinos, Mexican, Chinese, and Anglos (as we might say now) from the Midwest. He was drawn to them, "the handsomest men I have ever seen in my life," in contrast to the indigenous people, "The Indians down here are short, thick, dumpy." And against all these stereotypes he recognized "the people here look on me as some freak." He didn't socialize much. He read and he wrote, in September, ten thousand words in one day. From August to November 1948 C.L.R. translated Guérin on the French Revolution and composed his *Notes on Dialectics*. The ranch was on a lake, Pyramid Lake.

His critique of state capitalism was written in surroundings of a struggle, invisible to him, of a guerrilla war for the common lands of the Paiute. Denis Dworkin, a social historian at the University of Nevada (Reno), wrote of this episode in *History Workshop* and appreciates its ironies. "As a Marxist and a British imperial subject, it is certainly plausible that James would view the Paiutes as shaped by the same world-historical process of capitalist imperialism as he himself. Yet aside from his acknowledging that the ranch's location was on an Indian reservation, there is not a shred of evidence that James concerned himself with its inhabitants, let alone the land conflict."

Silver was struck in Virginia City in 1857. Cattle ate the piñon nuts, so the ranchers cut the piñon trees, as indirect attack on the indigenous people. In 1860 white men abducted two Indian women. The Indians fought back at Pyramid Lake that year. Sarah Winnemucca tells the story in *Life Among the Paiutes* (1883), said to be the first book by a Native American woman. A year later, Jack Wilson, better known as Wovoka, who had worked for a white rancher cutting trees for mine shafts, cord wood, and fence posts, had his vision that "the Messiah is coming to earth again and will put the Indians in possession of the country" and began his dance, "the Friendship Dance of the Indian Race" as he called it but known to the world as the Ghost Dance, shuffling along inch by inch, men and women in a circle with fingers interlocked, bodies painted in red and white pigments in order to eliminate illness and bring the dead closer. It was this dance that so frightened the USA that it massacred the Plains Indians at Wounded Knee in 1890. The dance was held in late spring in association with the fish runs.

Mary Austin wrote in 1924, "The Indian problem is of world dimension." She wrote feelingly of the Paiutes and their defeat at Bitter Lake, "they died in its waters, and the land filled with cattlemen and adventurers for gold." In *The Land of Little Rain* (1903) she described one of the ways they commoned. "In the river are mussels, and reeds that have edible white roots, and in the soddy meadows tubers of joint grass; all these at their best in the spring. On the slope the summer growth affords seeds; up the steep the one leafed pines, an oily nut. That was all they could really depend on, and that only at the mercy of the little gods of frost and rain. For the rest it was cunning against cunning, caution against skill, against quacking hordes of wild-fowl in the tulares, against pronghorn and bighorn and deer. You can guess, however, that all this warring of rifles and bowstrings, this influx of overlording whites, had made game wilder and hunters fearful of being hunted. You can surmise also, for it was a crude time and the land was raw, that the women became in turn the game of the conquerors."

Their land was surveyed at the time of the Civil War and President Grant gave this reservation legal status in 1874. Mary Austin describes the actuality of the enclosure: "the beginning of winds along the foot of Coso, the gathering of clouds behind the high ridges, the spring flush, the soft spread of wild almond bloom on the mesa . . . these are the Paiute's walls and furnishings."

The Bureau of Indian Affairs in 1941 published a study of *The Northern Paiute Indians* by Ruth Underhill. "Just as the white man looks for a job, so that he can support his family, the Indian looked to the resources of the country for enough to support his family." But it's not the same at all—the job-seeker finds a wage only with a boss, the Paiute finds resources only if these are conserved. Anyway, in 1941 the white *man,* it is true, found the job, but it was the Indian *woman* who was expert at subsistence. Another study of the Paiute reports that "gathering firewood became part of the ceremony for a young Indian girl when she became a woman," says. Like other proletarians, the young Paiute in the 1940s worked in the defense plants. In an experience described by N. Scott Momaday in *House Made of Dawn* (1966) the proletarian subjectivity of the California defense plants could not eliminate the native hunger, the metaphysics, for land.

A year after C.L.R. left Nevada, the New Yorker writer, A.J. Liebling, visited the Pyramid Lake Ranch, for much the same reason C.L.R. had also established a temporary residence in the "divorce haven." But, unlike C.L.R. who Zeus-like was hurling theoretical thunderbolts through the clouds of the Cold War, Liebling, a food and sports writer, was utterly absorbed by the dispute of the Paiute that he returned with an interest in the legality of the various claims and in the Paiute in general. He wrote a series of articles published in 1955 about the Paiute Indians and "the longest running Indian war in U.S. history." The lake was home to a unique species of fish, the kwee-wee, whose spawning run was the major annual event for the native people living there. These "the kwee-wee eaters" as the Paiute were called settled around this bounty about a thousand years ago. They spoke an Aztec language.

Their principal opponent was Senator Pat McCarran who for as long as anyone could remember introduced bills into the U.S. Senate in favor of a few squatters on the last remaining lands of the Paiute. Six hundred acres were left and in 1948 the Paiute moved back into them but found them dry as a bone. Their neighbors claimed water rights and had cut the water off. In this context the anti-communism of McCarran takes on deeper meanings for not only did he admire notorious international anti-communists like the Franco and Chiang Kai-Shek, in the U.S. he was a close ally of Joe McCarthy and the sponsor of the 1952 McCarran Act which specifically denied entry into the U.S. of Communists, "subversives," and "fellow travellers." In 1985 the U.S. Supreme Court ruled that belief that Nevada was aboriginal could not be litigated, denying any claim at all to land which the Paiute had inhabited for a millennium.

C.L.R. was examined under the Internal Security Act of 1950. In 1952 C.L.R. was imprisoned in Ellis Island. His appeal was rejected under the McCarran Act on the grounds that James was a Communist. He was not, though he was a Marxist revolutionary, but the distinction was lost on most people at the time, including the judge in the case. James wrote while in Ellis Island awaiting deportation that the main aim of the Department of Justice was "the extermination of the alien as a malignant pest."

Senator McCarran wanted to destroy the Indian commons and he wanted to prevent the entry of communists into the USA. Quibble as James might that he was not a Communist as in Communist Party member, he certainly was an opponent of capitalism and an advocate of working-class revolution. As such, however, he did not appreciate the commoning inherent in the Paiute way of life, even though he sat in the midst of the struggle for it. Writing on the edge of Pyramid Lake, neither the muse of Winnemucca nor the ghosts of Wovoka and the dance that that came out of defeat, disease, famine, and confinement to send shivers through the federal government—none apparently affected James. As James, Grace Lee, and Cornelius Castoriadis wrote in *Facing Reality* (1958), "a spectre is haunting Marxism." Now a spectre haunts the self-activity of the working class—the spectre of the commons.

To be fair to James, in 1971 he published in the student radical journal, *Radical America*, an essay from his *The Gathering Forces* in which he quoted D.K. Chisiza, a leader of the independence movement of Tanzania, from *Realities of African Independence* (1961). Why won't Africans settle down into industrial employment? "The loneliness which comes close to being a torture." Life in the village was based on "mutual aid and cooperation." "Like land, it is the equivalent of banks, savings, insurance policies, old age pensions, national assistance schemes, and social security." Or, as we might, the commons.

So. There are three examples of the invisibility of the commons. What obstructed the vision of these otherwise acute not to say profound observers, Orwell, Wordsworth, and James? I do not know for sure. What are your ideas? All I've come up with is that each failed to engage in conversation, in a true dialectics where each party in the discussion is changed by it. Orwell might have found a way to ease the burden of kindling, learned the language, and taken an interest in the lives of the women, and thereby reported for us the origins of the wood. Wordsworth too might have stayed on in France (I think of Samuel Beckett living a peasant's life in a dreary French village during World War II) helped out with Annette and his child and learned where milk and roast beef came from even in times of scarcity. And James? Would he have had to forsake his intellectual penetration as a Marxist thinker and his contributions to the pan-African revolt already in embryonic form by including the struggle for the indigenous common?

We must ask, too, how is it that we are able to see these commons when they did not? Considerable scholarship has unearthed the customary rights in the taking of forest wood for fuel, and it has made us sensitive to so-called "wood theft" as a form of commoning. Likewise, with the custom of herbage, or grazing commons, where the scholarly literature is vast and extends around the world. As for the indigenous commons, it has become a subject of international law even for those who were blind to the struggles initiated at Pine Ridge (1973) or Chiapas (1994).

The usufructs of each of these examples—fuel, protein, and land—are different, just as their ecologies are specific and just as the social relations of each are separate. What is gained by seeing them as commoning? An answer arises in the universality of expropriation, and a remedy to these crimes must be found therefore in reparations for what has been lost and taken.

Yours for commons for all,
Peter
August 2008

Notes

Introduction

1   It is an emergency cry that still can work. Abdul Alkalimat and I used it during lunch at the cafeteria of the University of Toledo to get folks' attention on behalf of the political prisoner and journalist Mumia Abu-Jamal.

2   E.J. Hobsbawm, *Primitive Rebels: Studies in Archaic Forms of Social Movement in the 19th and 20th Centuries* (New York: W.W. Norton, 1959); and from the Warwick School of Social History, our collective's *Albion's Fatal Tree: Crime and Society in Eighteenth-Century England* (London: Allen Lane, 1975) and E.P. Thompson's *Whigs and Hunters* (London: Allen Lane, 1975). Verso published a second edition of *Albion's Fatal Tree* in 2011, and Breviary Stuff published a new edition of *Whigs and Hunters* in 2013. See also the "Frankfurt School" study by Georg Rusche and Otto Kirchheimer, *Punishment and Social Structure* (New York: Columbia University Press, 1939), and the influential work by Michel Foucault, *Discipline and Punish: The Birth of the Prison*, translated by Alan Sheridan (New York: Vintage, 1977).

3   *The New Enclosures*, Midnight Notes, no. 10 (Jamaica Plain, MA: Midnight Notes, 1990).

4   *Radical History Review* 56 (Spring 1993): 59–67.

5   Thanks to Alexis Boyce of Cornell's Institute for Comparative Modernities for confirming these details.

6   *Principles of Political Economy* (1848), book 4, chap. 6, p. 2.

7   V. Gordon Childe, *Skara Brae: A Pictish Village in Orkney* (London: Kegan Paul, 1931), and Aeschylus, *The Prometheus Bound*, ed. and trans. George Thomson (Cambridge: Cambridge University Press, 1932).

8   James Seaver, *The Life of Mary Jemison: Deh-he-wä-mis*, 4th ed. (New York: C.M. Saxton, 1859), 15.

The City and the Commons: A Story for Our Times

1   I thank the Museo Nacional Centro de Arte Reina Sofía in Madrid and the GradCam in Dublin for occasions in May 2013 to discuss the ideas in this essay, particularly Ana de Mendes and Patrick Bresnihan.

2   This is a leading theme of David Graeber's account of Occupy Wall Street. See *The Democracy Project: A History, A Crisis, A Movement* (New York: Spiegel & Grau, 2013).

3   Elinor Ostom, *Governing the Commons: The Evolution of Institutions for Collective Action* (Cambridge: Cambridge University Press, 1990); and J.M. Neeson, *Commoners: Common Right, Enclosure, and Social Change in England, 1700–1820* (Cambridge: Cambridge University Press, 1993).

4   V. Gordon Childe, "The Urban Revolution," *The Town Planning Review* 21, no. 1 (April 1950): 3–17. Childe coined the term earlier in his book *Man Makes Himself* (London: Watts & Co., 1936).

5   John Horne Tooke, *Diversions of Purley*, 2 vols. (London: J. Johnson's: 1786–1805).

6   George Gould, *Righthandedness and Lefthandedness* (Philadelphia: Lippincott, 1908). The USA went right.

7   Anthony Vidler, "The Scenes of the Street: Transformations in Ideal and Reality, 1750–1871," in Stanford Anerrson, ed., *On Streets* (Cambridge: MIT Press, 1978), 58. See also, Bentham, *Panopticon Postscript* (1791), Bowring, vol. 4, 86.

8   Karl Polanyi, *The Great Transformation: The Political and Economic Origins of Our Time* (Boston: Beacon Press, 1957).

9   James Malcolm, *Londinium Redivivum* (London: J. Nichols, 1803), 436, as quoted in Daniel M. Abramson, *Building the Bank of England: Money, Architecture, Society, 1694–1942* (New Haven, CT: Yale University Press, 2005), 125, 130.

10   Col. George Hanger, *Reflections on the Menaced Invasion and the Means of Protecting the Capital* (London: J. Stockdale, 1804) 107–19.

11   Susan Buck-Morss, *Hegel, Haiti, and Universal History* (Pittsburgh: University of Pittsburgh Press, 2009), 60.

12   Frederick Engels, *Socialism: Utopian and Scientific with the Essay on "The Mark,"* trans. Edward Aveling (New York: International Publishers, 1994), 36, 43.

13   E.P. Thompson, "Disenchantment or Default? A Lay Sermon," Conor Cruise O'Brien and William Dean Vanech, *Power & Consciousness* (New York: New York University Press, 1969), 150.

14   Laocoön and marginalia on Thornton's "Lord's Prayer."

15   *Visions of the Daughters of Albion* (1793).

16   George Caffentzis, "The Work/Energy Crisis and the Apocalypse," in *In Letters of Blood and Fire: Work Machines, and the Crisis of Capitalism* (Oakland: PM Press, 2013) 11–57.

17   William Robertson, *The History of the Reign of the Emperor Charles the Fifth* (1769), book 6.

18   Thomas More, *Utopia*, translated by Raphe Robynson (1551), (Everyman's Library: London, 1910), 53.

19   Henry Quaquaquid and Robert Ashpo, *Petition to the Connecticut State Assembly* (May 1789). See also, Iain Boal et al., eds., *West of Eden: Communes and Utopia in Northern California* (Oakland: PM Press, 2012).

20   June Nash, *We Eat the Mines and the Mines Eat Us: Dependency and Exploitation in Bolivian Tin Mines* (New York: Columbia University Press, 1993), xxxiii. See also Michael Taussig, *The Devil and Commodity Fetishism* (Chapel Hill: University of North Carolina Press, 1980) Steve J. Stern, "The Age of Andean Insurrection, 1742–1782: A Reappraisal," in *Resistance, Rebellion, and Consciousness in the Andean Peasant World, 18th to 20th Centuries* (Madison: University of Wisconsin Press, 1987).

21   Laurent Dubois, *Avengers of the New World: The Story of the Haitian Revolution* (Cambridge: Harvard University Press, 2004), 20, 48, 162, 230.

22   F.H.A. Aalen, Kevin Whelan, and Matthew Sout, eds., *Atlas of the Irish Rural Landscape*, 2nd ed. (Cork: Cork University Press, 2011), 86–91.

23   John Prebble, *The Highland Clearances* (London: Secker and Warburg, 1963).

24   The literature is vast, but see E.P. Thompson, "Custom, Law, and Common Right," in *Customs in Common* (London: Merlin, 1991); and Bob Bushaway, *By Rite: Custom, Ceremony and Community in England, 1700–1880* (London: Breviary Stuff, 2011).

25   Peter Linebaugh, *The London Hanged*, 2nd ed. (London: Verso, 2003).

26   Alexander von Humboldt, *Personal Narrative of Travels to the Equinoctial Regions of America* (1805), 121–22 and Greg Dening, *Mr Bligh's Bad Language: Passion, Power, and Theatre on the Bounty* (Cambridge University Press, 1992).

27   Richard Holmes, *The Age of Wonder: How the Romantic Generation Discovered the Beauty and Terror of Science* (New York: Pantheon, 2008), 16–17. In Tahiti, the exchange between a stone age and an iron age culture, not to put to fine a point of it, was: One nail = one fuck.

28   Georges Lefebvre, *The Coming of the French Revolution*, trans. R.R. Palmer (1967), 140–41. Lefebvre says that the nearly universal use of the sickle, as opposed to the scythe, left the stubble generously high for the gleaners.

29   Jules Michelet, *History of the French Revolution*, translated by C. Cocks (London: H.G. Bohn, 1847), 66.

30   William Hazlitt, "The French Revolution" John Thelwall, *Poems . . . Written in the Tower and Newgate* (1795).

31   Dr Robert Watson was the secretary to Gordon and wrote his biography in 1795. Douglas

Hay, "The Laws of God and the Laws of Man: Lord George Gordon and the Death Penalty," in R.W. Malcomson and John Rule, eds., *Protest and Survival: Essays for E.P. Thompson* (London: Merlin Press, 1993).

32 Ralph A. Manogue, "The Plight of James Ridgway, London Bookseller and Publisher, and the Newgate Radicals, 1792–1797," *Wordsworth Circle* 27 (1996): 158–66.

33 A.D. Morris, *James Parkinson: His Life and Times* (Boston: Birkhäuser, 1989). "If the population exceeded the means of support, the fault lay not in nature, but in the ability of politicians to discover some latent defect in the laws respecting the division and appropriation of property."

34 *The Autobiography of Francis Place*, edited by Mary Thrale.

35 R.H. Thompson, "The Dies of Thomas Spence," *The British Numismatic Journal* 38 (1969–1970): 126–67.

36 Richard Mabey, *Flora Britannica* (London: Sinclair-Stevenson, 1996), 444.

37 Clifford D. Conner, *Arthur O'Connor: The Most Important Irish Revolutionary You May Never Have Heard Of* (New York: iUniverse, 2009), 115.

38 Arthur O'Connor, *The State of Ireland*, ed. James Livesey, (Dublin: Lilliput Press, 1998), 22.

39 James Dugan, *The Great Mutiny* (London: Deutsch, 1966).

40 [Arthur Young], *General View of the Agriculture of the County of Norfolk* (1804).

41 G.E. Mingay, *Parliamentary Enclosure in England: An Introduction to Its Causes, Incidence, and Impact 1750–1850* (London: Longman, 1997), 22.

42 John Gazley, *The Life of Arthur Young* (Philadelphia: American Philosophical Society, 1973), 440. He proposed that children at the age of four be taught how to plait straw.

43 Leon Radzinowicz, *A History of English Criminal Law and its Administration from 1750*, vol. 3, *The Reform of the Police*, 310.

44 Patrick Colquhoun, *A Treatise on the Commerce and Police of the River Thames* (1800), 195, 369.

45 Frederic H. Forshall, *Westminster School: Past and Present* (London: Wyman, 1884), 284–85.

46 Ibid., 199.

47 R.W. Malcolmson, *Popular Recreation in English Society 1700–1850* (Cambridge: Cambridge University Press, 1973), 110–11. See also John and Barbara Hammond, *Age of Chartists 1832–1854* (London: Longmans, 1930), 114, 118.

48 C.L.R. James, *Beyond a Boundary* (London: Hutchinson, 1963), 159–60; and *The Future in the Present* (Westport, CT: Lawrence Hill, 1977), 221.

49 Janet Semple, *Bentham's Prison: A Study of the Panopticon Penitentiary* (Oxford: Oxford University Press, 1993), 3, 16.

50 Communication from Elizabeth Wells, archivist, Westminster School, April 24, 2013.

51 Londa Schiebinger, *Plants and Empire: Colonial Bioprospecting in the Atlantic World* (Cambridge: Harvard University Press, 2004).

52 Luke Howard, *On the Modification of Clouds* (London: Taylor, 1803).

53 Simon Winchester, *The Map That Changed the World: William Smith and the Birth of Modern Geology* (New York: HarperCollins, 2001).

54 *In the Mirror of the Past: Lectures and Addresses, 1978–1990* (New York: Marion Boyars, 1992), 227. Jean-Baptiste Lamarck, *Système des animaux sans vertèbres* (Paris: Deterville, 1801).

Karl Marx, the Theft of Wood, and Working-Class Composition: A Contribution to the Current Debate

1 I wish to thank Norman Stein, who provided me with some material assistance in the preparation of this article. My deepest thanks to Gene Mason, Bobby Scollard, and Monty Neill, my comrades in the New England Prisoners' Association, for their criticism of an earlier draft of this paper.

2 I have found the article by Paolo Carpignano, "U.S. Class Composition in the Sixties," *Zerowork* 1 (December 1975): 7–32, invaluable in the development of this theme.

3 Hirst, "Marx and Engels on Law, Crime and Morality," 29; Phillipson, "Critical Theorising

and the 'New Criminology,'" 400; Melossi "The Penal Question in *Capital,*" 31; Currie, "Review: The New Criminology," 113.

4   One thinks here of those "deviancy specialists" influenced by Althusser (see, for example, Hirst, "Marx and Engels on Law, Crime and Morality," 28–56). It may be that Marx "never developed an adequate philosophical reflection of his scientific discoveries." However, some account of those discoveries is in order, especially when by Marx's own account one of his most important contributions over the advances made by Adam Smith and David Ricardo was that of the principle of historical specification of the categories of political economy (Marx, *Capital,* 1:52–54).

5   Melossi "The Penal Question in *Capital,*" 26ff.

6   Crime and Social Justice Collective. "The Politics of Street Crime," 1–4; Herman and Julia R. Schwendinger, "Delinquency and the Collective Varieties of Youth."

7   I would like to thank E.J. Hobsbawm and Margaret Mynatt at Lawrence and Wishart who kindly assisted me in making available the English translation of these articles before their publication.

8   Cornu, *Karl Marx et Friedrich Engels,* 2:68.

9   *A Contribution to the Critique of Political Economy,* 10.

10 There does exist a small literature on Marx's articles (see, for example, Cornu, *Karl Marx et Friedrich Engels,* 2:72ff., and Vigouroux, "Karl Marx et la législation forestière rhénane de 1842," 222–33) but its chief interest is in the intellectual passage of Marx's thought from Kant, Rousseau, and Savigny to Feuerbach and Hegel.

11 Cornu, *Karl Marx et Friedrich Engels,* 2:72–95; Mehring, *Karl Marx: The Story of His Life,* 37ff.

12 Treitschke, *A History of Germany in the Nineteenth Century,* 4:538.

13 Marx, "Proceedings of the Sixth Rhine Province Assembly," 747.

14 Wilson, *To the Finland Station,* 124.

15 These works are discussed in more detail in section V below. See also Fuld, *Der Einfluss der Lebensmittelpreise auf die Bewegung der Strafbaren Handlungen;* Mayr, *Statistik der Gerichtlichen Polizei im Königreiche Bayern;* Starke, *Verbrechen und Verbrecher in Preussen 1854–1878;* and Valentini, *Das Verbrecherthum im preussischen Staat.*

16 Lenin, *The Development of Capitalism in Russia,* 590.

17 Perrie, "The Russian Peasant Movement of 1905–1907," 128–29.

18 Bowring, "Report on the Prussian Commercial Union," 1.

19 Henderson, *The Zollverein,* 129–30.

20 Treitschke, *A History of Germany in the Nineteenth Century,* 7:201.

21 Banfield, *Industry of the Rhine, Series 2: Manufactures,* 55–56.

22 Banfield, *Industry of the Rhine. Series 1: Agriculture,* 142.

23 Palgrave, *Dictionary of Political Economy,* 2:814–16; Lengerke, *Die Ländliche Arbeiterfrage.*

24 Droz, *Les Revolutions Allemandes de 1848,* 78.

25 Milward and Saul, *The Economic Development of Continental Europe, 1780–1870,* 147.

26 Mayr, *Statistik der Gerichtlichen Polizei im Königreiche Bayern,* 136–37.

27 Milward and Saul, *The Economic Development of Continental Europe, 1780–1870,* 147.

28 Ibid., 82.

29 Treitschke, *A History of Germany in the Nineteenth Century,* 7:301.

30 Cornu, *Karl Marx et Friedrich Engels,* 2:78–79.

31 Banfield, *Industry of the Rhine, Series 1: Agriculture,* 157.

32 Ibid., 159.

33 Manwood, *Manwood's Treatise of the Forest Laws,* 2.

34 Heske, *German Forestry,* 241.

35 Bowring, "Report on the Prussian Commercial Union," 137.

36 Henderson, *The Rise of German Industrial Power, 1834–1914,* 54.

37 Banfield, *Industry of the Rhine, Series 1: Agriculture,* 109.

38 Noyes, *Organization and Revolution,* 23.

39 U.S. Department of State, *Forestry in Europe,* 74.

40 Even at the end of the nineteenth century the Italian, French, and English literature on forestry subjects presented a dearth in comparison to the German. This is the conclusion of the American silviculturist Bernhard Fernow (*Economics of Forestry*, 492).

41 Quoted in Heske, *German Forestry*, 254.

42 Schwappach, *Forstpolitik, Jagd- und Fischereipolitik*.

43 U.S. Department of State, *Forestry in Europe*, 53.

44 Banfield, *Industry of the Rhine, Series 1: Agriculture*, 115.

45 Treitschke, *A History of Germany in the Nineteenth Century*, 7:302.

46 Hughes, *A Book of the Black Forest*, 36.

47 Quoted in Howitt, *Rural and Domestic Life in Germany*, 89–90.

48 Cornu, *Karl Marx et Friedrich Engels*, 2:74; Wilson *To the Finland Station*, 41.

49 Banfield, *Industry of the Rhine, Series 1: Agriculture*, 111.

50 Mayr, *Statistik der Gerichtlichen Polizei im Königreiche Bayern*, chap. 4.

51 Starke, *Verbrechen und Verbrecher in Preussen 1854–1878*, 88.

52 Valentini, *Das Verbrecherthum im preussischen Staat*, 58.

53 Droz, *Les Revolutions Allemandes de 1848*, 151–55.

54 Adelman, "Structural Change in the Rhenish Linen and Cotton Trades at the Outset of Industrialization," *passim*.

55 Noyes, *Organization and Revolution*, chaps. 9 and 13.

56 Heske, *German Forestry*, 240ff.

Frau Gertrude Kugelmann and the Five Gates of Marxism

1 This paper was delivered on March 30, 2007, at Cornell University, Ithaca, New York, at a conference called Between Primitive Accumulation and the New Enclosures Conference. I thank Barry Maxwell, the organizer, and my colleagues Iain Boal and George Caffentzis.

2 Marx to Engels, February 13, 1866, in Karl Marx and Frederick Engels, *Collected Works*, vol. 42 (New York: International Publishers, 1987), 227.

3 Karl Kautsky published Marx's letters to Kugelmann in 1902. Five years later they were published in a Russian translation with a preface by Lenin. In 1934 they were published in an English translation by the Cooperative Publishing Society of Foreign Workers in the USSR, as Karl Marx, *Letters to Dr. Kugelmann*. Marxist Library, vol. 17 (New York: International Publishers, 1934).

4 Marx to Engels, May 7, 1867, in Marx and Engels, *Collected Works*, vol. 42.

5 He wrote Engels in January, "the baker alone is owed £20, and there is the very devil with butcher, grocer, taxes, etc." Ibid., 371, 343.

6 Letter of Karl Marx to Dr. Kugelmann, November 30, 1867, in ibid., 489. So many commentators since have dealt with this problem of "incomprehensible terminology" by suggesting some other sequence of reading than chapter by chapter.

7 Walter Rodney, *How Europe Underdeveloped Africa* (Washington, DC: Howard University Press, 1981); and Silvia Federici, *Caliban and the Witch: Women, the Body, and Primitive Accumulation* (New York: Autonomedia, 2004).

8 Hugo Gellert, *Karl Marx's 'Capital' in Lithographs* (New York: Long & Smith, 1934).

9 The introduction has been translated by T.M. Holmes, and is published in Karl Korsch, *Three Essays on Marxism* (London: Pluto Press, 1971).

10 Marx to Kugelmann, October 12 and Decermber 12, 1868, in *Letters*, 78, 83.

11 Yvonne Kapp, *Eleanor Marx*, vol. 1 (New York: Pantheon, 1972), 167.

12 David McLellan, *Karl Marx: His Life and Thought*, 428.

13 Rosdolsky believes that Marx intended to write a "*Book on Wage Labor*," which he abandoned because he had already conducted in volume one "the extensive empirical and historical analyses, which underpin the sections on absolute and relative surplus-value and on the process of accumulation." Roman Rosdolsky, *The Making of Marx's 'Capital*,' translated by Pete Burgess (London: Pluto Press, 1977), 61. The Marxist exegetes of the late 1970s had nothing to do with the Kugelmann chapters, G.A. Cohen, *Karl Marx's Theory of History: A*

Defence (Princeton: Princeton University Press, 1978), or Ellen Meiksins Wood, *The Pristine Culture of Capitalism*, or *The Origin of Capitalism*.

14 This is what is so remarkable about Harry Cleaver's *Reading Capital Politically*.

15 E.P. Thompson, *The Poverty of Theory* (Merlin Press: London, 1978), 257.

16 David Goodman Croly and George Wakeman, *Miscegenation: The Theory of the Blending of the Races, Applied to the American White Man and Negro* (New York: H. Dexter, Hamilton & Co., 1864); Elise Lemire, *"Miscegenation": Making Race in America* (Philadelphia, University of Pennsylvania Press: Philadelphia, 2002), 116–18, 140.

17 Scott Reynolds Nelson, *Steel Drivin' Man: John Henry, the Untold Story of an American Legend* (Oxford: Oxford University Press, 2006)

18 G.D.H. Cole, *Socialist Thought: The Forerunners 1789–1850*, vol. 1 of *A History of Socialist Thought* (Macmillan: London, 1953), 248. See also Eric Hobsbawm's introduction to Karl Marx and Frederick Engels, *The Communist Manifesto: A Modern Edition* (London: Verso, 1998).

Ned Ludd & Queen Mab

1 This pamphlet began as a lecture at a bicentennial conference called "The Luddites, without Condescension" held at Birkbeck College, University of London, May 6, 2011, and a précis was subsequently offered at a conference held in Amsterdam, June 16–18, 2011, called "Mutiny and Maritime Radicalism during the Age of Revolution: A Global Survey." I thank Iain Boal and Marcus Rediker for inviting me to these two occasions. Niklas Frykman, Forrest Hylton, David Lloyd, Charles Beattie-Medina, Gordon Bigelow, Manuel Yang, and Colin Thomas provided helpful suggestions.

2 I am grateful to Jesse Olavasky for bringing this crime to my attention. See Marion B. Lucas, *A History of Blacks in Kentucky: From Slavery to Segregation, 1760–1891* (Lexington: The Kentucky Historical Society, 1992), 47–48.

3 Frank Peel, *The Risings of the Luddites*, 4th ed. with an introduction by E.P. Thompson (London: Cass, 1968), 1.

4 E.J. Hobsbawm, *Labouring Men: Studies in the History of Labour* (New York: Basic Books, 1964).

5 "Report on the State of Popular Opinion and Causes of the Increase of Democratic Principles," *The Tribune* 28 (September 1795).

6 Linda Colley, *Britons: Forging the Nation, 1707–1837* (New Haven, CT: Yale University Press, 1992), 239, 256 ("In Great Britain, woman was subordinate and confined. But at least she was safe").

7 Book V, chap. 1 in Adam Smith, *The Wealth of Nations* (1776), ed. Edwin Seligman, 2 vols. (London: Dent, 1958), 2:264.

8 C.A. Bayly, *Imperial Meridian: The British Empire and the World, 1780–1830* (London: Longman, 1989), 129.

9 At the beginning of book nine.

10 David Noble, *Progress without People: In Defense of Luddism* (Chicago: Charles H. Kerr Publishing Co., 1993).

11 Muhammad Ali's state-sponsored long staple cotton industry did not begin until 1821. Afaf Lutfi Al-Sayyid Marsot, *Egypt in the Reign of Muhammad Ali* (Cambridge: Cambridge University Press, 1984), 145; and Henry Dodwell, *The Founder of Modern Egypt: A Study of Muhammad 'Ali* (Cambridge: Cambridge University Press, 1931), 32.

12 Alan Richards, *Egypt's Agricultural Development, 1800–1980: Technical and Social Change* (Boulder, CO: Westview Press, 1982), 12.

13 Stephen Randolph Gibbons, *Captain Rock, Night Errant: The Threatening Letters of Pre-Famine Ireland, 1801–1845* (Dublin: Four Courts Press, 2004), 59, 60.

14 *The Autobiography of William Carleton* (London: MacGibbon & Kee, 1968).

15 Kevin Binfield, ed., *Writings of the Luddites* (Baltimore: Johns Hopkins University Press, 2004), 209–11. While my own knowledge of the Luddites begins with Thompson's *Making*

of the English Working Class (1963) and Kirkpatrick Sale, *Rebels Against the Future: The Luddites and Their War on the Industrial Revolution: Lessons for the Computer Age* (New York: Addison-Wesley, 1995), recent local history enlarges our knowledge. Katrina Navickas, "Luddism, Incendiarism and the Defence of Rural 'Task-Scapes' in 1812," *Northern History* 48, no. 1 (March 2011), deepens knowledge of the dual economy, farming, and textiles.

16 R.G. Kirby and A.E. Musson, *The Voice of the People: John Doherty, 1798–1854, Trade Unionist, Radical and Factory Reformer* (Manchester: Manchester University Press, 1975), 2, 14.

17 W.B. Crump, ed., *The Leeds Woollen Industry, 1780–1820* (Leeds: Thoresby Society, 1931), 229–30.

18 Richard Holmes, *The Age of Wonder: How the Romantic Generation Discovered the Beauty and Terror of Science* (New York: Pantheon, 2008), 157, 162.

19 Malcolm Chase, *The People's Farm: English Radical Agrarianism, 1775–1840* (London: Breviary Stuff Publications, 2010), 46, 56, 59.

20 Peel, *Risings of the Luddites*, 14–15.

21 Richard Holmes, *Shelley: The Pursuit* (New York: Dutton, 1975), 98.

22 George Orwell, "Marrakech" in *Essays*.

23 David Lee Clark, ed., *Shelley's Prose; or, The Trumpet of a Prophecy* (Albuquerque: University of New Mexico Press, 1954), 108, 122.

24 See Mercutio's speech in *Romeo and Juliet*, I.iv.

25 Bayly, *Imperial Meridian*, 6, 14, 80, 121; Peter Carey, *The Power of Prophecy: Prince Dipanagara and the End of the Old Order in Java, 1785–1855* (Leiden: KITLV Press, 2007), 33, 179, 258.

26 Eugene D. Genovese, *The Political Economy of Slavery: Studies in the Economy & Society of the Slave South* (New York: Vintage, 1967), 55; *Roll, Jordan, Roll: The World the Slaves Made* (New York: Pantheon, 1974), 300.

27 Adam Rothman, *Slave Country: American Expansion and the Origins of the Deep South* (Cambridge, MA: Harvard University Press, 2005), 34–39.

28 Daniel Rasmussen, *American Uprising: The Untold Story of America's Largest Slave Revolt* (New York: HarperCollins, 2011).

29 Karen Racine, *Francisco de Miranda: A Transatlantic Life in the Age of Revolution* (Wilmington, DE: Scholarly Resources, 2003), 216, 226, 232.

30 Marixa Lasso, *Myths of Harmony: Race and Republicanism during the Age of Revolution* (Pittsburgh: University of Pittsburgh Press, 2007), 1; John Lynch, *The Spanish American Revolutions, 1808–1826* (New York: Norton, 1973), 205.

31 John Lynch, *Simón Bolívar: A Life* (New Haven, CT: Yale University Press, 2006), 54, 56, 63, 68.

32 "A Provincial Library in Colonial Mexico, 1802," *Hispanic American Historical Review* 26, no. 2 (May 1946): 162–83. The library belonged to one of his associates in Guanajuato. Volney's *Ruins* is not among the books listed.

33 Eric Van Young calls them "village soviets." See his *The Other Rebellion: Popular Violence, Ideology, and the Mexican Struggle for Independence, 1810–1821* (Stanford: Stanford University Press, 2001); and John Lynch, *The Spanish American Revolutions, 1808–1826* (New York: Norton, 1973), 309.

34 Oscar Lewis, *Tepoztlán Village in Mexico* (New York: Holt, Rinehart and Winston, 1960), 27; see also, Robert Redfield, *Tepoztlán: A Mexican Village: A Study of Folk Life* (Chicago: University of Chicago Press, 1930), 62ff; Brian R. Hamnett, *Roots of Insurgency: Mexican Regions, 1750–1824* (Cambridge: Cambridge University Press, 1986), 90.

35 Tenskwatawa blamed the defeat on his menstruating wife who contaminated the ceremonies before the battle. John Sugden, *Tecumseh: A Life* (New York: Henry Holt, 1997), 257.

36 John D. Hunter, *Memoirs of a Captivity Among the Indians of North America* (London: Longman, Hurst, Rees, Orme, and Brown, 1824), 257–58.

37 Thompson, *The Making of the English Working Class*, 487, 497.

38 Holmes, *Shelley: The Pursuit*, 164.

39 Anne Kelly Knowles, *Calvinists Incorporated: Welsh Immigrants on Ohio's Industrial Frontier* (Chicago: University of Chicago Press, 1997), 95.

40 Maxine Berg, *The Machinery Question and the Making of Political Economy* (Cambridge: Cambridge University Press, 1980), 15.

41 T.A. Critchley and P.D. James, *The Maul and the Pear Tree: The Ratcliffe Highway Murders, 1811* (London: Constable, 1971).

42 John Bohstedt, *Riots and Community Politics in England and Wales, 1790–1810* (Cambridge: Harvard University Press, 1983), 162.

43 Francis Grose, *A Classical Dictionary of the Vulgar Tongue* (1796), edited by Eric Partridge (New York: Barnes & Noble, 1963), 184.

44 John Harriott, *Struggles through Life*, 2 vols. (London: C. and W. Galabin, 1807), 2:337, 340.

45 *Parliamentary Papers*, vol. 17 (1795–1796), xxvi.

46 *Parliamentary Papers*, vol. 4, 225.

47 William Tatham, *The Political Economy of Inland Navigation* (London: R. Faulder, 1799), 133.

48 Thompson, *The Making of the English Working Class*, 544.

49 Critchley and James, *The Maul and the Pear Tree*, 174: "the key questions still unanswered"; and Leon Radzinowicz, *A History of English Criminal Law and Its Administration*, vol. 3, *The Reform of the Police* (London: Stevens, 1956), 322: "He was, without doubt, the murderer . . ."

50 During the Parliamentary debate on the police, Cochrane ascribed increase in crimes to "the Pension List and to the various other modes by which individuals of the higher classes . . . partook of the public money, without performing any public service" which demoralized the lower classes and drove them to the commission of offences. Radzinowicz, *A History of English Criminal Law and Its Administration* 3:336.

51 Critchley and James, *The Maul and the Pear Tree*, 200.

52 Rozina Visram, *Ayahs, Lascars and Princes: Indians in Britain 1700–1947* (London: Pluto Press, 1986), 34, 39, and 45. In 1806 Chinese and lascar sailors erupted in riot in Ratcliffe Gardens when the captain of their ship ordered a lascar to flog a Chinese sailor. I am grateful to Iona Man-Cheong and her paper, "Chinese Seafarers & Acts of Resistance in the 'Age of Revolution,'" (presented at the Conference on Mutiny and Maritime Radicalism, Amsterdam, June 2011).

53 *The Times*, January 1, 1812, 166.

54 I owe this knowledge to Niklas Frykman, who studied Captain Kennedy's log for 1811.

55 Emilia Viotti da Costa, *Crowns of Glory, Tears of Blood: The Demerara Slave Rebellion of 1823* (New York: Oxford University Press, 1994), 40, 99, 111, 175.

56 Richard Watson, *A Defence of the Wesleyan Methodist Mission in the West Indies* (London: Blanshard, 1817), 75.

57 As quoted in Walter Rodney, *A History of Guyanese Working People, 1881–1905* (Baltimore: Johns Hopkins University Press, 1981), 128.

58 Kenneth Joyce Robertson, *The Four Pillars: A Genealogical Journey* (Bloomington, IN: Xlibris, 2010), 160. A remarkable book of valuable inventories, archival labor, and pointed anecdote written by a Guyanese market fruit-juicer of Toledo who traces his ancestry to Ignatius Sancho, the grocer and man of letters of eighteenth-century London.

59 Michael Fisher, "Finding Lascar 'Wilful Incendiarism': British Arson Panic and Indian Maritime Labor in the Indian and Atlantic Oceans" and Nicole Ulrich, "Local Protest and International Radicalism: the 1797 Mutinies at the Cape of Good Hope," (paper presented at the Conference on Mutiny and Maritime Radicalism during the Age of Revolution, Amsterdam June 2011).

60 Binfield, *Writings of the Luddites*, 1.

61 Humphry Davy, *On the Fire-Damp in Coal Mines and on Methods of Lighting the Mines So As to Prevent Explosion* (Newcastle: E. Charnley, 1817).

62 Holmes, *The Age of Wonder*, 304, 325.

63 John Charnock, *An History of Marine Architecture* (London: Faulder, 1800).

Foreword to E.P. Thompson's *William Morris: Romantic to Revolutionary*

1   "Diary," *London Review of Books* 32, no. 15 (August 2010): 28–31.

2   "How I Became a Socialist," *Justice* (1894), reprinted in A.L. Morton, *Political Writings of William Morris* (London: Lawrence & Wishart, 1973), 241.

3   E.P. Thompson, Making History: Writings on History and Culture (New York: The New Press, 1994), 70.

4   William Morris, "How I Became a Socialist."

5   E.P. Thompson, *Persons & Polemics: Historical Essays* (London: Merlin Press, 1994), 67.

6   Perry Anderson, *Arguments Within English Marxism* (London: Verso, 1980), 163.

7   Thompson tells this story in *Beyond the Frontier: The Politics of a Failed Mission: Bulgaria 1944* (London: Merlin Press, 1997).

8   Mike Merrill, "Interview with E.P. Thompson," Mid-Atlantic Radical Historians Organization (1976), reprinted in Henry Abelove et al., eds., *Visions of History* (New York: Pantheon, 1983), 13.

9   Theodosia Thompson and E.P. Thompson, eds., *There Is a Spirit in Europe . . . A Memoir of Frank Thompson* (London: Victor Gollancz, 1948), 170.

10   Jack Dash, *Good Morning Brothers!* (London: Lawrence & Wishart, 1969), 24.

11   E.P. Thompson, *William Morris: Romantic to Revolutionary* (Oakland: PM Press, 2011), 727, 810.

12   Michelle Weinroth, *Reclaiming William Morris: Englishness, Sublimity and the Rhetoric of Dissent* (Montreal: McGill University Press, 1996).

13   *William Morris: A Vindication* (London: Martin Lawrence, 1934).

14   This was a story we told in *Zerowork* 1 (December 1975) & 2 (Fall 1977).

15   Tony Judt, *Postwar: A History of Europe since 1945* (New York: Penguin, 2005), 161.

16   Captain A.A. Brickhouse Jr., "Tapline's Sidon Terminal," *World Petroleum* (June 1957).

17   C.L.R. James, "State Capitalism and World Revolution" (1950) reprinted in *The Future in the Present: Selected Writings* (London: Allison & Busby, 1977), 128, 131. James, too, turned to literature in *Mariners, Renegades and Castaways* (1952), to *Moby Dick*, as a means of developing his theory of an autonomous socialist black movement and as a critique of the democratic centralism of the Marxist organization.

18   Jeffrey Meikle, *American Plastic: A Cultural History* (New Brunswick, NJ: Rutgers University Press, 1995), 82, 85, 154; and Claire Catterall, "Perceptions of Plastics: A Study of Plastics in Britain, 1945–1956," in Penny Sparke, ed.), *The Plastics Age* (Woodstock, NY: Overlook Press, 1993), 67–68.

19   Andy Croft, ed., *A Weapon in the Struggle: The Cultural History of the Communist Party in Britain* (London: Pluto Press, 1998) and Kevin Morgan, Gidon Cohen and Andrew Flinn, *Communists and British Society, 1920–1991* (London: Rivers Oram Press, 2007).

20   Orwell used the term "cold war" in the "You and the A-Bomb," *Tribune* October 19, 1945.

21   Frances Stonor Saunders, *The Cultural Cold War: The CIA and the World of Arts and Letters* (New York: The New Press, 1999), 2, 65, 129.

22   David Kynaston, *Austerity Britain, 1945–51* (New York: Walker & Co., 2008), 344.

23   David Renton, *Dissident Marxism: Past Voices for Present Times* (London: Zed Books, 2004), chap. 5.

24   "The Historian's Group of the British Communist Party," in Maurice Cornforth, ed., *Rebels and Their Causes: Essays in Honour of A.L. Morton* (Lawrence and Wishart: London, 1978), 22.

25   The Party Congress of 1952 passed a resolution calling for increased "activity against the Americanisation of Britain's cultural life, against reactionary film and lurid and debased literature and comics" but overlooked the opening of Coca-Cola bottling plants. Quoted by Andy Croft, "Authors Take Sides: Writers and the Communist Party 1920–56," in Geoff Andrews, Nina Fishman and Kevin Morgan, eds., *Opening the Books: Essays on the Social and Cultural History of British Communism* (London: Pluto, 1995), 92. I happened to be in school in north London at the time and remember that the hostility greeting the use of the ballpoint pen was mixed with "American" modernism.

26   "Through the Smoke of Budapest," *The Reasoner* 3 (1956): 3.

27   John Rule quotes this in his fine biographical entry on Thompson in The *Dictionary of National Biography.*

28   "Edgel Rickword," *Persons and Polemics*, 238.

29   John Goode, "E.P. Thompson and 'The Significance of Literature,'" in Harvey J. Kaye and Keith McClelland, eds., *E.P. Thompson: Critical Perspectives* (Philadelphia: Temple University Press, 1990), 194–96. F.R. Leavis hammered the nails into Shelley's coffin in *Revaluations: Tradition and Development in English Poetry* (London: Chatto and Windus, 1949), chap. 6.

30   I do not know the source of Thompson's aversion to Shelley.

31   Perry Anderson, *Arguments Within English Marxism* (London: Verso, 1980), 176, 189, 206–7.

32   Frank Hamilton Cushing, *My Adventures in Zuni* (New York: Century Co., 1882).

33   Michelle Weinroth, *Reclaiming William Morris: Englishness, Sublimity and the Rhetoric of Dissent* (Montreal: McGill University Press, 1996), 4. Although she does not take the story much beyond the 1950s her judgment of Thompson is inexplicably harsh: "his redemptive efforts are aristocratic and foreclose the possibility of engendering a real democratic movement; his following is always compelled to surrender irrationally to his judgment," 244.

34   Thomas Hughes, *The Scouring the White Horse* (London: Macmillan, 1859).

35   A recent biographer of Morris states, "The kitchen had always been his favorite of rooms." Fiona MacCarthy, *William Morris: A Life for Our Time* (New York: Knopf, 1995), 517.

36   MacCarthy criticizes Thompson for excluding anarchist influences on Morris, for missing "his qualities of waywardness and danger," 543.

37   Morris continued to visit the White Horse annually to the year before he died. See MacCarthy, 654.

38   Terry Eagleton, *The Idea of Culture* (Oxford: Blackwell, 2000), 1.

39   Morton, *Political Writings of William Morris*, 193.

40   Ashby, 281–83.

41   Sheila Rowbotham, *Edward Carpenter: A Life of Liberty and Love* (London: Verso, 2008), 20.

42   Mary Lago, *"India's Prisoner": A Biography of Edward John Thompson, 1886–1946* (London: University of Missouri Press, 2001), 128–29.

43   Theodosia Thompson and E.P. Thompson, eds., *There Is a Spirit in Europe . . . A Memoir of Frank Thompson* (London: Victor Gollancz, 1948), 48, 51, 118.

44   Ibid., 20.

45   Caroline Arscot, *William Morris and Edward Burne-Jones: Interlacings* (London: Yale University Press, 2008), 21, 25, 93.

46   Thompson, *William Morris*, 636.

47   "The Late Mr. William Morris: Interment at Kelmscott," 1896, Walthamstow: William Morris Gallery collection.

48   G.D.H. Cole, *The History of Socialist Thought*, vol. 2 (London: Macmillan, 1954), 424.

49   Thompson, *William Morris*, 566.

50   It is the title of a Sierra Club classic. Thoreau published his in *Atlantic Monthly* (1862) though he'd been lecturing on "Walking, or the Wild" for ten years.

51   Karl Marx, "A Contribution to the Critique of Hegel's Philosophy of Right," first published 1843–44, in *Early Writings*, translated by Rodney Livingstone and Gregor Benton (London: Penguin Books, 1974), 244.

52   Thompson's account is in *William Morris: Romantic to Revolutionary*, 437–45.

53   Thompson's relies on the local newspaper's account (*Newcastle Chronicle*) as confirmed by Morris's diary.

Preface to the Korean Edition of *The Magna Carta Manifesto*

1   Jessica Mitford, *Hons and Rebels* (London: Gollancz, 1960), 191.

2   George Katsiaficas and Na Kahn-chae eds., *South Korean Democracy: Legacy of the Gwangju Uprising* (New York: Routledge, 2006).

3   David Rollison, *A Commonwealth of the People: Popular Politics and England's Long Social Revolution, 1066–1649* (Cambridge: Cambridge University Press, 2010).

4   The Latin is *"Nempe reverso domum, cum uxore fabulandum est, garriendum cum liberis, collo-quendum cum ministris."*

5   Silivia Federici, *Caliban and the Witch: Women, The Body, and Primitive Accumulation* (New York: Autonomedia, 2004).

6   *Black and White: Land and Labor in the South* (New York: Fords, Howard & Hulbert, 1884), 217, 233.

7   *America Is in the Heart* (New York: Harcourt, Brace, & Co., 1946).

8   Ronald Briley, "Woody Sez: The People's Daily World and Indigenous Radicalism," *California History* 84, no. 1 (Fall 2006), 35.

9   *Wall Street Journal*, March 8, 2007.

10 Elinor Otrom, *Governing the Commons: Evolution of Institutions for Collective Action* (Cambridge University Press, 1993)

11 Or in a different register of meaning entirely, the "commons" might refer to Parliament or sewage, the House of Commons or the "necessary house." Francis Grose, *A Dictionary of the Vulgar Tongue* (1785).

12 See E.P. Thompson, "Christopher Caudwell," *Persons & Polemics: Historical Essays* (London: Merlin Press, 1994). They quoted Lenin at the fourth Congress of the Communist International (1922).

Enclosures from the Bottom Up

1   See Silvia Federici, *Caliban and the Witch: Women, the Body, and Primitive Accumulation* (Brooklyn, NY: Autonomedia, 2004); Maria Mies and Veronika Bennholdt-Thomsen, *The Subsistence Perspective: Beyond the Globalised Economy* (London: Zed Books, 1998); Michel Foucault, *Discipline and Punish*, trans. Alan Sheridan (London: Alan Lane, 1975); David Harvey, *The New Imperialism* (New York: Oxford University Press, 2003); and David Bollier, *Silent Theft: The Private Plunder of Our Common Wealth* (New York: Routledge, 2003).

2   Raj Patel, *The Value of Nothing: How to Reshape Market Society and Redefine Democracy* (New York: Picador, 2009), 172.

3   Antonio Negri and Michael Hardt, *Commonwealth* (Cambridge, MA: Harvard University Press, 2009).

4   Elmer Kelton, *The Day the Cowboys Quit* (1971; New York: Forge Books, 2008).

5   Alexander Cockburn, "A Short, Meat-Oriented History of the World from Eden to the Mattole," *New Left Review* 215 (1996): 16–42.

6   Midnight Notes Collective.

7   Pramoedya Ananta Toer, *The Mute's Soliloquy: A Memoir*, trans. Willem Samuels (New York: Penguin, 2000), 78.

8   Gregory King, *Two Tracts*, ed. G.E. Barnett (Baltimore: Johns Hopkins University Press, 1936).

9   Raymond Williams, *The Country and the City* (New York: Oxford University Press, 1973).

10 J.M. Neeson, *Commoners: Common Rights, Enclosures, and Social Change in England, 1700–1820* (New York: Cambridge University Press, 1993), 5.

11 E.P. Thompson, *The Making of the English Working Class* (New York: Pantheon, 1964), 218.

12 Maurice Beresford, *The Lost Villagers of England* (New York: Philosophical Library, 1954).

13 Elinor Ostrom, *Governing the Commons: The Evolution of Institutions for Collective Action* (New York: Cambridge University Press, 1990).

14 Neeson, *Commoners*.

15 Bernard Reaney, *The Class Struggle in Nineteenth Century Oxfordshire* (Oxford: Ruskin College, 1970), 12.

16 Vladmir Ilich Lenin, *A Characterization of Economic Romanticism: Sismondi and Our Native Sismondists* (1897; Moscow: Foreign Language Publication House, 1951), n.3.

17 Garrett Hardin, "The Tragedy of the Commons," *Science* 162 (1968): 1243–48. Googling the phrase "tragedy of the commons," in January 2010, I found 197,000 references—a disturbing number, somewhat allayed by Googling "silent spring," which yielded 457,000 references.

18 Reaney, *Class Struggle in Nineteenth Century Oxfordshire*, 4.

19 William Lloyd, *Two Lectures on the Checks to Population Delivered before the University of Oxford in Michaelmas Term 1832* (Oxford: Oxford University Press, 1833). Page citations to these lectures will be indicated in the text.

20 John Barrel, *The Idea of Landscape and the Sense of Place, 1730–1840* (New York: Cambridge University Press, 1972), 134.

21 John Clare, "Autobiography," in *John Clare: Selected Poetry and Prose*, ed. Merryn Williams and Raymond Williams (London: Methuen, 1986), 90.

22 Robert Bloomfield, *The Remains of Robert Bloomfield*, 2 vols. (London: Baldwin, Cradock & Joy, 1824), 1:85.

23 Richard Mabey, *The Common Ground: A Place for Nature in Britain's Future?* (London: Hutchinson Books, 1980), 166.

24 Ibid.

25 These terms are given a historical explanation in the glossary to Peter Linebaugh, *The Magna Carta Manifesto: Liberties and Commons for All* (Berkeley: University of California Press, 2008).

26 Mabey, *Common Ground*, 166.

27 Neeson, *Commoners*, 291, emphasis mine.

28 John Hammond and Barbara Hammond, *The Village Labourer, 1760–1832: A Study in the Government of England Before the Reform Bill* (London: Longmans, Green, 1913).

29 Reaney, *Class Struggle in Nineteenth Century Oxfordshire*.

30 *Jackson's Oxford Journal*, September 11, 1830.

31 James Boyle, "The Second Enclosure Movement and the Construction of the Public Domain," *Law and Contemporary Problems* 33 (2003): 33.

32 Reaney, *Class Struggle in Nineteenth Century Oxfordshire*, 25.

33 Sheila Rowbotham, *A Century of Women: The History of Women in Britain and the United States* (London: Penguin, 1997), 401.

34 Sally Alexander, *St. Giles's Fair, 1830–1914: Popular Culture and the Industrial Revolution in Nineteenth Century Oxford* (Oxford: Ruskin College, 1970), iii.

35 Ibid., 53, 55.

36 Eric Hobsbawm and George Rudé, *Captain Swing* (New York: Pantheon, 1968).

37 Reaney, *Class Struggle in Nineteenth Century Oxfordshire*, 48.

38 Sarah Wise, *The Italian Boy: A Tale of Murder and Body Snatching in 1830s London* (New York: Henry Holt, 2004).

39 Reaney, *Class Struggle in Nineteenth Century Oxfordshire*, 57.

40 Karl Marx, *Capital*, 2 vols., trans. Ben Fowkes, (London: Penguin, 1976), 1:92.

41 Ibid.

42 Ibid., 873.

43 William Cobbett, *A History of the Protestant "Reformation" in England and Ireland: Showing How That Event Has Impoverished and Degraded the Main Body of the People in Those Countries, in a Series of Letters Addressed to All Sensible and Just Englishmen* (London: C. Clement, 1824).

44 Marx, *Capital*, 873.

45 Reaney, *Class Struggle in Nineteenth Century Oxfordshire*, 28.

46 Livy, *The Early History of Rome*, 5 vols., trans. Aubrey De Selincourt (New York: Penguin, 2002), 4:59.

47 John Berger, *Hold Everything Dear* (London: Verso, 2007), 88.

48 Ian Wright, *The Life and Times of Warren James: Free Miner from the Forest of Dean* (Bristol: Bristol Radical History Group, 2008); and Steve Mills, *A Barbarous and Ungovernable People! A Short History of the Miners of Kingswood Forest* (Bristol: Bristol Radical History Group, 2009).

Wat Tyler Day: The Anglo Juneteenth

1 *De civili dominio.* "All good things of God ought to be in common. The proof of this is as follows: Every man ought to be in a state of grace; if he is in a state of grace he is lord of the world and all that it contains; therefore every man ought to be lord of the whole world.

But, because of the multitudes of men, this will not happen unless they all hold all things in common: therefore all things ought to be in common."

2   *An Appeal from the Old Whigs to the New Whigs* (August 1791).

3   Peter Ackroyd, *Blake* (New York: Knopf, 1996), 328–30.

4   *An Appeal from the New to the Old Whigs.*

5   R.B. Dobson wrote an introduction to an anthology of primary sources, called *The Peasants' Revolt of 1381*, 2nd ed. (London: Macmillan, 1983). It is in the series "History in Depth," edited by the late, great Gwyn A. Williams. All my citations to primary sources (Walsingham, Knighton, the Anonimall Chronicle) are found in this convenient collection.

6   Henry Knighton, in Dobson, 382.

7   Norman Cohn, *The Pursuit of the Millennium* (London: Secker & Warburg, 1957), 211.

8   Dobson, 164.

9   Ibid.

10 Ibid., 186.

11 "The Men of Kent and Essex—1381," in Yuri Kovalev, ed., *An Anthology of Chartist Literature* (Moscow: Foreign Langauges Publishing House, 1956).

12 Ibid., 156.

13 Rosie Dias, "Loyal Subjects? Exhibiting the Hero in James Northcote's 'Death of Wat Tyler,'" *Visual Culture in Britain* 8, no. 2 (Winter 2007): 21–43.

14 In 1794 it was put on permanent display in the Council Chamber of Guildhall where it remained until destroyed by bombs in World War Two.

15 E.P. Thompson, *William Morris: Romantic to Revolutionary* (Oakland: PM Press, 2011), 717.

16 Fiona MacCarthy, *William Morris: A Life for Our Time* (New York: Knopf, 1995).

Introduction to Thomas Paine

1   Thomas Paine, *The American Crisis*, no. 1, December 19, 1776, in Paine, *Collected Writings* (New York: Library of America, 1995), 91.

2   Obama quoted from Paine, ibid., in his inaugural address of January 20, 2009.

3   Richard Mabey, *Flora Britannica* (London: Chatto & Windus, 1997).

4   Alan Davison, *Norfolk Origins: 5: Deserted Villages of Norfolk* (North Walsham: Poppyland Publishing: 1996).

5   Oliver Rackham, *The History of the Countryside* (London: Weidenfeld and Nicolson, 1995), 302.

6   Moncur Daniel Conway, *The Life of Thomas Paine* (New York: Benjamin Blom, 1970, first published in 1892).

7   Tom Williamson, *Rabbits, Warrens and Archaeology* (Stroud: Tempus, 2007), 12.

8   Ronald Blythe, *Akenfield: Portrait of an English Village* (London: Allen Lane, 1969), 42.

9   Jessica Kimpell, ed., *Peter Linebaugh Presents Thomas Paine: Common Sense, Rights of Man, and Agrarian Justice* (London: Verso, 2009), 224.

10 May 13, 1775, list printed in Peter Force's *American Archives*, series 4, vol. 2, 646.

11 Kimpell, *Peter Linebaugh Presents Thomas Paine*, 33.

12 Andy Wood, *The 1549 Rebellions and the Making of Early Modern England* (Cambridge University Press, 2007).

13 Francis Blomefield, *An Essay Towards a Topographical History of the County of Norfolk*, 2nd ed. (London: W. Miller, 1805), 2:44; 3:223.

14 Olive Cook, *Breckland* (London: Robert Hale Ltd., 1956), 166

15 George Charles Cocke, *English Law; or, A Summary Survey of the Household of God on Earth* (London, 1651), 64–69; and an *Essay of Christian Government* (London, 1651), 154.

16 E.P. Thompson, "The Moral Economy of the English Crowd," in *Customs in Common* (London: Merlin, 1991), and A.J. Peacock, *Bread or Blood: The Agrarian Riots in East Anglia: 1816* (London: Gollancz, 1965), 77–79.

17 Robert Doyle, *Waisted Efforts: An Illustrated Guide to Corset Making* (Halifax: Sartorial Press, 1997).

18 R. Campbell, *The London Tradesman* (London, 1747), 212.
19 William Hogarth, *The Analysis of Beauty* (1753), edited by Ronald Paulson (New Haven, CT: Yale University Press, 1997).
20 Londa Schiebinger, *Nature's Body: Gender in the Making of Modern Science* (Boston: Beacon Press, 1993).
21 Arguments against the corset ("whalebone prisons") reached one of their peaks in the cult of motherhood in the 1770s and 1780s with Rousseau (it will "eventually cause the race to degenerate"). Marie Antoinette adopted the uncorsetted, natural look when in fact working women wore stays. See David Kunzle, *Fashion and Fetishism: A Social History of the Corset, Tight-Lacing and Others Forms of Body-Sculpture in the West* (Totowa, NJ: Rowman and Littlefield, 1982).
22 Peter Linebaugh and Marcus Rediker, *The Many-Headed Hydra: The Hidden History of the Revolutionary Atlantic* (London: Verso, 2000).
23 Kimpell, *Peter Linebaugh Presents Thomas Paine*, 11.
24 Kimpell, *Peter, Linebaugh Presents Thomas Paine*, 140.
25 John Thelwall, *Rights of Nature, Against the Usurpations of Establishments*, part II (London: H.D. Symonds, 1796), 430.
26 Proverbs 30:9.
27 Rodger Deakin, *Wildwood: A Journey Through Trees* (London: Hamish Hamilton, 2007).
28 John Keane, *Tom Paine: A Political Life* (London: Bloomsbury, 1995), 7.
29 Thomas Paine, *The Crisis*, no. 7, November 11, 1778, in Paine, *Collected Writings*, 208–9.
30 His major writings were published at this time of year. *Common Sense* in January 1776, *The Crisis* no. 1 in December, *Rights of Man* part one in February 1791, and *Rights of Man* part two exactly a year later, *The Age of Reason* was published in January 1794, and *Agrarian Justice* was published in the early months of 1797.
31 Thomas Paine, *The Crisis*, no. 7, November 11, 1778, in Paine, *Collected Writings*, 194.
32 Thomas Paine, ibid., 193; and *The American Crisis*, no. 2, January 13, 1777, in Paine, *Collected Writings*, 108.
33 See *The Pennsylvania Ledger*, December 9, 1775; January 6, 1776; and February 17, 1776.
34 Thomas Paine, "Letter to George Washington," July 30, 1796.
35 Kimpell, *Peter Linebaugh Presents Thomas Paine*, 179, 202, 240.
36 Ibid., 115.
37 Ibid., 152.
38 Kevin Whelan, *The Green Atlantic* (forthcoming).
39 George Smith, *The Life of Alexander Duff*, volume 1 (William Briggs, 1882), 143–47; Bimanbehari Majumdar, *History of Political Thought from Rammohun to Dayananda, volume 1, Bengal* (Calcutta: University of Calcutta, 1934), 80–85; and Tapan Raychaudhuri, *Perceptions, Emotions, Sensibilities: Essays on India's Colonial and Post-colonial Experiences* (Oxford: Oxford University Press, 1999).
40 K'tut Tantri, *Revolt in Paradise* (Heinemann, 1960), 172–3, and Timothy Lindsey, *The Romance of K'tut Tantri and Indonesia* (Oxford University Press, 1997).
41 Kimpell, *Peter Linebaugh Presents Thomas Paine*, 218.
42 Ibid., 299.
43 William Blake, *Annotations to Watson*, 1798.
44 Peter King, "The Origins of the Great Gleaning Case of 1788," in *Crime and Law in England, 1750–1840: Remaking Justice from the Margins* (Cambridge: Cambridge University Press, 2006).
45 Paine, *The Crisis*, no. 6, October 20, 1778, in Paine, *Collected Writings*, 183.
46 Kimpell, *Peter Linebaugh Presents Thomas Paine*, 239.
47 Ibid., 238–39.
48 Ibid., 140.
49 Ronald Blythe, *Akenfield: Portrait of an English Village* (New York: Pantheon, 1969)
50 William Blake, *The Four Zoas*, ix, 132: 8–9.
51 Gregory Claeys, *Thomas Paine: Social and Political Thought* (Boston: Unwin Hyman, 1989),

196; Gwyn Williams in *New Society*, August 6, 1970. Keane, *Tom Paine: A Political Life*, and Craig Nelson, *Thomas Paine: Enlightenment, Revolution, and the Birth of Modern Nations* (New York: Penguin, 2006).

52   John Thelwall, *Sober Reflections on the Seditious and Inflammatory Letter of the Right Hon. Edmund Burke to a Noble Lord* (London: H.D. Symonds, 1796), 336.

53   Kimpell, *Peter Linebaugh Presents Thomas Paine*, 295.

54   Ibid., 299.

55   Ibid., 300, 302.

56   Ibid., 303.

57   Ibid., 307.

58   Ibid., 311.

59   *Anecdotes of the Life of Richard Watson* (London: T. Cadell and W. Davies, 1817), 150.

60   Kimpell, *Peter Linebaugh Presents Thomas Paine*, 281.

61   Ibid.

62   Ibid.

63   Ibid., 274.

Meandering at the Crossroads of Communism and the Commons

1   Thirty years later this utopian commune dissolved and became the world's leading producer of stainless steel eating implements, Oneida flatware.

2   Lynn Marie Getz, "Partners in Motion: Gender, Migration, and Reform in Antebellum Ohio and Kansas," *Frontiers: A Journal of Women's Studies* 27, no. 2 (2006): 118.

3   *Keywords: A Vocabulary of Culture and Society* (1976).

4   The *OED* gives twenty-two meanings to the adjective "common," fifteen meanings to the noun, and eleven meanings to the verb.

5   *A Contribution to the Critique of Political Economy* (Chicago: Charles Kerr, 1904), 10.

6   Karl Marx, "Debates on the Law on Thefts of Wood: Proceedings of the Sixth Rhine Province Assembly," *Rheinische Zeitung* (1842) translated in Karl Marx and Frederick Engels, *Collected Works*, vol. 1 (International Publishers: New York, 1975), 224–63.

7   E.P. Thompson, "The Moral Economy of the English Crowd," in *Customs in Common* (London: Merlin, 1991)

8   James H. Billington, *Fire in the Minds of Men: Origins of the Revolutionary Faith* (London: Temple Smith, 1980), 243.

9   Ibid., 246.

10   Billington says he "became perhaps the most prolific—and surely the most forgotten—propagandist for communism anywhere." Ibid., 254.

11   Barbara Taylor, *Eve and the New Jerusalem: Socialism and Feminism in the Nineteenth Century* (New York: Pantheon Books, 1983), 176.

12   E.P. Thompson.

13   Billington, *Fire in the Minds of Men*, 248

14   Billington, *Fire in the Minds of Men*, 71–72.

15   See R.B. Rose, *Gracchus Babeuf* (London: E. Arnold, 1978) and Ian M. Birchall, *The Spectre of Babeuf* (New York: St. Martin's Press, 1997)

16   Taylor, *Eve and the New Jerusalem*, 175.

17   Thomas Frost, *Forty Years of Recollections: Literary and Political* (London: S. Low, Marston, Searle, and Rivington, 1880), 74.

18   W.H.G. Armytage, *Heavens Below: Utopian Experiments in England, 1560–1960* (London: Routledge and Kegan Paul, 1961), 204.

19   Ibid., 196.

20   Ann Hagedorn, *Beyond the River: The Untold Story of the Heroes of the Underground Railroad* (Simon & Schuster: New York, 2002)

21   Getz, 21. The *Oxford English Dictionary* gives two meanings for "lawing": litigation (going to court) or expedition (cutting off a dog's claws). It is unclear which was intended here.

22 Johann Georg Kohl, *Kitchi-Gami: Life among the Lake Superior Ojibway* (1858), chap. six, "they are almost communists."

23 Claude Lévi-Straus, the prominent twentieth-century anthropologist, as a teenager wrote a pamphlet called *Gracchus Babeuf et le communisme* (Brussels: L'Églantine, 1926).

24 Its subsequent incarnations were the St. Charles Seminary, home of Missionaries of the Precious Blood, then a senior living center.

25 William Cheek and Aimee Lee Cheek, "John Mercer Langston and the Cincinnati Riot of 1841," in Henry Louis Taylor Jr., ed., *Race and the City: Work, Community, and Protest in Cincinnati, 1820–1970* (Urbana: University of Illinois Press, 1993), 33.

26 Nikki Taylor, "African Americans' Strive for Educational Self-Determination in Cincinnati Before 1873," in Gayle T. Tate and Lewis A. Randolph, eds., *The Black Urban Community: From Dusk Till Dawn* (New York: Palgrave Macmillan, 2006), 289.

27 Peter Stallybrass, "Marx and Heterogeneity: Thinking the Lumpenproletariat," *Representations* 31 (Summer 1990): 69–95.

28 George Martin, *Collections of the Kansas State Historical Society, 1911–1912* (Topeka: Kansas State Historical Society, 1912), 12:429–30.

"The Red-Crested Bird and Black Duck"—A Story of 1802: Historical Materialism, Indigenous People, and the Failed Republic

1   Some of the ideas of this essay were germinated with Iain Boal as we followed Tecumseh's route along the Thames (Ontario) and the Scioto (Ohio), then developed at Professor Louis Cullen's modern history seminar, Trinity College (November 2000), and subsequently clarified in discussion with Staughton Lynd in Youngstown, Ohio.

2   John Dunne, "Notices Relative to Some of the Native Tribes of North America," *Transactions of the Royal Irish Academy*, vol. 9 (Dublin, 1803).

3   Richard White, *The Middle Ground: Indians, Empires, and Republics in the Great Lakes Region 1650–1815* (New York: Cambrdige University Press, 1991),

4   *The Northern Star*, March 17, 1792.

5   Kevin Whelan, *The Tree of Liberty: Radicalism, Catholicism and the Construction of Irish Identity, 1760–1830* (Cork Univsersity Press, 1996).

6   Frederick Engels, *Socialism; Utopian and Scientific*, appeared in French in 1880 and in English in 1892.

7   Johannes Fabian, *Time and the Other: How Anthropology Makes Its Object* (New York: Columbia, 1983).

8   Gregory Evans Dowd, *A Spirited Resistance: The North American Indian Struggle for Unity, 1745–1815* (Baltimore: Johns Hopkins, 1992), 135.

9   Anthony F.C. Wallace, *Jefferson and the Indians: The Tragic Fate of the First Americans* (Cambridge, MA: Harvard University Press, 1999), 11.

10 David Hurst Thomas, *Skull Wars: Kennewick Man, Archaeology, and the Battle for Native American Idendity* (New York: Basic Books, 2000). Jefferson began writing *Notes on the State of Virginia* in 1781 but they were not published until 1787.

11 Kerry S. Walters, *The American Deists: Voices of Reason and Dissent in the Early Republic* (Lawrence: University of Kansas Press, 1992).

12 Reverend Robert Hall, *Modern Infidelity Considered with Respect to Its Influence on Society* (1801).

13 Rowan, *The Autobiography of Archibald Hamilton Roman*, ed. William Hamilton Drummond (Dublin: T. Tegg, 1840), 291.

14 R. Dismore in *The Irish Magazine* 3 (January 1809): 36.

15 David A. Wilson, *United Irishmen, United States: Immigrant Radicals in the Early Republic* (Dublin: Four Courts, 1998), 115.

16 In truth, in 1802 the Surrey railroad opened, the first plate-edge iron railway for the public.

17 Jocye Appleby and Terence Ball, eds., *The Political Writings of Thomas Jefferson*.

18 Michael Durey, "John Lithgow's Lithconia: The Making and Meaning of America's First 'Utopian Socialist' Tract," *William and Mary Quarterly* 44, no. 3 (July 1992): 661–68.

19   John Anthony Scott, ed., *The Defense of Gracchus Babeuf before the High Court of Vendome* (University of Massachusetts Press: 1967), 58.

20   William L. Stone, *Life of Joseph Brant (Thayendanegea)*, 2 vols. (New York: A.V. Blake, 1838), 2:481.

21   Logan Esarey, I, 459. Joseph Barron is the translator. John Sugden, *Tecumseh: A Life* (New York: Holt, 1997), 204; Dowd, *A Spirited Resistance*, 140.

22   Here his path crossed Napoleon's and Buonarroti's. Napoleon dissolved Babeuf's conspiracy of the equals. Buonarroti defended the "ancient customs." Volney tried to establish "a rural establishment of a singular kind"—a plantation? Yes, he purchased in 1792 a domain, "Little India" it was called, for cotton, coffee, and sugarcane.

23   Clarence Glacken, *Traces from the Rhodian Shore* (1967)

24   White, *The Middle Ground*; and Anthony F.C. Wallace, *The Death and Rebirth of the Seneca* (New York: Knopf, 1969), 24–29.

25   Information supplied by C.J. Woods, Dictionary of Irish Biography, Royal Irish Academy.

26   William H. Drummond, ed., *The Autobiography of Archibald Hamilton Rowan* (Irish University Press: Shannon, 1972), 137.

27   Oliver MacDonagh, *States of Mind: A Study of Anglo-Irish Conflict, 1780–1980* (London: Allen & Unwin, 1983).

28   Kevin Whelan, "Three Revolutions and a Failure," in Cathal Póirtéir, ed., *The Great Irish Rebellion of 1798* (Dublin: Mercier Press, 1998), 34.

29   William H. Safford, *The Blennerhassett Papers* (New York: Arno Press, 1971; original 1864).

30   A commentator at the Treaty of Greenville compared one of the Indian orators to Nestor.

31   Lynn Hunt, *Politics, Culture, and Class in the French Revolution* (Berkeley: University of California Press, 1984), 59; and Madelyn Gutwirth, *The Twilight of the Goddesses: Women and Representation in the French Revolutionary Era* (New Brunswick, NJ: Rutgers University Press, 1992), 298, 302.

32   Thomas Malthus, *An Essay on the Principle of Population* (1798), chap. 3.

33   Charles Brockden Brown, *Three Gothic Novels* (New York: Library of America, 1998).

34   James Kelly, *"That Damn'd Thing Called Honour": Duelling in Ireland 1570–1860* (Cork: Cork University Press, 1995).

35   John Johnston, *Recollections of Sixty Years* (Dayton: J.H. Patterson, 1915).

36   Wallace, *The Death and Rebirth of the Seneca*, 24.

37   Paul A. Hutton, "William Wells: Frontier Scout and Indian Agent," *Indiana Magazine of History* 74 (1978): 183–222.

38   Wilcomb E. Washburn, *The American Indian and the United States: A Documentary History*, 4 vols. (Greenwood Press: Connecticut, 1973), 4:2295.

39   White, *The Middle Ground*, 479.

40   Leonard U. Hill, *John Johnston and the Indians in the Land of the Three Miamis* (Piqua, OH, 1957), 17.

41   Dowd, *A Spirited Resistance*, 4–5.

42   Hill, *John Johnston and the Indians in the Land of the Three Miamis*; John Johnston, *Recollections of Sixty Years*.

43   Olivia Smith, *The Politics of Language 1791–1819* (Oxford: Clarendon Press, 1984), chap. 1, *passim*.

44   Johannes Fabian, *Time and the Other: How Anthropology Makes Its Object* (New York: Columbia University Press, 1983).

45   George C. Caffentzis, "On the Scottish Origin of 'Civilization,'" in Silvia Federici, ed., *Enduring Western Civilization: The Construction of the Concept of Western Civilization and Its "Others"* (Westport, CT: Praeger, 1995), 33.

46   James Connolly, *Erin's Hope: The End and the Means* (Dublin: Socialist Labor Party, 1897).

47   Gibbons, in *The Field Day Anthology of Irish Writing* (Derry: Field Day Publications), 2:954.

48   Karl Marx, *Capital*, vol. 1, chap. 10, sec. 5.

Index

ABOUT PM PRESS

PM Press was founded at the end of 2007 by a small collection of folks with decades of publishing, media, and organizing experience. PM Press co-conspirators have published and distributed hundreds of books, pamphlets, CDs, and DVDs. Members of PM have founded enduring book fairs, spearheaded victorious tenant organizing campaigns, and worked closely with bookstores, academic conferences, and even rock bands to deliver political and challenging ideas to all walks of life. We're old enough to know what we're doing and young enough to know what's at stake.

We seek to create radical and stimulating fiction and non-fiction books, pamphlets, T-shirts, visual and audio materials to entertain, educate and inspire you. We aim to distribute these through every available channel with every available technology — whether that means you are seeing anarchist classics at our bookfair stalls; reading our latest vegan cookbook at the café; downloading geeky fiction e-books; or digging new music and timely videos from our website.

PM Press is always on the lookout for talented and skilled volunteers, artists, activists and writers to work with. If you have a great idea for a project or can contribute in some way, please get in touch.

PM Press
PO Box 23912
Oakland, CA 94623
www.pmpress.org

FRIENDS OF PM PRESS

These are indisputably momentous times—the financial system is melting down globally and the Empire is stumbling. Now more than ever there is a vital need for radical ideas.

In the six years since its founding—and on a mere shoestring—PM Press has risen to the formidable challenge of publishing and distributing knowledge and entertainment for the struggles ahead. With over 250 releases to date, we have published an impressive and stimulating array of literature, art, music, politics, and culture. Using every available medium, we've succeeded in connecting those hungry for ideas and information to those putting them into practice.

Friends of PM allows you to directly help impact, amplify, and revitalize the discourse and actions of radical writers, filmmakers, and artists. It provides us with a stable foundation from which we can build upon our early successes and provides a much-needed subsidy for the materials that can't necessarily pay their own way. You can help make that happen—and receive every new title automatically delivered to your door once a month—by joining as a Friend of PM Press. And, we'll throw in a free T-shirt when you sign up.

Here are your options:

- **$30 a month** Get all books and pamphlets plus 50% discount on all webstore purchases

- **$40 a month** Get all PM Press releases (including CDs and DVDs) plus 50% discount on all webstore purchases

- **$100 a month** Superstar—Everything plus PM merchandise, free downloads, and 50% discount on all webstore purchases

For those who can't afford $30 or more a month, we're introducing **Sustainer Rates** at $15, $10 and $5. Sustainers get a free PM Press T-shirt and a 50% discount on all purchases from our website.

Your Visa or Mastercard will be billed once a month, until you tell us to stop. Or until our efforts succeed in bringing the revolution around. Or the financial meltdown of Capital makes plastic redundant. Whichever comes first.

William Morris: Romantic to Revolutionary

E.P. Thompson
with a foreword by Peter Linebaugh

ISBN: 978-1-60486-243-0
$32.95   880 pages

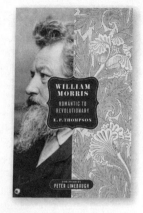

William Morris—the great 19th century craftsman, architect, designer, poet and writer—remains a monumental figure whose influence resonates powerfully today. As an intellectual (and author of the seminal utopian *News from Nowhere*), his concern with artistic and human values led him to cross what he called the "river of fire" and become a committed socialist—committed not to some theoretical formula but to the day by day struggle of working women and men in Britain and to the evolution of his ideas about art, about work and about how life should be lived.

Many of his ideas accorded none too well with the reforming tendencies dominant in the Labour movement, nor with those of "orthodox" Marxism, which has looked elsewhere for inspiration. Both sides have been inclined to venerate Morris rather than to pay attention to what he said.

In this biography, written less than a decade before his groundbreaking *The Making of the English Working Class,* E.P. Thompson brought his now trademark historical mastery, passion, wit, and essential sympathy. It remains unsurpassed as the definitive work on this remarkable figure, by the major British historian of the 20th century.

"*Two impressive figures, William Morris as subject and E.P. Thompson as author, are conjoined in this immense biographical-historical-critical study, and both of them have gained in stature since the first edition of the book was published… The book that was ignored in 1955 has meanwhile become something of an underground classic—almost impossible to locate in second-hand bookstores, pored over in libraries, required reading for anyone interested in Morris and, increasingly, for anyone interested in one of the most important of contemporary British historians… Thompson has the distinguishing characteristic of a great historian: he has transformed the nature of the past, it will never look the same again; and whoever works in the area of his concerns in the future must come to terms with what Thompson has written. So too with his study of William Morris.*"
— Peter Stansky, *The New York Times Book Review*

"*An absorbing biographical study… A glittering quarry of marvelous quotes from Morris and others, many taken from heretofore inaccessible or unpublished sources.*"
— Walter Arnold, *Saturday Review*

Capital and Its Discontents: Conversations with Radical Thinkers in a Time of Tumult

Sasha Lilley

ISBN: 978-1-60486-334-5
$20.00   320 pages

Capitalism is stumbling, empire is faltering, and the planet is thawing. Yet many people are still grasping to understand these multiple crises and to find a way forward to a just future. Into the breach come the essential insights of *Capital and Its Discontents*, which cut through the gristle to get to the heart of the matter about the nature of capitalism and imperialism, capitalism's vulnerabilities at this conjuncture—and what can we do to hasten its demise. Through a series of incisive conversations with some of the most eminent thinkers and political economists on the Left—including David Harvey, Ellen Meiksins Wood, Mike Davis, Leo Panitch, Tariq Ali, and Noam Chomsky—*Capital and Its Discontents* illuminates the dynamic contradictions undergirding capitalism and the potential for its dethroning. At a moment when capitalism as a system is more reviled than ever, here is an indispensable toolbox of ideas for action by some of the most brilliant thinkers of our times.

"These conversations illuminate the current world situation in ways that are very useful for those hoping to orient themselves and find a way forward to effective individual and collective action. Highly recommended."
— Kim Stanley Robinson, *New York Times* bestselling author of the *Mars Trilogy* and *The Years of Rice and Salt*

"In this fine set of interviews, an A-list of radical political economists demonstrate why their skills are indispensable to understanding today's multiple economic and ecological crises."
— Raj Patel, author of *Stuffed and Starved* and *The Value of Nothing*

"This is an extremely important book. It is the most detailed, comprehensive, and best study yet published on the most recent capitalist crisis and its discontents. Sasha Lilley sets each interview in its context, writing with style, scholarship, and wit about ideas and philosophies."
— Andrej Grubačić, radical sociologist and social critic, co-author of *Wobblies and Zapatistas*

Catastrophism: The Apocalyptic Politics of Collapse and Rebirth

Sasha Lilley, David McNally, Eddie Yuen, and James Davis with a foreword by Doug Henwood

ISBN: 978-1-60486-589-9
$16.00   192 pages

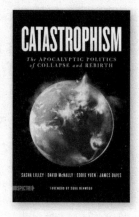

We live in catastrophic times. The world is reeling from the deepest economic crisis since the Great Depression, with the threat of further meltdowns ever-looming. Global warming and myriad dire ecological disasters worsen—with little if any action to halt them—their effects rippling across the planet in the shape of almost biblical floods, fires, droughts, and hurricanes. Governments warn that no alternative exists than to take the bitter medicine they prescribe—or risk devastating financial or social collapse. The right, whether religious or secular, views the present as catastrophic and wants to turn the clock back. The left fears for the worst, but hopes some good will emerge from the rubble. Visions of the apocalypse and predictions of impending doom abound. Across the political spectrum, a culture of fear reigns.

Catastrophism explores the politics of apocalypse—on the left and right, in the environmental movement, and from capital and the state—and examines why the lens of catastrophe can distort our understanding of the dynamics at the heart of these numerous disasters—and fatally impede our ability to transform the world. Lilley, McNally, Yuen, and Davis probe the reasons why catastrophic thinking is so prevalent, and challenge the belief that it is only out of the ashes that a better society may be born. The authors argue that those who care about social justice and the environment should eschew the Pandora's box of fear—even as it relates to indisputably apocalyptic climate change. Far from calling people to arms, they suggest, catastrophic fear often results in passivity and paralysis—and, at worst, reactionary politics.

"This groundbreaking book examines a deep current—on both the left and right— of apocalyptical thought and action. The authors explore the origins, uses, and consequences of the idea that collapse might usher in a better world. Catastrophism *is a crucial guide to understanding our tumultuous times, while steering us away from the pitfalls of the past."*
— Barbara Epstein, author of *Political Protest and Cultural Revolution: Nonviolent Direct Action in the 1970s and 1980s*